Seven Frontier Women and the Founding of Spokane Falls

Seven Frontier Women and the Founding of Spokane Falls

Barbara F. Cochran

Edited by Suzanne Bamonte and Tony Bamonte

Tony and Suzanne Bamonte
P.O. Box 8625
Spokane, Washington 99203
(509) 838-7114, Fax (509) 455-6798
www.tornadocreekpublications.com

First edition published 2011
by Tornado Creek Publications

Printed by Sheridan Books, Inc.
Chelsea, Michigan

ISBN: 978-0-9821529-2-8
Library of Congress Control Number: 2011921836

Photo Credits

Front cover photo:

Clockwise from Susan Glover (center), Anna Browne, Mary Latham, Carrie Adell Strahorn, Alice Houghton, Jennie Cannon, Clara Gray. *(For photo credits, please see the corresponding chapters.)* The background photo is a view of Spokane Falls in 1883. (*Photo from Mark Danner's Patsy Clark Album, courtesy Tony and Suzanne Bamonte*)

Back cover photo:

Looking south along Howard Street from the Spokane River, circa 1886.
(Photo from Spokane and the Inland Empire *by N. W. Durham, 1912)*

Photos from the collection at the Northwest Museum of Arts & Culture/ Eastern Washington State Historical Society are noted as **MAC/EWSHS**

Photos from the collection at the Northwest Room of the main branch of the Spokane Public Library are noted as **SPLNWR**

Other credits are as noted in the photo captions.

Table of Contents

About the Author

Barbara F. Cochran was a lifetime Washington resident, having been born in December 1922 in Vancouver, Wash. After graduating from high school in Vancouver in 1940, she attended Washington State College (now Washington State University) and graduated with a Bachelor of Arts in Speech in 1944. A year later she received a Master of Arts in Speech Therapy from the University of Wisconsin. She was married to her husband, Joseph A. Cochran, in the summer of 1945. While her husband served in the U.S. Army in Japan after the end of World War II, Barbara worked for the Portland, Oregon, school district as a speech therapist. During the 1946-47 school years, she was a speech instructor at WSC while her husband attended school there for additional coursework in accounting.

Barbara Fleischman Cochran
(1922 - 1987)

In 1947, Barbara and her husband moved to Spokane, where they raised a family of four children. Barbara was active in the Spokane Alumnae Chapter of Kappa Delta sorority, including serving as its president. She also worked at the national level of the organization, including eight years as a national officer. She also was very active with Camp Fire, Inc., for twenty years and served on the board of directors for the local council.

Barbara was a longtime member of the board of trustees of the Eastern Washington State Historical Society and served as a chairman of the library committee. She was interested in the history of the Spokane area and authored the book *Exploring Spokane's Past, Tours to Historic Sites*. Her interest in the early women settlers of Spokane led her to do the research and write the manuscript that became this book. She completed the manuscript just months prior to her death in 1987 in Spokane.

Foreword

Certain challenges arise when publishing a book posthumously, such as occasional questions regarding text or the source of information. It was serendipitous that the publishing project came to us. Because of the many years we have devoted to studying and writing about the Inland Northwest's history, we were able to correct a few factual errors we noted and resolve some questions by additional research. Nevertheless, some questions had to remain unanswered. In most cases, the unanswered questions were relatively insignificant and did not take anything away from the author's immeasurable contribution to the preservation of Spokane's early history. Although any piece of work of this magnitude requires rather extensive editing, we endeavored to preserve the author's style and, for the most part, did relatively little rewriting.

The ever-expanding volume of digitized historical records now available on the Internet has dramatically increased the availability of resource material to present-day researchers. However, at the time Barbara Cochran was gathering her material for this book, all she had available to her was the "old-fashioned" method of sleuthing through hardcopy materials at repositories that housed them. Since those days, the number of books, journals and articles written about Spokane's founding years have increased in number. But even now, there is relatively scant information available about women of early Spokane. Despite the constraints and tedium, Mrs. Cochran's research was thorough and well-documented. She succeeded in compiling an impressive amount of personal information about the women she chose to feature.

As explained in the author's preface, availability of material, or lack thereof, played a key role in the selection of the women she chose to write about. She did not intend the book to be a comprehensive or general history of life on the western frontier from the women's perspective, but rather about seven remarkable women who made notable contributions to the founding of Spokane. Their roles in life ranged from homemaking to professions typically reserved for men. Yet each, in her own way, was instrumental in contributing to the social structures that transformed a rustic *settlement*, meeting only basic human needs, into a thriving *community* that was attractive to families. Along with her interesting discourses about these strong, determined – and yet vulnerable – women, Cochran also painted a clear picture of what the gritty little town of Spokane Falls was like when they arrived and how it rapidly grew into a thriving metropolis.

Sadly, Mrs. Cochran died before this fine piece of work could be published and, for various reasons, it languished for over two decades. Fortunately, however, the material is timeless, and the technology has improved the ability to reproduce quality images, which enhanced the author's narrative, each with the proverbial "thousand words."

Suzanne and Tony Bamonte, editors

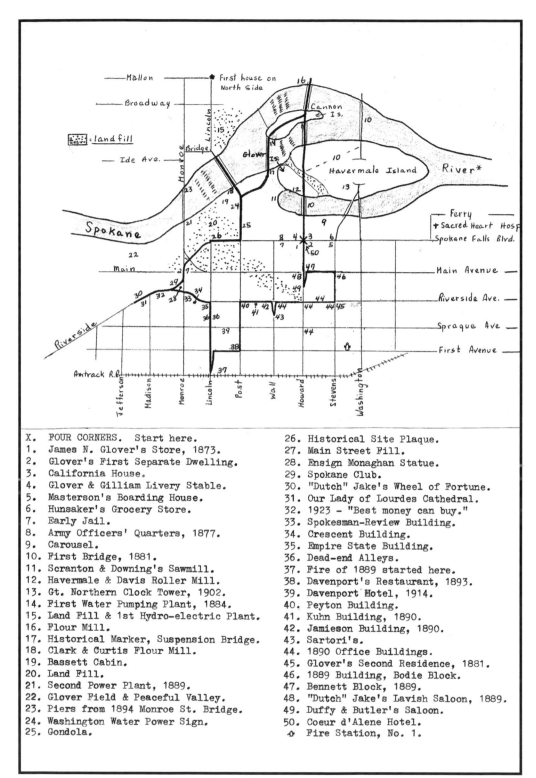

X. FOUR CORNERS. Start here.
1. James N. Glover's Store, 1873.
2. Glover's First Separate Dwelling.
3. California House.
4. Glover & Gilliam Livery Stable.
5. Masterson's Boarding House.
6. Hunsaker's Grocery Store.
7. Early Jail.
8. Army Officers' Quarters, 1877.
9. Carousel.
10. First Bridge, 1881.
11. Scranton & Downing's Sawmill.
12. Havermale & Davis Roller Mill.
13. Gt. Northern Clock Tower, 1902.
14. First Water Pumping Plant, 1884.
15. Land Fill & 1st Hydro-electric Plant.
16. Flour Mill.
17. Historical Marker, Suspension Bridge.
18. Clark & Curtis Flour Mill.
19. Bassett Cabin.
20. Land Fill.
21. Second Power Plant, 1889.
22. Glover Field & Peaceful Valley.
23. Piers from 1894 Monroe St. Bridge.
24. Washington Water Power Sign.
25. Gondola.
26. Historical Site Plaque.
27. Main Street Fill.
28. Ensign Monaghan Statue.
29. Spokane Club.
30. "Dutch" Jake's Wheel of Fortune.
31. Our Lady of Lourdes Cathedral.
32. 1923 - "Best money can buy."
33. Spokesman-Review Building.
34. Crescent Building.
35. Empire State Building.
36. Dead-end Alleys.
37. Fire of 1889 started here.
38. Davenport's Restaurant, 1893.
39. Davenport Hotel, 1914.
40. Peyton Building.
41. Kuhn Building, 1890.
42. Jamieson Building, 1890.
43. Sartori's.
44. 1890 Office Buildings.
45. Glover's Second Residence, 1881.
46. 1889 Building, Bodie Block.
47. Bennett Block, 1889.
48. "Dutch" Jake's Lavish Saloon, 1889.
49. Duffy & Butler's Saloon.
50. Coeur d'Alene Hotel.
⚑ Fire Station, No. 1.

Map of the walking tour of early Spokane from Barbara F. Cochran's book *Exploring Spokane's Past, Tours to Historical Sites*, published by Ye Galleon Press, 1979.

Preface

For years I was fascinated by Spokane's beginnings and, in reading historical accounts, observed that women seemed to be identified only by their relationship to men. For the first twenty years, our city directories carried these sorts of entries: "Jane Jones, spinster;" a divorcee would be listed as "Jane Jones (widow of Thomas)," although Thomas might have been very much alive and with a second spouse. A widow was still linked to her dead husband: "Jane Jones (widow of Jas)." Married women fared the worst. Until 1912, they were not listed at all, the only exceptions being women who operated businesses: millinery, dressmaking, piano teaching, etc.

Even today we still hear: "What women were of *historical* significance in Spokane?" The inference is that to be important a woman had to have designed the first building, or built the first bridge, or even taught in the first school. It is rather certain that a woman gave birth to the first child, created the first home, scrubbed the first laundry, swept the first floor, and probably endured the greatest loneliness.

The very fact that women were here *from the beginning* makes them historically significant. No town was ever built without women. With women in residence, the smallest hamlet can become a town. Towns attract people. People need buildings and services. People can provide the architects and carpenters and brick layers and store keepers and dentists with something to do.

For all of the above reasons, I started looking for Spokane's petticoated pioneers. How lucky for me! It has been an exciting treasure hunt filled with wonderful people I would not have met otherwise. To a certain extent I was limited by archival material available, and choices were made as to which persons to include within what time period. With one exception, all of these women were here prior to 1890. In the case of Susan Glover, no information was known, but I found her, or perhaps she found me. The indomitable "Mrs. Hercules," May Arkwright Hutton, was not included because she has been previously well-documented.

It has not been my intention to write a complete history of Spokane, but in order to visualize the ladies in "their" period of time, it was necessary to present enough material to provide a historical background. Questions never answered before kept popping up, such as "where did the people go who were at the Spokane Falls when Glover arrived?" The result may at times create a scattered or uneven flow to the story, for which I apologize in advance.

One of the greatest frustrations in this research has been conflicting information, especially on dates and events. Whenever possible, I have resorted to the newspaper of the day for accuracy. Ironically, the newspapers have been the greatest perpetuators of misinformation by reprinting, over and over, generation after generation, articles written decades after an event. These old stories containing myths and legends rather than facts serve to obscure what actually happened. Frequently, the reporters who use them have not done the most basic research: checking the news articles published *at the time* the event occurred. But even that basic research is not always enough. One also needs to consult other sources. Participants, even Glover or W. C. Gray, did not have infallible recall. Hence, I have used notes to explain differences in dates and to document my sources. For a nitpicker on detail, this has been a necessity. Without the use of specific dates, there is no time sequence to events.

Whatever else, my goal has been to further the knowledge about early Spokane, to correct as many misconceptions as possible, but most of all to introduce some of the ladies who also pioneered the town by the Falls.

Barbara F. Cochan
Written late 1986 or early 1987

Acknowledgements

From Barbara F. Cochran, author:
No one does a research project without the assistance and encouragement of many people. I am indebted to Jean Amy Adams, Spokane; Frances Maurer Schneider, Sacramento, California; Ruth Maurer, Portland, Oregon; Susan Bell, Salem, Oregon; George S. May, Fair Oaks, California; and the historical societies and staffs of Eastern Washington State, Oregon, Idaho, Chicago, Illinois State, and California. I also owe many thanks to son Michael and my husband, Joe.

From Tony and Suzanne Bamonte, editors/publishers:
We are forever indebted to our friends Laura Arksey and Doris Woodward, who faithfully have assisted us with nearly every writing and publishing project we have undertaken. Both are excellent writers, editors, indexers and proofreaders, and are also knowledgeable about Spokane history. Their commitment to this project was nothing short of outstanding.

We also wish to thank Marsha Rooney, Senior Curator of History, and Rose Krause, Johnston-Fix Curator of Special Collections, of the Eastern Washington State Historical Society/Northwest Museum of Arts & Culture (MAC), for proofreading the manuscript, and to Jane Davey, MAC Archives, for her help in resolving several questions that arose concerning some historical material. Barbara Cochran used the MAC (then called the Cheney Cowles Museum) extensively in her research and, without its resources, this project could not have been done.

Chapter I

Spokane Falls – 1870s

The earliest known photo of the Spokane Falls. *(Photo from the Jerome Peltier Collection, courtesy Tony and Suzanne Bamonte)*

The upper inland country of today's Washington State, that area north of the Snake River and between the Rocky and Cascade mountains, was among the last regions of the continental United States to be developed by the white man. Not until the 1870s did northeastern Washington begin to be settled.

Down in Salem, Oregon, lived a young man of thirty-six years by the name of James Nettle Glover. In the spring of 1873, he decided Oregon had become "stupid and sleepy." Being full of adventure, he was quite willing to pull up stakes and move on. When a friend returned with glowing reports of the Palouse region at the eastern edge of Washington Territory, Glover decided to go see for himself. Jasper N. Matheny[1] accompanied him.

James N. Glover, around the time of his arrival at Spokane Falls. *(Photo from Mark Danner's Patsy Clark Collection, courtesy Tony and Suzanne Bamonte)*

On the first of May, the two reached Lewiston, Idaho Territory, having traveled up the Columbia and Snake rivers by boat. After spending the night at the Hotel DeFrance, they purchased some needed equipment before heading north: a couple of Cayuse ponies, blankets and food.

"Between Colfax and Ft. Colville lay a wilderness broken only at long intervals by the 'post' of some Indian trader or the squalid cabin of a stray squatter," recalled Glover in later years.[2] For several days, Glover and Matheny rode north. Near the site of present-day Rockford in Spokane County, they met Harvey Brown, a mail carrier. "Little" Brown, it was said, was knowledgeable about the area and its inhabitants between Lewiston and Kendall's Spokane Bridge, located on the Spokane River near today's Washington-Idaho boundary. Kendall's toll bridge and trading post were for sale. However, Brown's best and prophetic advice to Glover was not to leave the country without seeing the falls.[3]

Approaching Spokane Bridge eighteen miles above the falls, the travelers' first view of the Spokane Valley prairie was most spectacular, and one Glover remembered all his life. As they came over the rather barren south ridge, Seltice Lake[4] (a shallow lake just north of Liberty Lake that was drained in the early 1900s) lay below them sparkling in the sun. There were deep green fields of magnificent grass filled with sunflowers of the brightest gold just bursting into bloom.

Glover and Matheny arrived at Spokane Bridge just as A. C. Kendall was being buried. Nine years earlier Kendall had erected a bridge across the river and developed the south end of the river near the shoreline. The twelve buildings included a store, hotel and dining room, built mostly of logs. Nearby was a Coeur d'Alene Indian village of twenty-five or thirty log houses and a number of tepees.

Across the river, Thomas Ford and Michael M. Cowley also operated a trading post. After looking the situation over, Glover decided he did not care for the trading post/bridge arrangement and turned his horse downstream. Later, Cowley bought out the Kendall holdings and moved all the goods to the north side of the bridge, abandoning the buildings on the south side.

The trail Glover and Matheny followed led to Joseph Moran's farm on Moran Prairie (near today's 51st Street and Ben Burr Road). Here a makeshift road ran about five miles northwest to the little settlement by the falls. Although steep and rocky as it led over a high basaltic bluff,[5] this track was the only way to reach the falls from the east. The sun was just setting as the weary men arrived at their destination on Sunday, May 11, 1873.

The falls from which the town took its name consisted of three parts: the upper falls near present Browne Street, the middle falls between Howard and Post streets, and the lower falls at Monroe Street. The total drop of water measured 158 feet. Numerous islands, dominated by Cannon Island (now Canada Island) and the Big Island (Havermale), dotted the river and divided it into three main channels with smaller side ones.[6]

Havermale Island, 1881. Inset the Reverend Samuel G. Havermale, for whom the island was named. *(Photo courtesy SPLNWR; inset from* Spokane and the Inland Empire *by N. W. Durham, 1912)*

There was not a great deal to be seen in the way of civilization. A small mill with a "muley" saw[7] run by a water wheel stood near the river. Slightly southwest was a double log cabin occupied by the Benjamin family with five children.[8] Close by was a box house, sixteen-feet square, in which the Swifts lived. Toward the east stood three unfinished log cabins. Altogether the entire hamlet consisted of no more than a half-dozen board and log houses. Only one had a wooden floor. But the people entertained Glover and Matheny with the best that they had.[9] A wagon track connected the houses and the mill. This road eventually became Front Avenue.

Nine adults were living at the falls: John J. Downing with his second wife, Marie, and her daughter Nellie, better known as "Babe"; A. C. and Della Swift; Richard M. and Elmira Benjamin; and two bachelors: Walter France and Seth

The old sawmill built by Scranton and Downing in the early 1870s. It was Spokane's first commercial business. *(Photo courtesy SPLNWR)*

P. Scranton. The Benjamin family consisted of two boys and three girls ranging in age from five to twenty.

Two years earlier when Scranton and Downing had come over the Mullan Road from Montana, they had picked out homesteads on Moran Prairie. A Montana acquaintance, G. W. Bassett, visited them there in April 1871, while driving some horses from Walla Walla to Montana. Accompanied by Bassett, Scranton went down to see the falls for the first time. It was then he decided the falls had more potential. By October, when Bassett came through again, Scranton and Downing had nearly completed the little sawmill.

When he arrived at the falls, James Glover was hardly the novice, happenstance traveler sometimes described. It was well known that the Northern Pacific Railway Company had received a government charter to build a main line from Lake Superior to Puget Sound. By the time Glover left Oregon, the western end had been completed from Tacoma to Kalama on the Columbia River; in the east from Duluth, Minnesota, to Bismarck, Dakota Territory.

After examining the falls early the next morning, Glover was determined to buy out Scranton and Downing, often referred to as squatters,[10] if he could get satisfactory terms. Closer inspection of both sides of the river confirmed Glover's first impressions. "I never doubted," he recalled some forty years later, "that it must soon become part of the route of a transcontinental railroad or that the falls would ultimately be the site of an important city – a manufacturing and distributing center for a rich and populous area."[11]

Actually, at first glance, the site lacked geographical importance. It was poorly situated to serve as a trading post – no main road led to the falls. The Mullan Military Road from Fort Walla Walla to Fort Benton, Montana Territory, came no closer than five miles southeast on Moran Prairie, and it crossed the Spokane River eighteen miles upstream. The next river crossing was thirty miles down-stream at LaPray Bridge,[12] where the most frequently traveled trail connected Walla Walla and Fort Colville.

Certainly the area of the falls was known, but it was not considered as anything more than a scenic attraction. The rocks and gravel in the Spokane Valley to the east showed no promise as good farmland. Occasional migrants camped but moved on. Then Scranton and Downing decided to put the power of the falls to use.

During the summer or early fall of 1871, a family named Wolford briefly joined Scranton and Downing at the falls. Clinton Wolford was fifteen when his family shared half the double log cabin with the J. J. Downings.[13] Then came the Wil-bur Fiske Bassetts. On January 2, 1872, their daughter, Minnie Maria, became the first white child born at the falls.[14] After a five-month stay, the Bassetts took up a homestead near Granite Lake and were replaced by the Benjamins. The Benjamins were ready to leave when Glover showed up.

Glover was determined to buy out the current owner and had the advantage of knowing from mail carrier Brown that Downing was anxious to sell. Downing had, in fact, agreed to sell his half to Benjamin for $2,500. However, after mak-ing a $400 down payment, Benjamin had been unable to make further install-ments, and Downing refused to return the deposit or transfer ownership.

Glover's proposal to buy out Downing was met with favor, and the price was set at $2,000. Glover accepted, but stipulated the first $400 was to repay Benjamin. That Glover knew of the previous transaction caught Downing by surprise, and he hesitated. After consulting with his wife, he agreed to the condition.

Since A. C. Swift claimed to be a lawyer, Glover asked him to draw up papers for everyone to sign that would relinquish any claim each might have had to Downing's half-interest in the land. With the $400 from Glover, Benjamin hap-

Seth R. Scranton was appointed to the position of Spokane's first postmaster. This photo montage prepared by William Edris lists the postmasters of Spokane from 1872 to 1912: Top row, left to right: C. F. Yeaton, appointed September 16, 1873; S. R. Scranton, July 5,1872; James N. Glover, February 5, 1877. **Second row:** Sylvester Heath, October 14, 1880; J. J. L. Peel, October 26, 1886; Thomas B. Warren, August 2, 1889; Arthur J. Shaw, July 24, 1890. **Third row:** Howard T. Mallon, May 9, 1894; George W. Temple, July 14, 1898; Millard T. Hartson, February 5, 1902. **Bottom portrait**, W. P. Edris, July 26, 1909. *(From* Spokane and the Inland Empire*, 1912, by N. W. Durham)*

pily left with his family to homestead on Rock Creek. Arranging with Scranton to run the mill in his absence, Glover and Matheny headed back to Salem.

Glover was willing to make a "long-shot" gamble in buying out Downing, although he did not think the odds were all that formidable. Jim Glover was a patient man and perhaps a bit stubborn as well. The seat of his pants might get thin, but his family would not go hungry, as there was plenty of game close at hand. Eleven small lakes were sprinkled to the east of the falls between today's Sprague and Seventh avenues, and from Pine to Arthur streets. The ponds, later drained and filled, were alive with ducks, geese, curlew, crane, heron, and even whooping crane. There were willow pheasants and blue grouse in the cliff section to the south, and cottontail and snowshoe rabbits all over the hills. In winter the whitetail deer came down to the river to browse on the cottonwood and willow trees. The river provided rainbow and cutthroat trout anytime one threw a hook in, and there were a number of salmon runs each year. Prairie chicken could be found on either side of the river. But, beyond an ample supply of meat, Glover's future hinged on that railroad coming through.

With machinery for a larger mill, supplies for a store, and household goods including an organ, Matheny and Cyrus Yeaton returned to Spokane (sometimes spelled without the "e") Falls in July.[15] Having had some business experience while a stationer in Salem with J. K. Gill, Yeaton had been taken on as a third partner to run the trading post. Accompanying them were a millwright, a couple of assistants, Yeaton's wife, Lizzie Bates Yeaton, and their daughter, Luella, age five.

Scranton was found hiding near the Keith ranch located on Keith's Prairie six miles north of Spangle,[16] and word was sent to Glover to come as soon as possible. Glover hastened his preparation and arrived with his wife, Susan T. Crump Glover, August 19th. He quickly paid $2,000 to Scranton for the other half of the unregistered preemption. Scranton headed for California.

Now that Jim was back, some of the other residents also moved on. "Babe" Downing followed Scranton to California where they were married. Her parents returned to their original homestead on Moran Prairie but sold out two years later. Taking some cattle and horses, the Downings moved farther west to Grand Coulee.[17] Walter France took up a homestead southeast of the falls on Glenrose Prairie. He kept in contact with the people at the falls, as Glover and Yeaton hired him to haul merchandise for their store from Walla Walla once or twice a year with his team of oxen. He also brought up some fruit trees from the Ritz Nursery for Rev. H. T. Cowley.[18] In the early 1880s, France moved to town again, but always remained a bachelor. The Swifts stayed a couple of years before moving to Santa Ana, California.

The immediate concern of the new owners at the falls was to enlarge the mill at the foot of Mill (Wall) Street. By the middle of September, it was in operation. Next, a store was erected on the west side of Howard Street between Front Street and the river.[19] It has been described as two "box" structures put together. A box house is built without a frame. Instead of erecting a frame and covering it with outside sheeting, the boards in a box house are placed vertically and comprise both the frame and the sheeting. The Glovers lived in one side of the building while the Yeatons' quarters were in the rear of the store. The little cabin on the southeast corner of Howard and Front (Coeur d'Alene Hotel site) was completed for Matheny, who had returned to Salem that fall to close up his sheriff's business and bring his family back. His wife, Mary, had passed away March 3, 1872, at the age of thirty-five, leaving Matheny a widower with seven children.[20]

Spokane's first store opened at the beginning of November. Trade was not very brisk. Having anticipated that the Indians would comprise his clientele for a while, Glover stocked those items they would want: calico dress goods, shawls, cheap blankets, tobacco (which the Indians mixed with the dried leaves of the kinnikinnick plant), and lots of cheap beads used to trim moccasins and pouches. Glover later commented that one hardly ever saw an Indian, male or female, "who wasn't painted up."[21] Consequently, a large supply of paints, which the Indians mixed with water to decorate their faces and heads, was kept on hand. Groceries consisted of staples: coffee, tea, sugar and flour. A small amount of hardware such as nails and other items the settlers might need was also carried.

It was six weeks after the store opened before there was any business with the Indians, and then it was the Coeur d'Alenes who came and remained their primary Indian customers. The Coeur d'Alenes were regarded by the settlers at the Falls as a prosperous, frugal and industrious people, whereas the Spokanes were considered an indolent sort who rarely seemed to rustle for anything.[22] Nevertheless, Glover and Yeaton had one firm policy: the scales were always honest, and the prices were the same regardless of the customer.

At first there was some trading in furs. The pelts of marten, muskrat, beaver, otter, black and cinnamon bear, coyote, and black or grey foxes crossed the counter in Glover's store. At one time, forty magnificent buffalo hides were brought in, which only brought $4.50 or $5.00 each.[23]

Most of the early settlers picked up enough Chinook jargon to converse with the Indians. Actually, it was not an Indian language, but a hybrid mixture of Spanish, French, English and Indian words (i.e. pidgin Indian). It came into use between the "Boston men" (early white sea traders on the coast and up the Columbia) and all the different tribes of the Northwest.[24]

An early Spokane Indian encampment. *(Photo* Spokane and the Inland Empire *by N. W. Durham)*

The falls on the Spokane River had been the great rendezvous for all the Indians in this part of the country, and continued to be for several years after 1873. Annually there were three great runs of salmon: steelhead, chum or dog salmon, and chinook. Few salmon could leap the falls, so the Indians came each autumn to lay in their winter's supply of dried fish. Besides setting traps at the mouth of Hangman Creek, they speared or hooked in a variety of ways the white salmon that came up the river from the Columbia. The fish were then dried without salt on high scaffolds built of willow limbs. Earlier in the spring when the sap began to run, the Indians peeled bark strips from the pine trees to use as wrappings for the dried fish. These packages were then swung high in a pine tree for storage. The Indians who came from other areas packed their fish to take home.

There was a definite division of duties among the Indians by which the women, viewed today, seemed to be veritable slaves. They brought in the firewood on their backs, carried the water, put up and took down the tepees, and cared for the other equipment in moving to a new camp. They dug and prepared the camas bulbs; caught, cleaned, cut up and dried or smoked the salmon. For their part, the men did the riding, hunting, carried on the physical aspect of their wars, and especially participated in their "recreation." Primarily, this consisted of gambling and horse races. Most Indian men loved to gamble and would bet their horses, blankets and anything else they possessed, which could include a wife. They played card games using regular decks of playing cards. Their real love was the horse race, the course being across the flat prairie along what later became Riverside Avenue from Cedar to Washington streets. Their hearts were in each race as they whipped their horses every foot of the way. Many Indians went home on foot while others got all the ponies brought to the celebration.

The Indians around the falls pitched their tepees along the river during the summer. In winter they moved back to Drumheller Spring, Cowley Park, Indian Canyon, or to a little knoll near Fourth and Cannon (originally named Pine Street) in Browne's Addition. Here they had a couple of old sheds in a dry and well-sheltered spot. Nearby was a cemetery where they buried their dead in the ground with Christian services as they had been taught to do years earlier by Rev. Cushing Eells, who with Rev. Elkanah Walker established the Tshimakain Mission northwest of Spokane.[25]

The little community came through that first winter without serious problems and prepared for a busy season. The site by the falls seemed like a natural one to James Glover, and he figured he would not have to wait long for the immigrants to come and buy his land. Since the 1840s, there had been a steady stream of immigration into Oregon and California. By the 1870s, the northern and "upper country" began attracting settlers from the Willamette Valley of Oregon by way of Walla Walla. But the hoped-for immigration to the falls did not appear.

The economic depression that befell the United States in the fall of 1873 made itself felt even at isolated Spokane Falls. Financier Jay Cooke's bank, the principal source of financing for the Northern Pacific Railroad, had closed, halting further construction. This was a major disaster to the investors at the Falls. Immigration in general slowed down. Even so, the men finished some of the log houses and were happy if an itinerant traveler used them. More lumber was added to the stockpile, but there was little demand and that mostly on credit.

The Panic of 1873

By 1873, the nation's economy had overexpanded, particularly in railroad construction. The main economic problems were overproduction, a declining market and deflation. Investors in Europe, where a depression was already underway, began to call in American loans. The New York Stock Exchange closed its doors for ten days, numerous businesses failed, and railroad construction was curtailed, with some railroads defaulting on their bonds.

The weak link turned out to be the banking house of Jay Cooke and Company, which helped the U.S. government finance the Civil War and also underwrote the construction of the Northern Pacific Railroad. Jay Cooke and Company, a large and respected banking house, declared bankruptcy and announced its failure on September 18, 1873. The bank's collapse precipitated the "Panic of 1873" and the ensuing three-year depression during which over 10,000 businesses failed. The unemployed began to move about the country seeking jobs, and bread lines appeared throughout the nation.

Cash in the pocket was nonexistent. Out in the farm areas, the crops were scant, having been chewed up by a swarm of crickets. All in all, it was a discouraging time for the entire upper country.

Perhaps the need to continue their own customs spurred the townspeople to stage their first celebration on July 4, 1874. People came from fifty to sixty miles away, bringing food and bedding to camp during the three-to-four-day festivities. There had to be a flag, of course. Made with materials from the store, it was raised on a flagpole erected near Front and Howard. The road in front of the store wound around the pine trees, but the men found room to put up a frame with a floor for dancing. Pine and fir boughs were twined around it, creating quite a pretty bower.

James A. Perkins came all the way from Colfax to be the orator, and a fine speech he made, too. In the afternoon and evening, dancing took place while the Indians watched through the evergreens. As soon as the white people quit, the Indians took over and performed until morning.

One of the better known local Indian leaders was Spokan Garry, who had been educated at Red River School near Winnipeg, Manitoba, many years earlier. At this Church of England Mission School, Garry learned to speak, read and write English, and to do some arithmetic. Other subjects taught were European history, geography and religious instruction. An unfortunate side effect was exposure of an impressionable teenager to the rivalry between Protestants and Catholics. Garry acquired a strong prejudice against the Roman Catholic Church.

Spokan Garry.
(Photo courtesy SPLNWR)

Even though it occurred forty years later, the conversion of Chief Peone and his band of Upper Spokanes to the Catholic faith was not met with favor by Garry. Father Joseph Cataldo had begun his missionary work among the Upper Spokanes in 1864 with a tiny church on Peone Prairie. Equally disturbing to Garry was his increased awareness of territorial laws that affected the lives of his people. The traditional Indian customs were not adequate.

In his early years, Garry had worked with Walker and Eells at their mission station northwest of Spokane during the 1840s. By the 1870s, the only non-Catholic minister Garry knew was Rev. Henry H. Spalding, an associate of Walker and Eells who visited the Spokanes during the early years. Accordingly, Garry asked Richard Benjamin, an early settler at Spokane Falls, to write to Spalding for him. His letter of March 27, 1873, requested Spalding to come and baptize his people and marry them according to the white man's laws. Garry said his people numbered 447.

A second letter, very possibly written by Garry himself, was sent the first of May changing the meeting place with Spalding. He further requested that Chief Lawyer and other Nez Perce chiefs attend as well. Spalding's subsequent visit of three weeks was highly successful. Spalding returned again in July and August of 1873. In September, he brought a government inspector for Indian Affairs, Colonel E. C. Kemble. Since Kemble was also an Episcopalian, Garry appealed through him for an Episcopal teacher for his people. This request was not granted. Spalding recognized the need and the interest among the Indians for a Protestant missionary, and discussed the situation with his Presbyterian associate, Henry T. Cowley.

A third letter went to Rev. Spalding in February 1874. Although this has also been credited to Benjamin, the handwriting, spelling and punctuation of the three letters indicate three different people wrote them.[26] Again, Garry requested a visit from Spalding. As illness prevented his coming, Spalding sent Rev. Cowley in June to investigate the feasibility of a mission among the Spokanes. The Oregon Presbytery and the Mission Board in New York had appointed Cowley a missionary to the Spokanes. However, neither Baptiste Peone, a Catholic on Peone Prairie, nor Garry living with his people east of Hillyard and still hoping for an Episcopalian missionary, wanted Cowley to settle among the Spokanes. However, most of the Spokane bands were in favor: Enoch's band at the falls, William Three Mountain's group east of Hangman Creek, Paul's band on the Little Spokane, and Lot's band between Walker's Prairie and the Columbia River.

Rev. Henry T. Cowley.
(Photo Spokane and the Inland Empire *by N. W. Durham, 1912)*

Like Glover, Cowley's initial view of the Spokane River and valley was awe-inspiring and moving. He wrote: "My first glimpse of the site of the future magnificent city was unfurled to view from the cliff near the head of Washington Street and was so enchanting, that I dismounted and spent several moments enjoying its grandeur and beauty. Here seemed to be the setting of the elements of an ideal city – even a corner of Paradise. To the east and west the panorama of the tranquil and majestic Spokane Valley stretched out before me, while beneath lay an extensive pine grove, golden with the wild sunflower, and the ear caught the melodious murmur of the series of waterfalls."[27]

Differences with John Montieth, the Lapwai Indian agent, had already caused Cowley to move to Mount Idaho after a year at Kamiah on the Clearwater River. Another year was spent among the Nez Perce, but now the yearning of the Spokane Indians for more Christian knowledge appealed to Cowley, as did the looks of the country. A second trip in August convinced him to reside among Enoch's band, because he offered the most assistance to the mission in the way of oats, furs, horses and labor to construct the buildings needed. In October 1874, Cowley brought his wife and four small children in two wagons over the 300-mile journey, thus becoming the fourth family to settle permanently at the falls. (Two more children would be born to them at Spokane Falls.) Cowley would play a prominent role in the development of the town, partly because Chief Garry[28] earnestly desired not so much a teacher as a minister to "immerse the boys and marry the girls."

A house and school were built, largely by the Indians, for the Cowleys on land held by Chief Enoch Selquawia. The house stood on Sixth between Browne and Division with the school a little further east on Sixth Avenue between Division and Pine. When the school opened in the Cowley house in January 1875, six children of the town also attended: Edith, Fred and Grace Cowley, Lulu Yeaton, and the two Poole girls. William Poole, who arrived the day after the Cowleys, was a carpenter and helped with the construction of Cowley's buildings. Among the Indian pupils were three of Garry's relatives.

The Cowley home in Spokane.
(Photo courtesy SPLNWR)

Grace Cowley wrote later: "Don't think they [the Indian pupils] behave in school any better than we do, for they pinched, whispered and stuck pins through the cracks of the door and pricked the people on the other side. Just normal humanity, perhaps more keen eyes, more sensitive to sound, but with a finer sense of humor as they understood it, than the white people."[29]

It soon became apparent that the Indian school took up so much of Cowley's time that he could not attend to his other missionary work. Mrs. Swift took over the white school in her home for the rest of the three-month term. By this time, the Swifts had built a log house northwest of the Cowleys between Third and Fourth, and Bernard and Browne.

The spring and summer of 1875 went dragging along: the financial depression was still being keenly felt. Enterprise drooped listlessly, and no improvements were made. One consolation encouraged James Glover, however; the previous summer James Tilson Sheets, a government surveyor working to the west on Crab Creek, had come on to the falls in July to survey Glover's claim. The odd-numbered sections had been reserved for the railroads as an inducement for them to extend their lines west. Although Glover did not file for a deed until April 5, 1878, he at least knew his land claim lay within an even-numbered section. He had the south half of the southwest quarter, the southwest quarter of the southwest quarter, and the northwest quarter of the southwest quarter of Section 18, Township 25 North, Range 43 East comprising just under 158½ acres. It made an inverted "T" shape with the stem going as far north as Broadway and taking in most of the bay by his sawmill. The line ran north of Front, east to Bernard, south to Sprague (the section line) and west to Cedar.[30]

During the summer of 1875, Samuel G. Havermale, an itinerant Methodist minister stationed in Walla Walla, chanced through Spokane Falls on his way to Colville. Liking the area around the falls, he picked out the quarter section adjoining Glover's on the east and filed on it while in Colville. It formed a little "L" of the northeast corner of Glover's land and included the largest island in the Spokane River, which subsequently was given his name. By November, Havermale returned with his wife Elizabeth Goldthorp Havermale and their sons, Schuyler and Wilbur. However, they continued to spend a large part of their time in Walla Walla where their daughter Laura, the wife of Dr. Benjamin F. Burch, lived.

There still was no direct route into Spokane Falls. The mail carrier followed the Mullan Road. He left the mail, sometimes amounting to no more than a few letters, in the care of Joe Moran on the prairie bearing his name south of town. Moran or one of the neighbors delivered the mail to town, or Lee Matheny rode out to get it. Pack trains also crossed Moran Prairie with merchandise for the area stores: Cowley's and Ford's at Spokane Bridge; Dick Fry's at Seneaquoteen on the Pend Oreille River; and Galbreath's at Kootenai (Bonners Ferry).

Early in 1876, Charles Bell, his son Oliver, and Chauncey Gutches came to the falls looking for a place to locate. They found Glover at the mill dressed in an old shirt, yellow overalls covered with black splotches of pine pitch and an old hat on his head. Oliver did not think he look very prepossessing. "Glover was a great greeter," admitted Oliver, "and insisted we stay at his house." Glover sent Lee Matheny with young Bell to pasture the horses on the prairie to the south. Mrs. Glover got their meals, and they spread their blankets on the kitchen floor of the little four-room house near Yeaton's store. The next day, while Glover took Bell and Gutches across to the north side of the river, Oliver and Lee became acquainted. The boys were of a similar age, around eighteen. Lee confided to Oliver that everyone at the falls wanted to get away. "I'm going to Waitsburg to work in E. L. Powell's store," Lee said, "and my father is going to Utah. Everyone here is all tangled up and wants to leave." Learning that Gutches had some ready cash, Lee thought it would be a fine thing if the folks at the falls could unload on Gutches.

That evening Yeaton, Matheny, Glover, Rev. Cowley and Rev. Havermale gathered at Glover's home to persuade Bell and Gutches to settle at Spokane Falls. But as the soil did not look good for agriculture, the invitation was turned down. Bell located at Latah and Gutches at Wyola, near Palouse City. Oliver recalled in later years: "Of all the original settlers here at Spokane then, Mr. Yeaton impressed my youthful mind as being by far the smartest man in the bunch."[31]

It was becoming increasingly clear that the partnership was not progressing as had been hoped, and the relationships were far from satisfactory. Matheny was the first to make the decision to leave. Having seven children to support, he declared he could no longer live on water and air. In the spring of 1876, Matheny asked Glover to buy him out for a few hundred dollars, which he did.

Keeping the store stocked was no small task. Year after year, Glover had been hauling flour from Waitsburg, the nearest flour mill. Although L. W. Meyers had built a mill at (present) Kettle Falls in 1872 on the Colville River, Glover preferred to go south. It was no wonder that when Frederick Post came to Rathdrum with the greater portion of a flour mill, he became the most popular man around. Every community in the area tried to get him to locate in its town. Glover also negotiated with Post. Finally he made an offer Post could hardly turn down: forty acres of land. This gift was the stem of Glover's inverted "T". It covered the area west of Post Street, north of Main Avenue and extended across the river to Broadway, giving Post the entire lower falls. Post paid Glover $217 for the property.[32] Glover did retain one block, however, the northwest corner of Main and Post streets. Post offered to buy that lot for $350 to even off his forty acres. This "deal" became a standing joke between the two men as every time Post needed money, he would sell the block back to Glover, then buy it back again. Back and forth it went four or five times before finally being sold to Anthony M. Cannon and John J. Browne several years later.

Little was done in the fall of 1876 toward getting the flour mill into operation, other than the excavation of a flume and the cutting of timber. However, it was enough to spur Glover into building a new story-and-a-half store on the southwest corner of Howard and Front. The Glovers moved into the house vacated by Matheny across the street to the east of the new building. Eventually the house was enlarged and remodeled into a five-room dwelling of half logs and half boards with a picket fence around it.

From time to time, families continued to drift in and out. Even though Glover did everything he could to encourage residency by giving everyone a free lot in town, most of the people moved on after a year or two. One of these was W. H. Downer, who left and took up a farm southeast of town. Mr. and Mrs. R. M. Smith had a lot on the southeast corner of Front and Mill streets, but they, too, left. W. R. Evans opened a cabinet shop on the south side of Front between Howard and Mill. Evans, his wife, son and daughter stayed long enough to receive a deed to his property when Glover platted the town in January 1878. Permanent settlers out on Moran Prairie were Robert G. and Sarah Williamson, who arrived with their family of three sons and two daughters in the fall of 1876. Nevertheless, the population reported at various times during those early years always seems to be more than the names that are now known.

If nothing else discouraged settlers, an Indian scare arose periodically. Unfounded rumors of an expected uprising were magnified by the Portland and southern Washington Territory newspapers, causing some of the populace to push the panic button. Men abandoned their homesteads and moved their families to larger communities for greater security. Others gave up completely and returned to former homes. Yeaton stuck it out until the latter part of 1876 when he, too, approached Glover with a request to be bought out. His wife, who was an invalid, seemed to be more frail than ever. The nearest doctor was at Colfax, 65 miles away. Upon at least one occasion, they sent an Indian with a message to a Dr. Bonnell, who arrived 24 hours later. With the departure of Yeaton, James Glover became the sole proprietor of his enterprises.

The winter of 1876 and the spring of 1877 were perhaps the most trying of all for the dedicated couple by the falls. Little progress, if any, had been made to increase the population. In fact, there were fewer people in town than when they had arrived. There seemed to be faint prospects for any greater activity in 1877. Glover's mill could produce over 150,000 feet of lumber in four or five days – enough to meet the demand for an entire year. Grimly, they held on.

Unbeknownst to them, a storm was brewing to the south that spring. Embittered by an army ultimatum to relocate them to the Lapwai Reservation from their beloved Wallowa Valley in northeast Oregon, three young Nez Perce killed several white men in the Salmon River Valley. The inevitable reprisal came June 17 at White Bird Pass, where the Army was defeated. Now it was a break-and-run situation for the Nez Perce. Rumor had it that Chief Joseph was planning to go from the Wallowas in Oregon to Canada to join Sitting Bull. The shortest route lay through Spokane. The entire upper country was terrified in anticipation of a general Indian outbreak throughout Eastern Washington, Oregon and northern Idaho. Many settlers gathered at the nearest village for safety. Stockades were erected at Spangle, Colfax, Palouse and Moscow. Other homesteaders and ranchers in the outlying areas, not trusting these primitive precautions, fled with their families to the larger communities of Dayton and Walla Walla.

In July, a band of Nez Perce came to the falls to generate some sympathy for their cause and to stir up the Spokanes to strike against the white people. The Nez Perce camped near First and Bernard streets in the vicinity of the present Spokane Intermodal Facility (originally the Northern Pacific Depot). About dusk each day, a smudge was built around which the Indians circled. Over the fire was held a hoop covered with a stretched animal skin. By beating on this drum, the Indians marked time for their dancing and songs. This performance continued until just before dawn. Two weeks of these nightly shenanigans, as Glover described them, were more than enough to make the settlers' hair stand on end as nerves wore thin.

From the stoop of his store, Glover could plainly see the Indians about four blocks to the southeast. If there were to be an attack, Jim figured it would be in the early hours. On the second night, as he sat up to watch, an apparition appeared near Howard and Riverside streets at around three in the morning. "I guess our time's come," Glover told Ed Bradbury, an employee of Frederick Post's who was standing guard with him. However, neither one had any firearms. "Run over and tell them at the house." A horse and rider came into sight with a wagon following, so Jim knew it was not Indians, but homesteaders. When Bradbury returned to the Glover home, where most of the townspeople had gathered, he found some crying, others praying. Holding two of her children in her arms was Laura Havermale Burch, who was visiting at Spokane Falls for the first time from her home in Walla Walla.

Before the day was over, more settlers arrived, some on horseback, some on foot, and some riding in wagons with their scanty household goods. A few came from as far as 45 miles away. Glover had a skiff from which a raft was constructed to move the fleeing homesteaders and townspeople to Havermale Island. There they built a thirty-foot log-and-rock fortification around a little enclosure about a hundred feet north of the present Great Northern clock tower. Noses were counted and thirty-one able-bodied men and boys responded. They had a militia company under Glover's direction. Al Williamson was sent to do scout duty along the Mullan Road and Lapwai Trail southeast of town. Frederick Post and his employee, Ed Bradbury, did not go onto the island, as Post claimed he was too busy building his mill.

According to Williamson, the island was the least safe place the people could have chosen. Any Indian could have hidden behind a rock and picked them off one by one. Furthermore, it was impossible to get off the island as the current was too swift to swim and a canoe would have been a "sitting duck."[33]

During this time, the Spokane Indians kept abreast of events on the Indian battlefields around the Palouse Country by runners going between their camp and the fighting. Curly Jim or another of the older Indians then informed Mr. Glover. Even so, Jim decided something had to be done. With great personal courage, he called some of the older Spokanes to his store. He told them the Nez Perce had better *klat-a-wah* (a Chinook word for "go") by noon of the next day, or he would call for the boys with the "brass buttons." The ruse worked, as the memory of Colonel Wright's campaign of September 1858 was still vivid, and the Nez Perce left. Fortunately, after a week of camping out, the settlers were able to return home as the local Spokanes assured them of their peaceful intentions. Rev. Cowley wrote afterwards: "From the 27th of June til the 10th of August the suspense was painful in the extreme."[34]

By the sheerest coincidence, several companies from the Second Infantry under Colonel Frank Wheaton, who became the second commander of Fort Coeur d'Alene (later renamed Fort Sherman) marched into town shortly afterwards. Wheaton's role was twofold: to block the possibility of the Nez Perce, who were now in Montana, from doubling back via the Mullan Road, and to protect the small communities. After a council with the local Indians, Companies H and I were left at the falls for six weeks.

After the soldiers left to rejoin their regiment at Lapwai, word was received that General William T. Sherman of Civil War fame would soon stop at Spokane Falls. He was on an inspection tour of the army posts in the northwestern states and territories. Determined to give him a grand reception as befitted his rank, every household contributed its best for the meeting and noontime dinner to be held at the Glovers' home. Naturally, the talk that day turned to the recent disturbing incident of the Nez Perce visit in July. Red-headed General Sherman let it be known in no uncertain terms that "pioneers to such a remote region could not reasonably expect the government to follow each weak settlement with a company of United States troops nor establish posts every hundred miles or so on such a vast

General William T. Sherman. *(Library of Congress photo)*

frontier. If adventurous people would penetrate the wild west and venture their lives among the hostile savages, they must do it on their own means of defense as did Daniel Boone in the early Kentucky days. The Indian was by nature a savage, treacherous and bloodthirsty."

It was Sherman's personal opinion that "the region as far as he could see, coming down the Spokane bottom [valley] was little but a sterile, gravelly waste, not suitable for cultivation, and no white man could make a decent living from it. It never could be settled and successfully occupied by whites, and those already here were rash intruders into the Indians' domain, who had better prepare to vacate."

General Sherman did not inform the populace that he had been instructed by the War Department to locate a suitable site for a post in the vicinity of Spokane Falls. He already had one in mind – at Lake Coeur d'Alene. Nevertheless, in order to have his men on hand for construction of the new fort in the spring, General Sherman allowed Companies H and I to return to Spokane Falls and go into winter quarters.[35]

The increased business generated from building quarters and furnishing supplies for the soldiers inspired new confidence in the community – quite a contrast to other winters. The barracks were built on Main Street (later changed to an avenue) with the officers' quarters on the north side of Front near Mill.

The fall of 1877 saw a few more permanent immigrants arrive: the Percival brothers, Herbert and Myron; Lorenzo W. Rima; Dr. James and Margaret Masterson with three sons: John, Oscar and David; mail carrier Lewis Yale; and several other persons. Rima opened a little jewelry store on the east side of Howard between Front and Main streets. That was true optimism! Doc Masterson started a small boarding house on the southwest corner of Stevens and Front streets, which later was called the Western House. By November, Post's flour mill finally was in production.

Hearing that the soldiers were wintering at the falls, Yeaton wrote from Salem asking to return and take charge of Glover's store again. He was also interested in being appointed the post trader at the new fort. Yeaton got the job with the Army and stayed at Fort Coeur d'Alene six or seven years. In the meantime, Glover contracted to furnish the Army with flour, grain and whatever else they needed. This he continued to do for a number of years, competing with Michael M. Cowley at Spokane Bridge.

Glover decided the time had come to plat a real town. The preliminary survey was made by Lorenzo Rima in January and February, with the filing done at

Lorenzo Rima, who made the first survey of the early Spokane Falls town site and opened the first jewelry store. *(Photo* Spokane and the Inland Empire *by N. W. Durham, 1912)*

the county seat in Colville on February 13, 1878. The streets were named by Glover: Washington, Stevens, Mill and Post from east to west, and from north to south: Front, Main (which he expected to be the principal business street in town), South (Riverside) as it was the last street south at that time, and then Sprague. In 1880, when there was a new survey by a professional surveyor, Glover named the streets west of Post to Cedar in honor of the presidents of the United States. Even so, there were no proper streets or roads – merely wagon tracks haphazardly following the easy grades up or down any inclines. Basically, the flat prairie south of the river was still a wide, empty wilderness, a gravelly plain growing bunch grass in the summer.

If the wintering of the two companies of soldiers was the turning point in the economic survival of the small community, their departure in the spring of 1878 coincided with the arrival of a pair of men who would mark the beginning of the town's growth. Anthony M. Cannon and John J. Browne, both of Portland, approached Glover about buying a half-interest in his claim. Glover's first land claim was a preemption, but he had also taken 160 acres west of it as a homestead. (This he relinquished to J. J. Browne.) Recognizing that these two men possessed the aggressive qualities needed to move things along, Glover agreed to their proposition. A contract was drawn up on April 26 whereby Cannon and Browne promised to pay Glover $3,000-$3,200. The down payment was only $50, but it was all they had apart from the amount necessary to bring their families to Spokane Falls. It would be five or six years before the final payment would be made. Glover said of these two:

A detail from the front page of Spokane's first newspaper, *The Spokan Times*, which published its first issue on April 24, 1879. *(Courtesy Tony and Suzanne Bamonte)*

> The newcomers were to play conspicuous parts in the great drama of city building by the wild cataracts of the Spokane, and it may well be doubted if two men better fitted by courage, enthusiasm, and knowledge of western life and western conditions could have been found, either east or west, to take up that work and carry it forward to success and brilliant achievement.[36]

These three men, who were to be good friends for the rest of their lives, played key roles in guiding, directing and leading the tiny upper country hamlet of less than one hundred people to what soon became a thriving metropolitan city.

In addition to Browne and Cannon, by the end of November 1878, the following families or individuals had made their way to Spokane Falls: the Woods, Polks, Ellis, Capt. James M. Nosler and family, Dr. Leonard Waterhouse with his wife and daughter, and two unrelated families named Oliver.

Renewed surveying by the Northern Pacific Railroad in 1879 brought fresh optimism to the inhabitants of Spokane Falls for a speedy construction through town. Several new businesses, although mostly one-story shacks, sprang up along Howard, Front and nearby streets. On the west side of Howard, across the street from L. W. Rima's jewelry store, Jack Squier ran a saloon. The first jail was located west of that. John T. Graham's sat on the corner of Main and Howard. As proof the town was growing, a second general merchandise store, Friedenrich & Berg's, opened on the opposite corner. (Simon Berg, one of the proprietors, was the first known Jewish settler in Spokane Falls.) On Main, Louis Ziegler opened a hardware store. The place was beginning to look like a town, with Howard Street as the center of business. Cannon's sawmill at the foot of Mill (Wall) Street and Post's gristmill at the foot of Post Street completed the industrial area. Some apple trees were planted on Riverside east of Washington. The closest bridges to cross the river were still twenty miles upstream at M. M. Cowley's, or thirty miles downstream at LaPray's. Robert W. Forrest established a ferry about Division Street just where the river makes a bend. Unfortunately, he did not have much business.

The first schoolhouse for the white children, a small one-room frame structure, was erected in a little grove of pine trees south of town near Lincoln Street. School opened on April 1, 1879, with Miss Anna Waterhouse as the first teacher.[37] Twenty-two pupils answered roll call. In 1881, it stood in the way of the Northern Pacific right-of-way and had to be moved a block north to First Avenue in the middle of the block between Post and Lincoln streets.[38] Two years later, a four-room school was built on the present Lewis & Clark High School site, and the *Spokane Falls Review* then began operation in the abandoned schoolhouse.

The first two churches for the white settlers in Spokane Falls were established in 1879: the Congregational Church was started by Rev. H. T. Cowley and the first Methodist Church by Rev. J. H. Leard. Among the eight founding Methodist members were Rev. and Mrs. Havermale. Because Rev. Cowley's first responsibility was to the Indian mission, when he was prevailed upon to start a church for the white settlers, he agreed on the condition it would always be open to Indians as well as whites. When it was organized on May 22, 1879, Enoch Selquawia and his wife were among the ten charter members. Rev. Cowley also agreed to serve as its "acting" pastor until a permanent pastor could be found. For two years, the members met in the little schoolhouse. After their first regular pastor, Rev. F. T. Clark, arrived, a church was built on the southwest corner of Sprague and Bernard and dedicated on December 20, 1881. The Methodists built a church at the southwest corner of Sprague and Washington in 1882.

Also in 1879, a somewhat more official post office was initiated in Warner's store. It consisted of a three-foot slant-top box placed on top of the dry goods counter. Its back was toward the public with a slot cut out to insert the letters. To remove the mail, Sylvester Heath, who became postmaster in October 1880, simply lifted the hinged lid. An apple box next to it served to hold newspapers. A smaller box was for the letters of the Chinese. One of the duties of the postmaster was to address letters for the Chinese in English for forwarding. Heath, who also clerked for Mr. Warner, used the same counter to do the bookkeeping for the store.

The first newspaper in Spokane Falls, the *Spokan Times*, appeared April 24, 1879, with Frances H. Cook as owner, editor and publisher. Cook was a strong proponent of spelling the town's name without the "e" on the end. He argued that including the "e" was not phonetically correct and would be mispronounced by outsiders. Consequently, he used his preferred spelling for his newspaper.

Cook had first looked over the prospective city in the spring of 1878. He returned the next year and accepted a lot from Glover on Front Street. An experienced newspaperman, Cook had worked on several eastern papers. At the age of 23, he bought the *Olympia Echo*, and started the *Tacoma Herald* three years later in 1877. Although setting up shop in Spokane Falls, Cook continued to publish the *Herald* for another year. Apparently his constituents considered him more a citizen of Tacoma than the Falls as they elected him to the Territorial Legislature from Pierce, Mason and Chehalis counties in the fall of 1879. Chosen to be president of the House of Representatives, Cook was the youngest member of that body and the youngest person to preside over joint meetings with the Senate. However, from the first issue of the weekly *Times*, Cook promoted the upper inland country by printing an article on how to reach it:

> 1) With a team, wagon and stock, drive from Omaha to Ogden, then by wagon road to Spokan Falls which takes two to three weeks from Ogden when the roads are good.
> 2) Rail[road] to Kelton: $50; stage to Walla Walla: $75; to Colfax: $10; to Spokan Falls: $7.
> 3) Rail[road] to San Francisco: $50; ocean steamer to Portland: $2 - $30 according to cabin and state of opposition [competition?] on the route; to Almota (on the Snake River) by river steamer from Portland: $18. This is the easiest and cheapest."[39]

The *Times* also printed the schedule for the stagecoach lines: "Stages leave Colfax at 6 o'clock on Tues. and Friday traveling north. Stages leave Colville at the same time heading south. Ninety-six hours are allowed between the two points. Most stages make it in less time."[40] Spokane Falls passengers arrived at or departed from the stage barn by the livery stable owned by James Glover's brother John Glover.

The town was so small that it took everyone working together to produce any improvements. The *Spokan Times* ran a notice in 1879 for workers to build a road east of the town to the prairie:

> Come one, come all, both great and small,
> Ye handsome and ye gay;
> Come, go your length; display your strength,
> In rolling rocks away.

Capt. Nosler, assisted by Lorenzo Rima and William Parks, laid out the route while Capt. George Pease, Herbert Percival and Sam Arthur rounded up tools. Jennie Cannon, Clara Gray, Margaret Masterson (Dr. James Masterson's wife), and Elizabeth Havermale (Rev. Samuel Havermale's wife) organized the dinner for the workers.

The following week a large number of people gathered to donate a day's labor, and the first road to Union Park[41] became a reality. It was described as being a little circuitous but quite passable.[42] A similar call resulted in a bridge over Hangman (Latah) Creek, probably at Riverside Avenue.

The falls on the river that had attracted the early settlers continued to draw people to its banks. In spring, the tall cottonwood trees along the river east of town sweetened the air with their perfume while in June the cottony blossoms collected like miniscule clouds settling on the earth. Pleasant coves among the pines and granite boulders invited the women and children to picnic. While the men fished, young boys teased the lively crawdads in the shallow water. Town picnics were held downstream at what was later known as Poverty Flats, and renamed Peaceful Valley in 1893.

Of course there were favorite swimming holes for the boys, young men and Indians. The first was above the sawmill between Bernard and Division. Then they moved farther upstream where the river makes a big bend, just west of the Gonzaga campus. As more and more houses were built, the swimming places had to relocate, since bathing suits were nature's own. Another good spot was below the falls at a bay in the river (later filled in) at Elm and Main streets. They also swam two miles or so up Hangman Creek.

Anytime of year horse racing was a popular sport. Both Indians and white men participated. Every Sunday afternoon (until the Sunday Laws made it illegal), nearly all the men would be out running their fast horses. There was a quarter-mile track from Howard and Main diagonally to a point on Riverside. For a half mile, they would tear down Sprague to Cedar or on out as far as J. J. Browne's fence in Browne's Addition. At one time, Riverside Avenue was the track. In the early 1880s, no significant community event was complete without a horse race. Rich and poor, young and old, all enjoyed watching the serious riders, the buggy races, and the Indian free-for-alls with the same degree of enthusiasm. Of course, betting was as much a part of it as the races.

By the close of the 1870s, Spokane Falls was beginning to take on the appearance of a real town. The official U.S. Census the following year recorded a population of 350. Perhaps it was all the new commerce that prompted J. J. Browne to prophesy that someday the town would have a population of five thousand. At the time, Browne was sitting on a log by the river. Bill Gray and two other men who heard him were all for throwing Browne into the water for making such an exaggerated statement.[43] Browne was far off the mark; by 1890 Spokane Falls climbed to nearly twenty thousand! Both these men would live to see Spokane over the 100,000 mark.

Chapter II

Susan Crump Glover

Susan Crump Glover around 1881.
This photograph, taken in Portland, was
found among Clara Gray's possessions.
(Photo courtesy MAC/EWSHS, L93-66.134)

In all the recordings of Spokane's beginnings, James Glover's first wife, Susan, has remained a mystery – a ghost-like person who seems not to have been here at all. So completely has she been ignored that Glover has been labeled a "widower" or even a "bachelor." Not so!

Susan Glover shared with her husband all the hardships, deprivations and loneliness that characterized pioneer towns whether in the eastern, midwestern or western areas of the United States. Yet most writers would have us believe that in the beginning Jim Glover lived here virtually alone without friends or companions. Never at anytime was Glover the sole white person at Spokane Falls. That the isolation proved to be harder on Susan than on Jim, who was continually occupied in the construction, development and promotion of his town, became only too evident as the years went by. She never managed to overcome a feeling of extreme loneliness.

Susan Tabitha Crump was born in St. Charles, Missouri, late in 1842 or 1843, the third child of J. Turner Crump and Tabitha Remey. Mrs. Crump's first marriage, to Frenchman Henri A. Saucier, had ended in divorce. Missouri did not remain Susan's home for long as the Crumps joined the long migration across the plains to Oregon in 1846. They traveled at times with a number of other families, including the Donner-Reed party who would suffer a terrible winter tragedy in California's Sierra Nevada Mountains. In the same group was the former governor of Missouri, Lilburn Boggs and his family.[1]

The Crumps traveled to Oregon, while the Donner-Reed party took the ill-fated Hastings Cutoff en route to California. The Crumps, however, had severe problems of their own, being among the first parties to follow the so-called Applegate Trail through southern Oregon. The new route, advertised as a shorter and easier route than the well-known Oregon Trail route through the Blue Mountains and down the Columbia River, actually proved to be a hundred and fifty miles longer, and took an additional four months to travel. The Crumps had traveled nearly 2,355 miles in a journey that took nine months.[2]

The Crumps finished their overland adventure and remained in Dallas, west of Salem, until spring 1847. That all the Crumps made it through was a blessing not accorded all families on the overland trail, as hundreds of unmarked graves lined the route. But a high price would later be paid by three-year-old Susan Crump.

When spring came, Crump moved his family into Salem, a town consisting of only three or four houses built by Methodist missionaries, the first of the Oregon missionaries, who were led by Rev. Jason Lee. In the fall, Crump went into business with Thomas Cox and his youngest son, William, recent arrivals from Illinois. They opened Salem's first store in what was known as the "Judson House." This two-story house was built by Jason Lee around 1841 and is now located in the Thomas Kay Historical Park in Salem.[3]

During the six years the Crumps lived in Salem, Turner Crump served as a probate judge and the second postmaster, serving from February 21, 1851, to

October 11, 1852. When William Cox decided to close the store in 1853 because of poor health and move out to his father's farm, Crump, too, moved to a 645.30-acre Donation Land Act claim on top of the hill above the Coxes.[4] The road today closely approximates the old one of over a hundred years ago, and the location of the Crump homestead is about two miles south of Hylo Road on Liberty Road in Marion County, Oregon. Here Susan Crump grew up.

Although nothing is known about her formal schooling, it is unlikely that any education was available beyond some elementary grades. For many years education in the pioneer country was a problem. Students studied on their own, hoping a teacher would be found so school could commence. Susan matured into an attractive, slender young woman who was well liked. Her brother William and a dark-haired fellow by the name of James Nettle Glover apparently worked for William Langhead, possibly as carpenters. Both men had joint accounts with Langhead at the South Salem Steam Flour and Lumber Mills. Thus, Susan met the handsome Jim, who sported a black mustache and goatee.

On the first of September 1868, Susan T. Crump, age 25, and James N. Glover, 31, were married.[5] Minister P. R. Burnett conducted the ceremony at which James T. Crump and a J. Brown served as witnesses. Just before his marriage, Jim, along with Richard[6] and E. Williams, purchased a half-interest in a ferry. In 1863, the other owner, Jasper N. Matheny, had established this first steam ferry across the Willamette River. It connected Marion and Polk counties, with the landing in Marion County at the foot of Trade Street in Salem.[7] In addition to this commercial enterprise, in 1869 Jim served as a Salem alderman and the following year was employed as the city marshal at an annual salary of $650.

After selling the ferry business, Glover and Matheny headed for the upper country looking for a new business opportunity. During this trip, Glover purchased the potential town site at Spokane Falls and the sawmill owned by Seth Scranton and James Downing. The two men then returned to Salem for supplies. Glover sent Matheny and Cyrus Yeaton ahead on the return trip to Spokane Falls with the equipment for a larger, more modern sawmill and with merchandise for their trading post. Jim and Susan left the Willamette Valley in August 1873.

The Glovers' route was by train to Portland, then by steamer up the Columbia River. Boats with comfortable cabins and staterooms plied the river with passengers and freight. At the cascades (Cascade Locks), they were transferred to a narrow gauge railroad run by mule power for a six-mile portage. Then another steamer sailed upstream to The Dalles, where the Glovers stopped overnight.

A second portage, a fifteen-mile wagon ride from The Dalles, was necessary to bypass Celilo Falls. A third boat trip took them to Old Wallula, where Glover hired a wagon and driver to take them to Spokane Falls. Upon their arrival on August 19, a country of scab rock, bull pine and sagebrush greeted Susan. The Glovers moved into the log cabin vacated by the Downings, who left for Moran Prairie.

Frontier life was not unfamiliar to Jim Glover. At the age of twenty, he had taken fruit to the Yreka mining district in northern California where he operated a fruit stand for a year. In 1862, he went to the mining districts of eastern Oregon with his brother Samuel. Near Canyon City, just south of John Day, they made the first discovery of gold in eastern Oregon.[8] Miners immediately poured into the John Day "diggings" from the California and Nevada mines and elsewhere.

The following spring the two Glover brothers moved on with a group of miners to Griffin Gulch near Auburn on the Powder River, southwest of present day Baker, Oregon. Lady Luck favored them again with another pocket of gold. From there, the Glovers and Wash Palmer continued northeast to Eagle Creek, where they built the first house in that valley. From Eagle Creek, they ran a pack train between Sparta and Weiser, Idaho Territory, during the rush to the Salmon River mines. From these various enterprises, the brothers accumulated about $12,000.

Since mining camps where not exactly noted for comfortable living conditions, Jim was as prepared as anyone could be for whatever lay ahead in the Spokane country. But for Susan, it was a new experience. How many times did she dream of home? The entire neighborhood of Salem where Susan grew up had consisted of a large, extended family. Now her neighbors in Spokane Falls were Mr. and Mrs. Swift, Mr. and Mrs. Yeaton with five-year-old Lulu, and Mr. Matheny – all strangers. As soon as the store building was completed, Jim and Susan moved into one side of the two "box" structures where a living room, bedroom and a little kitchen had been partitioned off. Later, Glover built a barn behind their house and store.

The first few years established a precedence of holiday gatherings and social activities at the Glovers' home. No matter how bleak the year or the weather, decorations were made of Oregon grape, a feast magically appeared from their meager supplies, and gifts were created for the children. For these occasions Susan loved to play the parlor organ. There was one difference from former Christmases, however. The curious Indians also came and watched. The townspeople always made certain there was enough food to share with these neighbors.

During the early years before the arrival of the railroads, Glover had to haul his merchandise by wagon from the Columbia River. For eight years, he and/or Walter France traveled to Wallula to pick up the supplies ordered from Portland. Laborious as this was, it did present a change of activity and a chance to see and talk to other people. For the women at the Falls, only the short stay of an occasional traveler changed their routine of "scrubboard" laundry on sunny days, quilt making, bread baking and "patching." They sewed their own clothes, mentionables as well as unmentionables. Every scrap was saved for use; old garments were cut up for new ones. Flour sacks especially were most versatile and were often used for patches.

Lucius G. Nash recalled the first time he met Mr. Glover. Jim was bent over a campfire cooking a steak in a long-handled skillet. Glover's trousers had been well mended with a flour sack. It must have been a ludicrous picture to a nine-year-old, as emblazoned across the seat of Glover's pants in big blue block letters were the words "self rising."[9]

James Nettle Glover, circe 1881
(Photo courtesy MAC/EWSHS, L93-66.120)

Mail delivery to the upper country was irregular. In good weather, if they were lucky, the mail came once a week. In winter it could be weeks between deliveries. This only contact with the outside world and loved ones at home made every mail day a holiday, with everyone wearing his best clothes. Newspapers were immediately scanned carefully for any news of progress on the Northern Pacific Railroad.

Welcome as it was, a precious letter could make one even more lonely and homesick than before. By letter, Susan learned her youngest brother, Lilburn, had died at age twenty-four on July 4, 1874, leaving a year-old son. Perhaps this letter again brought back the shock, pain and heartache of an earlier letter. Before her brother James committed suicide February 21, 1870, he had written to their mother from a Portland hotel. In a lengthy and melodramatic letter the 32-year-old Jim explained that he was unemployed and so deeply in debt it would take a gold mine to pay off. "Read this to Lilburn," he wrote, "and tell him, receive no credit for anything unless he knows where and when he can get the money to make his word good. And above all, tell him never to acquire a habit of playing any game at cards or billiards for whiskey." He also asked his mother to break the news of his impending action as gently as possible to his "angel wife," nineteen-year-old Julia Wilson, to whom he had been married only a couple of months.[10]

Now Susan had lost a second brother and was so far from home she could be of no solace to her mother. Good health could never be taken for granted. Frequent illnesses and disease prevailed among the pioneers: scarlet fever, measles, typhoid fever, diphtheria, rheumatism, consumption (tuberculosis), dysentery, sore throats, chilblains and complications from childbirth. Death of the very young to the elderly had to be accepted.

If Christmas was a time for celebrations and merrymaking by the citizenry at the Falls, Independence Day was even more so – especially the nation's centennial birthday of 1876. Although no telephones, telegraphs, radios or other forms of mass media existed, the news got around; excitement was keen. On the third of July, wagonload after wagonload of families from all directions pulled in to camp beneath the pine trees.

The Fourth of July dawned clear, bright and warm with a spicy aroma in the air. Only the forest of trees would keep the afternoon from seeming sultry. Long before noon, a table nearly a hundred feet long was spread with barbecued turkeys, dozens of hens, large tubs of delicious strawberries and gallons of cream. Pies of every description and a galaxy of frosted cakes had been prepared.

From Rosalia came sixteen-year-old Ella Masterson with an older sister, her brother-in-law and their three children. It was a reunion with their parents, Dr. and Mrs. James Henry Masterson, who would move to the Falls from their ranch at Trent the following year and open a boarding house (the Western House). With the parents were another daughter (seventeen-year-old Rilla) and sons John, Oscar and David.

Years later Ella wrote: "Mrs. Glover, the charming wife of Mr. Jim Glover, found my sister and me early in the day, and declared she knew all about us, embracing us fondly and keeping us close by her for the remainder of the day. She had loaned her organ for the occasion, and she and my sister led the festivities by singing "The Star Spangled Banner" and other patriotic songs."[11] The Declaration of Independence was read, followed by games for the children. Every child old enough to walk was given a flag and marched around in a circle. It was a day they never forgot.

When evening came with the moon and stars outside, kerosene lamps and candles lit up the hall in Glover's newly finished building on the southwest corner of Howard and Front streets. Flags, bunting and evergreens decorated the room while an orchestra of two violins and an organ provided music for dancing until daybreak. The children and older people had long since gone to bed in the campsites among the pines where here and there shone dim lights from their lanterns.

No celebration was held the following year because of the long-remembered scare of an Indian uprising. The fear and potential horror of the Nez Perce rebellion spreading to local Indian tribes automatically drew people together at the nearest village. In Spokane Falls, the logical place to congregate was at the largest house in town, that of Jim and Susan Glover, but as the numbers grew, most retreated to Havermale Island for safety (see Chapter I for detailed account).

The year 1879 ushered in several changes in Susan's life. Her husband had leased his store and sawmill to Anthony M. Cannon and Cannon's brother-in-law, Alexander (Jack) Warner. Jim went to work for the Northern Pacific Railroad erecting whatever buildings the railroad construction camps needed. He also served as their forage agent, purchasing most of the hay and grain at Farmington, fifty to sixty miles from Spokane Falls. In order to receive the funds needed for his purchases or to be reimbursed for his expenses, Jim had to travel to Colfax where the Northern Pacific land office was located. This work required him to be frequently absent from home.

Another important occurrence altering Susan's life was the arrival of some family from Salem. Glover's recently widowed youngest brother, John,[12] came to the Falls accompanied by eleven-year-old George, the son of another brother, Philip Glover Jr. Both made their home with Jim and Susan. While attending school during the year or so he lived here, George proved his academic abilities by making the honor roll. John opened a livery stable with Lane Gilliam on the northwest corner of Howard and Front and also started the first stage line to Colville.

Early in 1880, Jim and Susan sold the lot where their house stood to Frank Rockwood Moore,[13] who planned to build a store on the site with August Goldsmith. The Glovers were relocating uptown on the southeast corner of Riverside and Stevens. As yet, no mill for finished wood existed in town, so all the woodwork had to be planed by hand. In fact, all building materials were difficult to get. Nevertheless, at a reputed cost of $11,000, the *Spokan Times* reported their new home eclipsed anything of its kind in the city. One of the conveniences was having their own well, as water had been found at sixteen feet. Other residences were going up on South Street (Riverside). By August, in addition to the Glovers' house, construction was underway for Rev. Havermale and George Brandt.

The early 1880s may well have been the happiest in Susan's life. Their social life was a whirl. There were grand balls such as the one held on Valentine's Day at the Northern Pacific Hotel. The Cannons hosted many large and elegant parties, with the Glovers, the J. J. Brownes, the Louis Zieglers and the W. C. Grays heading the guest list. When the Sprague House opened with a grand ball, it was

The Glover home, from 1880 to 1887, was located at the southeast corner of River-side and Stevens and later moved to the corner of First and Oak in Browne's Addition. It was subsequently extensively remodeled and converted to apartments.
(Photo detail from Mark Danner's Patsy Clark Album, courtesy Tony and Suzanne Bamonte)

heralded as the great social event of the 1882 season. (The hotel's tenure ended when it burned in August 1884 and was not rebuilt.) They also attended dances and lectures sponsored by local fraternal lodges, as well as performances by the occasional theatrical troupe that came to town.

That Susan had many friends was certainly evident when forty-two people gave her a surprise party the evening of August 8, 1881. Everyone met at the city hall before proceeding en masse to the Glover residence on Riverside Avenue. The guests included single people as well as married couples. Music, parlor games and waltzing in the spacious parlors provided the evening's entertainment. Ice cream and cakes were served. The *Spokan Times* reported the next day that "the visitors were hospitably received and generously entertained as might be supposed by all who know Mr. and Mrs. G." Arrangements for the party had been made while Susan was enjoying the recreational facilities at Medical Lake that day with some lady friends.

It could have been for a birthday gift that Jim ordered a $500 piano from Portland as soon as the railroad reached Spokane Falls in June 1881. It was now possible to reach the Willamette Valley far more easily than before, but it still required a combination train and steamer ride with train ferries across the Snake River. In October, Susan made the two-day trip to the Oregon metropolis in the company of Cyrus and Lizzie Yeaton. Yeaton was now employed as the post trader at Fort Coeur d'Alene. Susan visited family in the Salem area before returning to Spokane Falls in November with her husband. From time to time, Jim went to Portland on business, but it is not known how frequently Susan was able to accompany him. Sometime between June 1881 and 1883, the Glovers took an extended trip by ocean steamer from Portland to San Francisco.

Susan Glover in San Francisco around 1882. Inscribed on the back of the photo was "Aunt Susan Glover, Uncle Jimmy's first wife." *(This photo was found in Barbara Cochran's research files and is presumed to have come from the family of Glovers' niece Venia Culver Maurer)*

Hospitality remained a key ingredient at the Glover home. Frequent guests were the H. W. Fairweathers from Sprague. Mr. Fairweather was a superintendent for the Northern Pacific Railroad, and they had formerly lived at Ainsworth. Fairweather has been described as a "prince among railroad men." A longtime friend of Jim's, he was also an officer in the Spokane Lodge of the Masonic Order. Another brother Mason who stayed at the Glovers' was Levi Ankeny of Walla Walla, the Grand Master for Washington Territory.

This was a time, certainly, when everyone knew everyone else. A wedding was universally celebrated and a death mutually mourned. A picnic by two young ladies, Jennie Ziegler and Olga Brandt, at Medical Lake was a newsworthy item reported in the weekly newspaper. Spokane Falls was that kind of town in the early 1880s.

Just when Susan's spells of despondency began is hard to say. Perhaps it was in Salem after the possible loss of a child. Whether there was a miscarriage or a stillbirth is not known.[14] However, there would be no living issue from Jim's and Susan's marriage. A number of years later, an attending physician indicated her depression dated back to childhood. Certainly there are several references to suggest she had not been well in Oregon. One of the considerations prompting Glover to come to the inland country, recorded Spokane's earliest printed history, was the health of himself "and his wife." In May 1884, a J. J. Murphy from Salem stopped to visit the Glovers. He thought Mrs. Glover looked so much better than when she lived in Salem, he claimed he didn't recognize her. Indeed, he kidded Jim about having married some young girl and that Susan was "his second" wife!

However, a pall of intense loneliness had continually plagued Susan's existence in Spokane Falls. No doubt Jim's frequent and sometimes lengthy absences on

The identity of the women in this photograph is unknown, but the carriage was the typical of the primary means of transportation in the early days of Spokane Falls and probably similar to the one used to meet James and Susan Glover's niece Lovenia Culver at the train depot in 1883. *(Photo from the Don Neraas Collection, courtesy Tony and Suzanne Bamonte)*

business, coupled with a possible family-related emotional instability, played major roles in her inability to cope in later years. Whatever the cause, the Glover family always referred to her affectionately and with great sympathy as "poor" Aunt Susan.

Finally in 1883, Louisa Culver, Jim's youngest sister, offered to send her daughter Lovenia to keep her sister-in-law company. Both Susan and Jim were pleased with the idea and extended a welcome to Lovenia for as long as she would like to stay. As Jim was going to Portland on business in June, he could provide an escort for his niece, affectionately known as Venia. Jim's nephew Wyley, John's seventeen-year-old son, came to spend the summer also. John met the train with a carriage when it arrived early in the morning of June 27. However, when they got home, they found Susan still in bed. Venia wrote to her parents that "Uncle Jimmie rousted her out in a hurry by turning down the cover and spanking her."[15]

Jim's niece added a new dimension to the house at Riverside and Stevens. The very first day, Susan took Venia shopping for a light hat and some ribbons. While she lived with them, they bought her lovely clothes, including a black cloak trimmed with black silk plush.

It was the practice of the ladies in Spokane Falls to visit friends and neighbors in the afternoon. As many as four or five calls might be made depending upon how many women were in, and upon returning home one frequently found that someone had stopped by. Eventually this custom evolved into a more formalized ceremony with certain areas of the town having specific "at home" days. Visits became shorter and the ladies no longer brought their mending or embroidery to share over tea. But in the 1880s, calls were a form of daily feminine companionship, a much needed support group.

From the day of Venia's arrival, Susan proudly took her to meet the Glover friends. One day they found Mrs. Sarah Davenport of Cheney with her three-year-old daughter, Eva, waiting to visit them. The Davenports had lived in Salem before moving to Colfax in 1873 where John Davenport built the first flour mill and ran a mercantile store. Seven years later, they moved to Cheney where Davenport opened a bank.

Venia also met the members of the mixed choir when they gathered to practice at the Glover home for the Fourth of July. There had not been a celebration in town for two years, so this one was going to be a bang-up good one. For six weeks the nineteen members of the choir rehearsed in each other's homes. When they met at the Glovers' home, Susan accompanied them on the organ. Clara Gray and Laura Havermale Burch also sang with the group. The festivities were so successful, it took nearly a full page in the *Spokane Falls Review* to describe them all.

It was several weeks before Venia saw the falls and rode across the bridges. She had to wait for Uncle John to bring the barouche[16] from his livery stable as not everyone in town owned a carriage, and Uncle Jimmie was no exception.

Venia's 15th birthday on July 31 was an occasion for a great deal of teasing. At breakfast Uncle Jimmie and Uncle John participated in the time-honored custom of spanking the birthday celebrant. But Aunty laughed and said she was afraid Venia would not live through the day if she whipped her also. John presented his niece with a nice bouquet of wax flowers in a vase, and Jim and Susan gave her a pair of gold bracelets. Later, Venia recorded her thoughts about being five hundred miles from home and the first birthday away from her parents. Sitting on the end of her trunk with her journal resting on the washstand, she wrote:

> But I am among those who are kind, ah, more than kind to me, with my dear aunt and uncle whose kindness shows itself by kind words, nice presents, and everything that they know of to make me feel at home and happy. May the blessings of a gracious Lord be theirs. Ah! God alone knows what the coming years may bring or just where I may be and how feel in another short year.... When I think of what may happen and what not before I am called sweet sixteen, it almost scares me. But all things that are, are for the best and we have no right to complain.[17]

Lovenia Louise Culver, shown here at age 14, lived in Spokane Falls 1883–1885 with her Aunt Susan and Uncle Jimmie Glover. *(Photo courtesy Frances Maurer Schneider)*

The Glover home faced Stevens Street with large porches on the west and north sides. That spring Jim had replaced the dirt path in front of the house with a substantial sidewalk. Trees grew along the picket fence while in the garden roses bloomed in profusion. This year no vegetable garden had been planted, although in the past there had been one. Vegetables could be bought at the store, but it wasn't like having them right at your door, Susan told Venia. They did have a chicken coop. Out in the woodshed, Venia found five kittens to play with and love. Venia's room was upstairs, to the right as one faced the house, where she had a good view of the town with just a peep at the "new bank." Uncle Jimmie was putting up a two-story brick building, the second in town, on the site of his former store. Scheduled for completion by fall, the building measured fifty by seventy-seven feet and cost around $19,000.

Over the years, Jim's involvement with politics and the city had continued unabated. At a Republican convention for the Spokane Falls precinct, Jim, William C. Gray, George Davis, A. M. Cannon, J. T. Lockhart, C. B. King and Louis Ziegler attended as delegates. Their purpose was to elect delegates to the state convention in Vancouver. Although he was nominated, Glover declined, as he refused to go as an instructed delegate. Apparently, he preferred his own opinions to those of his constituents.

In the spring of 1883, Jim became Spokane's second mayor, and his official duties kept him doubly busy. On August 2, some important visitors arrived from Fort Coeur d'Alene: Generals Sherman and Miles, and Associate Chief Justice Wade. Glover hired the barouche for the occasion, but General Sherman indignantly refused the ride, saying he preferred to walk around town. That evening a "general handshaking" was held two blocks from the Glover home at Cannon's Hall. However, as Susan did not attend the reception, Venia also missed seeing the celebrities.

Before Wyley had to return to Salem in August for the beginning of school, he and his father, an avid sportsman, took the Northern Pacific train to Spirit Lake for a week of hunting and fishing. Their trip proved successful as John killed two deer, but was able to bring only one home. They reported the gnats to be in great supply and very hungry!

School began for Venia, too, on September 19 in the Methodist Church. Located just two blocks away on the southwest corner of Sprague and Washington, it was close enough for Venia to walk home for lunch. Professor Isaac C. Libby was the teacher for the thirty-five students. The classes were held in the basement of the church and included: Latin Fifth Reader, Peck's Complete Arithmetic, algebra, spelling and writing. Venia shared a seat with Julia Post in the first "town" school she had ever attended.

A major problem developed in the household that fall when Waw, the Chinese cook, unexpectedly announced he wanted to go to the Coeur d'Alene mines. He had been with the Glovers for two years. However, he brought another Chinese man to take his place. The fellow prepared a reasonably good dinner, but breakfast the next morning was so bad no one could eat any of it. Jim out-and-out told him to "git!," as Venia recorded the incident in a letter to her parents.

For the next ten days, Susan and Venia fixed breakfast, which Venia did not think was much of a chore since they bought their bread. In fact, she thought it rather fun as everything was so handy in the kitchen. For the noon meal, she and her aunt prepared whatever they liked while the men ate downtown. For dinner everyone went to Carson's Restaurant.

Jim next hired a big, stout-looking girl, Minnie Thompson, who bragged that she wouldn't ask a cent in wages if she couldn't beat anyone in Spokane cooking. Obviously, she did not make much money at the Glovers' because two months later they were without a cook again. Although Venia helped as much as she could, Susan felt as if she had been driven up the wall over the lack of hired help, or in her words: "gone up the spout."

It is interesting to note that Jim did the hiring of the domestic help. While other women in town handled this chore, Susan either rejected the responsibility or Jim wanted to have control of everything. For someone who had made her own bread and was willing to help newcomers in that art only ten years earlier, Susan seemed to become unduly upset with this interruption in the household. Louisa Culver even wrote from Salem to suggest Susan hire a good German girl, as cousin Lou always had good help and relied only on German women. However, the filling of this position had to wait for Jim to return from Olympia.

Chapter II

Finally, a new girl came on the 19th of November. Venia reported that Susan's spirits had risen, but how long her happiness would last depended upon whether or not the girl worked out. Since Venia no longer mentioned the situation in her journal or in letters home, the new cook must have been satisfactory.

As mayor, Glover had gone with Colonel C. F. Morgan to Olympia in October 1883, to lobby for a further division of Spokane County. In letters to his wife, Jim did not know when he would be able to leave the territorial capital. They had been gone exactly four weeks when the two men returned. Glover expressed the hope that he would not have to go back again as his business always got behind when he was out of town. Nevertheless, a week later he and Louis Ziegler were again on the way to Olympia in spite of Jim's having a bad cold and a fever. The weekly *Chronicle* reported their journey as being for the purpose of "throwing oil on the troubled waters of the county division legislation." It must have worked as Grant, Douglas and Lincoln counties were separated from Spokane, and Spokane County has not changed in size since. It was hoped the county seat would go along with the new boundaries as Spokane Falls already possessed the Land Office. The county seat was considered a choice plum to bring into town from outlying areas potential customers who might also have business at the court house. This did not happen, however.

Being away from home was not always easy for Venia, and homesickness took over. She was the middle child in a very close and loving family. Letters from home were never frequent enough, often two months apart. Venia usually wrote on Sundays after returning from church. She always inquired about all the many cousins, friends and neighbors.

Although Venia greatly appreciated the solicitude and kindnesses of her uncles and aunt, she greatly missed her mother and her home remedies, especially when she was not well. At one time, Venia had a case of diarrhea for over a week that kept her feeling miserable, and she lost some weight. Eventually her health improved. Susan and Venia weighed themselves, and in the first eight months with the Glovers, Venia had gained twenty-four pounds. This made her four pounds heavier than Susan, whose weight was a trim 121 pounds.

Susan and her niece attended most of the Sunday morning services at the Methodist Church where the Reverend R. E. Bisbee was the pastor. They also went to any evening lectures at the church. One visiting minister was Father Wilbur, an older Methodist preacher who must have practiced in Salem as Susan remarked to Venia that she had known him since she was as "big as a piece of chalk."

At Thanksgiving, their church held an old-fashioned dinner at noon. The ladies and girls, including Venia, waited tables dressed in Pilgrim costumes. Venia found it amusing to "dress-up and pretend" for such occasions. At home, two fat old hens were cooked for the holiday.

Religion seemed to be important to Susan although no evidence has been found that she was ever a member of any church or that she necessarily attended after Venia left. This is surprising since the first sermon in the little town was held in the Glover home November 14, 1875. Jonathan Edwards stated that the Reverend Samuel Havermale's first sermon was held "in a 'box house' used for a residence just west of where the city hall now [1900] stands." The Yeatons lived behind the store while the Glovers' home was in the other half of the box-house. Although Mrs. Yeaton is credited with playing the organ and leading the singing on that occasion, it is far more likely that it was Susan who performed those services.

Jim Glover was the sixth son in a large family. His parents, Philip and Sarah Koontz Glover, had eleven children. Jim's home was always headquarters for visiting brothers. William, the firstborn and oldest brother, came through Spokane to investigate the Idaho mines. Sammy, the third son, arrived in time for Christmas 1883 and stayed through the spring. Then he, too, went to the mines. Ironically, Sammy declared the Coeur d'Alene mines to be overestimated! He was a frequent house guest and eventually made his home with Jim for the last thirty years of Jim's life. John, the tenth child and youngest brother, lived with Jim and Susan for six years. He returned to Salem frequently and tried to spend the Christmas holidays with his son Wyley and daughter Mary.

Venia's letters to her parents provide a glimpse of Spokane College, its faculty, curriculum and activities. The school became a center for social gatherings for the young people and their families especially after it moved into its own building across the river at College Avenue and Jefferson Street. Moving day was December 13, 1883, the day before the term ended for the Christmas recess. Venia expressed her pride at being one of the first students to attend the school.[18]

The two-story building had high towers and a mansard roof. Because the rooms were not quite finished and contained no seats, the library had to be used for a recitation room. Venia walked to school and took her lunch. Sometimes the girls wandered down to the river during the lunch break, and even found buttercups in bloom while the snow still covered the ground.

Spokane College operated on the quarter system. Tuition cost $9 for the preparatory students, $7.50 for the primary, and $15 for the commercial course. Languages and music required extra fees. After the spring break, the attendance in Venia's section dropped to less than half as some of the boys had to quit school to work on home farms. Being able to go to school full time never ceased to be a marvel to Venia, who was most appreciative of the educational opportunities her uncle and aunt had made possible.

Professor Libby served as president of the college, but was succeeded by Rev. R. E. Bisbee the second year. Other faculty members included Professor Boulton from Montreal, L. D. Westfall, Mrs. Waltz, the music teacher, and Professor Pangborn. Some of Venia's classmates at Spokane College were Lulu Kelley, Roy Clarke, Minnie Morgan, Nettie Piper, Will Smiley, Ida Kirkman, Jennie Crystal and Julia Post.

From time to time during the school year, "sociables" were sponsored by the college either in their chapel or at the Opera House. These get-togethers provided most of the activities for the youth. The faculty attended and even presented some of the entertainment. Mr. Westfall liked to write amusing prophecies about the students. Refreshments were provided by the young ladies. Group singing seemed to be informal sing-alongs rather than an organized choir. Athletics played no part in the school's curriculum or activities.

Some of the older students were invited to "give a piece" at lodge meetings, civic gatherings for visiting dignitaries, or other town functions. Each term at the college concluded with what was called an "entertainment" or declamation contest. These varied little in content: original or paraphrased essays, poems, stories and selected readings. A debate would be in the form of essays with no rebuttals. Sometimes a few musical selections on the violin or piano would be included. What was missing were dramatic skits, monologues and one-act plays. These occasions were well attended by Susan and Jim, Uncle Sammy and the other parents.

The program ending the winter term March 25, 1884, turned out to be a very special occasion. Three prizes were offered: two for elocution and one for composition, which were to be determined by three judges for each category. Venia had rejected the topics suggested by Professor Libby as being too hard to write about, so she came up with a story about a dewdrop. It did seem like a silly little subject to her, but her originality paid off as the prize in composition was awarded to the writer of "The Dewdrop."[19] When the astonished Venia received a bright new five-dollar gold piece, her aunt and uncle were just as thrilled as she was. Jim even accused his wife of crying, she was so happy.

A typical Sunday afternoon at the Glover home would find Aunt Susan and Venia writing letters while uncles Jimmie and Sammy napped. John, on the other hand, was probably downtown visiting widow Margaret Seaman Paynton, a nice-looking woman whom John had met in Colville before she moved into Spokane with two of her children. She operated a dressmaking business from her apartment in the Union Block. John claimed Mrs. Paynton was a good talker, and Venia figured he ought to know. John got a good deal of teasing from the other family members which he took good-naturedly when he began squiring Maggie around.

City affairs kept Jim busy following his reelection as mayor for a second one-year term in the spring of 1884. Cousin Wyley also returned to town. He went to work at $40 a month for H. C. Hayward, who ran a sporting equipment store.

Down the street west of the Glover house stood Louis Ziegler's hardware store. On March 26, 1884, the Masonic Lodge moved into the hall above it with a big dedication party. All the Glovers attended. Of course there were speeches: O. F. Weed gave the main address followed by Levi Ankeny of Walla Walla, the Grand Master of Washington Territory. Then Louis Ziegler took the rostrum. H. W. Fairweather of Sprague had a turn as did ten other speakers. Interspersed among the talks were selections by a choir under the direction of Dr. Penfield. When the exercises were concluded, a supper was served about 11:00 p.m. Then the band struck up a tune for dancing, which continued until three in the morning.

Venia described the occasion to her parents: "You should have seen Uncle and Aunty get around. They were as light on their feet as any of the young folk ... We are well acquainted with Mr. Ziegler and family who owns the building." (The Zieglers lived one block south of the Glovers on the southeast corner of Stevens and Sprague.) "I danced more than anytime since I have been here, and had a very nice time ... I expect you all are beginning to think I am getting very wild and spoilt. I know I am petted enough to be spoilt, if such a thing is possible."[20] It is easy to understand why this lovely, unsophisticated young lady was a very special person in the home and hearts of her aunt and uncle.

Venia had hoped for a visit home during the summer, but she had to wait until Jim had time to leave. Finally on July 9, Jim, Susan and Venia boarded the Northern Pacific train for Portland and a reunion with her family.

The winter of 1884-1885 came in earnest with deep snow and cold weather. By Christmas, the snow reached two to three feet deep with temperatures plunging to eighteen below zero. The trains stopped running, making it impossible for John to leave on his customary holiday trip to Salem. The weather made good sleighing, but Venia thought it too cold to be pleasant. It was so cold, she wrote home, that she and Aunt Susan did not do much but "laugh and grow fat."

Chapter II

The Glovers did not have a tree that Christmas. Yet Venia found her chair at the breakfast table on Christmas morning stacked with boxes and bundles. She received a diamond ring, a lovely pair of bracelets, a nice large scrapbook, a neck comforter and, from Uncle John, a pretty Christmas card. Susan unwrapped a very handsome pin and Christmas card while Jim found a nice moustache cup and saucer with forget-me-nots and strawberries on it.

As 1884 came to a close, Venia wrote in her journal: "As I look back and note the events of the past year, how many changes can be seen. I can now play on the piano. I am quite well acquainted with the people up here, I am getting along well in my studies, and my health is quite good. Oh! how many, many blessings I have to be thankful for. It seems almost impossible that it is I who am receiving such advantages and such kindness."

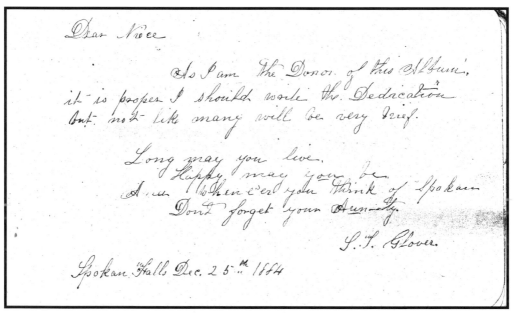

The first page of Venia's plush autograph album, which was given her by Aunt Susan when she lived with them in Spokane. *(Courtesy MAC/EWSHS, MsSc220)*

One sad obligation marred the new year. Mrs. Schuyler S. Havermale (Florence or "Kitty"), the twenty-eight-year-old daughter-in-law of Rev. Havermale, passed away suddenly of a brain disease after a short illness. She left two children: a boy of eight and a four-year-old daughter. All the Glovers attended the funeral services held January 1.

One of the New Year's Day customs in Spokane Falls was to visit one's friends. The ladies stayed home to receive the callers, however, while the gentlemen did the calling. Although Susan expected some visitors, Jim said he would also call on her as he was going out with four or five other men.

A Spokane street scene in 1885. *(Photo from* Spokane and the Inland Empire *by N. W. Durham)*

In the spring of 1885, Jim left for an extended business trip back east. Even though he was the mayor and missed several city council meetings, he was not expected back until the latter part of April. How fortunate for Susan that she had the company of Lovenia as well as John and Wyley during this long absence of her husband.

Summer brought an exciting event when John Glover, age 43, and Maggie Paynton were married June 11, 1885. His longtime friend and business associate, Lane Gilliam, and Maggie's sister, Carrie M. Seaman, stood up with them. One son, Sherman, would be born of this marriage.

In July, Jim's mother died of a stroke at the age of 82. She was buried next to her husband and other members of the family in the Macleay Cemetery. Venia graduated from Spokane College in June and returned to her family home.[21] What a void her departure must have left in Susan's life. Venia was a sweet, charming young lady and, always willing to please, had been a pleasant companion. She was dearly loved by both her aunt and uncle and reciprocated that feeling throughout her life. In fact, one of James Glover's last letters was written to Venia just eight weeks before his death November 18, 1921.

Jim's interests continued to take him out of town in the fall of 1885. Besides trips to Portland, he went to Olympia in December to badger the Territorial Legislature for another election on the location of Spokane County's government. "May success crown his efforts," wrote the *Spokane Falls Review.* Eventually the pressure paid off as an election in 1886 moved the county seat permanently to Spokane.

By the latter part of the 1880s, Spokane had passed its babyhood. The population swelled to several thousand. The mines in the Coeur d'Alenes brought new people to town every month. Railroads were spreading in all directions. If the city by the falls had been slow in starting, it was making up for lost time by racing to become a "boom" town. The frenzy in building, the opening of new banks, and the start of more businesses were paced equally by the social structure with enlarged social activities, the organization of women's clubs and church groups, local entertainments, and the appearances of professional troupes.

In the middle of all this was warmhearted, affable Jim Glover. This was still "his" town, and he was taking an active part in shaping and guiding it. But had it grown too big for Susan, who seemed to be the very antithesis of her husband? There were other, better voices to sing the hometown renditions of operettas, and other hands to prepare the receptions and plan the get-togethers. More and more of the newcomers, leaders in business and finance, came from the eastern states, were college educated (as were a surprising number of their wives), and from a background of moderate to wealthy families. Perhaps there was little in common with the emigrant child from an Oregon farm. Could it have been because of her insecurity that Susan seemed to fade into the background?

Another niece came to keep Susan company in the summer of 1886. When Jim returned from Portland on May 4, he brought twenty-year-old Ada Cox, the youngest child of Susan's sister. However, by the following winter, Jim and Susan were living alone without any other family members.

In January, Jim received an offer from F. M. Tull of Kansas to buy the lot on which their house sat for $7,500. This seemed too good an opportunity to pass up. Later, Jim admitted going around town telling everyone he had caught a "sucker." Tull planned to put up a brick building on the site that was appraised the following year by a San Francisco mortgage firm for $100,000. Some sucker!

One of the agreements of the sale was to move the house to Browne's Addition.[22] After completing the negotiations, the Glovers moved downtown into quarters over Jim's bank building – practically right back where they had started. The house was moved slowly down Riverside Avenue during July 1887, block by block, interrupting the telephone lines. Finally, by the fourth of August it was settled on the southeast corner of First Avenue and Oak Street, the property of William Pettet who had purchased it for his daughter and son-in-law, Grace and J. P. M. Richards.

Jim and Susan attended the Christmas party given by the Masonic Lodge in mid-December 1887. The next day, the *Spokane Falls Review* reported that the

J. N. Glovers would be leaving soon for California to enjoy the "tropical climate of the Golden State during the middle months [of winter]." The Southern Pacific Railroad had begun advertising its Shasta Route connecting Oregon and California. However, something must have prevented their departure, as two weeks later their attendance at the Ladies Benevolent Society's Charity Ball on New Year's Day was also duly noted in the newspaper. This may have been the last time Susan and her husband appeared together in public socially. However, Susan continued to accept invitations from her friends for euchre card parties, luncheons, etc., although she seemed not to entertain in return. No mention in the newspapers appeared about any social events at the Glover home as a couple or singly.

On February 8, Jim left for the east with a stop in Helena before continuing on to Hot Springs, Arkansas. There he joined his good friend Hanford W. Fairweather, who with George Brooke had founded a bank in Sprague, which they named the First National Bank of Sprague, in 1886.[23] Glover's health had not been good for some time, and it was thought the hot mineral waters might be beneficial. The previous summer he had been ill with a touch of malaria, and from time to time, he suffered from a sore and swollen throat and ran a fever. His extensive business interests in mining, real estate and banking carried heavy responsibilities. With James Monaghan, he often made inspection trips to the mines at Wardner. Glover was probably exhausted and needed a quiet rest.

Jim had incorporated the First National Bank of Spokane in November 1882, with F. Rockwood Moore, its first president; Horace L. Cutter, longtime cashier; H. M. McCartney; Dr. L. H. Whitehouse; and August Goldsmith. Glover served as the bank's first vice-president. They opened on the southwest corner of Howard and Main.

The next month A. M. Cannon moved his Bank of Spokane Falls and the mercantile store into his new wooden building on the northwest corner of Riverside and Mill, vacating Glover's building on Howard and Front. This opened the way for Jim to tear down his six-year-old, one-and-a-half-story wooden frame in order to erect, in 1883, his two-story brick Glover Block, which became the new location of the First National Bank.

Glover obviously recognized and appreciated the value of architectural planning as he hired a new arrival, Herman Preusse, to design the Glover Block. This was Preusse's first assignment, as would be architect Kirtland K. Cutter's work with Glover a few years later. J. T. Davie's brickyard in Stafford's Addition between Twenty-eighth and Twenty-ninth avenues and Inland Empire Way furnished the bricks. Henry Brook supervised the laying of them.

The Glover Block, built by J. N. Glover in 1883, on the southwest corner of Front and Howard was the second brick building constructed in Spokane Falls. For a few years, it housed the First National Bank of Spokane. The wagon train was loaded with supplies for the military Fort Spokane. *(Photo from* Spokane and the Inland Empire, *1912, by N. W. Durham)*

In 1886, the First National Bank, of which Glover was president, moved into a four-story frame building leased from John and Mattie Hyde Blalock at the

The First National Bank Building, 1888, built by Glover at the northwest corner of Howard and Riverside. *(Sketch from* Spokane Falls Illustrated, *1889)*

northwest corner of Howard and Riverside, which was closer to the center of commercial activity. In 1888, a three-story brick building, known as the First National Bank Block, was erected on the same site. The Spokane National Bank was diagonally across the street, thus establishing Howard and Riverside as a banking corner.

In 1887, Glover increased his holdings along Howard Street by purchasing a two-story brick adjoining his bank building to the south from Dr. B. F. Burch for $9,000. At the same time, his First National Bank sold a sixty-foot lot to R. T. Daniels on the southwest corner of Howard and Main for $20,000. This site had been the bank's temporary location five years earlier.

When the First National relocated in 1888, F. M. DeWitt's wholesale cigars and tobacco shop rented the vacated space. The drugstore had previously moved, and M. H. Whitehouse used that location for a jewelry, optical, and book store. For two years, Jim and Susan lived above the ground floor shops.

Jim's wisdom in constructing a brick building paid off when a fire broke out September 14, 1888. Starting in the Pioneer lunch counter on Main, the fire ate its way along Main to Mill and down Howard to Front. Lost also were the Queen Chop House, the Star Lodging with a saloon underneath, the Senate Saloon, Mrs. Hunt's hair dressing establishment on Front, and Dr. John Morgan's office and residence on the northeast corner of Mill and Main. The only building remaining in that entire block was Jim's little brick. Amidst all the confusion of smoke, cinders, firefighters and frightened people came the call that a child was lost. Jim happened to find the little girl, whose face was burned. Susan immediately took over and cared for the child.

That year Jim purchased a tract of land along Eighth Avenue from the Northern Pacific Railroad. It reached from the head of Washington Street east to McClelland and south to the rimrock. Glover, who was now a millionaire, commissioned K. K. Cutter, a teller in his bank and a nephew of the First National's cashier, to design a home worthy of Glover's wealth and station in life.

At a reputed cost of $80,000 to $100,000 including furnishings, it was grand indeed! Gone were the woodshed, chicken coops and familiar "outhouse." Now there was "inside" plumbing, a carriage house, sweeping lawns and formal gardens. The most impressive structure of all, the manor house, sat against a bank of outcropping rock. Built of native granite with the English style of half-timbered gables, the mansion contained twenty-two rooms. The main entrance through a stone arch fifteen feet in diameter opened directly into the large two-story reception hall that measured twenty-four by twenty-five feet. Elaborate hand-carved woodwork in antique oak with two large arches was an outstanding feature of this room. Under the open grand staircase, which covered the south wall, one arch lined with benches led to the conservatory. The other one at the foot of the staircase gave entry to a back hallway and a sleeping room in the southwest corner of the first floor. At the northeastern end of the hall stood a large granite fireplace with a five-foot opening. Lion heads adorned each side.

All the wainscoting in the room contained a set-in square design including the side jambs and yoke of the deeply recessed north windows, almost giving a basket-weave appearance at first glance. A mezzanine overlooked the hall on three sides while on the west wall a baronial balcony extended from the master suite above the great hall. Directly beneath the balcony, double doors opened

The Glover mansion at Eighth Avenue and Washington Street. *(Photo courtesy SPLNWR)*

into a lovely ladies' parlor with white and gold woodwork and delicate blue upholstery in the Marie Antoinette style. A small fireplace daintily decorated a corner. Across the north side of the mansion from the great hall to the east were the library and dining rooms, each leading into the next through double doors hung with heavy velvet portieres. Finished in a warm cherry wood, the library wainscoting continued the recessed square design. Architect Cutter reversed this pattern in the dining room with the squares set-out. The built-in buffet and ceiling beams of oak were stained a dark, almost black color.

A billiard room, finished in pea green and oak, a pantry and kitchen completed the first floor. There were only five fireplaces in the house, a small number in relationship to the number of rooms. A central steam heating system heated the entire house.

On the second floor a large dressing room, or possibly the mistress's sitting room, adjoined the master bedroom. All the other sleeping chambers were re-moved from the master suite by the width of the entry hall and were located above the eastern half of the mansion. To the rear of the house through the porte cochere stood the $8,000 barn and carriage house with a matching granite arched entry.

Magazines featured this fine home with its unobstructed view of the Spokane Valley: "The delight of its occupants and the pride of the town."[24] The greatest innovation of all, of course, were the three bathrooms, inside plumbing being uncommon in 1889. The Glovers moved in shortly before the Great Fire. It was a far cry from the cramped partitioned-off part of "two box structures put together" of some sixteen years earlier.

After the devastating city-wide fire of August 4, 1889, the following year brought such a burst of building that local pride wanted the world to see the "new" Spokane that had swept aside ashes, rubble and tents. With Spokane acclaimed as the only gateway to the Northwest, the Northwestern Industrial Exposition was planned to "acquaint the world with the enormous advantages and unsurpassed natural resources of the entire Pacific Northwest." The Exposition Building stood on the northeast corner of Sprague Avenue and Hatch (then Grant) Street, a gigantic three-story edifice with an imposing roof line, a turret on top and flying flags. Unfortunately, with opening day scheduled for October 1, the carpenters went on strike September 17. A call went out for volunteers to report with hammers and tools. Susan's husband was one of the more than 350 men to show up. Prominent citizens loaned nonstriking carpenters from their own buildings to get "the job" done.

At the suggestion of Lane Gilliam to enlist the aid of the ladies, the president of the exposition, F. Lewis Clark, invited the wives of the city's most prominent social leaders to meet in the parlors of the Hotel Spokane. He asked them to provide an elegant luncheon at the expo building for the volunteer workers. This they did. Entering into the spirit of the occasion, Susan was among the ladies who waited on the tables.

To say that the personal relationship between the two occupants of the mansion at the head of Washington Street was eroding would be an understatement. In fact, it had been deteriorating for quite some time. One wonders whether or not Susan was ever happy in their fancy house. Loneliness had plagued her before, but now she rattled around in a gigantic stone palace. She was hardly needed to manage the household, let alone bake the bread or patch her husband's trousers. At age 47, Susan's moods could easily have fluctuated from highs of good cheer to the depths of depression and irritability.

It seems significant that neither Jim nor Susan was a founding member of any church or listed as even being affiliated with any denomination. Yet Glover had contributed generously to many church building funds. It seems unusual that, although the Glovers were the original pioneers of the town, Susan is not included as a founding member of any of the women's social or philanthropic organizations, not even the Ladies Matinee Musicale group. Could her name have been deliberately deleted from the annals of history to protect her husband from embarrassment? We will never know. However, by the beginning of the 1890s, this couple, once the very core of community activities, was becoming conspicuous by their absence.

The fabulous Auditorium Theatre built by Cannon and Browne had its Gala Premier on September 16, 1890. Anybody who was anybody was there, but the Glovers were not. Although Jim was on the committee and Susan named as a patroness of the Grand Ball that marked the opening of the Exposition, they were again among the non-attending.

The entire situation came to a head and erupted in August 1891. Jim's attorney, James R. Smith, drew up a four-page "Articles of Separation." The Glovers took this means of legally declaring their future relationship rather than suffer the publicity of a divorce. They both agreed there had been a total lack of compatibility evidenced by differences and frequent disputes for more than ten years, and that continuing life together would be completely untenable.

According to the agreement, Jim would not sue Susan for living apart or compel her to live with him, nor would he sue, molest, disturb or trouble any person for receiving, entertaining or harboring her. Furthermore, he would not, without her consent, visit her or knowingly enter any house or place where she might be. Nor would he send or cause to be sent a letter or message to her. It was to be as if she were a "feme [*sic*] sole" and unmarried. Jim lived up to the letter of this contract.

Jim further agreed to provide a well-furnished and comfortable home for Susan at or near Mrs. L. J. Culver's (Venia's mother) about four and a half miles east of Salem. He was also to provide a horse and carriage. For her support and maintenance, he would pay her one hundred dollars a month for the "rest of her life."

So eager was Susan to leave that, except for her jewelry, personal effects and apparently a few household goods, she waived any claim to property rights and interests then or at the time of Jim's death. Should either of them at a future time proceed with a divorce, she could claim no alimony.

It would seem the separation could have been Susan's idea, as her sister, Adeline Cox, came from Salem to help her move and was a witness to the "Articles of Separation." However, the legality – the actual drawing up of a contract, duly signed, witnessed and notarized – was probably Jim's or his attorney's. Susan was not represented or advised by a separate counsel. In so signing, she relinquished any right to her millionaire husband's fortune or property.[25] Susan left for Salem August 28, 1891.

Presumably, Jim met Esther Emily Leslie sometime during the fall of 1891. Having come to Spokane Falls the previous year from Lewiston, Maine, Esther was employed as an insurance agent with offices in the Auditorium Building. She resided on the north side of Broadway Avenue in the block west of Home

(Chestnut). Esther had four sisters including a twin, Emma, Delia Smith, Mina Rowell, Doram Hull and a brother, William Franklin Leslie. Except for Emma who remained in Maine, Esther's family, including her parents, Samuel Chase and Mary Ann Leslie, emigrated to Spokane after 1892.

Deciding that marital happiness was still available to him, Jim filed for divorce January 11, 1892. The Divorce Complaint charged that the defendant was and had remained impotent, barren and incapable of reproduction, which was unknown to the plaintiff at the time of the marriage.

A second allegation clearly spelled out what life had been like between Jim and Susan. Stating that the marriage had been unfortunate in every respect, the extreme incompatibility of temper, differences in tastes and inclinations, habits of life and bend of mind and aspirations made them wholly unsuited and uncongenial with each other. "This incongeniality [sic] which existed between the parties was so extreme that it rendered cohabitation and social intercourse between them repulsive, beyond endurance on the part of either, and in fact, impossible."[26] About ten years after their marriage, around 1878, because of the incompatibility and complete repugnance to each other, the plaintiff and the defendant had not lived together as husband and wife. Both parties recognized this fact, rendering it impossible for them ever to live together again.

The "Articles of Separation" were included in the divorce complaint as evidence that there had been a property settlement and there was no community property of the said spouses in spite of the fact the State of Washington had had a community property statute since 1869. This contention was based on Glover's claim that his real estate holdings and capital stocks had all been acquired by him from income earned or proceeds from property owned by him "prior" to their marriage. Hence, the return from that original purchase of land by the falls, he said, enabled him to now own eighty acres at Galena (one-half mile west of Fairchild Air Force Base), three hundred twenty acres in Lincoln County, nine acres along Hayden Lake, Idaho, a half-interest in two quartz claims in Stevens County, plus lots in Medical Lake and in five separate additions throughout Spokane, as well as the property with his residence and parcels of property in the downtown area. Glover further claimed that the large amount of personal property that he owned – including household furniture, useful and ornamental objects in his house – was all separate property of the plaintiff. He also claimed as separate property shares of capital stock in the First National Bank of Spokane, the Spokane Savings Bank, Traders' National Bank, Washington Water Power Company, the Seattle, Lake Shore & Eastern Railway Company, and the Spokane and Northern Railroad, plus notes, mortgages and other securities.[27]

Susan was duly served with process, but failed to respond. On March 31, Jim was allowed to amend his Complaint for Divorce with the following paragraph: "IV. That defendant has been guilty of cruel treatment towards plaintiff and has heaped personal indignation upon him without fault on his part, and that there is such incompatibility and lack of congeniality between them that they cannot live together as husband and wife."[28]

The rules governing divorce in 1892 were the same as the laws for civil procedures insofar as a waiting period was concerned. However, in cases of abandonment for a year, adultery within a year, or "cruel treatment," there was no time specified, and a divorce could be granted upon application. Therefore, Glover amended the original complaint with the charge of cruel treatment in order to expedite the obtaining of his divorce. S. G. Allen, prosecuting attorney, was appointed to represent Susan; Lucius B. Nash represented Glover. Mrs. Glover's failure to appear to answer charges was adjudged by the court to be a confession of guilt. Glover claimed and the court confirmed that all the property previously described was the separate property of the plaintiff. In addition to the one hundred dollars a month, if Susan should lose the house in which she was then living through no fault of her own, Jim was to erect on any land owned by Susan in the states of Oregon or Washington as she designated, a dwelling house equal to the one she currently had of no less value than three thousand dollars.

These papers serve a double purpose: they not only describe the legal proceedings taken at that time but also reveal a side of Glover's character and personality not seen before. Although the briefs were drawn up by his attorney, Glover concurred with the contents by signing his name and swearing in court to their validity.

Described as being unpretentious in spite of his wealth, Glover, in actuality, was a very ambitious man. His tastes and aspirations were geared to the "affluent" life in direct conflict with Susan's. From the beginning, Jim always had the largest house in town and had it first. The mansion on Eighth Avenue was intended to be a "show place" to exhibit his great wealth instead of a home, as evidenced by its entry into a vast baronial great hall. Had Susan reveled in their social status, she would never have traded a $100,000 mansion for a $3,000 home and $1,200 a year, even with a horse and carriage!

It is possible that Susan had nagged Jim to return to Salem from the earliest days in Spokane until in later years she became a viperous shrew. By the same token, it may have been Jim's perseverance, or just plain stubbornness, that made him stick it out in Spokane until he became financially successful. He kept it all – even the household furniture and art. Where was the friendly,

James and Esther Glover. *(Photo courtesy SPLNWR)*

easygoing, generous "Papa" Glover? Toward Susan he extended no charity. He was stubborn, and she was moody and querulous; no wonder life together was untenable, leaving each intensely bitter toward the other.

The divorce was granted March 31, 1892, by Judge W. G. Langford. On Saturday, April 2, James N. Glover, 55, and Esther E. Leslie, 33, were quietly married in Rathdrum, Idaho.[29] The *Coeur d'Alene Press* carried the following paragraph April 9, 1892: "James N. Glover, president of the First National Bank, of Spokane, was married at Rathdrum, last Saturday, to Miss E. E. Leslie also of Spokane. This is the finale of a very unsavory scandal in which he figures as the principal. He was recently divorced from his first wife with whom he had lived for forty [actually twenty-four] years."

Unfortunately, the story does not end happily. For a reason known only to herself, Susan Glover returned to Spokane two weeks after Jim's marriage. Described as being of slender build, pale with a look of melancholy in her eyes, Susan was met at the Union Pacific train and driven to a prominent residence on Pacific Avenue – the Zieglers' perhaps. The Glover separation and subsequent divorce had not occurred without creating waves. Friends of both had tried to dissuade them from the course of action taken eight months earlier. So intense were some of the loyalties that friendships had been severed. Now the lines were being drawn again.

Chapter II

It seemed to be no secret that Susan had been receiving medical treatment for mental problems in Salem during her absence from Spokane. That her closest friends considered her vastly improved was noted in an article in the *Spokane Review* reporting her return April 15, 1892. (Interestingly, this article was found in Maggie Ziegler's scrapbook along with all the family items. Obviously, Maggie considered Susan a longtime and dear friend.) The journalist proceeded to speculate on Susan's motives and commented that Jim's recent marriage had been considered reason enough to keep the former Mrs. Glover away. Now it was conjectured that Susan's return was to contest the legality of their divorce. She supposedly claimed irregularities and duplicity in the proceedings, as the attorney who had obtained the divorce for Jim had actually been employed by her as her legal advisor. Furthermore, the article indicated Susan was dissatisfied at the unequal distribution of property.

Determined friends of Jim's, it was said, were trying to persuade Susan to desist and return to Salem by offering her an increase in the financial arrangements. On the other side were those who were equally determined that fair play should prevail. These alleged statements led the reporter to observe that "a lively time may be anticipated."

What the reaction was from the honeymooners in the mansion on the hill to this Sunday morning article is unknown. Susan, however, annoyed by this gossipy, malicious writing, requested an interview with the newspaper to dispel any false impressions that might have been created. At John Glover's home where she was then staying, Susan informed the public via the *Spokane Review* that she planned no such legal action. Nor was any hearing ever heard in court.

It must have been an even lonelier existence for Susan during the next seven years. One wonders how many "old" friends continued the friendship. Perhaps they tried as she was a trustee of the Ladies Benevolent Society in 1893 (later the Washington Children's Home), although the roll book shows she did not attend their meetings.

Susan moved from one downtown apartment to another. She stayed at the Hotel Spokane for a while, then moved to 403 West Fourth Avenue between Washington and Stevens, and later lived at 207 Fourth between McClelland and Bernard. Nothing seemed to be satisfactory. By 1896, she had packed up again and moved to number 76 in the Granite Block which, ironically, was on Washington and Riverside at the eastern end of the block where she had lived ten years earlier. Another relocation put her back home: number 233 in the Tull Block, built on the site of her former home where perhaps she had been the happiest and most comfortable. Here she stayed a couple of years.

In the meantime, Jim, too, had been forced into a couple of moves. The Panic of 1893 hit the Bank of Spokane Falls on the 5th of June when it failed to open its doors. July 26, the First National went into liquidation. In 1895, Simon Oppenheimer bought the Glover mansion for the Hypotheekbank. Jim and Esther rented Clara Gray's large home on Fifth and Washington until the house at 702 South Washington was ready. Here the Glovers lived for approximately thirteen years before moving in 1909 to a Cutter-designed bungalow at 1408 North Summit Boulevard.

One would not expect to find Susan a member of their former social sphere as society became more and more elaborate, wealthy, elegant and isolated. But then, neither were Jim's and Esther's names to be found in the society columns. They did attend the 50th wedding anniversary reception for Rev. and Mrs. Samuel Havermale on November 1, 1899, which was more like a pioneer family reunion. However, the J. N. Glovers were not among the guests at the Louis Zieglers' 30th and 40th anniversary parties in 1892 and 1902, although the J. J. Brownes and the W. C. Grays were present. Jim and Susan had attended the Zieglers' 20th celebration. Divorce and remarriage seem to have altered Jim's life far more than did his loss of capital, which he regained to a certain extent.

Toward the end of June 1899, Susan decided to buy a house owned by the proprietor of the Grand Hotel, C. B. Strong, at 316 South Ash for $1,500. However, when no money had been paid by the end of a week, he sold the house to someone else. Unknowingly, on the following Saturday, July 1, Susan had a wagonload of furniture, including a piano, taken from her rooms and placed on the first floor of the house on Ash Street. When Strong heard of this, he took a workman to the house who helped him move the furniture and piano out onto the sidewalk. Susan found her possessions there in the open air when she returned that evening. Confused, upset and in a daze, she wandered around the neighborhood for several hours before coming to rest on the front steps of the McCrea home at 1623 West Fourth Avenue.

On Monday, July 3, 1899, the *Spokesman-Review* carried the story:[30]

SUSAN T. GLOVER IS INSANE
Found in a Demented Condition and Placed in Custody

Crazed and in a partially helpless condition, Susan T. Glover was picked up by the police last Saturday night and taken in the patrol wagon to the county jail, where she was confined, pending today's session of the superior court, when her mental responsibility will be examined into.

Officer Beals made the arrest as a result of a telephone message from the home of ex-City Treasurer McCrea, requesting that an officer be sent to remove a demented woman from the front steps, where she had been sitting for some time, resisting all attempts at approach.

Office Beals found Mrs. Glover sitting on the steps. He tried to induce her to go home, offering to accompany her. She refused. Then the officer said he would send for a carriage and have someone in citizen's clothes go home with her. She violently replied that she did not want to go home, or go anywhere, and that she would allow no one to lay a hand on her. When the patrol wagon arrived, Mrs. Glover refused to enter it. The officers lifted her bodily into the patrol. The crazed woman was placed in a cell in the women's department of the county jail ... Friends of Mrs. Glover say that within the last year her mental affection has been growing worse and that at times she became almost abusive. Physicians will now examine the unfortunate woman and determine whether or not she is capable of having the care of herself. Mrs. Glover was formerly the wife of Councilman J. N. Glover.

The headline in *The Chronicle* that evening was no more kind.[31]

SHE CAME TO SPOKANE MANY YEARS AGO
Twenty-Six Years Since Susan T. Glover Came Here – Doubts as to her Sanity

Mrs. Susan T. Glover, formerly wife of Councilman J. N. Glover, will be examined this afternoon by Dr. Freeman and [Dr.] Mary Latham to determine as to her sanity. Mrs. Glover was taken in custody yesterday, and has since been confined in the women's department at the county jail, where she is being cared for by Mrs. Thompson, wife of one of the jailers. The warrant charging Mrs. Glover with insanity, was sworn to this morning by C. B. Strong of the Grand Hotel. Mrs. Glover is very restless in the jail and has kept her hat and wraps on all the time, saying she has some important business which she must attend to at once. She spends all of her time at the barred door, ready to go out as soon as it is opened.

Mrs. Glover was one of the first white women to settle in this country, and said this morning that she came here in 1873. She is said by her friends to have been acting queerly for some time past, and on one or two former occasions it was decided to try to have her committed to the asylum, but no action of this kind was taken, as she always seemed to get better right away. A short time ago she seemed to get an idea in her head that she had purchased a house from Mr. Strong and moved in. Later Mr. Strong sold the house to other parties and Mrs. Glover refused to move out when requested to do so. She said this morning that they had moved her goods out into the street and she was homeless, but as soon as she was released she would be able to settle the matter and would regain possession of her house.

After a hearing and testimony from several witnesses, including her former husband, who were paid $2.20 for appearing in court, Susan was judged to be suffering from melancholia (depression). Although considered neither suicidal nor dangerous, she was declared unable to care for herself any longer. At the age of fifty-six, Susan Crump Glover was admitted to Eastern State Hospital at Medical Lake on July 3, 1899. Here she would remain for the rest of her life.

Events move in strange ways. The second heaviest stockholder after Jim Glover when the crash of 1893 closed the First National Bank had been Jules L. Prickett. He also lost everything. Later, Prickett became active in the Cariboo Mining, Milling, and Smelter Co. in the Camp McKinney District of British Columbia, serving as its secretary. The president and manager was James Monaghan. The close friendship of the Monaghans and the Michael M. Cowleys is well known.

Eastern State Hospital above Medical Lake. The first building opened for patients in 1891. Susan Glover was admitted in 1899 and remained there for the rest of her life. *(Photo from the Magee Collection, courtesy SPLNWR)*

As devout Catholics, they would never have sanctioned a divorce action like the Glovers.' At the time of her medical examination by doctors Latham and Freeman, Susan had given the name of M. M. Cowley as a friend. It is possible that Cowley and Monaghan prevailed upon Prickett to apply for appointment as Susan's guardian.[32] In any event, he was so designated by the court on July 13, 1899.

Susan's meager possessions had been placed in the hands of the Northwest Storage and Transfer Company. They consisted of a piano (very old), a bed and two dressers, a few chairs including a rocking chair, a valise (empty), two rolls of carpet (very old), some miscellaneous items and two bucketsful of kitchen utensils – all old, much worn and of little value. In addition to these, her only other asset was 160 acres of unimproved land in Lincoln County located a mile and a half east of Harrington.

Because there was no income to pay the taxes and the administration of her Lincoln County land or the $2.50 per month storage fee, let alone provide for her personal needs, the court ordered that Susan's assets be sold except for what furnishings she was permitted to have at Eastern State Hospital. These amounted to a trunk of clothing and a chair. We do not know what happened to the hundred dollars per month for life that Jim Glover agreed to pay her.

Prickett sold the land for $1,500, the piano for $180, and the other items brought in $25. This amount he invested for Susan at four-percent interest. For twenty-two years, Prickett purchased out of this fund the clothing Susan needed: dresses, aprons, shoes, stockings, sweaters, nightgowns, yardage, etc. He shopped at quality stores: Kemp & Hebert's or the Palace Department Store. Each time an order was sent to the hospital, he also included candy, nuts and fruit for Susan. Nor did he ever forget a gift at Christmas time. Every year, Prickett submitted an accounting to the court, including all the sales receipts and the value of her estate.

October 11, 1921, Susan succumbed to lobar pneumonia, having been considered senile for years. Jim Glover passed away only thirty-eight days later on November 18. Her death certificate gives no date of birth, lists her as having been single and other personal data as "unknown." Did no one care? The day following her death, with no mortician in charge, she was buried in the hospital cemetery. Although it would have been kinder had arrangements been made, even years earlier, to have her body returned to Salem where other members of her family rest, Susan's grave site is not forlorn. Marked only by a small concrete brick bearing a number, as are all the graves, she lies at the foot of a pine tree in a large field that slopes down to the shore of West Medical Lake. The area is probably similar to the prairie that had stretched in front of her first home at the falls. The wind still ruffles the tall grass and murmurs through the pine trees. There are wild flowers that bloom, and birds that sing.

James Glover in 1914.
(Photo from Mark Danner's Patsy Clark Album, courtesy Tony and Suzanne Bamonte)

At the time of her death, Susan's estate totaled $2,796.25, but she left no will. Prickett requested her estate since he had never been paid for managing her affairs for over twenty years. Surely no one could have done more for Susan in providing for her needs and wisely investing her nominal funds. After being notified of her death, Susan's survivors filed suit a year and a half later for her estate. The court paid Prickett $300 for his services of twenty-two years. An attorney received $75, and the balance went to family members.

The life of Susan Crump Glover is the story of a woman who had suffered incomprehensible hardship as a child on the Oregon Trail, whose husband founded a city and became a millionaire, but who spent the last quarter of her life in a mental institution. Tragic and sad as it was, what greater insult could there be than to deny her very existence – this lonely woman who at the very best was "the First Lady of Spokane Falls," and at the very least was one "who also pioneered a town."

EPILOGUE

In 1979, Venia's daughters, with the assistance of the author and Jean Amy Adams, placed a granite marker in Spokane's Greenwood Memorial Park cemetery in memory of their Great-aunt Susan.

Anna Stratton Browne

Anna Stratton Browne as a young woman.
(Photo courtesy MAC/EWSHS, L93-66.38)

In her writings, Anna Stratton Browne reminisced about her first impression of Spokane Falls.[1] "When I saw all the pine trees, I knew I had no regrets in leaving Spangle and Colfax. I loved Spokane from then on." Even so, as she and her family drove down the track called Howard Street in July of 1878 and pulled up by the little wooden store, her heart sank. Roughly dressed men in frontier garb came out on the platform to get the mail, and Anna felt she had arrived at a very desolate place.[2] They had just left Portland, Oregon, their home for the past four years.

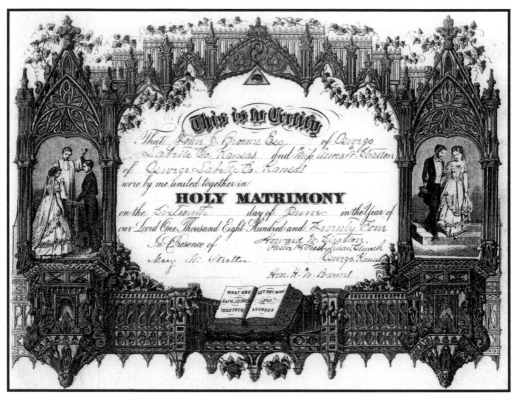

John J. and Anna Stratton Browne's marriage certificate. *(Courtesy Joanne Kohler Rieger, great-granddaughter of J. J. and Anna Browne)*

Anna Whittlesey Stratton and John J. Browne had been married in Iola, Kansas, on June 16, 1874. Although not quite 19, Anna defied her father by marrying Browne, almost thirteen years her senior. They immediately left for the West. Although it was never stated, it is likely they traveled by train to San Francisco. From California they would have taken an ocean steamer to Portland.

By the next year, Anna's parents, Rev. Howard W. Stratton and Mary Ann White Stratton, with her three younger brothers Charles, Alfred (Alf) and Clarence (Clad), also emigrated to Oregon. Stratton was the pastor of a combination Presbyterian and Congregational church in Albany.

In Portland the young couple experienced a difficult financial struggle. Although J. J. had hung his shingle out, his law practice was not profitable. Their only source of steady income, albeit minimal, came from Browne's election as superintendent of schools for Multnomah County. So penniless were they that J. J. did not have the fare to visit Anna at Christmas in Albany, where he had sent her to recuperate from the loss of their firstborn son in November 1875. It was several months before he could save enough to pay her passage on a river boat back to Portland.

Attorneys, like circuit riders, went where their calls took them. In the spring of 1878, Browne was in court in The Dalles, Oregon. Expecting to be there several months, he tried to find a place to rent so that Anna and baby Guy, born August 9, 1877, could be with him. Nothing was available. He even approached a carpenter about building a cabin for them. But, as the fellow wanted seventy-five to a hundred dollars to put up a box house only ten by twenty feet, plus a monthly rental fee of eight dollars, Browne turned him down.

About that time, providence, in the form of Anthony M. Cannon, played a role in determining the Brownes' future. Cannon was heading for a place called Spangle in the upper inland country and suggest-

John J. Browne, whose portrait was taken in San Francisco, circa 1874.
(Photo courtesy MAC/EWSHS, L85-45)

ed Browne go along. Having had frequent bouts of bronchitis from the damp coastal air, Browne decided it might be advisable to seek a drier climate.

Browne and Cannon left The Dalles on April 12, 1878. From Colfax, Washington Territory, they twice traveled to Spokane Falls. Pooling their resources, the two men made a fifty-dollar down payment against the total purchase price of three thousand dollars on half of James Glover's town site.

J. J. wrote to Anna: "I had hoped to write full descriptions of the places I visited and give you some account of the people. Let me say, however, generally that the people whom I have met have been hospitable and kind even to a fault. I was never treated better anywhere. I have been received as a friend and brother."[3]

With only enough money left to move their families to Spokane Falls, Browne and Cannon returned to Portland. By early July, J. J., Anna, and eleven-month-old Guy set out for their new home. They were able to go by boat as far as Almota on the Snake River. The bald rolling hills tapering sharply to the river were a direct contrast to the evergreen forests they had known in Portland. Nor did the scenery improve very much as a lumber wagon took them on the next leg of their journey.

They reached Colfax, fifteen miles north of the Snake River, about dusk on an unusually cold third of July. The town was crowded in anticipation of the coming holiday, and the Brownes were fortunate to secure one room in the only hotel. As this room seemed to be the only one with a fire in the grate, other women crowded into the room to get warm. They chatted late into the night making it difficult for Anna to get Guy to sleep. The ladies unanimously expressed their opinion that the Brownes were foolish to consider taking a baby to a place as wild as Spokane Falls, especially since Colfax was the only town of any promise in the area.

Nevertheless, on the morning of the fifth, the Brownes left on the stage, so-called although it was only a light spring wagon that carried the mail as well as passengers. As they reached the top of the long climb out of Colfax, a wheel broke. Passengers, baggage and mail were dumped on the prairie while the driver went back to Colfax for repairs.

When they finally arrived in Spokane Falls, the question of a place to stay arose immediately and was answered as quickly. On Browne's previous visit, he had stayed with Frederick Post, the miller. Again, Mr. Post invited the new arrivals to his large home on a bluff overlooking the river and his grist mill (northwest corner of Post and Front, now Spokane Falls Boulevard). The Brownes occupied the two unfinished rooms upstairs. Unfortunately, the windows that had been ordered from Portland had not arrived, making it necessary to cover the openings with boards whenever it rained.

The Brownes remained with the Posts until the following spring and found them to be the truest of friends. "Mr. Post was the very soul of uprightness and honor, a man whose word could always be trusted implicitly," Anna later related. "His wife and grown daughters were hospitable, kind, and generous like himself."[4]

Browne filed a preemption claim to the quarter section west of the town site. He opened a law office in two rented rooms upstairs in Glover's building overlooking Front Street (later to be called Front Avenue).

Anna found that J. J.'s description of Spokane Falls had been accurate. There was a nucleus of a town: a gristmill, sawmill, a store, saloon, and post office with some half dozen residences. So, too, had been his vivid description of the falls:

> You will see that the river comes from the east, turns to the southwest and runs in that direction about three hundred feet when it again turns to the west and flows toward the setting sun a mile-and-a-half where it turns to the northwest. [This rock] is forty feet high and perpendicular. It is just above the "great falls." Look! Where? Anywhere! Look to the south, to the east, to the northeast, and north! Magnificent! Sublimely grand! Great Good is this breaking up of the mighty deep! See the great waters as they leap and jump and beat themselves into angry foam white as the driven snow, and then whirl and jump and leap again. Down over the rocks splashing and foaming the waters come with a mighty power

and force, heaving and swelling and thundering until earth and air and everything seems one moving, heaving, thundering, frothing, angry mass bent on destruction![5]

One day as Anna was busy in the main room of the Post home by the thundering falls, she heard a faint noise. Looking around, she was terrified to see a half-dozen big Indians lined up against the wall. They had entered as silently as cats and were as quietly watching her. Although this happened frequently after that, she never ceased to be startled by it. They seemed to be fascinated by baby Guy and always asked to see the "white papoose," a novelty to them.

Having lived in Portland, a city of 15,000 where most everything was readily available, Anna found the shortage of food to be the greatest hardship that first winter. In particular, milk could only be procured on an irregular basis. Rev. Cowley's cow wandered at will and only came in to be milked about once in three days.[6] At such times, Anna might be able to get a pint of milk. Guy's principal source of nourishment was bread soaked in warm water or weak tea, but he seemed to thrive on it. Butter was nonexistent from December to April. They even ran out of potatoes that first winter. Anna carefully hoarded one peck to plant in the spring when they moved into their own house.

J. J.'s law practice took him to Colfax, Colville and even as far as Walla Walla. When he was called to try a case in the Crab Creek area, Anna begged to go along. In a light spring wagon rented from Mr. Glover, they followed the un-populated road fifty miles southwest to Crab Creek. Although they arrived in the evening at the two-room home of the justice of peace, it was decided to proceed with the trial immediately. Browne was defending a man accused of shooting a neighbor over disputed property rights. Anna and Guy went to bed while the trial, held in the next room, lasted most of the night.

The next day J. J. decided to return to Spokane via Deep Creek. Although he received explicit instructions for the unfamiliar road, Browne needed to rely upon the sun for directions. A heavy rain obscured the sky, and by the end of the day the Brownes found themselves at the Columbia River, eighty miles from Spokane.

Fortuitously, a ranch appeared where they were welcomed to spend the night. The one-room shack with a fireplace and earthen floor was the home of a white man, his Indian wife, and six children. Dinner consisted of boiled hog's head, fried cakes of flour and water, and tea, but there was milk for Guy. The beds were bunks against the wall with buffalo robe coverings. As tired as they were, they were grateful for a place to rest. It was a two-day journey back to Spokane Falls. This time they spent the night at the farmhouse they had missed the day before.[7]

On April 24, 1879, the *Spokan Times* announced that J. J. Browne had just erected a very neat dwelling in one of Spokane's most pleasant suburbs, soon to be called Browne's Addition. Anna described the house, which faced east, as "just a box structure of rough boards with four rooms and rough board floors."[8] Their property went from Pacific Avenue on the north to Second Avenue on the south, and extended one block west, where the horses and cow were pastured. To the north of the house was a patch of alfalfa. An orchard grew on the southeast corner near the house.

Being isolated a mile and a half from town had some definite disadvantages. During the first summer the Brownes were on their homestead, J. J. had to make a trip to Colville. Anna, Guy and the young girl Anna had hired to help with the baby were left alone. A carpenter had been working on the house, enlarging the windows and putting on new doors

A sketch of the Brownes' home, 1879-1887, at 1717 West Pacific. *(From* The West Shore: An Illustrated Journal of General Information Devoted to the Development of the Great West, *April 1884)*

since these materials had become available locally from a new planing mill.

As evening approached, the carpenter expressed concern about leaving Anna alone with open windows. Although she assured him she was not afraid and the Indians had always been friendly, he propped some large boards against the window openings.

Just after nightfall a knock came at the door. When she did not respond to several inquiries and more rapping, a man's voice asked her to open the door as he wanted to see Mr. Browne. She suggested he see her husband at his office in the morning. Whereupon the man asked if Mr. Browne was out of town and in Colville. Anna admitted that he was. The man moved a few feet from the door, and Anna heard a click that might have been a match striking or the cocking of a revolver. Either thought was equally terrifying. Anna quickly grabbed the baby, motioned to the girl, and climbed to the second floor. The stairway only reached the landing with a ladder to the room above. After scrambling to the top, Anna returned for an ax and a mattress, then pulled the ladder up into the loft.

All night Anna and the girl lay on the mattress, too terrified to speak or sleep. About three in the morning, the man walked around the house several times trying the doors. Finally he left. Fortunately, he never tried to push against the boards leaning over the window openings. Anna never found out who he was or what he wanted.

The Indians were frequent visitors to the Browne homestead, especially when they were ill. Anna believed she put more mustard plasters on Indians than anyone else. It was a common treatment for any kind of ailment. The most usual complaint of the Indians was a stomachache, and a mustard plaster was as good a remedy as any other.

Chief Garry visited their home, as did Chief Seltice of the Coeur d'Alenes. Seltice was a benevolent Indian with a kindly face. Guy took to him and would stand by the hour looking up at his face although he was afraid of all the other Indians. One day Chief Seltice asked Anna for a dress for his wife. She either made one or somehow acquired a dress, which Seltice's wife wore day and night.

When Christmas came, Anna wanted to do something for the boys: two-year-old Guy and baby Earle, born on October 5. She popped corn and strung it on a small tree. J. J. went downtown, but all he could find was a box of blocks and a book for Guy and a jacket for the baby. Meagre as it was, that Christmas of 1879 was the one Anna remembered more than any other. "It isn't what you have," she later remarked, "it is what you feel that really counts."[9]

Anna's husband, in his late thirties, was energetic, ambitious, active in community affairs, totally in love with his wife, and proud of his growing family. He had been born April 28, 1843, in Greenville, Ohio. After his mother's death when J. J. was two, he was reared by his maternal grandparents in Columbia City, Indiana.[10]

Following graduation from Wabash College, Browne began his lifelong commitment to education. He was in charge of the high school in Columbia City and also served as the superintendent of schools in Goshen, Indiana. He decided there was greater remuneration in the field of law and, accordingly, attended the University of Michigan Law School, graduating in 1868.

His reputation as an educator followed him to the upper inland country. Following the formation of Spokane County in 1879, Browne, who was responsible for drawing up the bill to create the new county, was appointed as its first county school superintendent.[11] He served on the Spokane school board for sixteen years, often as president

Browne's active involvement in education continued throughout his life, in and out of Spokane. Prior to 1893, he was appointed to the Board of Regents for the University of Washington and was elected president. He was a regent for Eastern Washington University (then the State Normal School at Cheney). After six years, the governor transferred Browne to the board of Washington State College in Pullman, where he also held the offices of president and vice president.

Chapter III

The Brownes' first daughter, Alta May, was born April 8, 1881, after a difficult delivery. Anna's mother remarked that it was not to be wondered at when she heard of Anna's doing all the out-of-doors work: milking the cow, taking care of the horses, planting the vegetable garden, and never neglecting the flower beds. "You are the same imprudent girl, aren't you?" her mother wrote.

Anna never changed. Blessed with two "green thumbs" and not afraid of hard work, she had a lifelong love for and interest in growing things, especially flowers. Her flourishing garden was so well known in town that the newspapers commented on it. She even sent C. B. Carlisle, editor of the newly organized *Chronicle*, an eight-pound turnip, which prompted him to print that Mrs. Browne's garden was the envy of all.

Anna's father, perhaps lured by the enthusiasm of the Brownes for their new homeland, became the first of a number of her relatives to settle in Spokane. Brothers Alf and Charles followed shortly afterwards. Rev. Stratton took out a homestead about five miles north of town that later became known as Stratton's Addition. At best, he was a difficult man. Although a Presbyterian minister, he never had a congregation in Spokane. Conflict with his parishioners had led to moves from Ohio to Kansas to Oregon and finally to the little town by the falls. Stratton had a hot temper, constantly driving himself, expecting perfection in others, and feeling great pain when they fell short. He once wrote to Anna: "I hope you will never know the constant sense of failure and disappointment which I feel because my family falls so far below my ideals and hopes. Probably for this I am largely responsible, but 'that' does not lessen the pain."[12]

The most revealing insight into Rev. Stratton's personality came from his wife, Mary, when she told Anna that her father was the busiest man physically, mentally and "religiously" that she ever saw – poor man. She hoped he would be rewarded for his increasingly untiring sacrifice and wear of body and mind. "I was wondering the other day," she wrote, "how much of Spokane he had contracted to plough, scrape, and shovel this summer and how many churches, missions, etc. he had to shoulder."[13]

Regardless of Mary Stratton's understanding of her husband's foibles, she stayed in Oregon when Rev. Stratton relocated in Spokane. Moving to Portland, she took in boarders to support herself. Although she occasionally visited her daughter and sons, Mary and Howard Stratton never again lived together. H. W. did a variety of things in Spokane: he taught school, farmed, preached once in a while, and with Rev. T. G. Watson started the Centenary Presbyterian Church on the north side, although he was never its pastor.

Anna Stratton Browne was a romanticist, and she found a lifelong love in the man she married. If the Victorian era was marked by a formality between husband and wife, this was never the case with Anna and J. J. He wrote to her as "My dear Tart [Sweetheart]" and signed his letters "Lovingly, Hub." She affectionately called him "Brownie." Over the years their loneliness at being parted, and their desire to be together, never diminished. They both expressed themselves fluently and never failed to say the thoughts the other one wanted to hear. When they were separated, each expected the other to write frequently, if not daily.

Anna's letters could be gently scolding as when she chided him for going away in cold weather leaving her to sleep alone. She almost froze. Or she could be most sentimental, recalling their early years together with every scene written in her heart. Best of all, she told J. J., was the love he showered upon her through every act, word and look.

Browne was no less wistful. When Anna was visiting in Portland, J. J. tenderly wrote to his wife: "That place on the west side of town is not home, it is a lonely dark spot. It will probably be 11 or 12 by the time I leave the office and when I get home, it will only be to find a dark tenantless house and as silent as the tomb except for the rattle and bunk of that everlasting never sleeping wood rat. No wife, no babies, nothing but darkness and the dismal, horrid gnawing of my unobserved and unobservable rat."[14]

Obviously devoted to his wife and family, Browne often took one of the children with him on his business trips, the girls as well as Guy or Earle. Even when he had to be away for several weeks, he included a child whenever he could. He never failed to tell Anna how proud he was of his companion, the attention they attracted on the train, and their good deportment.

Anna's children and husband were always the central part of her life, but never more so than during those early years on their homestead, especially when J. J. was out of town. If the weather was cold and snowy, she spent a lot of time playing with the children. She would dance and take turns waltzing each one around the room. When the boys broke the head from the body of Alta's doll, she tied it on and made an apron for the doll to comfort Alta. She consoled Irma Spokane (who had joined the family May 10, 1883) when she fell out of the rocking chair and bruised her lip and nose. Anna laughed at Earle, who was developing a talent for mimicry. Once she rented a sleigh and took the children for a ride.

Should one of the youngsters become ill, Anna was beside herself with worry. It seemed someone always had a cold, sniffles, earaches, or something else.

Hazel, Alta and Irma Browne, circa 1890.
(Photo courtesy MAC/EWSHS, L87-98)

Their bout with scarlet fever left Anna feeling that she could endure no more. Dr. N. Fred Essig made frequent calls to the house on Pacific Avenue.

Even with her devotion to her children, Anna kept abreast of events in town and wrote to J. J. on the affairs of his office when he was absent. She mentioned who was building and where. This information meant more to Browne than a mere concern for the community. It involved his personal finances intimately. From the beginning, J. J. had invested heavily in property, not only in town, but out in the county as well. He had erected a two-story brick office building on the northwest corner of Post and Riverside in 1883. But, as business became slack, he felt discouraged. The Coeur d'Alene gold mines were attracting a great deal of attention, the town was full of people, yet no one seemed inclined to buy any property.

J. J.'s interest in the little town also included its politics, although he never ran for the city council or served as mayor. A staunch Democrat, Browne discussed his political views with his wife. It was another topic of mutual understanding that they shared in their correspondence. The spring elections of 1884 prompted Anna to write: "Afraid you won't get home in time to have any influence before the city election.... Everything will be in all probability 'cut and dried.' " (J. N. Glover was re-elected mayor for another year.)

In the fall of that year, Browne was again looking for capital to be invested in Spokane Falls. Finding none in Walla Walla, he headed east in October. In Minneapolis, Browne tried to interest C. A. Pillsbury of the milling firm to buy Post's flour mill in Spokane. In Chicago, he contacted no less than 20 loan agents without success.

In New York, he struck out again. A Mr. Wright told him very frankly that nothing could be done in the way of negotiating loans at the present time. "I do not think that any money can be had on property in your town before January next. In the present state of the market I would be unwilling to attempt to raise money for you."[15]

The one bright spot for J. J. was the results of the 1884 presidential election. From New York he graphically described the scene:

> This city is wild with enthusiasm – joy is unbounded – all night last night the people stood in the rain around the *Herald & World* offices many thousands in numbers to receive the news and as favorable reports came in the immense throng cheered and cheered again and again until the very walls of the massive buildings seemed and in fact joined in the echo. [Grover] Cleveland and [Thomas] Hendricks elected – The republic saved!

From Spokane Falls, Anna passed on the news that the Democrats claimed victory of Charles S. Voorhees's bid to Congress. She most earnestly hoped so, if for no other reason than to defeat Glover & Co.[16] When Browne heard that Vorhees had been elected from Washington Territory, he tossed his hat in the air in the lobby of his hotel and gave a good rousing "hurrah!" much to the amusement of the other guests.

On the home front Anna managed as best she could. She had to collect the rents, about $160, pay the most pressing bills, and send the rest to her husband who was desperately in need of cash. At the house Anna saw that Henry, the hired man, butchered the last pig, but she took care of the meat and rendered the lard. If it was time to fill the ice house, Anna arranged for that, too.

The house on Pacific Avenue grew as the family grew. Hubert Dale Browne arrived January 17, 1885. Anna laughingly recalled that people claimed an addition to the house was built every time there was a birth in the family – and that was pretty often. The two-story white house had a living room or parlor and a big dining room with a fireplace and large table. Two bedrooms, a woodshed that was also a summer kitchen, and a washroom behind the kitchen occupied the main floor. Upstairs were more bedrooms. There was no inside plumbing, and baths were taken in a wooden tub in the kitchen. A couple of hired girls and Henry, who worked for his board, helped Anna take care of the growing household, the garden and Cherry, the cow.

Browne's business endeavors often involved A. M. Cannon as a partner. Their original purchase of half of Glover's 120 acres included the middle falls (now referred to as the Upper Falls), which was half the water power in the river. Later they purchased part of Frederick Post's land, which gave them a half-ownership in the Lower Falls.

While Browne was in New York, Cannon and Mr. Brandt bonded all of the waterpower together. Acting for Browne and themselves, they put a purchase price of $30,000 for all their interests in the river and all that pertained to it. In December 1884, F. Lewis Clark, with whom Browne had started negotiations the previous summer, bought Post's mill and the water rights. The next year, Clark and Frank Curtis built the C&C Flour Mill to the north of Post's mill.

By 1885, J. J. realized he could no longer handle a law practice and the increased demands of his real estate and other business enterprises. After seven years, he closed his law office. However, his financial situation did not seem to improve. While J. J. was in Portland, he again relied upon Anna to collect the rents. It took a determined stand to get money from people who were equally determined to stall or bid for more time. As Christmas approached, Browne wrote that he expected Anna to take out what she needed for Christmas purchases, but admonished her to let the sum be as small as possible.

Scarcely were the holidays over before Browne again journeyed east. He arrived in Washington, D. C., with a two-fold purpose: to promote the annexation of northern Idaho to Washington Territory, and to obtain a charter to build a railroad from the Northern Pacific line to Coeur d'Alene City with a steamer connection across the lake. A second line was to run from the Old Mission at Cataldo up the south fork of the Coeur d'Alene River to the mines. In New York Browne had interviewed the Northern Pacific and Oregon Railway and Navigation officials requesting their support and influence in Congress.

Browne was fortunate in being able to depend upon a wife as intelligent and understanding as Anna to take care of business and domestic affairs in his absence. She was as good as an office manager, following his instructions on the kinds of receipts to get and what notes to deposit. One new renter, F. E. Curtis, however, gave Anna a hard time by demanding that she have the floors, doors and windows fixed. Nor would he pay his rent in advance. Browne apologized to his wife for not having taken care of those things before he left. He realized that Curtis would not be a profitable tenant. "He belongs to that class who are never satisfied or if satisfied it would only be when he was furnished with accommodations worth $50 per month for $15."[17]

Although Browne frequently reminded Anna to get along as cheaply as she could, he did not want her to run out of money. He felt it was better to buy on credit, if necessary, than to run out of funds in case any of their employees needed or wanted some money.

The bill to annex northern Idaho passed the House of Representatives February 25, 1886. It never got beyond that point. On the railroad matter, Browne spent two and a half months in Washington trying to lobby a bill through Congress that would permit him to build. He was told his company had to have $250,000 in its treasury before the Secretary of the Interior would give his consent for

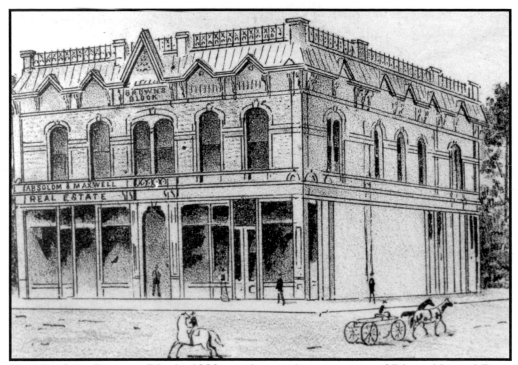

Sketch of the Browne Block, 1883, on the northeast corner of Riverside and Post.
(From The West Shore: An Illustrated Journal of General Information Devoted to the Development of the Great West, *April 1884)*

Browne to build on public land. While Browne waited, D. C. Corbin and Sam Hauser received the backing of the Northern Pacific in July, and in the fall built the two railroad lines Browne had proposed.

The Brownes welcomed a third daughter, Hazel Jay, October 15, 1886. Anna had already decided they needed a new home. They hired Frank Johnson, a neighbor who lived farther west of them on Pacific, as the architect. The location chosen made a six-block area bordered by Pacific on the south, Riverside on the north, Hemlock on the east, and Coeur d'Alene Street on the west.

The original construction estimate of $20,000 nearly doubled by the time of completion almost two years later. About 200 houses of all kinds and sizes were built in Spokane in 1886, the most expensive being banker Horace Cutter's dwelling on Seventh Avenue at $6,000. The Brownes' house was said to be the finest residence between Helena, Montana, and the Cascade Mountains. It was indeed elegant.

The house rose three stories with a mansard roof and a brick veneer. The foundation consisted of cut granite blocks. The basement with nine-foot ceilings had been divided into six rooms for a furnace, laundry and cellars for food storage.

A sketch of the Browne mansion, located half a block west of Hemlock on First Avenue, where the family lived from 1888 to 1902. *(Sketch from the* Northwest Magazine, *April 1890)*

Two parlors with twelve-foot ceilings were located on the first floor along with a sitting room, library, dining room and kitchen. Through the use of sliding doors, most of the main floor could be made into one large room. The hall from the main entrance and the stairway were large and spacious.

On the second floor were located seven bed chambers with eleven-foot ceilings. The third floor also contained seven rooms, but the ceilings were only nine and a half feet high. Each floor was furnished with the most modern appliances for heating and lighting, patent bathtubs and toilets. Although boasting central heating, each room contained a fireplace for auxiliary heat. Grates, fireplace mantles, tiles and other furnishings had been purchased in Chicago.

The main portion of the house was 42 feet square with a 20-by-24-foot wing. Connected to the house was a glass conservatory. Porches ran along four sides of the building. Situated in a grove of pine trees, the house also had a tower with a commanding view.

The grounds included the usual ancillary buildings: a barn, an ice well and chicken coops. One hundred and fifty fruit trees were ordered from Mr. Ritz's nursery in Walla Walla. Besides a number of horses, there were also a cow, rabbits, turkeys, chickens and goats. A two-acre deer park and a large vegetable garden completed the complex.

In addition to their home in town, Browne owned an operating farm on Moran Prairie and a smaller one at Spangle, each with a resident manager.

While the house was under construction, Anna and J. J. decided to consult the doctors in New York about two-year-old Hubert's health. Taking baby Hazel, Guy and Earle, they went east in January 1887. On the way, they hired Katie O'Neill in St. Paul as a nurse for the two younger children. As Hubert's treatment took a long time, Anna and Katie, with the two babies, stayed in Brooklyn for several weeks while J. J. returned to Spokane with the boys.

Sketch of the Browne farm on Moran Prairie, looking southeast, in 1892. Browne's Mountain is shown left center. *(Sketch from the* Northwest Magazine, *June 1892)*

One day Hubert went into one of their adjourning rooms in the hotel, got a box of matches, and built a bonfire on a chair. When Katie found him, the blaze was eighteen inches high while Hubert kept feeding it with more matches. Anna was most thankful Hubert's clothes had not caught fire. In her letter to her husband telling him about this incident, Anna did not express the least concern or even give a passing thought to the potential danger to the other occupants of the hotel.

This was typical of Anna and J. J.'s reaction. If there was one flaw in their devotion to their children, it was their inability to see any of their faults. They refused to listen to any criticism of them; therefore, there could be no problems. Not only was there no attempt at discipline, the children were not given any responsibilities such as household tasks or chores, not even the care of the pets. This lack of discipline and overindulgence contributed to the children becoming, in the common vernacular, "just plain brats," especially Guy and Earle.

After the move into the big mansion January 28, 1888, and with additional domestic help, Anna could travel with her husband more frequently. With their parents gone, the two older boys acted out. Their idea of fun was to tear the beds apart and then have the maids remake them. They would get up in the middle of the night and race up and down the stairs until everyone was awake. One early morning, Guy and a friend entertained themselves by moving the furniture around in a guest chamber. Nor were the girls exempt from misbehavior. When they were a little older, they would get up at 3:30 a.m., jumping and pounding until great-grandmother, who had come to live with the Brownes in the spring of 1889, was awakened in her room under theirs. (For five years after Anna Marie Whittlesey Stratton, Mrs. Browne's paternal grandmother, lost her husband in 1884, she lived alternately with one or another of her six living children, three of whom – Anna's father Howard, son H. Granville and next-to-youngest daughter, Alice V. Hull – lived in Spokane Falls.)

Just for fun, all the children turned everything topsy-turvy in the two libraries and closet, leaving Katie, who had returned from Brooklyn with Mrs. Browne, to straighten the room up again. The boys were verbally abusive to the servants, and at one time Guy hit Katie on her face and neck with a stick.

With Browne's keen interest and active participation in education, one would expect him to emphasize academics and insist on regular attendance at school. This was not the case. His children went to school when they felt like it. Earle could play a "headache." Alta stayed home because she had to recite a piece. The weather was too cold, the snow too deep, the roads too muddy, or the rain too wet. As Guy and Earle got older, their attendance became more irregular. When finally sent east to private school, they had academic problems.

In January 1890, Guy began attending Spokane College across the river, but his attendance was quite erratic. He might go three days, stay home seven, or leave school at noon. In the first three months he spent less than half the school hours in the classroom. A year later his parents transferred him to Way's Military School, which Earle attended.[18]

Shortly after Grandmother Stratton came to live with the Brownes, she expressed her concerns about the children in her diary. As a recent addition to the household, she could see clearly what was happening. In the form of a prayer she wrote: "O, shew [sic] they servant [Mr. Browne] what he is doing with his sons to ruin them body and soul and all his children." Another time her earnest plea was to help Mr. Browne see what his indulgence and love was doing to his children. "Help him see before it is forever too late."[19]

Grandmother was 76 years old. The first few years she helped with the household chores as much as she could. She dried the dinner dishes, stemmed the gooseberries for pies, put up the pickles. Her hands were never idle. She helped with the endless mending of the children's clothes, knit dozens of pairs of mittens each year: silk ones, others made of saxony, dougle mittens, or coarse ones for the men. She also knit slumber robes (afghans), hemmed tablecloths and dozens of napkins for Anna, and wrote many letters to her large family of children, grandchildren, sisters and brothers.

During the six years Grandmother Stratton lived with the Brownes, she kept a daily diary recording her thoughts, the activities in the mansion, the antics of the children, always beginning each day's entry with a scripture. Although she often expressed her irritation about how late the family rose, particularly on Sundays, and that seldom did anyone in the household attend church or sabbath school, she frequently prayed for patience and to hold her tongue. Many times she wrote of her appreciation for her comfortable home and asked blessings for this dear family who had been so kind to her in her helplessness and destitution. When Grandmother was able to attend church, Anna would give her some coins for the collection.

The summer of 1889 was a particularly busy and important one for J. J. Browne. He had been elected to serve on the committee to write the state constitution. The Brownes took the children with them to Olympia for the two months it would take for the committee to do its work.

The year before, J. J. had been a delegate from Washington Territory to the National Democratic Convention in St. Louis. This was the second time Browne had attended a national convention, having been elected a delegate from Kansas in 1872.

On the way home, J. J. stopped in Chicago where the National Republican Convention was in progress. There were a great many people in attendance and a great deal of enthusiasm, but not as much, he commented to Anna, as at the Democratic Convention. "Certainly the St. Louis Convention was more in earnest," he wrote, "[it] had more genuine feeling and determination."[20]

The Brownes returned from Olympia August 8, 1889, to find Spokane in ashes following the great fire. When they went to get Grandmother at the Hulls, it took three hours to drive from the north side to Browne's Addition because of the dust and smoke. The next day Anna took her grandmother to see the burnt district. Mrs. Stratton remarked that the city looked so sad and desolate. The smoke and dust hung over the city and residential areas for weeks as the dry weather continued.

Nevertheless, Anna made preparations for the annual camping trip to Blake's (Eloika) Lake in northern Spokane County. A man was sent ahead to make tent platforms, put up the tents, make tables and benches, repair the boat, and put up swings. The bedding, mattresses, trunks, provisions, satchels, rifles, fishing gear and chairs filled two large wagons. There were usually a couple of ponies tied behind one of the wagons, as well as a dog. In Mr. Browne's carriage rode J. J. and Anna, Alta, Irma, Hubert and Hazel – one time with each child holding a puppy for the thirty-mile ride. Guy and Earle often rode ahead on horseback, frequently accompanied by neighbor boys. A hired carriage took the cook, two maids and box lunches for all. Cousins, aunts and friends were invited to spend a week or more at camp.

Mr. Browne's stay at camp was intermittent, as pressing business kept him away. Periodically someone was sent to the farm on Moran Prairie for fresh vegetables, milk and butter. The campers relied upon small game and fish for their meat. Once a week a wagon made the journey into town with their dirty clothes for the Brownes' laundress to wash and send out clean ones.

This annual vacation became more complex each year as the children grew older and invited more friends. Invitations were seldom turned down. Eventually, Browne bought property on the east side of the lake.

Although it would seem that the Browne household, with its burgeoning number of children and innumerable live-in servants, would constitute a full house, there always seemed to be house guests or boarders. Visiting ministers and their wives stayed with the Brownes, as did several teachers who boarded for a few months to a year. The longest non-family residents were Mr. and Mrs. Simon R. Flynn, Dick and Mertie, who arrived September 28, 1889. Flynn had been a correspondent for the *Baltimore Sun* in Washington, D. C. Prior to Flynn's coming to Spokane, Browne had met him in Tacoma where he had worked for the *Tacoma Ledger*, reporting on the progress of the new state constitution committee. The Flynns remained lifelong friends and were very much a part of an extended Browne family.

Washington Territory entered the Union on November 11, 1889. Leaving the Flynns in charge of the children, Mr. and Mrs. Browne went to Olympia to witness the inauguration ceremonies of the 42nd state's new officers on November 18. As the Brownes always shared interesting experiences with their children, Anna wrote to Earle describing the historic events and their opportunity to shake hands with the new governor, Elisha P. Ferry.[21]

In the fall of 1889, J. J. Browne was beginning to enjoy a period of great financial success. That it would last less than five years was unforeseen. He had a greenhouse built just south of the deer park, much to the delight of Anna and the gardener, Ben Sweatman. It meant fresh vegetables and a profusion of flowers all year long. In December Browne ordered gas light fixtures installed throughout the house. Although total disorder and confusion reigned with every room on the second and third floors torn up, Browne wanted the work completed by Christmas. Like everything else in the Browne household, preparations for Christmas became more involved. Grandmother commented that Mrs. Browne had more on her hands and mind than six women could handle. A number of the gifts were made by the ladies and girls in the family.

The family filled the parlor Christmas Eve for the customary exchanging and opening of gifts. Anna's brothers, Charles and Alfred, and their families, her father, and her aunt, Alice Hull, and cousins were present. Besides the six Browne children, Mr. and Mrs. Flynn and Grandma Stratton completed the circle. Anna presented her husband a $60 clock, while J. J. gave her two splendid gilt frame pictures from Denver for the parlor. On Christmas Day, 26 people ate dinner at the Brownes' home. However, Anna, as always, did not forget the poor families of the city, and sent several baskets of food to them.

New Year's Day, 1890, found the Brownes entertaining the employees of the Browne National Bank that J. J. had founded in 1888 with a capitalization of $60,000. The menu was typical of what Anna served. First course: raw oysters, slices of bread, salted olives, water; second course: soup, crackers, almond meats; third course: turkey, potatoes, cauliflower with gravy, peach pickles, celery, cranberry sauce, bread, butter, gravy; fourth course: chicken salad, warm soda biscuits; fifth course: mince pie and cheese; sixth course: nuts; seventh course: sliced oranges and cake; eighth course: coffee; ninth course: finger bowls with a rose geranium leaf. The guests sat at the table for two hours at a meal served by several servants.

Big houses and big families required large domestic staffs to run them, perhaps not always smoothly, but at least to keep things going. Anna had a virtual army of help to oversee. When they were in the house on Pacific, the Brownes usually had two men to do the outside chores, and two girls to help with the children, cooking and laundry. The mansion, however, seldom had less than a live-in staff of six. Katie was with them for nearly six years and basically looked after the younger children. She cared for them when they were ill, took them to town for haircuts, bathed them, saw they were dressed properly for school, helped with their parties, and often spent her evenings mending their clothes. When the laundress quit, Katie would help with the washing and ironing. She waited table when the second girl quit. More often than not, it was Katie who built the morning fire in Grandmother's room and took meals to her. Katie was a jewel and received thirty dollars a month.

Chapter III

Ben Sweatman was another employee of long duration. Although he begrudgingly allowed his greenhouse flowers to be cut for the house, Ben saw that grandmother had at least one bouquet of fresh flowers in her room. Ben and Anna planned the flower beds for the yard. Mrs. Browne spent many an hour planting and potting in the greenhouse.

Most of the other servants came and went. The cooks were the most transient. The hours were long and the work hard. Breakfast could last from 7:00 a.m. to 10:00, depending upon when the children felt like coming downstairs. The fare usually included mush, meat, potatoes and warm biscuits. Lunch and dinner often meant a minimum of sixteen people at each meal. A typical family dinner included fresh fish, fried potatoes, bread and butter in the first course. Then came roast pork, mashed potatoes, spinach with cold boiled eggs, gravy, lettuce, radishes and tea followed by custard boiled in a muffin crust for dessert.

However, extra guests seemed to be the norm: business associates of Browne's, or some of Anna's relatives, and almost certainly several of the neighbors' children. So rare was it not to have an extra child or more at the table that Grandmother always commented about it in her diary.

The Brownes had several Chinese cooks. Zip quit because Katie got after him for washing chickens in the dirty dishwater. Then Anna hired Don who was crosser than Zip. He lasted two days. A woman named Anna came next. Mrs. Browne paid her thirty dollars a month and Martha, the dining room girl, five dollars a week. Two months later the cook left because there was too much to do and the cement floor was hard on her feet. They were sorry to see her go as she had been a good cook, quiet and pleasant. Tilly, the laundress, took over as cook, and Hildah came to work for the Brownes.

One year Anna hired Maggie Gibson on December 11. Three days before Christmas Maggie left. Minnie came on the 22nd and quit on the 27th. The next day another cook arrived. The following month was not much better. They had six different cooks and four laundresses in four weeks. One new cook did not even take her hat off before she quit – after two strong men had carried her heavy trunk up to the third floor. The stable men were not any more reliable.

There were some exceptions. Even after leaving, Tilly would come back to help out. Hannah Dahl was with the family for a year before she left to learn dressmaking. Jennie, the black cook, worked for six months until she married. The ceremony, conducted by the minister from the First Baptist Church, took place in the Brownes' home.

Besides the daily meals for a cook to prepare, there were the parties. Each Browne child had a birthday party with lots of friends. A typical one was the picnic Alta and Irma had on the lawn for fifteen girls. Katie served two kinds of cake, sandwiches, lemonade, candy and nuts. After Earle's eleventh birthday party, his mother reported to Grandmother that the guests only broke three chairs, an easel, something "about the mantel," and a tumbler.

On Hubert's fifth birthday, January 17, 1890, thirty-two boys and girls helped him celebrate. They sat at a long table in the dining room for the refreshments: warm soda biscuits, cold turkey, pickled peaches, oranges, three kinds of cake, nuts, candy, lemonade and ice cream.

The next evening Guy, age 13, entertained twenty-seven of his friends plus his brothers, sisters and cousin Leah, Charles's daughter. The party did not break up until after midnight. Even the young children stayed up to have supper after 10:00 p.m. Grandmother's reaction: "Lord have mercy."

One evening, when Guy was not yet sixteen, his friends threw a surprise party for him at the Browne home. Forty young people attended with dancing and card playing. Grandmother commented: "O God!" On Guy's seventeenth birthday, ninety guests crowded the mansion.

For the largest party, including 350 guests, ever held in the mansion, Anna served two large fruit cakes baked in tins, chicken salad, various cakes including angel food, bread, butter, coffee and ice cream.

When they were without a cook, Anna could be found in the kitchen preparing the meals. She worked hard even with a large staff. One busy day when she helped with the ironing, it took five women to get the job done by noon. In the afternoon they baked ten cakes and boiled three hams for the Press Association luncheon the next day.

In the summer and fall when the crops were harvested and the berries picked, Anna did a lot of the canning. It was not unusual for her to put up 110 glasses of currant jelly, 134 glasses of red raspberry jelly, 17 quarts of blackberry jam, 9 quarts of gooseberry jam, and 7 quarts of currant jam. She also canned cherries, apricots, pears, plums, raspberries, strawberries, gooseberries and even made three gallons of homemade currant wine.

Twice a year the house was thoroughly cleaned from top to bottom. Carpets were sent out to be cleaned, bedding aired, windows washed and floors waxed. This not only involved every woman in the household but extra day help as well. Anna was not above scrubbing floors on her hands and knees.

In the summer, awnings were put up over the south side windows to keep out the heat. Screens were absent, apparently, as Grandmother complained that she could not sleep because of the flies. Painting was periodically done inside and out. Mice were common occupants. In one four-day period, ten mice were trapped by the radiator in Grandmother's room and seven more in the parlor.

Winter presented other major situations. A few days after the dinner for the bank employees, Grandmother discovered smoke in her room and closet. It took the firemen an hour to find the source. They located it burning under the tile in the dining room hearth that was directly above the furnace. In gratitude Browne gave the firemen a hundred dollars.

When the pipes froze and burst less than a week later, water was sent cascading down the walls in the parlor. Not only did the workmen have to take up the carpet, they also had to remove the wet plaster from the wall.

Leaving the Flynns again in charge of the children and household, on January 23, 1890, Mr. and Mrs. Browne left for the East. They were to meet the Cannons in New York where the gentlemen planned to order the fittings and furnishings for the Auditorium Theatre they were building. On the outward journey the Brownes stopped in St. Paul where they purchased two Shetland ponies, a set of harnesses, and a cart for Hubert and Hazel. They sent Irma a side saddle like Alta's. Grandmother confided in her diary that such extravagances were unnecessary, and commented tersely that she did not think Alta had used her saddle four times in the entire year.

When she traveled, Anna always carried pictures of the children that she placed in her hotel room, claiming it was the only way she could bear to be apart from them. She wrote faithfully to each child. In a letter to Alta, she expressed quite explicitly how she and J. J. felt toward their children:

> You children are our all in this world. We live for you, work for you, love and think about you all the time. We want you to be good, and wise, and useful men and women – yes! and good and wise and useful girls and boys too, that the world may be better and wiser because you have lived in it. God bless you, my darlings, and grant that our prayers and desires for you may be fulfilled. – Very much love and many kisses to you all. Your loving Mother.[22]

J. J. also wrote to the children as often as he could. His letters were full of descriptions of the countryside as the train sped along, of towns passed through, but especially how much he missed each child and loved him or her.

On their return home, the Brownes stopped at J. J.'s boyhood home in Collumer, Indiana. J. J. wrote of this experience to Earle:

I was again at the old homestead and walked upon the river bank where I had, when a boy, played and loitered many an hour. I saw the grounds of the old sugar camp where I had spent many a happy hour making sugar but alas the woodsman's ax has been there and the grand old trees of the forest including sugar trees (maple) have been cut down and carried away and the "camp" dumped into a wheat field. I felt like weeping over the desolation as every tree of the old camp had seemed to me as a sentinel and friend.

During the Brownes' absence, the temperature dropped again in late February. Although John, the furnace man, turned the water pipes off at 5:00 p.m., they still froze. The thermometer registered 32° below zero, the coldest night of the winter. The bouquet on Grandma's windowsill froze, and ice formed in her tumbler.

The cold weather was good for forming ice to cut on the streams and lakes. Fifteen loads from Hangman Creek were put in the ice house at a cost of $1.25 a ton. On the other hand, the furnace had already burned 70-75 tons of coal that winter. Hard coal sold for $12.50 a ton and soft coal cost $7 to 7.50. The stoves in the kitchen and laundry used wood. Even so, the upstairs was so cold, fires had to be kept going in the grates constantly.

The Shetland ponies arrived in Spokane March 10, the same day Grandmother tripped over a hassock in the sitting room. This was the beginning of her back problems. Although she spent six weeks in bed, it was two and a half months before she was able to walk downstairs to eat with the family. In the meantime, trays were brought to her room, usually by Katie. Dr. Essig called frequently to see her.

Before leaving on this business trip, Browne had been trying to buy back the *Evening Chronicle,* which he had founded in 1881 with Cannon and Glover. During J. J.'s absence, Flynn had continued negotiations, keeping Browne informed of the progress. Flynn's perseverance got the price down to $22,000. The Brownes returned to Spokane Falls March 15, 1890. Two days later Browne purchased the *Chronicle* from W. D. Knight and J. S. Dickerson.[23] Twenty-seven year old S. R. Flynn became its managing editor.

Activities in the mansion continued at their busy pace with the return of the heads of the household. The Shetland ponies each gave birth to a colt in the spring. There were new fawns in the deer park. The Brownes took the children to minstrel shows, circuses, on picnics and to the opera. Later there were bicycle races and horse races at the fairgrounds.

The most gala event of 1890 was the opening of the new opera house, the Auditorium Theatre, September 16. The Brownes, Mr. and Mrs. Flynn, Guy and

Chapter III

Earle occupied the Browne box. The next evening Anna sent some of the maids to see the building and hear the program. She was always generous with tickets to all their hired help.

Anna often took the children to a matinee and would return again to the theatre in the evening with her husband. Although the Brownes had a number of carriages and horses in the barn, they frequently rode the "cars" to the theatre.

Browne's popularity and financial success were unequaled. He was reported to be the largest property owner in town with an assessed value of $1,200,000 – three times what Cannon's property was worth. F. Rockwood Moore's holdings amounted to $200,000. Even so, cash flow was another matter, and it kept Browne hustling to make his tax payments every year. Nevertheless, J. J. continued to be generous with his family. He presented Anna with a diamond ring on her 35th birthday, and Earle received a $135 bicycle. Alta got a $50 gold watch and chain for her 11th birthday. On Grandmother's 78th birthday Mr. and Mrs. Browne gave her a beautiful writing desk complete with paper, envelopes, pens and a glass inkstand.

Anna was pregnant again, but it did not slow her down. When the Northwestern Industrial Exposition opened October 1, 1890, she drove her grandmother to see the huge building and the rebuilt city. Six weeks before Anna's due date, she entertained with a nine-course luncheon for twelve to honor a Mrs. Chambers.

Son Garland arrived at 2:15 a.m. on December 12. Dr. Essig spent 27 hours at the house with Anna. In preparation for the new baby, Anna had bought a crib for $12. The next spring she paid $52 for a splendid buggy with a brown satin parasol trimmed with white lace. It was several months before Garland received a name – not an uncommon practice at the time. Sometimes a baby might not be named for a couple years. Garland was very likely named for a friend of Guy's who had died the previous year.

Although Garland was a good baby, he was not a robust, healthy child. Anna hired a special nursemaid to care for him. Grandmother frequently mentioned what a lovely baby he was, but there was a constant worry about his health. By the next summer, he seemed to be frequently ill with high fevers and nausea. Nevertheless, Anna took Garland camping with the family for the month of August.

As September turned into October, it became increasingly clear that Garland was a very sick child. After several days and nights of extreme suffering, he died in his mother's arms at 5:30 a.m. on October 7. Ben put two buff-colored roses and some white daisies in Garland's little hands. Katie was heartbroken. Minnie, the seamstress, came to finish a dress for the little boy before he was laid in

Auditorium Building, c. 1920, built by Browne and Cannon at the northwest corner of Main and Post in 1890. Besides the theatre, it housed the Browne National Bank, the federal courtrooms, the post office and some apartments on the upper floors. It was razed in 1934. *(Photo from the Jerome Peltier Collection, courtesy Tony and Suzanne Bamonte)*

a white casket in the parlor. Anna's brother, Charles, and Mr. Heine, a neighbor and vice-president of the Browne National Bank, sat up all night with the body.

Grandmother wrote in her diary:

> The Angel of death has come to this house, and taken the youngest only ten-months old while I am almost 79 years old am spared. Why is it so? The funeral was set for 10 o'clock October 9. Many kind friends and neighbors came to sympathize with the family. The Beautiful flowers tied with beautiful ribbons and with the name of the doners [sic] on a card were very pleasing to Mr. and Mrs. Browne. Charles helped me downstairs for the first time in 18 days. Mr. Browne led me to the little casket to look on Garland for the last time. . . . Family and friends rode to Fairmount Cemetery and laid our sweet baby amid a bower of vines and flowers Minnie and the Sexton had spread in and about the grave.

Anna went to the cemetery weekly with flowers for the little grave. One time the gate was locked, but she climbed over the barbed wire fence, ignoring the mud.

The year 1891 was also marked by the divorce of Anna's parents. Rev. Howard Stratton had become increasingly discouraged with his solitary life over the past ten years. In a last effort at a reconciliation, he had visited Mary in Seattle, where she had moved in 1890. For years Grandmother had prayed for Mary to see her duty and live with her husband. It was not to be.

Following the divorce, Stratton traveled to California for a wife, as he needed someone to take care of him. On July 29, 1891, Rev. H. W. Stratton and Louise Brier exchanged vows in Centerville, California. In Seattle on October 3, 1892, Mary Stratton married John B. Fisher, a man nineteen years her junior.[24]

Anna was extremely generous with her time and good fortune. At Christmas time she sent boxes east to her aunts and cousins and to Portland to her brother Clad and his family, in addition to remembering the growing number of relatives in Spokane. At Easter Mrs. Browne would color eggs for the children in the neighborhood.

Her contributions to charity were not limited to holidays. She had been a promoter of the Ladies Benevolent Society's efforts to provide for orphans. In 1889, Browne donated two lots worth $3,100 on Boone and Calispel for the construction of the Home for the Friendless, forerunner of the Washington Children's Home. Anna knocked on doors and called on offices for donations. One day she gathered $1,200 in subscriptions and the offer of furnishing a room. Other days her soliciting brought in $300 and $650.

Anna also spent countless hours working on bazaars for the Presbyterian Church and waiting tables at church dinners. J. J. did his part by paying $75 for a doll for

Alta at a fundraiser. Anna also served as president of the church sewing circle, a group of ladies who provided clothing for families in distress. Her selfless consideration of others prompted Grandmother to comment: "She is very thoughtful of all her family and of all her relatives, the poor. God bless her kind heart. All the dear ones will 'rise up' and call her and her husband 'blessed.' "[25]

Perhaps at no other time were the Brownes' social activities greater than the back-to-back parties held at the turn-of-the-year, 1892. On New Year's Day, they entertained all the *Chronicle* employees: newsboys as well as managers, reporters, etc., totaling 79 persons. The newspaper carried a detailed description of the reception. The parlor was decorated with festoons of smilax descending from the elegant mantle, the arch having been transformed into an evergreen arcade. The dining room and library were ornamented with banked masses of green foliage, vases of cut flowers, and trailing vines. The long dining table had rose bowls and smilax on the snowy damask cloth. Bonbon souvenir baskets were provided for the newsboys, who had been treated to a sleigh ride, games and a merry entertainment.

The menu featured raw oysters, three roasted pigs, nine roasted turkeys, twenty loaves of bread, cranberry sauce, green corn, sweet potatoes, mashed potatoes, cabbage salad, plum pudding with brandy sauce, mince pie, vanilla ice cream, pineapple ice, candy and nuts, and coffee.

The next day the Brownes held another dinner party for all the employees and their wives from the Browne National Bank. Twenty people sat at the dinner table for two hours to consume the meal.

The day after the bank party, Browne brought home Will Collins, a *Chronicle* employee who was ill with typhoid fever. He hired the sisters from the hospital to nurse the sick man at night. They were there more than three weeks. When Collins's brother came from Seattle, he also stayed at the Brownes' home. Will spent nine weeks there, finally leaving March 6, 1892.

The presence of Collins in their home did not prevent the Brownes from inviting the neighbors to the mansion on First Avenue for an evening, and their home seemed to be headquarters for all the neighborhood youth. With all the people coming and going, the Browne household could have appeared to an outsider to be a three-ring circus, yet Anna seemed to take it in stride. She managed to do what she wanted to do whether it was spending an entire day in the greenhouse or digging in the flower beds, working for the church or attending club meetings. If a family member arrived as she was leaving, she continued on her way and let them visit Grandmother.

Both Mr. and Mrs. Browne made their home available for meetings. In the spring of 1892, a group of ladies met there to organize a society to do good and to encourage labor among the poorer classes of women and girls. With "tongue-in-cheek," they chose a Chinook word *Cultus* (meaning "worthless") as the name of their club. Membership was limited to thirty ladies, and meetings were held bimonthly.

Although her activities would seem to indicate a strong and vigorous person, Mrs. Browne frequently spent a number of days in bed with a sick headache or other ailments. Anna's health and well-being greatly concerned Grandmother. After a particularly annoying visitor one afternoon, Grandmother was prompted to write in her diary: "I did not get to sleep until after one o'clock, I was so nervous and excited, wondered how anyone that ever had the headache could be so thoughtless as to sit down & talk & laugh before one that had & was nearly wild for two hours & not stop. Why cannot a woman learn when to be still?"

Even though Dr. Essig came to the house regularly, many home remedies were used. When Irma had an earache, Uncle Charles blew cigar smoke in her ear. Dried mullen leaves were smoked by adults for a sore throat. (Even houseplants had smoke blown on them to kill the insects.) A cough was treated with onion syrup. Katie rubbed Grandmother's bad back with chloroform when she was laid up. An upset stomach called for a stomach rub with chloroform liniment and Pond's extract, while camphor and water was taken internally. A sore eye was washed with salt water and bound with tea leaves at bedtime. Other remedies included fig syrup to move the bowels, turpentine rubbed on the chest for a cough, or a flax seed put in an eye when a foreign object got in it. Once Anna bought a "bottle of electricity" for $2.50 to give to her aunt to relieve a sick headache and pain in her stomach.

In spite of professional medical attention and home remedies, death reached into the Browne family again. Eight-year-old Hubert died February 7, 1893, after a week's illness with scarlet fever. Hazel, too, came down with the disease, but she recovered.

A year and a half later, the Angel of Death called once more when Anna was delivered of a stillborn boy July 12, 1894. A month earlier, she had fallen down the stairs. Alta, age 13, wrote to her mother from Camp Eloika: "We all felt very bad when [cousin] Grace told us about the little boy we were destined never to see."

The children's activities changed as they grew older. Instead of a passion for marbles, which had led Guy to charge his little friends marbles to ride his pony, he became an avid bicycler. With other fellows he went on bicycle excursions for a week or longer, rode his bike out to Blake's Lake, or to the farm on Moran

Prairie. Eventually, Guy became good enough to race, traveling as far as Portland to compete.

On a warm summer's day the three girls with some neighbor children set up a store by the front gate (and near the streetcar line) to sell lemonade, strawberries, currants and flowers. They made enough money to buy some candy, which Hazel shared with Great-grandmother and Minnie.

Alta and Irma began taking piano lessons from Susie Stratton, Anna's uncle's wife, who had been teaching music for several years in New York State while Granville was trying to establish himself in Spokane.

Like the rest of Spokane, J. J. Browne worried about the economic crisis that clouded the country in 1893. His bank struggled along until November 23, 1894. At the time, Browne was in Portland trying to borrow money. He had known for months that he was unable to pay the bank's debt to the city. Since June of the previous year, the Browne National Bank had paid off more than $300,000 to its depositors.

On November 22, Anna had gone downtown to see her father. When she learned about the condition of the bank, she called on a number of businessmen to see whether or not she could do anything to prevent the approaching disaster. Anna was devastated and looked as if she had a siege of sickness. Grandmother unburdened herself in her diary: "What will become of me? I am only a burden upon them. They have been for years, so kind & thoughtful for my comfort."

Economies were taken at home. Browne no longer hired a man just to keep the grounds looking good. In December they began killing the deer for food and because it was too expensive to feed them. The deer park was never restocked. However, the number of domestic staff was not reduced.

Even Spokane had its problems. In December of 1894, the city could not afford to pay for lighting the city streets. At night all was darkness.

There were other worries for the Brownes besides finances. In the fall, Anna's father became seriously ill, which an operation in December did not seem to improve. He found it necessary to take morphine at night to ease the pain. Rev. Howard W. Stratton passed away from Bright's disease on August 23, 1895, at the age of 62, leaving his wife and a three-year-old daughter.

Whether or not the hard times influenced Grandmother Stratton's move to her son Granville's apartment in the Auditorium Block is hard to say. She lived with him and his wife two years until her death on August 16, 1897. On the day of her funeral, an article appeared in the *Spokesman-Review*: "Her Christian character was of the greatest beauty." This would have pleased Grandmother very much. At the time of her death, Anna Whittlesey Stratton was nearly 85 years of age, with seven children (five of whom were still living), twenty-three grandchildren, and eighteen great-grandchildren.

In spite of their reduced economic situation, in September 1895, Browne sent Guy and Earle to Orchard Lake Military School in Michigan. The boys complained bitterly that it had the reputation of being the strictest military school in the country next to West Point. The academics were hard, and the boys were constantly working off demerits. Guy had taken his "wheels" with him, which he rode 40 miles to Ann Arbor to see a football game. However, he returned to school on the train with the team.

Although Earle had to complete the school year at Orchard Lake, Guy was permitted to enroll at Washington Agricultural College in Pullman for the spring semester. Guy's roommate was football star Boyd Hamilton, whom he described as being "all right." College did not seem to have a strong appeal for Guy, as a year and a half later, he was on his way to the Yukon. J. J. accompanied his twenty-year-old son as far as Vancouver, B. C. On October 15, 1897, he wrote to Anna describing Guy's approaching trip:

> The steamer City of Seattle ... will leave at 8 p.m. for Fort Wrangel carrying <u>our dear boy</u> and his companions.[26] At Wrangel they will take canoes for a hundred and fifty miles up the Stickeen River to Telegraph Creek – thence by toboggins [*sic*] with dog and man power to Leslin Lake and other points in the Yukon country. I have had the best visit with Guy that I have ever had since he was a small boy. You can not realize how much I have enjoyed this continuous companionship – a union of hearts and perfect harmony and confidence. No son was ever better or more genial and in every way agreeable. He has filled my heart to over flowing.

There is no record as to whether or not Guy and his friends did any prospecting or whether they were successful if they did. However, two years later Guy married Caroline (Carrie) Mayer of Wenatchee. That same year, 1899, Irma and Hazel were sent to the Visitation Convent in Georgetown, Washington, D. C. Even though Ella and Katherine Clark, daughters of Patsy Clark, and Mabel and Eleanor Welch, daughters of Patrick Welch, were also attending, the Browne girls were dreadfully homesick. They were completely unused to the discipline of a convent school. Although the Sisters were kind, the biggest problem was a total lack of spending money. In Spokane, Browne tried to juggle income with expenses, seemingly a continual struggle.

At Christmas, Browne did not have the money for the girls to come home. At the insistence of Irma and Hazel, their mother went to Georgetown to spend the holiday with them. Much as the girls pleaded with Anna to return home, they remained at the convent for the full school year.

None of the children were at home, as Alta and Earle were attending Washington State College. As a member of the football team, Earle made a name for himself in the Battle of the Palouse between the Agricultural College and the University of Idaho. Along with Boyd Hamilton and fellow player Goodsell, Earle starred in the game. A typical college student, Earle bought a mandolin and sent the bill to Papa. J. J. admonished him to get his lessons and play afterwards!

With the development of the mines in British Columbia, Republic and a renewal of work in the Coeur d'Alenes, the general economy in Spokane experienced an upswing as the end of the century neared. The neighborhood around the Brownes' home was changing dramatically. Instead of being rural and isolated, J. J.'s homestead was rapidly becoming a leading residential area with a lot of new construction. Where the deer park had been, A. B. Campbell was building a mansion designed along English Tudor lines: half brick topped with stucco and timber. Farther west W. J. C. Wakefield's mission-style home was going up, while at the end of First Avenue, John Finch was erecting a huge Colonial Revival home. All were designed by architect Kirtland K. Cutter.

At the Brownes' home, preparations were under way for the marriage of Alta May to Boyd Hamilton, which took place in their home September 20, 1900. A little more than a year later, Boyd was working for J. J. in one of his banking enterprises. He eventually became the cashier for the Coeur d'Alene Bank & Trust Co., of which J. J. was the president and his sons were vice presidents.

Guy and Carrie lived in Wenatchee where Guy was the vice president and manager of the family bank, the Columbia Valley Bank of Wenatchee. He was also the president of the Cashmere State Bank.

A big change took place in 1902 when the Brownes decided to move to the Moran Prairie ranch and sold their First Avenue home to Robert Strahorn. The following year J. J. built a large three-story white house to the north of the old farmhouse, which was then torn down. Formal landscaping surrounded the new house with a large heart-shaped flower bed on the northeast corner, two stone pillars stood at the entrance, and the sidewalk to the house was lined with bushes, trees and flowers. When a new barn was built to the north in 1906, lilacs lined the land leading to it.

The family was growing up. Hazel graduated from high school in January 1903. Although her father wanted her to attend the University of Michigan, Anna

J. J. Browne, in his late 50s, and Anna Browne, about 40 years old. J. J. became one of Spokane's first capitalists through his extensive property holdings. *(Photos courtesy MAC/EWSHS, (left) L-93-66.65 (reproduced from the* Magazine of Western History) *and L87-99)*

declared it was too far away, and Hazel enrolled at Washington State. For part of her time there, Earle was also a student at the college, but by 1905 J. J. employed him at the Bank of Oroville. Earle became the next Browne child to marry. He and Florence Littlefield of Wenatchee exchanged vows October 8, 1905. Once more, his parents came to Earle's aid by helping him buy Florence an engagement ring, then later buying furniture for their home.

In spite of periodic reverses, J. J.'s finances looked solvent by the middle of the first decade of the 1900s. The Brownes spent a month on Lake Coeur d'Alene, hiring a Japanese couple to do the cooking and laundry. Anna ordered a custom-made fur coat from Marshall Field and Company in Chicago. However, the greatest indication of success began December 1906, when J. J. sent Anna, the three girls, Alta's husband, Boyd Hamilton, and their year-old son Dale, to Europe for several months.

The following June, Hazel graduated from college, perhaps the only member of the family to do so. In September, she married her college sweetheart, Everett M. Sweeley, who had been an outstanding football player at the University of Michigan before transferring to Washington State. Typical of a Browne function, Hazel's wedding in their Moran Prairie home September 28, 1907, was one of the more elaborate social events of the year. The library, decorated in green and white, contained a large arch of asters banked by palms and ferns that formed the background for the ceremony.

Special trains were run on Spokane and Inland Railway's electric line from the city to accommodate the two hundred guests for the reception after the 8:00 p.m. ceremony. Davenport's Restaurant served the refreshments, and Senescu's orchestra provided the music during the evening. The decor in the subdued-lit reception room was red and white.

The Sweeleys lived in Twin Falls, Idaho, and later Boise where Everett practiced law. Although Irma had described herself as a Mama and Papa girl, she surprised the family by eloping with Marshall Ross in January 1908. Except for Sweeley and Ross, J. J. provided employment for all the male members of his family. Of all the children and sons-in-law, Sweeley was the only one who later tried to help Anna with financial or legal problems. The others took or added to her burdens, although Anna may not have recognized it as such or been willing to admit it.

Dissatisfied with what she could buy in Wenatchee, Guy's wife, Carrie, wrote Anna with requests to pick out wallpaper samples at Graham's for her, as well as buying a pattern, material, plus the necessary trimmings for a fine waist to wear to church or calling. She also hoped Anna might know of a cook, as three families wanted to share a cook whom they expected to do the dining room work as well as laundering the table linens and kitchen towels. They would pay her transportation to Wenatchee and $20 a month, $25 if they had to.

The prosperous years never seemed to provide a monetary carry-over for the lean years. Another recession hit the country in the winter of 1907-1908. Once more, Browne headed east searching for capital. He announced that there was no money for Christmas.

At the ranch, the Browne children were replaced with grandchildren.[27] All of them spent a great deal of time with their grandparents during the summers. J. J. kept a pony for the little ones and horses for the older ones. No camping trip was complete without a number of grandchildren at Eloika Lake.

As they grew older, J. J. and Anna both developed periods of poor health. Early in 1904, J. J. sent his wife, with Irma accompanying her, to San Diego where he hoped she could find relief from her severe headaches and rheumatism during the winter months. The following year Anna broke her collar bone while visiting in Wenatchee. Although it knit together properly, it continued to give her considerable discomfort under her shoulder blade.

J. J., too, was having physical problems. He wrote to his longtime friend Dick Flynn, who had moved to San Diego: "In the years that have past I am well aware now that I have stuck too close to business, and that I am practically worn out. I need rest, recreation, and a change of climate."[28] In January 1911, Browne sought treatment for his sciatica and neuralgia in Hot Springs, Arkansas.

Twenty years earlier, J. J. had been advised by his doctor to leave his business and cares for a couple months, if not a couple years, because he was coughing a great deal and spitting blood. Examination of his lungs showed the right one to be fine, but the left one was not entirely sound. His heart was normal. Since this consultation took place shortly before the great fire of August 4, 1889, Browne had had no opportunity to act upon his doctor's advice.

J. J. Browne in his later years.
(Photo courtesy MAC/EWSHS, L85-46)

On March 13, 1912, J. J. again confided in Flynn: "During the past two years there has been a very large amount of grading, sidewalking, and paving in Spokane, and as this work was done largely in localities where I owned a large amount of property, it has fallen very heavily upon me. Sales have not been good. It has kept me busy working pretty hard to meet the obligations. The taxes and assessments for the past 18 months have amounted to more than $100,000."

Twelve days later, just a month prior to his 69th birthday, John J. Browne suffered two heart attacks at his office and died. Earlier that Monday morning, he had hurried to catch the electric interurban car from his home. The doctors felt this action had contributed to the heart attacks that occurred shortly after he arrived at his office in the Paulsen Building.

That evening the *Chronicle* carried a banner headline: "J. J. Browne, City Pioneer, Dead." Telegrams and letters of sympathy poured in. Among them was a letter from Grace Campbell, who had just lost her husband, and a telegram from Gov. M. E. Hay. Mark F. Mendenhall, a Spokane attorney, wrote: "For I regard him as a citizen of most high and honorable purposes as well as a true friend throughout the twenty years of my residence in Spokane. I was always impressed with his sense of honor and his unselfish devotion to the public interests." Ina W. Collins sent a note from Seattle, part of which said: "You have been a wonderful woman, Mrs. Browne, in your untiring efforts to always think of Mr. Browne's comfort."

Funeral services took place at the ranch Friday, March 29, 1912. The Superior Court adjourned for the afternoon, as did all the banks in Spokane. The students at Washington State College received a half-holiday in honor of Regent Browne. The Inland Electric line ran a special train out to Moran Prairie. Automobiles lined both sides of the road with an overflow on the lawn.

The body lay in state in the parlor, surrounded by floral offerings that were described as being the most extensive and beautiful ever seen at a funeral of a Spokane man. In attendance was a delegation from the Knights of Pythias Lodge in Coeur d'Alene, of which Earle was a member, as well as graduates from the University of Michigan living in the Lake City. A group of business men came from Wenatchee, and a representative group of students from the state college journeyed from Pullman. Members of the Pioneer Society were among the mourners. Anna's mother and brother Alf were with the family.

Chairs were set up on the lawn and porches as well as in the house for the simple ceremony at which no major address was given. E. A. Bryan officiated, and Mrs. Pearl Hutton Shrader sang. Bryan offered the final prayer from the porch. Interment services at Fairmount Cemetery were private.

J. J. left no will. According to the inheritance laws of the state of Washington, his estate of approximately $450,000 would be divided with half going to his widow and half to his five children. Most of the property consisted of shares in banks and real estate companies.

Browne had organized the Columbia Valley Bank at Wenatchee in 1892 and the Coeur d'Alene Bank and Trust Co. in 1903 (acting as president of both); the Bank of Oroville, and the Cashmere State Bank with Guy as president. Browne's real estate holdings included the Columbia Investment Co., with taxable property of over $300,000, the Spokane Investment Co., the Browne-Post Investment Co. with Frank T. Post, and the Prairie Development Co. Browne owned more than 2,200 acres in the district of Spokane.

Impressive as these holdings sound, they did little to relieve Anna's financial situation. By January of the next year, the bank examiner gave Mrs. Browne 30 days to repair the capital stock at Coeur d'Alene. Her son-in-law Everett Sweeley wrote that this was no surprise as they had known for a year and a half that such action would ultimately be required. He felt that Boyd Hamilton, the cashier, had had enough time to go to Boise to straighten the matter out.

Two months later, Guy wanted his share of the estate to be figured on some just and equitable basis and set aside for him. Hazel was most indignant at this request and was ready to do battle, if necessary. Her husband wrote frankly and graphically to his mother-in-law:

There is a lady at my house who is a pretty able and conscientious scrapper, and to my certain knowledge she has got out her war bonnets, put a shine on her tomahawk, carefully picked out a place to put her foot down on, and proposes to keep the same there till sun down, or later, on that proposition. From my experience I can safely say that on occasion said lady can become considerably "sot" in her views, and my judgment is now that she has attained one of her "sottest" positions. There is an ancient maxim that "He who seeks equity, must do equity," and it is hardly to be expected that one who has appeared rather unresponsive to the call in his time should await prompt action when he lifts his voice. Especially when there are other matters first.

In addition to your own right there is the matter of Irma's house. She, alone of the children, has not had her share of the good things. It was, as we all know, Mr. Browne's firm intention to see that Irma had ultimately as much as the others. It could not, of course, be enforced, but it forms one of the elements to be considered in a just and equitable basis of settlement. There is a possibility that Earle has some ground of argument concerning his Coeur d'Alene stock, as when he traded his house for that, and Wenatchee stock, there was an understanding concerning some things that were to be done. It might, perhaps, be proper for the estate, as a whole, to consider these things, before any other action, which has the same basis for its seeking, be taken. No division can be sought at this time as a matter of right; it is at the most merely an accommodation, and if you'll forgive my bitterness this once, is only an attempt to capitalize unpleasantness past and possible.[29]

One of Anna's dearest friends was Carrie Adell Strahorn. They had a rapport that allowed Anna to confide her problems, particularly monetary ones. Mrs. Strahorn suggested several times that Anna motor with them to San Francisco and San Diego, but business matters kept Anna in Spokane. Adell's fondness for Mrs. Browne prompted her to write encouragingly: "You have done wondrously well and your wonderful power to smile through your troubles is a talisman that will be a power for good always."[30]

In spite of her business concerns, this courageous woman found time to remember her friends with bouquets of her beautiful flowers and to teach Sunday school. Some of her pupils wrote to her while in the army during World War I. Finally, Anna's financial situation became so critical that some sacrifices were necessary before she lost everything. In the fall of 1914, Mrs. Browne sold off the livestock: cows, pigs and hens. From the house went dressers and stands, filing cabinets and bookcases. Even jars of pears, apricots, plums and peach butter were sold. She received a little less than $3,000, but it was only a stop-gap aid.

An opportunity came along to acquire a property that brought in about $1,500 a month. For this, she traded 415 acres of the farm, 400 acres at Rathdrum, 240 acres north of town, and 100 feet on Riverside Avenue. In addition, she sold 17.5 acres for $1,300, and some farm equipment for $6,000. The next year

(1916) she was able to sell two apartment buildings for cash: The Helen at 173 South Adams and the Harvard at 117 West Third Avenue.

Along with the seemingly never ending financial matters facing Anna, family worries cropped up as well. Irma and Marshall Ross separated after J. J.'s death. An alcoholic, Ross agreed to take the cure, although Hazel felt he would never be able to support his family. Earle's marriage came to a crashing halt around 1918. The story is that Guy gave a party at which he hired some "girls" to entertain. One, named Agnes, plied her wiles on Earle, then threatened to ruin the family name unless he married her. Although Anna begged her son not to marry Agnes, Earle and Florence were divorced. Florence and her two daughters returned to Wenatchee.

Anna left the farm about 1920 and moved to 21st and Grand Boulevard, where she lived two years. Unfortunately, her bank problems were not over. The depression of 1921 closed the doors of the Coeur d'Alene Bank and Trust Co. In good faith, Earle had over-extended the bank's resources by making loans to a number of sawmills. When the bottom dropped out of the timber and plywood market, bankruptcy inevitably followed. Earle and Agnes moved to Oakland, California, where Earle found successful employment with the Bank of Italy, which later became the Bank of America.

After leaving the ranch, Anna leased the house to a group who named it "The Motor Inn." Her insurance premiums were high because the property was rated as a "road house." Early in December 1924, the prosecuting attorney started abatement proceedings against the farmhouse. He proposed to get a court order prohibiting the premises being used for any unlawful purpose.

The management of the Motor Inn had allowed, as road houses in the 1920s were apt to do, a disregard or bending of the law. Consequently, there were convictions on liquor charges against the people who lived there. Anna's attorney, Lester P. Edge, candidly recognized that it probably had been difficult to make the place pay without being somewhat free and easy in its conduct. Nevertheless, the prosecuting attorney's action did not preclude the property being used for any legitimate purpose. To save Anna's having to return to Spokane (she was then at Twin Falls, Idaho), Mr. Edge appeared at the hearings in her behalf.

Finally, after living in Los Angeles and possibly Twin Falls, Idaho, since 1923, Mrs. Browne returned to Spokane in 1927. Her diary following her return contains some interesting entries:

> January 11: Was married at 6:30. Mr. Van Nuys read a beautiful service. Dinner downtown with Irma and Ed. Left for New York at 8 p.m.

January 12: Am very, very happy.

January 14: [at St. Paul] Am getting settled, am happy and contented, and getting near normal.

Anna and her new husband, Edward G. Taber, a well-known railroad engineer, made their home at South 1910 Upper Terrace in Spokane. Anna was in the role she enjoyed the most – a homemaker. She planted multitudes of flowers and shared them with her friends. Although 72 years old, she still put up quantities of jam, jellies and fruit, even making rhubarb wine. Her home was open to grandson Dale Hamilton when visiting from Washington State College or to Irma's children from Liberty Lake.

For entertainment there were bridge luncheons at the Country Club, dinner at the Davenport Hotel, and lots of movies and theatre. Anna frequently traveled with Ed on business trips or to conventions. Like her own grandmother, she kept in touch with children, grandchildren, cousins and aunts through copious letter writing. These were happy years for Mrs. Taber, who could still remember the early years in Spokane Falls with a twinkle in her eye.

September 2, 1936, Anna Browne Taber passed away at the age of 81. Her descendants numbered five children, twelve grandchildren, and six great grandchildren. In January 1936, Herman Drewes bought the Moran Prairie farm. After the house burned in October, it was never rebuilt. However, J. J's large red barn to the north of the house site remained for another fifty years or more.

The J. J. Browne family barn on Moran Prairie, about 1980. It has since been torn down to make way for a housing development. *(Barbara Cochran photo)*

Chapter IV

Jennie Clarke Cannon

Jennie Clarke Cannon in her late thirties. *(Photo courtesy MAC/EWSHS, L87-96)*

One of the most important women in the early years of Spokane Falls was Jennie Clarke Cannon, wife of Anthony M. Cannon. Cannon's and Browne's names have been linked together in the annals of Spokane history from their arrival in 1878. However, no person was better known, better liked, or contributed more to the community than Jennie.

Although no firsthand manuscript material of Jennie's has survived, it is possible to trace her life in Spokane through her husband's mercurial career and various newspaper articles.

Born March 30, 1840, in Hudson, New York, Jane Frances "Jennie" Pease married Joseph Burlington Clarke in New York City about six weeks before her 21st birthday. In December 1862, they made the arduous move to Oregon City, Oregon. In this small western town their children were born: Marie, 1863; Ralph Lincoln, 1864; George P., 1867; Katherine, 1869; and Josephine, 1871. Joe farmed in the Willamette Valley. His death March 19, 1871, left Jennie with five small children to support.

Moving to Portland several years later, Jennie Clarke took rooms in the Centennial Block and went to work for the Howe Sewing Machine Company. One of her duties was to teach upper class Chinese women to sew. Calling at their homes, Jennie discovered she had a knack for other languages. Although it may have been only pidgin Chinese, she could communicate with people of another culture.

At the same time, there was a handsome, full-bearded gentleman who also lived in the Centennial Block and was an agent for the Howe Company: Anthony McCue Cannon, generally referred to as "A. M." Selling sewing machines was only the latest business enterprise for Cannon.

He had left the family farm near Monmouth, Illinois, in 1857 at the age of 20. Lured west, Cannon started for Pike's Peak with two yoke of oxen. At St. Joseph, Missouri, he joined a small group of emigrants consisting of forty-four men and eight women.[1] Elected captain, young Cannon led them successfully to Denver.

Finding the Pike's Peak gold fever diminishing, A. M. turned down an offer to buy one half of the Denver town site for $1,000 on credit and returned to Chicago. As one of the first members of the Board of Trade in the Windy City dealing in grain commodities, Cannon made several fortunes – and lost as many.

In 1869, he built a large flour mill in Kansas City but sold it two years later for $65,000. Again he journeyed west, this time to San Francisco. However, siren gold lured him to White Pine, Nevada. After a year in that mining district, Cannon returned to Chicago. Not satisfied, he once more tried San Francisco and Los Angeles. By 1874, he was in Portland working as a general agent for the Howe Company.

Cannon had married Julia Rupp before leaving Monmouth. They had two daughters: Mary, born in 1860, and Valina, three years later. A. M. and Julia were divorced in Portland. Cannon then met Jennie Clarke, the small, elegant widow with crinkly dark hair and very blue eyes. If nothing else, A. M. Cannon could sell himself. Jennie and Cannon were married July 21, 1878, three months after Cannon and partner J. J. Browne had purchased land in Spokane Falls.

In April 1878, Cannon had purchased one-half of the town site of Spokane Falls with J. J. Browne and was preparing to migrate to eastern Washington Territory. Cannon's primary motive in making the move from Portland had been his poor health. He liked to tell the story about how he lay on his couch suffering from inflammatory rheumatism when a friend called and told him about the upper country, the Spokane River and the great falls. Cannon was never one to let his occasional bouts of rheumatism interfere with his financial enterprises. The more he thought about the friend's suggestion, the more convinced he was to check it out. Within two days, he set out for Spokane Falls. His buggy only lasted as far as The Dalles. After joining up with Browne, they took the river steamer.

With plans to take over James Glover's general merchandise store, Cannon put together an inventory of goods and food items to be shipped. He sent his new brother-in-law, Alexander (Jack) Warner, with his wife, Maria (Jennie's sister), and family, to Spokane Falls in July to get the store in operation. Warner's half of the partnership in this venture included doing the bookkeeping.

The Cannons followed six weeks or more later.[2] Several other members of Jennie's family emigrated to Spokane Falls that year: her brother, George Pease, and his son, Archie, and Jennie's widowed sister, Harriet Pope, and her children. Their length of residence was not long, as by 1880 they had returned to Portland.

The Warners and Cannons moved into the two box-houses Glover had used for his first store and residence on the west side of Howard Street between Front and the river. A. M. also preempted a quarter-section of land to the west of the town site and south of Browne's. He put up a small shack and some posts in the way of improvements.

Even if Jennie had not been living near the main intersection of town, she would have been deeply involved in the town activities. She and Clara Gray, perhaps more than any of the other ladies in those early years, worked many hours to provide entertainment, food and decorations for the little community's social affairs.

It could be said Cannon began his empire in June 1879, when he hung out a sign on Howard Street on the side of the small addition Glover had built to the south of his building. Upon disembarking from the stage on his return from Colfax, Glover caught sight of the sign: Bank of Spokane Falls: A. M. Cannon, pres.

The "bank" consisted of a counter, a safe and $1,000 that A. M. had borrowed from his sister-in-law, Hattie Pope.

When Glover walked into the store, Alex Warner greeted him with: "Look what A. M. has done. He is head-over-heels in debt, and I won't have anything to do with it."[3] Cannon took the ribbing in good humor. He really stated his philosophy of life in explaining to Glover: "When a man is down, then is the time to put forth your best energies and show people that you are somebody in the world."[4] Besides, he reasoned, there was no bank north of the Snake River, and when the Northern Pacific railroad came through, there would be payroll checks to cash. Cannon believed in being ready.

With his characteristic genial smile, Anthony Cannon received instant acceptance by his fellow citizens. Slightly more than a year after his arrival at Spokane Falls, he was elected treasurer at the first Spokane County election. The following year he was re-elected for a two-year term.

After living in Glover's tiny three-room house for two years, Cannon built a small home for the family near Fourth and Walnut on his homestead. Now there was a little more room for social activities, which from then on seemed to center around the Cannon home. Jennie hosted the ladies of the Library

Anthony McCue Cannon, an energetic man of many enterprises and an early Spokane developer. *(Photo courtesy MAC/EWSHS, L85-44)*

Association and the Aid Society. Their dime sociables included games, singing and raffles. At one, A. M. won an afghan. At another, the receipts totaled $10.

But Mrs. Cannon did not devote all her time to social pursuits. She was an excellent nurse and could be found at the bedside of a sick friend whenever she was needed. Her idea of true happiness was to be doing for those she loved and caring for those who needed her care. Her presence in a sick room was likened to a ray of sunshine for the sick and suffering.[5] As a result, Jennie Cannon became one of the most respected and beloved members of the little town.

Her ministrations were not limited to the white population. The Indians, also, found her to be friendly, sympathetic, and one who spoke their language quite well. They frequented the Cannon home for many years, especially when in need of some doctoring.[6]

Jennie's generous contributions to charitable causes were to become widely known. She supported the Home of the Friendless, the Woman's Exchange, and the Fireman's Fund. It was said that she had a standing offer of $1,000 to any member of the *demimonde* (ladies of the night) who wanted to give up that profession, leave Spokane and start a new life. When the city of Seattle burned June 6, 1889, Jennie was one of fifteen women appointed to solicit relief funds. Jennie covered Cannon's Addition while Anna Browne canvassed Browne's Addition. More than $11,000 was collected in Spokane.

A. M. managed to convince his father, William Cannon, and two brothers to move from Illinois to Spokane. The elder Cannon came about 1880 and lived with his son and daughter-in-law. For a time, Thomas Cannon also made his home with his brother. The eldest brother, Aniel R. Cannon, took out a homestead on the north side when he arrived in 1885, naming it Cannondale. A sister, Emma, also lived in Spokane for a time and took an active part in the ladies' activities.

A. M. was appointed to the first city council of the newly incorporated Spokane until an election could be held. Although he did not win a position at that first city election, he was requested to fill a vacancy created when one of the members moved out of town. For four years, Cannon represented the Fourth Ward until being elected mayor April 8, 1885, an office he held for two years. This was the last time Cannon sought or was elected to public office. He still served on many civic committees. It probably could be said that little transpired in the community without his involvement.

A drawing of Cannon's Block, in 1882, at the northwest corner of Riverside and Mill (now Wall). The building housed Cannon's Bank of Spokane Falls and the store he had taken over from James Glover in 1878. Establishing the bank at this location moved the business center from Howard and Front to Riverside Avenue. *(From* Spokane Falls Illustrated, *1889)*

Typical of Cannon's far-sightedness or audaciousness was the location he chose for his own building – the northwest corner of Riverside and Mill (now Wall). This ornate two-and-a-half-story frame structure contained dormers on the third-story gambrel roof and a corner entrance from the streets. On the north end was a daylight basement, which bordered the head of a gully (Little Wolf Ditch).[7] Cannon's Block was considered well away from the center of town. Nevertheless, when A. M. moved his store and bank there in December 1882, business followed, and Riverside Avenue became the new commercial center. About a year later, Cannon sold the grocery and mercantile business to the Schulein Brothers and Simon Oppenheimer. The second floor of his building was occupied by professional offices.

If Cannon was not making money, he was certainly spending it. In 1883, he built a large home that, with its landscaped grounds, encompassed a full block between Third and Fourth avenues from Cedar to Walnut streets. (Until 1891, when the street numbering system was changed, the address was 813 West Third Avenue.) This city house was probably the first mansion in Spokane Falls. Although a carriage house and stable stood on the property, no written reference to other outbuildings, such as chicken coops or animal pens, was found.

The new Cannon home stood three stories high with dormer windows in the mansard roof. The main body of the house formed a rectangle facing north. A ten-foot-wide hall divided the first floor into four rooms with fourteen-foot ceilings and plate glass windows that almost reached the floor. Double parlors finished in cedar stood to the right of the hall, while on the opposite side were the reception room and library. Beyond the library was the dining room with frescoed walls done in oil. The butler's pantry and kitchen, both finished in cedar, adjoined the dining hall.[8] Through the use of folding and sliding doors, nearly all the ground floor rooms could be made into one large reception area. Four large sleeping rooms with twelve-foot ceilings occupied the second floor. Additional sleeping chambers made up the third floor. The bathrooms contained tin bathtubs set in mahogany.

At the end of the main hall, a stairway descended to the large and commodious billiard and smoking rooms in a half-basement. To the rear of the house, a two-story section contained an elaborate laundry and cheerful apartments for the staff. The carpets and furniture came from Portland. Costly oil paintings adorned the walls, hot air heated the house, and Jennie placed a Steinway grand piano in the living room. Eventually, gas lighted the rooms and electric bells were installed.

The house with its pebbled driveway sat back 140 feet from Third Avenue. Two verandas completely surrounded the house on both the ground and second-story levels. Flower beds, shade trees and lawn provided a proper setting for the handsome house. This was truly a show place in a town of barely 1,500 population. Later, when gas became available, Cannon installed high spouting fountains in the front yard. To add to the uniqueness, A. M. imported some live seals.

The Cannon mansion, built in 1883. Its landscaped grounds occupied a full block between Third and Fourth, Cedar and Walnut. *(Photo courtesy MAC/EWSHS, L95-12.184)*

Jennie, A. M. and three of the Clarke children moved into their modern, convenient and comfortable home toward the end of 1883.[9] (Marie, the eldest of Jennie's children, had married Bascom H. Bennett, cashier of the Bank of Spokane Falls, on April 26 of that year and son George had passed away three weeks prior.)

What better way to officially inaugurate their new home than with a Fourth of July ball the following year? Besides Mr. and Mrs. Cannon, the hosts for the gala party were: Ralph L. Clarke, his cousin Charles N. Warner, Will C. Stainsby, Lester D. Hawser and George E. Parker. Handsome and artistic invitations were sent to more than 50 young people.

The house sparkled with beautiful flowers and festoons of evergreens and bunting. Outside, fir and cedar garlands trimmed the wide verandas while overhead 200 Chinese lanterns radiated soft, multicolored light. A band played for dancing from nine until midnight at which time the guests gathered on the lawn to "ooh" and "ah" at the magnificent display of fireworks. After partaking of an elegant supper, the party-goers danced until dawn literally broke the eastern sky. The coverage in the newspaper was probably no more extravagant in its praises of this "event-of-all-events" than the actual function itself. As Susan Glover's niece Lovenia Culver, one of the guests, wrote to her parents, it was a very "tony" affair.

Jennie was an independent woman. It would certainly appear so when she traveled to Portland alone to accompany one of her daughters home from school. The journey was arduous at best before the railroad came through. It meant a ride to the Snake River or Wallula by stagecoach to get a river steamer. In mid-February such a trip would be quite miserable with open or poorly covered windows, drafty doors, and buffeted by wind, rain or snow. Comfort stops were not frequent. On the return trip five weeks later, Jennie's daughter's trunk fell off when the stage was crossing a swollen stream below Colfax. It remained in the water three hours.

In the fall of 1884, with winter approaching, Jennie began making plans to spend the winter traveling. She confided in a visit to Anna Browne that she knew times were hard, but she had made up her mind that they were going anyway.

In response to this bit of "news" from his wife, on October 24, 1884, J. J. Browne wrote to Anna:

> I think Mrs. Cannon very unwise in leaving home traveling for pleasure under the circumstances. It seems to me that they could pull through all right if they would do everything possible – and one of the things would be to stop expense as far as possible. And even in case of disaster, it is better by far to economize now – as economy such as they would be compelled to exercise under those circumstances would be more easy. It certainly would be hard for them to live on $800-$1000 a year which would be necessary then. Indeed it would be very difficult for us to come down to that.

Nevertheless, Jennie proceeded with her preparations. When Anna saw Mr. and Mrs. Cannon while out walking, Jennie said she possibly would start east in a week. A. M. said he had been sick for a week and was not going. "I don't think I ever saw him look so miserable," wrote Anna to J. J. "How she can even think of leaving him for a pleasure trip, I cannot understand."[10]

Whether or not Jennie actually left at this particular time is unknown. However, the Cannons did travel to Portland frequently, visited Victoria, a popular vacation spot, and wintered in California. There were also many trips to New York.

Apparently whenever Mr. and Mrs. Cannon entertained, the party was heralded as the social event of the season. So it was with the reception they gave June 29, 1887, for Jennie's son Ralph L. Clarke and his bride, Jennie G. Sheppard of Portland. Following their wedding in Portland June 15 and a wedding trip to Victoria, B. C., the Clarkes made their home in Spokane where Ralph was the assistant cashier at the Bank of Spokane Falls.

Japanese lanterns lit up the lawns and verandas, while evergreens and flowers decorated the inside of the Cannon home. The bride wore a beautiful pale blue moiré with a train and a handsome de Medici collar. The braid down the front of her gown was trimmed with pearls. Diamonds and a corsage of tea roses completed her attire. The groom wore the regulation black.

Two hundred twenty-four guests greeted the couple while the Spokane Brass Band played serenades in the background. About 11:00 p.m., after refreshments had been served, the band played waltz music for several hours of dancing. A newspaper write-up waxed eloquent: "The brilliant array of costumes has never been equalled in the city and would have done credit to a formal reception in the hub city of the universe."

On December 5, 1889, reporting on another wedding, the *Spokane Falls Review* began: "The most brilliant social event that ever occurred in Spokane Falls took place at the Cannon home last night." It was a double wedding ceremony. At 7:15 p.m. the stringed orchestra struck up "Mendelssohn's Wedding March." Down the broad staircase came Rev. Dr. Crawford of All Saints Church with the two grooms, followed by others in the wedding party. A. M. Cannon descended next with a bride on each arm. The two cousins, Katharine Clarke and Mary Evelyn (Mamie) Pope, wore identical dresses of heavy cream-colored silk with long trains trimmed with duchesse lace. About 30 people witnessed the ceremony. The list of guests for the reception that followed resembled the social register of Spokane.

Jennie Cannon in her mid-forties. *(Photo courtesy MAC/EWSHS, L87-97)*

Afternoon parties for the ladies were also held at the Cannon home. With daughter Marie Bennett and daughter-in-law, Jennie Clarke, Jennie often entertained 100 women at euchre – a popular card game of the time.

Not only were Jennie and A. M. active in community affairs and functions, but so were Mrs. Cannon's children. Ralph, Katie and Josie sang in the operettas, took part in church affairs, and attended all the balls. When the Young Ladies Guild of All Saints Episcopal Church put on a fund-raising program at the Opera House, Katie sang: "Coming Through the Rye." A reporter for the *Spokane*

Falls Review expressed the opinion that, to many, this was the success of the evening. Miss Clarke sang with "great sweetness and expression," he wrote.

Yet, sadness and bereavement did not bypass this family. Jennie's second son and middle child, George P. Clarke, died April 5, 1883, shortly before his sixteenth birthday.[11] Two years later, A. M. lost his father, William Cannon, at the age of 75. Surely, Jennie did not experience anything more heart rending than the death of little Marjory Clarke, her first grandchild, at the age of four in 1892.

In the spring of 1889, the Roseburg *Oregon Review* claimed that A. M. Cannon was the richest man in Eastern Washington with a worth of $4-6 million. This would appear to be slightly exaggerated. However, Cannon was enjoying enormous success, even if his health was not keeping pace. Besides his own Bank of Spokane Falls, Cannon helped organize and was elected president of the Bank of Palouse City. At the same time, he was an officer in several other banks.

In addition to banking, Cannon also realized railroads were prime movers in developing an area. He had earlier pushed for a Spokane and Palouse line. After advancing the money for a survey and preliminary work, Cannon traveled to New York in 1886 with A. A. Newbery and Paul F. Mohr to convince the Northern Pacific to build the road. Consequently, Cannon became president of the ensuing Spokane and Palouse Railroad. He also served as treasurer for the Spokane Falls and Idaho Railroad, a branch line to Coeur d'Alene that he promoted the next year.

There were also other varied investments. In 1881, largely in opposition to Francis Cook's *Spokan Times,* Glover, Cannon and Browne had started their own newspaper, *The Chronicle,* which culminated in a newspaper war that turned violent.[12] With Browne, Cannon had a half-ownership in the Spokane Cracker Company and the first streetcar line. He also became co-owner, with E. J. Brickell, of Glover's old sawmill (renamed Spokane Falls Mill Company). In 1888, he founded Greenwood Cemetery and became the cemetery association's president. He served as a director of the Eastern Washington and Idaho Fair Association, as he would for the 1890 Northwestern Industrial Exposition. Indeed, it seemed as if there was nothing Cannon could not do or try to do.

Cannon and Browne also partnered on the construction of the magnificent Auditorium Building at the northwest corner of Main and Post. Construction began shortly before the 1889 fire, but the building was spared because Little Wolf Ditch separated it from the fire's path of destruction. With their wives, the two men went to New York to order appropriate trimmings for their theatre. On the return trip the ladies stopped in Chicago to visit Josie Clarke, a student at the Lake Forest Seminary for Young Ladies.

The Auditorium Theatre proved to be everything its builders promised it to be. It contained the country's largest stage, 60 by 45 feet, held 1,400 strawberry plush seats and ten elegant hanging boxes. One of the stained glass windows contained portraits of Cannon and Browne. At a cost of a quarter of a million dollars, it took a year and a half to build.

Opening night September 16, 1890, Mr. and Mrs. Cannon took their seats in Box A with Mr. and Mrs. Hemenway. In Box B sat Mr. and Mrs. Ralph L. Clarke and Mr. and Mrs. B. H. Bennett. "Nanon" by the Carleton Opera Company was the bill of fare. After an opening address by Col. P. H. Winston complimenting the manager of the opera house, H. C. Hayward, the audience called for Browne and Cannon. It would be hard to imagine a greater moment of triumph and success that those two families enjoyed that evening. The glory reflected their hard work, faith in Spokane, and the goodwill of their fellow citizens.

After the Spokane fire of 1889, the Bank of Spokane Falls was located temporarily in the Review Building. It was then moved to a three-story brick on the west side of Mill, north of Riverside, until Cannon could build the Bank building on his old site, the northwest corner of Riverside and Mill. Again Cannon presented a unique concept – a building for only one business. Just one story high with a daylight basement, the little building had revolving doors and a great round skylight in the center of the roof. The exterior was faced with grey polished marble. Inside, marble had also been used generously. Although remembered by many Spokanites for its two large cast-stone crouching lions in front, these were not part of the original construction.

Cannon never had the opportunity to move into his Marble Bank building. Although construction began in 1892, it was not finished when the Bank of Spokane Falls failed June 5, 1893, thus becoming the first bank in Spokane to collapse in the national financial crisis known as the Panic of 1893.[13]

Cannon's Marble Bank, circa 1905, adjacent to the Crescent store, at the northwest corner of Riverside and Wall. *(Cropped postcard photo from* Vintage Postcards From Old Spokane *courtesy Duane Broyles and Howard Ness)*

It seemed as if Cannon's entire world began to fall apart. Jennie had been in poor health for two years. In June 1892, she had a serious but undefined operation. After an apparent recovery, a relapse occurred. Dr. R. Ludlam,

Interior of the Auditorium Theater. *(Photo from the Jerome Peltier Collection, courtesy Tony and Suzanne Bamonte)*

professor of surgical diseases of women at the Hahnemann Medical College and Hospital of Chicago, was brought to Spokane, and the operation repeated.[14]

By September 1893, Jennie was on her death bed. She had made a last-minute trip to Chicago hoping to improve her health, but became weaker and had to return home. Throughout her illness, it was said that she never complained and bore her suffering with great fortitude. The last few days she was in a coma. She passed away September 8, at the age of 53.

Jennie Pease Clarke Cannon lay in state in a beautiful casket draped in black broadcloth in the parlor of her home surrounded by a bower of flowers. Anna Browne sent a large basket of white and purple flowers that she had arranged with five ferns and vines tied with a white ribbon.

Jennie Cannon, circa 1892, about a year before her death. *(Photo courtesy MAC/EWSHS, L87-100)*

Dr. Watson, the Episcopal minister, said at Jennie's funeral: "We have lost one of Spokane's greatest citizens and benefactors. No one came to the city that she wasn't ready to be interested in, although she was not a public woman. Her home was emphatically her kingdom; its happiness, her happiness. There are two lessons from Mrs. Cannon's life: one, her large-heartedness and charity, the other her patience and faith."[15] No other pioneer woman was accorded the front-page coverage Jennie received when she died.

Cannon found it difficult to put his financial affairs in order, and his health failed accordingly. It seemed to him that life would be a useless burden unless he could find somebody to sympathize with him sincerely."[16] With this thought in mind, he went to Helena, Montana, and convinced the young Mrs. Eleanor Davis Ward, a divorcee of a year with three small children, to marry him. A. M. had first met Mrs. Ward a couple years earlier when she had an asphalt business in Spokane.

Although the marriage was kept secret, word of it leaked out. Spokanites were scandalized that Cannon would remarry, by some reports, within six weeks of Jennie's death. Certainly the union took place within two months. Mr. and Mrs. Cannon traveled to New York separately, but by early January, A. M. decided to end the rumors by talking to a reporter for the *New York Recorder*. The new Mrs.

Cannon was a vivacious blonde, attractive in face and figure. Cannon pointed to her "as the best proof that he was in his right mind when he contracted his second [actually his third] marriage."[17] The article printed in the *Recorder* was duly reprinted in the *Spokane Chronicle* the following week.

The economic crash of 1893 proceeded to divest Cannon of more than the Bank of Spokane Falls. He and Browne had mortgaged their substantial land hold-

ings to build the Auditorium Building. By February 26, 1894, the stockholders met to set a price on the Auditorium. Unable to meet mortgage payments and taxes, Cannon's land holdings began slipping away. He had guaranteed a $30,000 loan with 61 prime residential lots. In 1895, the Northwestern & Pacific Hypotheekbank foreclosed and bought the property at a sheriff's sale, thus "wiping out Cannon's last assets in the city."[18]

Suffering from heart problems and rheumatism, Cannon went to South America with F. C. Goodin in January 1895. His health improved greatly, and rumor said that Cannon was looking for a quick profit in railroading or mining in Brazil. Not

A. M. Cannon about 1890. *(Photo from* Spokane Falls and Its Exposition, *1890)*

finding it, he returned to New York, where he arranged with George Hutchinson to open an office, signing a year's lease. However, before anything further could be done, Anthony M. Cannon passed away in his sleep April 6, 1895, exactly one month shy of his 58th birthday, at the Sturdevant Hotel. With death came forgiveness, and Cannon's life and accomplishments were given widespread coverage in the newspapers.

His financial affairs did not fare as well. As Cannon left no updated will, Eleanor sued for a widow's one-half of his estate. In 1897, the court decided that hers was a preferred claim over all others, and she was to be paid out of the estate of A. M. and Jennie Cannon. This amounted to little. Within a few years, Eleanor moved back to Helena.

Chapter V

Clara Smiley Gray

Clara Smiley Gray in her mid-thirties.
(Photo courtesy MAC/EWSHS, L93-66.184)

Clara Foster Smiley was destined to live the longest life of any resident from embryonic Spokane Falls, Washington Territory. Born January 20, 1854, she spent her early childhood in Benton, Maine. Shortly after her birth, her father, Johnson Foster Smiley, was lured to the goldfields in California.

Eight years later, Clara, her mother Sarah Ann Richardson Smiley, and older brother Fred, embarked upon her first journey into the unknown. After a train ride to New York City, they emigrated to California via the Panama route. Arriving in San Francisco, they headed for the little mining town of Indian Valley on the Yuba River in central California, where Johnson Smiley had a general merchandise store. A year later, Sarah convinced her husband to move to Marysville where there were schools available for the children. It was here that Clara grew up.

As a teenager she attended Mrs. Poston's Seminary, a private school for girls in Marysville, one of the earliest secondary institutions in northern California. Eugenia Cornelia Poston had opened her school in 1857 and served as its principal. Clara, whose nickname was Caddie, received a classical education: Latin, music, grammar and history.

Caddie did not have far to walk to school as the family lived a block and a half away on Seventh Street between C and D. Her father was a city police officer, and brother Fred worked as a messenger for Western Union.

Clara graduated from the seminary with a teaching certificate. However, she had met a dashing young railroad man, William Chandler Gray, whom she married October 23, 1872. They made a handsome couple: slender, dark-haired, eighteen-year-old Clara, who stood about 5'5", and tall, blonde Bill, 27, sporting a fashionable mustache and goatee.

Bill was the oldest of six children and a former Easterner. At age 19, he made his way to the Far West and Virginia City, Montana. The next year, 1865, young Gray went to California and soon began a railroad construction career. He worked on lines from Sacramento to Redding and Oakland to San Leandro. He also laid track for the Southern Pacific out of Los Angeles, but by 1871, he was in Redding where he built the Depot Hotel. It was here he took his bride to live. Two years later, he sold the hotel and returned to railroad construction.[1] Whether or not he realized it at the time, Bill Gray had established the careers he would pursue for the rest of his life and which would earn him a niche in history in the yet unknown outpost of Spokane Falls, Washington Territory.

As a well-educated young woman, Clara was not about to be left behind when Bill went to work for the Southern Pacific building the line between Oakland and Martinez. She went to San Francisco and took a course in telegraphy that enabled her to travel with her husband as his clerk and telegrapher while also employed by the Southern Pacific Railroad. "In fact," she remarked in later years, "we became great pals as well as husband and wife."[2]

William Chandler Gray and Clara Smiley Gray, around the time they arrived in Spokane Falls, circa 1878. *(Photos courtesy MAC/EWSHS, L87-74 (left) and L93-66.183)*

Rumors kept sifting down to California about the upper inland area of Washington Territory, enough to incite the curiosity of Bill Gray. He decided to see for himself. Accompanied by J. H. Greiner, and a pack on his back and rifle over his shoulder, Gray reached the falls of the Spokane River on August 26, 1878. The men stayed in a livery barn on the northeast corner of Mill and Front.

The beauty of the falls impressed Bill but not enough to invest in the miniscule village. He was much more interested in Colfax, where he tried to buy the Baldwin Hotel. When that proposal did not develop, friends convinced Bill to return to Spokane for a second look. Deciding the town needed a hotel, Gray bought a 60 by 120-foot lot on the northeast corner of Howard and Front for the unheard-of sum of $200.[3] Upon returning to Walla Walla, the nearest outfitting center, he wired Clara in Oakland to come.

From San Francisco, Clara and her two younger brothers, William Smiley, 11, and Charles, 15, took the steamer *Great Republic* north to Portland. After their mother had died five years earlier at age 51 from "bilious fever," the boys had lived with Clara and Bill. Upon their departure on their long journey, Clara's friends were convinced they were going to the North Pole. To Clara it seemed likely; Spokane Falls was such a long distance away.

A river steamer took them up the Columbia River from Portland to The Dalles, a train skirted Celilo Falls, and another boat trip landed them at Wallula. Finally, aboard Dr. Baker's strap-iron narrow-gauge railroad, they arrived in Walla Walla on the last day of September 1878. The passenger car on that famous line was not much more than a box car with benches along the side – a tough looking outfit and just about as comfortable.

While waiting for his wife, Bill Gray had been busy purchasing items needed for the hotel: doors, windows, sashes, hardware, a large supply of groceries and no doubt some rudiments of household items. On the second day of October, the family headed north in a lightweight covered wagon pulled by two horses. All the supplies were carried in a big heavy prairie schooner drawn by six horses. They followed the Old Territorial Trail to Spokane Falls, up through Dayton and Colfax.

The main wagon road into Spokane Falls came in from the west. After fording Hangman (Latah) Creek, it crawled up the hill on the opposite side by a ravine that came out at Sixth Avenue. Then it angled in a northeasterly direction across the gravel flat, crossing the block (Third and Cedar) where the First Presbyterian Church stands. The track made the final approach down Howard Street. Before them lay the town, such as it was: one store, one small sawmill, one small flour mill and a blacksmith shop. No churches, no schools, only a cluster of shacks and unpainted buildings huddled beside the river. It could hardly be considered even a crossroads, as there were not two roads to cross.

Nearly everyone lived on Front Street (changed to an avenue in 1891) in order to get water from the river. These included the families of J. N. Glover, Frederick Post, J. J. Browne, Alexander Warner, Dr. Masterson, Sam Arthur, Mr. Lowery and Mr. Downer. The Reverend Cowley had his home at Sixth and Division, and the Reverend Havermale lived on his homestead near Front and Bernard. Some people by the name of Goodner lived across the street. Mr. and Mrs. Evans, who had a cabinet shop, were on Front between Howard and Mill. On the north side of that block, Mrs. Arthur had a little eating house while her husband, Sam, worked in Cannon's store. Next to them the Percival brothers ran a blacksmith shop. A few unmarried men made up the rest of the townspeople: the Dart brothers, Platt Corbolay, a Mr. Grant and Mr. Tervin. According to W. H. Smiley's account in 1936, the Grays increased the population to fifty-four.[4]

As they pulled up by Cannon & Warner's store, Frederick Post, the miller, walked out of the store. He insisted the Grays stay with his family instead of at Masterson's boarding house over on Stevens Street. Masterson's was suitable for an itinerant laborer, Post explained, but hardly the place for a lady and a couple of young boys. The accommodations were rather crude and rough. There was only a dirt floor, and Doc had a habit of relaxing after dinner by putting his feet on the table.

Although the Posts had four of their five daughters and a foster son, John Mitchell, at home, they gladly made room for four more. They had already extended their hospitality to Mr. and Mrs. Browne and baby Guy. It was suggested that Bill Gray could use two vacant log cabins near Mill and Main that had been built and occupied by the soldiers the year before during the Nez Perce Indian scare. The cabins were only log walls, as all the sawed boards from the roof and floor had been removed. However, in two days Gray had one cabin habitable, and the family moved in.

As they had no mattresses nor were there any to buy, Clara purchased material at Cannon's store to sew into mattress ticks. Bill gathered wild hay to stuff them, but it became lumpy and hard packed. One could not even stir it!

Work started on the hotel immediately, and Clara was presented with two carpenters to board in addition to her husband and brothers. This was not unusual. In a new country, women were expected to feed the extra men as boarding houses and restaurants were in short supply.

Clara was not exactly a recent bride; she and Bill had been married six years. But this was perhaps the first time she had had to set up housekeeping. Baking bread was a new adventure! Valiantly, Clara tried her best. She mixed baking powder biscuit dough, put it in pans and baked it like loaves of bread. But it did not turn out like loaves of bread. It must have been pretty terrible and word got around. Shortly afterward Susan Glover called and asked what she knew about making bread. After hearing what Clara had been doing, Mrs. Glover kindly explained how to make yeast. However, before Mrs. Gray got around to following her instructions, she had another visitor, Marie Warner, wife of the storekeeper. She, too, asked about Clara's bread making techniques. Again, the same sad story. "Don't worry about it," Mrs. Warner told her. "I'm teaching the Indian women how to make bread, and I'll furnish you with all the yeast you need."[5]

Indians were very much a part of the town scene, and if they were at first a curiosity to the townspeople, the latter were even more so to the Indians. One day an Indian woman went a bit further than idly watching. It was the day Jim Glover sent Nellie, Spokan Garry's daughter, to help Clara with a big washing. Mrs. Gray explained to Nellie what she wanted done, but Nellie instructed an older Indian woman she had brought with her, then left.

The Grays' cabin was so tiny Bill had made a shelf on one wall to serve as a table. Consequently, only three people could eat at one time. After finishing the noon meal, Gray and the workmen headed back to the hotel. Just as Clara and her brothers were about to sit down, Nellie returned and surveyed the food on the table. In a flash she scooped it all into her shawl: meat, potatoes, bread – everything. It happened that Bill returned for something about that time and intercepted Nellie as she tried to sidle out the door. Although he gave her a good shaking to return the food, she hung on and escaped. Clara ended up cooking another meal for herself and the boys.[6]

Since nearly everyone lived along Front Street between Washington and Post streets, it seemed to Clara that their little cabins were far out of town. The word "streets" was almost a misnomer. Most were either crude wagon roads or dirt paths and some existed essentially in name only.

The winter of 1878 was particularly cold. By mid-December winter came in earnest: minus twenty-degree weather and snow which eventually reached five feet. The town was shut off from the rest of the world with no mail delivery for six weeks.[7] In the Grays' little log hut, the steam from the tea kettle on the stove condensed into water. As the water fell to the floor, ice formed around the stove. Thinking she would clean up the mess, Clara poured a whole kettle of boiling water on the floor, only to create a skating rink. Bill had to use a shovel to scrape up the ice.

It was truly a happy day for Clara when the Grays were able to move into the lean-to kitchen of the unfinished hotel early in December. As there was no wardrobe or closet for her clothing, she improvised by tacking a sheet across the rough siding and hung her dresses on hooks. Then she tacked another sheet over the clothing.

When Christmas came, the Grays and the boys were welcomed to the traditional gathering at the Glovers' home. Mr. and Mrs. A. M. Cannon were there with her daughter, Marie Clarke; the Alexander Warners with their children, Charlie and four-year-old Hattie; the J. J. Brownes; Alice and Julia Post; bachelors Herbert and Myron Percival, and a few others. Susan Glover played carols on the organ for the group. To Bill Gray, the best singers were his wife, Susan Glover and Marie Warner. "A pretty intelligent set of people," he observed.[8] Refreshments served were cake and coffee with apples from Oregon.

With the growing number of children in Spokane Falls, it became apparent that a permanent school was needed. To raise funds a dance was held in Glover's Hall shortly after the New Year, 1879.[9] When Clara went to her improvised wardrobe to get her black lace dress, she found that the frost coming through the wall had frozen the sheet fast to the boards, and her polonaise,[10] trimmed with Spanish lace around the bottom, was also frozen to the sheet. Someone suggested heating a flat iron on the cook stove. Although it took quite a while, Clara literally ironed her dress off the wall, and the Grays made it to the dance.

Glover's Hall was a large room on the second floor over Cannon and Warner's store (the two-story building they leased from Glover), kitty-corner across the intersection from the hotel. All the social life of the town took place there. For dances and special occasions, homesteaders came from Deep Creek, Medical Lake, Four Lakes, Spangle and the lower country. There were soldiers from Fort Coeur d'Alene and Fort Colville (1858–1880). Music was furnished by two Arkansas fiddlers, sawing the beat for square dances. Not everyone attended the dance, as some of the people who were very strict in their religious practices disapproved of dancing.

During the evening, one of the officers asked Clara for a waltz. As the musicians played a three-four tune, they danced around the floor a couple of times before they noticed no one else was dancing. Clara always felt she and the young lieutenant danced the first waltz in Spokane. This was a story Clara told frequently in later years. It also set a pattern, as Mrs. W. C. Gray would be in the forefront of all the social activities for the next decade. The dance was a huge financial success, raising $80, enough to build the schoolhouse. It was completed in time for school to open on April 1, 1879. The Smiley brothers were among the twenty-two students.

In February 1879, Mrs. Warner had decided she was tired of housekeeping and suggested that if the Grays' hotel did not open pretty soon, she would open it herself. In addition to the fact that the building was not finished, Clara reminded her they had no cook. Mrs. Warner offered to take care of that. In a borrowed horse and buggy, Marie Warner drove to Westwood (Rathdrum) and hired an African American named "Duke." So in a sense, the Grays were forced to open their hotel the last of February 1879.[11] Having come from California, they named the hotel California House. Facing Front Street, the original frame building was only 26 by 40 feet, just eight feet wider than the ballroom later built on the third floor of the F. Lewis Clark home. The main floor of the hotel contained the office, dining room and bar, while the second floor had ten rooms.[12] The undivided attic contained a double bed in each corner and was known as the corral.[13] Here men could bunk down or curl up in blankets when the other rooms were full. The regular price was 50¢ per meal and 50¢ a bed, or $6.00 a week for room and board. Behind the hotel toward the river were the horse corrals, pigpens and wood yard.

A sketch of the California House, Echo Roller Mills, and Glover & Gilliam's Livery Stable, as they appeared in 1884. The Howard Street Bridge, the first bridge over the Spokane River in downtown Spokane Falls, is in the center of the photo. *(From* The West Shore: An Illustrated Journal of General Information Devoted to the Development of the Great West, *April 1884)*

Clara wanted the opening of California House to be a well-remembered event so she carefully set the table for breakfast the night before. By morning, the cream she had so thoughtfully poured was frozen and the pitchers broken into little pieces. It seemed she still had not learned to cope with Spokane's cold weather! However, when the buttercups along the riverbank heralded spring, she and Bill picked them to brighten the tables. Wildflowers out on the prairie south of town (Riverside Avenue) also found their way to the California House.

The star boarders at the hotel included Mr. and Mrs. Warner and their children; Capt. George Pease (a brother of Mrs. Warner's and Mrs. Cannon's) and his son Archie – both noted pioneer pilots on the Columbia River; Mr. Silver, a clerk at Warner's store; and two men who hauled logs to the sawmill. Clara had also taken in a Dr. Hornberger, who had been staying at Doc Masterson's boarding house. Hornberger had tuberculosis, and Clara took care of him until just before he died.

Meat for the hotel dining room was purchased from Steve Liberty at Liberty Lake. He would go out and kill a beef – not always his own. Eggs could be purchased at Deep Creek, and the settlers in the Pine Creek area raised some vegetables. Fish from the river was always plentiful. Other staples had to be freighted in from Walla Walla.

Although the hotel was operating, Gray had not completed construction. A basement was later finished in which he relocated the bar, thus converting the main entrance into a reading room. A porch along the entire west side was added. Then Gray spruced up the building with rustic siding and paint. Perhaps the most innovative project was with the stovepipe sticking out of the roof. There had been no bricks available when Coon Livingston of Colfax made the chimney for the hotel. Bill got tired of looking at the old pipe, so he had it painted to look like brick. Wood, of course, was used for fuel. From the beginning the hotel proved to be too small. Seven months after the opening, Gray built an 18 by 40-foot addition on the east end.

Located in the very center of the little community, California House afforded its proprietors grandstand seats to observe the growth of Spokane Falls and to participate in all the action. Participate they did. With enthusiasm, vitality and good humor, with open hospitality, honesty and integrity, this gracious couple played major roles in the heartbeat of the tiny town during the 1880s.

In the middle of the summer of 1879, a United States infantry band en route to Fort Coeur d'Alene from Fort Lapwai camped under the pine trees near Front and Post. Since all entertainment had to be locally produced, a wandering minstrel of any kind was warmly received. To the delight of the whole town, the band accepted Gray's invitation to give a concert. Standing in the center of the intersection near the hotel, the 22-member band played its best. In appreciation, Gray took the entire band downstairs in his hotel and, according to band member Professor T. W. Pynn, "treated them royally."

In spite of the fact the 1877 Nez Perce War was long over and the Sioux Wars had ended, there were still occasional Indian scares. To Clara Gray the greatest one occurred in the fall of 1879.[14] The Grays were sitting in the lobby of the hotel with some guests when an old trapper and hunter walked in about ten at night and said, "I've lived in this country nearly all my life, and I never saw things look as scary as they do tonight." When asked why, he said the Indians had not returned to their homes that night, but were lying behind rocks all over town while the women and children had been sent away. Clara was nearly frightened to death!

After recovering from the shock, the men decided the best thing to do was to bring in the few scattered families. Bill Gray and Harry, the bartender, got the J. J. Browne family from their homestead at 1717 West Pacific and alerted the Cannons at their residence. Other men went to the Cowley place or to the other few homes in the wilderness to the east. The Cannons and Brownes stayed at the store; the rest came to the hotel. As soon as the doors were barred, Gray stood his hunting rifle by the door. A few minutes later he started for the dining room, accidentally brushing against the gun. It discharged close to his head, the bullet lodging in the wall. If nerves were jumpy before, that was the finishing touch.

All that night, Clara sat on the floor near the window where she could look up Howard Street and also check in other directions. But no Indians appeared. The next day the Indians explained that they had sent their wives and children to dig camas roots.[15]

For the most part, the relationship between the settlers at Spokane Falls and the Indians was cordial. The Grays and many others employed Indians to wash and iron as there was no other help to be had. The Grays felt the Indians were honest and very capable of doing all kinds of work. In fact, as Clara commented later, she did not know how they could have gotten along without their help.

"Curly Jim was always one of my friends and did me a number of good turns. He was an honest, hard-working Indian and was well liked by all the white people," Clara recalled many years later. Another good friend of hers was Chief Moses, a famous character, and chief of the Sinkiuse (sin-kus), usually called Columbias, who lived at Moses Lake and the Moses Coulee area. It was said that although Chief Moses was on good terms with many influential white men, he never made friends with white women. On his way back from Washington, D.C., where he had seen the heads of government, Moses stopped at the hotel. Bill Gray went to get his wife, perhaps with tongue in cheek. Clara walked into the office with her hand outstretched, cordially greeting the chief. *"Halo wawa,"* he replied in Chinook.

The proprietress of the hotel had learned enough of the Indian trade language to invite him to have some dinner. Accepting, he stalked into the dining room where he was served the best meal they could prepare. "Now, Chief Moses," Clara told him when he was through eating, "whenever you come to town, you must come here for your meals." She apparently struck a responsive chord because from that time on Chief Moses never came to Spokane without visiting the lovely lady of California House.

In the early 1880s, the Spokane Indians had many little fields cultivated and enclosed. One garden was where Lewis and Clark High School now stands, and others were out toward Garden Springs.[16] Fish remained one of their staple foods, however. It was not unusual to stand on the porch of the hotel and watch hundreds of Indians fishing. On the north bank, the Indians hung a large basket-shaped net from a rock ledge to catch the salmon as they tried to leap the falls.

When Cannon & Warner's, formerly Jim Glover's little store, was the only merchandise store in town, there were frequent problems with supply and demand. It was more a case of what one could get than what one wanted, as Mr. Cannon was usually "just out." One lady needed a pair of shoes. She wore a size four, but the smallest size in stock was a six. That is what she had to buy. However, the biggest disappointment came when it rained – the soles of the shoes quickly disintegrated! Prices for food on the frontier were high: butter could cost as much as $5.00 a pound, eggs were $1.00 a dozen, and the only fruit to be had in 1879 was apples at 12½ cents a pound.

Clara never forgot the time she lost a needle and went across the street to get another. Mr. Cannon pulled out a packet of the requested size and asked how many she wanted. Clara had never bought less than a paper of needles at one time, but she was willing to adapt to the local customs. She supposed one would do. Very gravely, Mr. Cannon removed one needle and handed it to her. "How much is it?" she asked. "Ten cents." In handing over the dime, Clara must have looked rather skeptical because Cannon apologetically explained: "I suppose that seems a pretty high price to pay for one needle, but you know it's so expensive to get our goods up here. The freight rates are so high, having to freight everything in by wagon."[17]

The idea that the weight of one needle contributed to the overall freight struck Clara as being so immensely funny that she broke forth with a good laugh. But she got even. At various times the Grays were included at the Browne and Cannon homes when there were distinguished visitors from the east. The men, including A. M. Cannon, liked to amuse their guests by relating stories about what Clara did or said when she first came to the tiny town. She would usually retaliate by telling about the needle episode and the fantastic freight rates. Even Cannon joined in at the laughter directed toward him.

Hardships were many. Women wore sunbonnets to bed with netting over their faces to protect them from the mosquitoes. Housekeepers had to fry hotcakes in tallow which stuck to the roof of one's mouth. And it was common, as Clara later pointed out, to frost one's feet in winter.

But there were also good times. For the most part, dances with good hearty country suppers continued to be the favorite form of entertainment, and calico dresses were the proper attire for such events. A family of Harris boys, one named Lafayette from Granite Lake, usually did the playing. "There was always a lot of drinking at the dances, but we didn't have any shooting until the rough characters came with the N. P.," Bill Gray reminisced some forty years later. "There were always a lot of drunken Indians around town keeping things stirred up, that took the place of moving picture shows and vaudeville. Plenty of action here in the early days, believe me."[18]

The olden days are often referred to as times when men were men and women were women. Well, boys were boys. Although it is not recorded that any of the Spokane Falls chaps took buggies apart on Halloween and reassembled them on top of some neighbor's barn, Will Smiley acknowledged being the culprit who put red pepper on the stove at school. Class had to be dismissed until the room aired out. Another time Will spread Limburger cheese all over Katie Clarke's desk because she sat behind him and stuck pins in his neck. That time, school was dismissed for the day.

In snowy winters the Smiley brothers and their friends had a fantastic sledding course – down the long gully that stretched from Howard and Riverside north-westward to the river behind Frederick Post's grist mill. In the summertime, the boys amused themselves by playing baseball or fishing for trout off the Howard Street bridge. Over the hill on Hangman Creek crayfish the size of crabs were caught and boiled for a feast.

For a number of years California House was considered the only first-rate hotel in Spokane, if not north of the Snake River. They advertised in the *Spokan Times* as having ample accommodations for families. By the first of April 1880, there were forty permanent boarders.

Unfortunately, the Grays did not have much success with employees, especially the cooks, a position that changed personnel frequently. The cook known as "Duke" lasted about six months. Clara replaced him with a Chinese man who had come to Spokane Falls to start a laundry. Prejudice against Asians was so strong that he had been prevented from starting his own business. It did not make much sense to Clara that he was permitted to cook for them, but could not run a laundry. (By 1885, however, there were at least three Chinese laundries: Hop Lee's, Sang Lee's and Tong Lee's. Yant Long operated a Chinese store.) Unfortunately, the Chinese cook had one major problem – he occasionally got drunk. Clara's good neighbors, especially Mrs. Olga Brandt, who taught piano on the second floor of Glover's Block, and Mrs. Gilbert, wife of the blacksmith, often helped her out in such emergencies. When additional chambermaids were needed, Gray ran an ad in the newspaper: "Good wages paid for a good girl."[19]

During hot weather, iced tea and iced water were served at California House. All stages left from the hotel. One newsworthy item appeared in the local newspaper in August 1881, informing the public that Gray had installed an 1,800-pound safe. Similarly, the populace learned that Bob, a pet bear, was quartered at California House while entertaining the townfolks with his trainer.

Many well-known generals, including Sherman, Howard, Miles, Merriam and Wheaton, stayed at Grays' hostelry. Early railroad men, touring actors, lecturers and clergymen all enjoyed Bill's and Clara's hospitality. Regardless of competition or reputation, Bill Gray never turned a hungry man away because he could not pay.

In 1881, Fathers Cataldo and Joset were guests at the hotel when they bought 320 acres of land from the Northern Pacific for the future Gonzaga University and Mount St. Michael's Seminary for $3.20 an acre, with money donated, in part, by the men of the town.

The California House after the Grays enlarged it, circa 1886. *(Photo from the Jerome Peltier Collection, courtesy Tony and Suzanne Bamonte)*

Deciding that still more space was needed, in 1882, Bill Gray purchased thirty more feet along Front Street for $125, and put up an "L-shaped" addition. By elevating the roof, the building was made larger and more spacious. Three years later, Gray again had the carpenters working as he remodeled California House into a structure of three and a half stories.

Now more than double the size of the original building, the wood frame hotel had a three-story front with sixty feet along Front Street and thirty feet along Howard. A two-story wing continued north on Howard for another twenty feet. The pitched hip roofs of the main building were shingled. A large dormer window projected from the west and east ends of the attic. Numerous chimneys sprouted through the roof. Above the length of the wooden sidewalks on the west and south sides ran a balcony supported by ornate brackets and wood posts. Along the two streets, Gray planted a number of trees. In the rear of the hotel a narrow two-story stable wing extended from the east end.[20]

As the population of the little town increased, the social life became more sophisticated. Spokane Falls was no longer isolated. The Northern Pacific Railroad finally made it to town. The city was incorporated in 1881, and Bill Gray was appointed and then elected a member of the first city council, a position he would hold five more times.

Musicals and dramas, local and imported, and socials with card games entered the social scene. Two ladies who could always be found working on the decorations, music or reception committees were Jennie Cannon and Clara Gray. Although the J. J. Brownes were always prominently in attendance and the Glovers occasionally, Jennie and Clara entered whole-heartedly and enthusiastically into everything. It is interesting to note that the planning and sponsorship of these events were primarily the function of the men. They had not yet relinquished those positions to the fairer sex.

Clara's fine voice was always in demand. It has been recorded that at an entertainment on March 11, 1882, she was a member of a quartet that sang "Moonlight on the Lake." Her solo number was "Thou Art So Near and Yet So Far."

The dances were no longer hoedowns but balls that invariably began at 9:00 p.m. with a grand march. Elegant suppers were served around 11:30 p.m., after which dancing continued until the early hours of the morning. Masquerades with costumes and masks were held. At one, Clara dressed as a gypsy maid. The *Chronicle* reported a New Year's Eve dance at the hotel: "The sprightly hostess of the California House did the honors of the evening on the dance floor with her accustomed grace while Mr. Gray in the office was as genial and hospitable as ever."[21]

One entered the large gambling room and saloon through an open door in Bill's office. As in the rest of town, every imaginable gambling game was running full blast. Bill Gray was particularly good at the game of faro.

By 1883, there were five other hotels in town: the Northern Pacific run by Mel Grimmer and B. F. Shaner; the Western House with Hamilton and Ryan as proprietors (Doc Masterson, the former owner, had moved to Rathdrum); Sprague House near the railroad depot, managed by W. Kaiser; the Palace Hotel, managed by Mrs. P. A. Knox; and the Villard House operated by S. Littrell. None of them, however, came close to rivaling the reputation of California House.

Probably the hotel's guest who ultimately became the most famous was a Catholic nun, Mother Joseph of the Sacred Heart, who arrived May 1, 1886, from Vancouver, Washington Territory, to build a hospital. During her stay at the California House, she drew the plans for Spokane's first hospital (see chapter VI) while seated at the hotel's dining room table.

The year 1886 witnessed some notable events. On May 7, a fire started in the laundry room in the rear two-story wing of the California House. Romance bloomed as Charles Smiley, now age 24, married Lida W. Morris on July 15. They moved to Seattle where Charles worked for the Immigration Service.

A view of the backside of the California House, located at the northeast corner of Front and Howard. The photo was probably taken shortly before the California House was destroyed by fire in 1887. The Western House, facing Front at the far left of the picture, was the first hotel of sorts in Spokane Falls. It was built in 1877 by James Masterson. Room rates were fifty cents a night. *(Photo courtesy MAC/EWSHS, detail of L86-275.2))*

They had two daughters, Clara and Gladys. On December 6, 1886, Mrs. W. C. Gray became one of the initial thirty-five customers of the new telephone service inaugurated in Spokane Falls.

Although new businesses and most settlers had always been welcome, not all persons were accorded this hospitality. The *Spokane Falls Review* stated it very bluntly in an article that appeared March 17, 1887: "W. C. Gray is putting up a row of five frame buildings on Stevens between Front and the river to be rented to Chinamen. The purpose is to move China town as far away from the center of town as possible."

The real news in 1887, however, was that Bill Gray decided he had been in the hotel business long enough. In March, he leased his hostelry to Stephen S. Bailey and Reuben A. Freese. After redecorating, the new proprietors claimed to have the best hotel in the upper country. Even so, fire, that constant threat to wooden buildings and frontier towns in general, claimed otherwise. At 8:00 p.m. on May 17, 1887, the largest frame structure in town was ablaze. The fire seemed to be in the roof at the back of the hotel. By the time the volunteer fire

Pioneer Artist Pictures the Burning of the "California House"

An artist's concept of the California House fire of May 17, 1887, which was re-printed in the Spokane *Chronicle* on January 19, 1935.

department had rounded up long ladders from people's sheds and barns, the fire was well underway. Hoses were connected at Front and Howard, Stevens and Front, and Main and Howard. In order to reach the back of the hotel, the firemen carried hoses up through the building and onto the roofs of adjoining buildings. One of the hazards for those below was that the water poured into the fourth floor came down boiling hot. Carpets and blankets were hung in front of John Glover's livery stable across Howard Street to protect it from flying sparks or from the potential intense heat should all the hotel go.

Over on Pacific Avenue in Browne's Addition, Daniel H. Dwight was visiting his future father-in-law, W. G. Willis. In a letter to his father, Dwight described the incident:

> . . . when looking out, we saw a great smoke and blaze in the direction of the Arlington Hotel [where Dwight was staying], and heard the shouts and cries of fire. Forthwith my long legs sped away for the scene of the confusion for if the hotel was on fire I didn't care to lose our "traps" if they could be got out. It proved to be the California Hotel, just one block from this one. This [Arlington] is a brick building, but the California is made of wood, and the whole roof was all in a big blaze, – baggage and furniture was flying out of windows and everybody was running down there as hard as they could go. The great falls in the river

gave this town an excellent water system and no fire engines are needed because the falls give such a pressure on the pipes that all that is necessary to throw a stream over the highest building is just to hitch the hose on to the hydrant and turn on the water. In a short time there were so many big streams of water pouring onto the flames that they were put out and only the roof and the upper story were burnt off.

This morning the proprietor sat out in the street in a chair and looked at the ruins for a time, and then said, "Send for the architect; we will put it up a hundred feet bigger this time" and before the water had soaked out or the burnt timber hardly got cold they were measuring for a new building. Nobody was hurt and nearly all the baggage was saved.[22]

The *Morning Review* covered the fire in a full-column story the next morning. Among the items seen tossed out a hotel window was a pair of eye glasses. One helpful guest carefully lowered a piece of crockery on a rope. Just as it was about to reach the ground safely, a fireman came along and accidently struck it with a club, shattering it to pieces.

The flames had first appeared in room 71 on the fourth floor. Down on the second floor, a very hot fire had been built in room 6 to heat water in order to clean the silverware. The same flue extended up through rooms 28 and 71. The fire, caused by an over-heated flue, damaged only the roof and fourth floor. However, the other floors suffered heavily from water damage, and all the windows were broken. Policemen were left on duty all night to protect the furniture which was scattered about.[23]

Gray decided to rebuild and hired L. B. Whitten as his contractor. The new hotel was three stories high with a 90-foot L-shaped wing along Howard and 125 feet along Front Street. Two corner towers had cathedral windows of colored glass while the roof was encircled with a wrought-iron fence. Fire escapes were installed. Actually, they were nothing more than iron ladders against the building, extending to the roof. Close inspection would indicate they were intended more as an access for firemen to protect the wooden building than as a means of permitting guests to escape.

The *Morning Review* heralded the now-named Windsor Hotel upon the occasion of its grand opening October 1, 1887, as a "model of elegance and comfort."[24] The ground floor contained all the needed services for the traveling man: a bar, billiard room, club room and sample rooms – all large with handsome leather upholstered furniture. For the ladies, an ornamentally decorated parlor with an excellent piano was on the second floor. One could also find a sitting room and pleasant alcoves on the second and third floors. The elegant guest rooms were furnished in rich mahogany, oak and cherry with bright carpets. Electric lights, electric enunciators and call tubes were throughout the building, making all parts of the hotel in direct communication with the office.

The Windsor Hotel, successor to the California House, 1887-1889, at the northeast corner of Front and Howard. *(Photo from the Teakle Collection, courtesy SPLNWR)*

Gray again leased his establishment to the "Laurel and Hardy" team of Messrs. Bailey and Freese. The former was tall and lanky while Freese, according to the *Morning Review,* supported a rotundity that was the envy of every alderman in town. Bailey and Freese operated the Windsor Hotel in the superb manner people had come to expect. The dining room was large and had an excellent reputation for perfection. From the uniformed doorman, Rodgers, to the black waiters, to the free horse-drawn buses that ran to and from the trains, the Windsor was as near perfect an establishment of that kind can be, so said the *Morning Review.* (It would stand for only twenty-two months before going down for the last time in the Great Fire of August 4, 1889.)

Gray had other investments besides the hotel. Like others in Spokane Falls, he was involved with mining claims. The local newspapers eagerly printed any information about mining, even reporting when various prominent citizens went to check on their properties. The *Morning Review* for June 21, 1887, reprinted the following from the *Colville News*: "W. C. Gray accompanied by H. E. Allen of Spokane Falls took a buckboard for the Silver Crown mine where the boys are working an increased force of miners and taking out a volume of ore that is amazing to behold. It is reliably reported that there are 1000 tons in sight."

The Silver Crown and the Northern Light were located on the east side of the Columbia River about a mile and a quarter above Five Mile Creek in the Colville Mining District of Stevens County. By 1910, Bill had leased these two quartz mines to J. E. Wilcox of Kellogg, Idaho, for a ten-percent royalty. However,

Wilcox kept writing that the ore was too low-grade to ship. Any bonanza from these mines apparently had long since vanished.

After completion of the Windsor Hotel, Bill and Clara left to spend the winter in the milder climate of central and southern California. Although their original plans called for them to return in March 1888, Bill came back in February, leaving Clara to follow later in the spring.

Gray bought 720 acres in Stevens County, 4.2 miles north of Springdale toward Valley, where they moved. He ran stock, grew grain and had a few fruit trees. The farm was situated along D. C. Corbin's Spokane and Northern Railroad. Gray's Station or Siding was named for him.

For some time Clara had been in poor health. In 1890, the Grays either went to Milwaukee, Wisconsin, or were on a trip in that area when Clara entered St. Mary's Hospital on the Lake. Her medical problem required surgery, which turned out to be more serious than anticipated. From the best reconstruction of clues, it is likely that Clara had a hysterectomy. At that period of time it would have involved only a partial removal of organs. Although convalescence was slow, it ended years of painful suffering for her.

Clara's nurse, Lucy Shepherd, considered her to be a dear little patient with a jolly husband. Friends commented upon Clara's courage and bravery. In characteristic fashion Clara formed a close relationship with her doctors: O. W. Carlson of Milwaukee and Dr. R. Ludlam, a professor of surgical diseases of women at the Hahnemann Medical College and Hospital in Chicago.[25] In a letter the next year, Dr. Carlson reminded her of the bear skin she had promised to get for him and, upon a request from Clara, Dr. Ludlam sent a picture of himself.

In 1889, after selling the California House property for $67,000 to the city as a site for a new city hall, Bill bought the eastern half of the block on Fifth and Sixth avenues between Washington and Stevens streets for $13,000. Although they had the ranch, Bill still wanted a nice house in Spokane they could call home. In 1892, Gray, who was considered one of the wealthy men in the city, hired the noted architect Herman Preusse as his designer and Charles Wilbert as the contractor.

Situated on the southwest corner of Fifth Avenue and Washington Street, the two-and-one-half-storied house contained sixteen rooms. These included a drawing room, butler's pantry, alcove suites and other features. Immense heavy timbers, square nails, five kinds of brick in the chimney, and heavy panel work of cherry, mahogany and California redwood were used. The finishing materials came from Minneapolis cut to size. Imported marble lined the four fireplaces

Grays' house, southwest corner of Fifth Avenue and Washington Street, 1892–1931, which Clara referred to as "Gray's Folly." It was designed by architect Herman Preusse (inset). *(Photo from* A Race for Empire and Other True Tales of the Northwest, Spokesman-Review, *1896. Inset from* Spokane and the Inland Empire *by N. W. Durham, 1912)*

that had mantels of cherry, white oak or mahogany. One of the rooms was frescoed by an artist from Germany. Quarters for the servants were on the third floor, and on the west side of the house was the carriage entrance. Altogether the construction cost $20,000, with several thousand more spent in blasting the rock from the site and hauling in dirt to build the terraces that surrounded the house on the north and east. Steps were cut into the bank diagonally to the corner.

To be truthful, Clara did not want the house, but since her husband built it for her, she acquiesced. He may have presented it to her as a 20th wedding anniversary gift. In any event, Bill deeded the property to her outright.

The extremely cold winter of 1892-3 ran up heating costs of nearly a hundred dollars a month in spite of the fact the house was well built. As Clara's delicate health seemed to be better on the farm, and winters were frequently spent in California, they only occasionally used the house after the first year. Thereafter, Clara affectionately referred to their mansion as "Gray's Folly."

The Grays at Niagara Falls, probably on the occasion of their 20th wedding anniversary, in 1892. *(Photo from the Jerome Peltier Collection, courtesy Tony and Suzanne Bamonte)*

Will Smiley lived in the house as a caretaker while working in Traders National Bank as a teller. When Smiley left to attend law school in the East, Clara leased the house to Jim Glover in 1896 until his house at Seventh and Washington was completed. Mrs. James Clark, a sister-in-law of Patrick "Patsy" Clark, rented it around 1900 while her home was being built on the northwest corner of Third and Spruce in Browne's Addition. Eugene B. Braden, prominent in the ore-smelting business, also was a tenant at one time. There followed a succession of occupants, including Dr. George W. Libby and a Dr. Armstrong. Clara kept the house about twenty-five years until it became too much to take care of. In 1916, title to the property passed to Mrs. T. J. Wilcox. In later years, several doctors operated a sanitarium in it. Finally it became dilapidated and was torn down in June 1931 by its owners, the Endelman brothers.[26]

After spending the greater part of eleven years on the ranch, Bill sold it to D. C. Bonthuis in July 1902 and went into railroad construction again. In Idaho, he built six miles of track from Summit to Naples, nine miles from Summit to Athol, and six miles from Summit to Rathdrum for the Spokane and International Railroad. With John W. Chapman, Gray built ten miles for the Northern Pacific on the Lewiston branch. Then followed a contract for half of the fourteen miles of D. C. Corbin's coal road at Crow's Nest Pass in British Columbia. Gray's investments and interests became extensive. Besides mining and rail-roading, he held a directorship in the National Bank of Commerce.

In 1909, the Grays built a house at 414 West Sixth Avenue on lot nine, the only one available from their six-lot holding. It stood southwest of their mansion.

A girlhood next-door neighbor, Louise Derrickson (married name), wrote to Clara in 1909 with news of old friends and changes in Marysville. She commented that it was a good thing Clara had not married Irwin, Sue Lawrence's husband, because he had ended up having a drinking problem. Instead, Clara had been more successful than any of the girls in their crowd. "It always does me good to see a poor girl do well," wrote Louise.

Clara's success perhaps had as much to do with her own energy and vitality as with a happy marriage. At the age of 65, she took up the study of both French and Spanish, which she learned to read, write and speak fluently. She served as a trustee, vice president, and president of the Pioneer Society. At one annual picnic, Clara was described as being the most agile of all the pioneers. She was a young 82. She wrote her autobiography as well as articles on early life in the Inland Empire that were published by Washington State College (now University). Clara remained a prominent member of the First Episcopal Church and a member of its choir. After Bill's death in 1926 at the age of 81, Clara became

Clara Gray, circa 1912. *(Photo courtesy MAC/EWSHS, L87-75)*

a member of Westminster Congregational Church, only a short walk from her home. Church records show that she joined their choir that year.

At 75 years of age, Clara remarked: "I cannot understand why people should not make use of their spare time, even though they have reached an advanced age."[27] Clearly, the lovely lady of California House had remained a vivacious, charming and intelligent person. Indeed, she truly was an indomitable woman who matched the stature of her time.

Clara sold her house on Sixth Avenue to R. W. Cooper in 1941 before moving to St. Joseph's Home for the Aged. She passed away there on September 20, 1942, at age 88, having outlived all the early residents of Spokane Falls. The Grays are interred at Riverside Memorial Park.

Clara had been a "saver." Among items donated to the archives of Eastern Washington State Historical Society (Northwest Museum of Arts & Culture) were some telephone bills for 1912 sewed together (pre-staples), receipts for coal, plumbing repairs, window screens, ads in the newspaper, and small purchases. Among the pictures and snapshots were early-day photographs of Susan and Jim Glover and Jennie and Anthony M. Cannon, proving her loyal friendship. A trunk containing some of Clara's dresses and blouses dating from 1900 or earlier, and a beaded black evening cape from the 1870s, were presented to the historical society by one of her brothers.

Epilogue

William Smiley had worked as a bookkeeper and teller for Traders National Bank. At the age of 28, he left Spokane to enter law school at the University of Michigan, returning in 1897. Six years later, he married Melissa Meeks, sister of Adalena Meeks Cooper, whose husband, Dr. John Cooper (with O. O. Peck) initially grubstaked Noah Kellogg. Melissa and Will were childless. From 1924-1935, the Smileys lived in Hoquiam, where Will was associated with the Federal Land Bank. Upon returning to Spokane, they lived with Clara until she went to St. Joseph's Home. Will survived his sister by only two years.

Charles Smiley passed away in 1930. His daughter Clara was born in 1887 and Amy Gladys in 1894. At the time of Clara's death, Clara Thornhill lived in Tacoma and Gladys Gee in Seattle.

The oldest brother, Fred Smiley, lived in California, was married and had three children.

Chapter VI

Spokane Falls – 1880s

This photo of Spokane Falls, taken about 1885, is looking southwest from the Spokane River. The streets in the foreground are Front (running east and west) and Mill (now Wall) Street, which curved down along the river to the sawmill built by Scranton and Downing and purchased by James Glover along with the town site. The two-story building facing Front was the Carter brothers' machine shop. In 1887, Elijah Davenport, uncle of Louis M. Davenport of the Davenport Hotel, converted it into the U.S. Hotel. *(Photo from the Don Neraas Collection, courtesy Tony and Suzanne Bamonte)*

The decade of the 1880s has not been surpassed in importance to the little hamlet by the falls. It began inauspiciously enough but terminated in a manner so devastating that no one could wish it to be repeated. The years between were filled with growth, discovery, progress and glamour. It was truly a decade of new beginnings.

The advent of the railroad marshaled in phase two of Spokane Falls, ensuring its survival. Construction on the Pend Oreille Division of the Northern Pacific Railroad began October 2, 1879, when Director John W. Sprague turned the first shovelful of dirt at Ainsworth, Washington Territory, a construction town on the north side of the Snake River near its confluence with the Columbia.

Chapter VI

Teams of horses, muscle power, #2 picks and shovels did the actual work of grading. Any blasting had to be accomplished by hand drilling and dynamite. The main body of laborers, consisting primarily of Chinese, laid the ties; another squad placed the rails. A third force fastened them together, followed by the spike drivers and levelers. Thus, in follow-the-leader fashion, the iron rails inched across the prairies, gullies and streams at a rate of about two miles a day. By May 25, 1881, Cheney had been reached. From there the route skirted the east side of Fish Lake, passed through Marshall, and followed down Marshall Creek Canyon to the valley of Hangman (Latah) Creek.

Construction fell behind schedule when freight was delayed on the Columbia River. When the bridge timbers did arrive, they had not been cut to specifications. However, in ten days, J. M. Hayes managed to build a 180-foot span bridging Hangman Creek at about Thirty-second Avenue. From there the rail laying proceeded along the previously graded east bank of the creek to the plateau southwest of Spokane. Passing through the gap in the bluff near Seventh Avenue, the track extended through a grove of scattered pines, finally reaching Howard Street at four in the afternoon of June 25, 1881.

The townspeople gathered to watch the construction train reach town and cheered the long awaited "Iron Horse." It had been expected that H. W. Fairweather, the general superintendent for the railroad, would address the eager throng, but he was nowhere in sight. Jim Glover seized the opportunity to climb on top of a boxcar. Waving a red bandanna over his head, he led the crowd in three lusty hurrahs for the Northern Pacific. However, as Glover began to speak, the train crew, unaware of the impromptu oratory, started up the engine to continue their work. Jim grabbed a brake wheel and tried to talk louder as the crowd walked along the right-of-way to keep up with him. Soon the noise of the engine, the rattle of the wheels, and the increased speed of the train separated the father-of-the-town from the townsmen.[1] The first passenger train arrived at 7:14 that evening and was greeted by a crowd of six hundred.

The real celebration, however, was nine days later on the Fourth of July when the railroad officials arranged a free excursion ride of sixteen miles between Spokane Falls and Cheney. Folks gathered at the California House for the festivities. Led by the Spokane Falls Band and headed by Grand Marshal Jim Glover, the holiday began with the usual parade. Down Howard Street to Main Street marched the citizens, then east on Main to Stevens Street, and south on Stevens to Riverside (since April, the new name of South Street). Turning west on Riverside Avenue, the people continued on to Riverside Park, located just below the present day Monroe Street Bridge. Capt. James Nosler recorded in his diary that the picnic was held in a grove of trees below J. J. Browne's homestead.

A road construction crew working on Riverside Avenue in the mid-1880s. *(Photo courtesy SPLNWR)*

The free ride on the railroad highlighted the day. People came from miles around, as word of this celebration had spread as far away as Moscow, Idaho, and Uniontown, south of Pullman. Some, no doubt, had their first sight of a steam engine. The excursion train was made up of an engine and six wood-rack cars lined with pine planks.[2] It was not fancy, but Spokane Falls had a railroad!

The fare from Ainsworth to Spokane was $9.00, a fairly significant amount of money. A dollar would buy seven pounds of sugar, six pounds of coffee, twenty pounds of beans, three cans of fruit or jelly, twelve yards of sheeting, forty candles, a gallon of syrup, or two meals at California House. The common laborer's wage was $1.75 per day.

The first passenger depot faced Riverside between Post and Lincoln on the north side of the tracks. To the east of Post, the freight depot was later built with the Northern Pacific warehouse opposite it on the south side. A 15,000-gallon water tank was erected on the south side of the track near where Railroad and First avenues curved together at Bernard. The water came by pipe from Cowley's Spring, a little more than a half mile away. The location of the first tracks into Spokane has remained virtually unchanged for over 100 years. When the road-bed was elevated in 1914 in conjunction with the construction of the Union Terminal, heavier rails replaced the original ones (more about this in Chapter X).

As it had been on railroad property, the little one-room schoolhouse had to be moved. It was relocated a block north on First Avenue about in the middle of

Spokane's second schoolhouse, built in 1883. *(Photo from the Jerome Peltier Collection, courtesy Tony and Suzanne Bamonte)*

the block between Post and Lincoln. Here it remained until a four-room frame building was erected in 1883 on Fourth Avenue between Stevens and Howard streets. In 1891, it became the site of Spokane High School (name changed to South Central in 1908) and Lewis and Clark High School in 1912.

The first telephone line was installed in 1881, its distance reminiscent of the tin-can communication children used to string across vacant lots. A. K. Clark and Ed Knight opened Spokane's first hardware and tin shop on Main Street near the Howard Street corner. With Clarence White, they stretched a telephone wire from the hardware store up Howard a block to the newspaper office where White worked. One wonders what anticipated earthshaking conversations prompted the hookup of these two unlikely businesses. It would be another five years before a proper telephone service was installed.

The legislative session of 1879-1880, of which newspaper publisher Francis Cook was the presiding officer, passed House Bill #36 by which Spokane County was organized. The temporary seat was placed at Spokane Falls. Because the county was then responsible for providing a jail, James Glover and A. M. Cannon contracted

Francis H. Cook
(Photo courtesy Jan Edmonds, Cook's great granddaughter)

with the county to provide the facility. They constructed a 16 by 16-foot structure close to the courthouse, near the northwest corner of Main and Howard. They received their remuneration for the jail in the form of rent.

The elections in November 1880 gave the coveted prize to Cheney, which initiated a melodrama. There were counts and recounts and accusations of illegal procedures. The bottom line: Cheney won, and Spokane Falls did not like it. The location of a county seat was a greatly sought-after prize because it brought people into town who had business at the courthouse. As the Spokane Falls officials dragged their feet about turning over the county records, some Cheney residents felt they had but one recourse: to take matters into their own hands.

"THE GREAT STEAL"

The Scene:

Graham's building on the northwest corner of Main and Howard streets, Spokane Falls. The county offices were on the second floor.

The Time:

Early morning, about 1:00 a.m., on Monday, March 21, 1881.

The Cast of Characters:

The Bride and Groom: Unwittingly, Dick Wright and Bertie Piper, who were married Sunday evening. It seemed that all of Spokane Falls went to the wedding dance.

Auditor: William H. Bishop, who was working late in the county offices.

Citizens of Cheney, a nearby town: Avery A. Smith, probate judge; James (Mike) Hatton; John Sill, justice of the peace; Bill Griswold; Curley Doan; the Rich boys; Mr. Malloy of Malloy's Prairie; Frank Spencer, newspaperman; and probably L. E. Kellogg, editor of Cheney's newspaper, the *Northwest Tribune*; and unidentified horses.

Act I:

Three men remained with three light wagons and teams in seclusion near the Episcopal Church at Riverside and Lincoln. Seven men stealthily sneaked along the shortcut crossing Little Wolf Ditch from Riverside between Mill and Howard to Graham's building on Main. Once inside, they confiscated the county records and stole the auditor as well.

Act II:

Their arrival in Cheney three hours later was announced by firing their pistols and guns accompanied by lots of "chin music" (yahoos). It could not be called a thirstless night's ride. The records were piled in the dining room of the Cheney Hotel under the watchful eye of an armed guard. Auditor Bishop apparently moved to Cheney voluntarily to continue his elected position.

Chapter VI

Epilogue:

The *Northwest Tribune*, Cheney's newspaper, defended the men's leaving Spokane Falls at an early hour so they could reach Cheney the same day. Cook retorted in the *Spokan Times*: "Horse thieves and robbers have often made just as early starts, impelled by the same motives."[3]

The curtain fell on the "Great Steal." The county seat remained in Cheney until another election was held on November 12, 1886, at which point it was permanently returned to Spokane.

In addition to political drama, the citizens of Spokane Falls were also entertained by theatrical troupes that occasionally came to town. One popular group was the Kendalls, who put on "Rip Van Winkle," an amusing comedy. A local group, the Home Dramatic Club organized by Charles Cornelius, also drew the crowds. The town fathers were so pleased with one performer they published an open letter to him in the *Spokan Times*. Having recognized his ability as an actor, they requested Mr. Daniel D. Squier to perform at a charitable benefit at Cornelius and Davis's hall. The letter was signed by Geo. Davis, J. N. Glover, J. T. Lockhart, W. C. Gray, Louis Ziegler, Col. D. P. Jenkins, A. M. Cannon and J. J. Browne. The event took place Friday, March 12, 1880; the play: "Michael Earle, the Maniac Lover." Fraternal lodges also played a major role in providing entertainment for their members. In addition to the brotherhood of lodge meetings, they put on dances and sponsored lecturers from out of town.

The year 1881 witnessed many far-reaching events. In January, the Spokane Tribe of Indians finally received federal recognition. They had previously been included with the Coeur d'Alenes or ignored completely. On January 18, President Rutherford B. Hayes designated 155,000 acres 45 miles northwest of the falls as the Spokanes' territory. Although the Lower Spokanes moved onto the reservation immediately, the Middle and Upper bands stalled. They felt they were entitled to compensation for the land that they were having to give up. An agreement was finally reached March 18, 1887, whereby the United States government paid them $127,000 to be used for the purchase of homes, cattle, seed, farm implements, etc. Many holdouts then relocated on the Spokane and Coeur d'Alene reservations.[4]

Having ministered to the Indians since 1865, Father Joseph Cataldo, Superior of the Jesuits' Rocky Mountain Missions, envisioned a site near Spokane Falls as a center for the Jesuit mission schools. In 1881, he negotiated the purchase of two 320-acre parcels of land on the north side of the river: one became the site of the third St. Michael's Mission Church for the Indians (later becoming the site of Mt. St. Michael's Scholasticate) and the other the site of Gonzaga College (now University). However, Cataldo, like Rev. Cowley, succumbed to the needs of the white settlers. He purchased three lots on the northwest corner of Main and Bernard on May 8, 1881, for a church site in town. A tiny, primitive carpenter's shop on the site was converted into a makeshift chapel, christened the Church of St. Joseph. It served for five years until it was replaced by a new brick church. In 1884, Father Louis Ruellan became its first resident pastor.

With seven members, Rev. D. J. Pierce and Rev. S. E. Stearns installed a Baptist group on December 8, bringing the number of religious congregations in Spokane to five. The Baptists built a church on the southeast corner of Monroe and Sprague. Their third pastor would be a woman, Spokane's first female pastor, Mrs. May C. Jones. Her administration was noted for evangelical movements, such as the organization of the Pine Street Mission and the formation of a young men's missionary society.

The *Spokane Falls Review*, in an article headed "Good and Noble Women of Spokane Falls Goodly Works," described Mrs. Jones as an evangelist in the fullest sense of the word. Her church was always crowded with young and old and people from every walk of life. Her gentle presence was welcome in the homes of rich or poor, and she never turned from any appeal. However, when Rev. Jones wrote a letter to the newspaper a few months later condemning gambling, she received a different reaction. She maintained that the ministers in town had delivered sermons and prayed against it. She accused the newspapers of being partly to blame for the continuation of gambling because they did not take a strong enough stand against it.

The editors of the *Review* expressed their exception to her letter in an editorial saying she showed no charity. Furthermore, "condemnation of gambling must come from the entire community, not just the minister." Praying, said the editorial, was not going to put an end to it. It did weakly point out that gambling was evil.[5]

A female pastor did not please everyone, obviously, as eighteen persons asked to leave the church in 1890 to form a new one on the north side of town (which became Grace Baptist Church). During Rev. Jones's tenure, the sale of the Sprague Avenue property brought $25,000 with which lots were purchased on Second and Monroe. The timing was ill-advised, as shortly thereafter the church suffered heavy financial losses, making it necessary to remodel a store building on Second and Post for their use. After serving almost four years, Rev. Jones resigned in October 1891. Unfortunately, her financial acumen had not matched her missionary zeal and the Baptist group was left with serious fiscal problems. When Rev. Beavan took over January 1, 1892, he found the church in dire need of his executive abilities. He guided the church through four trying years.[6]

Bell's grocery and bakery at the corner of Riverside and Howard in the early 1880s. *(Photo from* Spokane and the Inland Empire *by N. W. Durham, 1912)*

One persistent legend centers around the spelling of Spokane: with an "e" on the end or without, which supposedly divided the townspeople into two camps. Francis Cook was one of the champion advocates of the latter group. It has been said the *Chronicle* was started as a result of this controversy. It would seem this is a myth that makes a good story. The vituperative feud that developed between Cook and Glover-Browne-Cannon occurred after the establishment of the *Chronicle* and concerned a difference of opinion over the handling of municipal affairs. Had there been any basis to a spelling controversy, Cook would not have hesitated to broadcast it loudly and clearly in his newspaper. No reference as to how Spokane should be spelled appears in any of the existing copies of the *Times* or the *Chronicle* for that period.

Part of the story contended that the argument was settled when the city was incorporated November 29, 1881, with an "e." That is, the handwritten Articles of Incorporation delivered to the territorial government used the "e," as did most of the local businesses that used the word "Spokane" in its name or as its address. However, the territorial printing office failed to make note of that spelling. Their official printing of the Articles of Incorporation indicates the city to be "Spokan" Falls. Although the source of an "e" controversy remains in obscurity, the one thing most everyone can agree with is there would be a great deal less confusion in the nation over pronouncing Spokane correctly if the "e" had been left off.

The incorporated town site encompassed the area from the north bank of the river south to Sprague, and Cedar east to Hatch, and the area from Sprague south to Sixth, with Chestnut as the west boundary and Chandler on the east, a

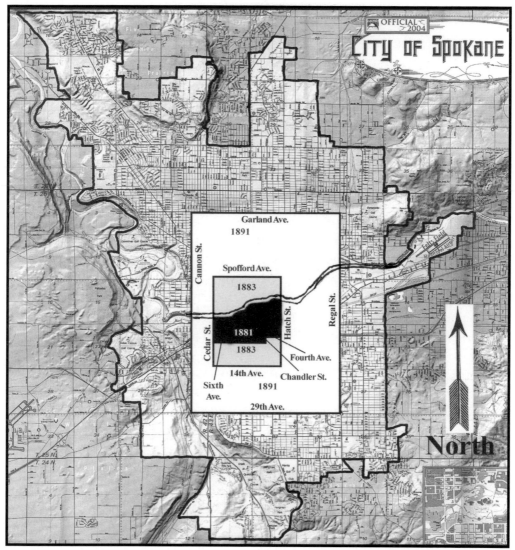

Outline of Spokane's incorporated city limits as of 2004. At the time this map was prepared, there had been sixty-eight additional annexations since Spokane's incorporation on November 29, 1881. The blackened area depicts the original city limits, which encompassed 1.56 square miles. Delineated within the 2004 boundaries are annexations made in 1883 and 1891. In 1907, the boundaries almost doubled the size of the city.

The original city limits extended south from the north riverbank between Cedar and Hatch streets to Sixth Avenue. At the southeast corner, the area south of Fourth and east of Chandler included land given by the Spokane Indians to Rev. Henry Cowley for an Indian school. The title to that land was somewhat clouded, which is why that corner was not included in the original incorporated city limits. Today the incorporated city encompasses nearly sixty square miles. *(Boundaries for map created in 2004 by Tony Bamonte for* Life Behind the Badge: The Spokane Police Department's Founding Years, 1881-1903*)* little less than a thousand acres.[7] Two years later, the city limits were extended to two square miles.

Article 2 of the Articles of Incorporation identified the elected officials to be a mayor and seven councilmen who would serve without salaries. They were to appoint a city treasurer, a city marshal, a clerk, and a justice of the peace, who also doubled as an assessor. Terms of office would be for one year beginning ten days after each election of the first Monday in April.

Organizing a fire department and a police department were among the responsibilities assigned to the council. They were also required to provide a jail, lighting for the streets and a workhouse. Matters of public health and safety were carefully delineated, as was the power to license, tax and regulate every manner of business, including those having to do with night-life entertainment (i.e. saloons, houses of prostitution and variety theatres).

The legislature appointed Robert W. Forrest to act as mayor until an election could be held. Councilmen also appointed included: Rev. Samuel G. Havermale, Anthony M. Cannon, Dr. Louis H. Whitehouse, F. Rockwood Moore, William C. Gray, Lorenzo W. Rima and George A. Davis (who built the Echo Flour Mill with Havermale). With the exception of Cannon, all of these men were subsequently elected to serve as the first government for Spokane Falls. Samuel T. Arthur, an emigrant of 1878, was the seventh councilman. However, shortly after the election, Arthur and his wife Nellie moved to Missoula, whereupon Cannon was appointed to replace him on the council.

Robert W. Forrest, Spokane's first mayor
(Photo from Spokane and the Inland Empire *by N. W. Durham, 1912)*

In contrast with today's complexities of government, economics, politics and everyday living, 1881 may appear to have been an uncomplicated, simple era. Yet tempers flared, frustrations existed, sides were taken on civic matters and vehemently defended. Newspaper publisher Francis Cook had become known as a "calls 'em as I sees 'em" person. At least he had the vehicle to express his opinions. This he did regardless of whose toes he stepped on. "Stepped" is a light word; "trod" might be more appropriate. It became obvious that he and the town fathers – Glover, Cannon and Browne – would be set on a collision course.

Glover called the *Times* an advertising sheet that Cook passed off as a newspaper.[8] Before long, J. J. Browne went to Portland and arranged with C. B. Carlisle to establish another newspaper. The *Spokane Falls Chronicle,* published every Wednesday, was founded by James N. Glover, J. J. Browne, and Anthony M. Cannon. The first issue appeared June 29, 1881.

Looking south in 1884 toward the main business section of Spokane Falls from one of the islands in the Spokane River. The large building at the upper center on Front Avenue (later Trent and now Spokane Falls Boulevard) at Howard Street (the main street running through the center of the photo) is the California House. The first bridge at the town of Spokane Falls was built in 1881 and actually consisted of three spans that zigzagged across the islands, connecting the nucleus of the town at Howard (as shown above) to the north bank at Washington Street.
(Photo Haynes Foundation Collection, Montana Historical Society)

By the fall of that year, the friction between Glover and Cook was headlining the editorial page of the *Spokan Times* in almost every issue. For example, Cook took exception to Glover's lack of or miserly support of the greatly needed first bridge across the river. Many intense discussions and debates were held on the merits of the three proposed sites: at Mill (now Wall) Street (the one favored by Glover), at Howard Street or at Washington Street. The location receiving the greatest support through monetary pledges would be selected.

A contract with A. S. Miller & Son of Portland was awarded for the winning Howard Street location on May 12, 1881. Scheduled for completion by the first of October, the bridge was actually three spans: the first one of 200 feet crossed the mill pond at the foot of Howard Street, while the next section of 100 feet went northeastward across the very rapid current of the second channel of the river from Glover's Island to the Big Island. A third bridge of 230 feet connected Havermale Island with the north bank of the river at about Washington Street.

Lt. Thomas Symons, engineer for the United States Army, had made an earlier survey for a bridge in 1879. In a letter dated September 18 of that year to his brother in Saginaw, Michigan, Lt. Symons praised Spokane, but added: "It is a long ways out of our world, however. [It is] the extreme frontier outpost of civilization and until the railroad is built, it is hard to get at."[9] Symons did invest in a lot on the southeast corner of Howard and Sprague. An office building bearing his name is still located there.

Cook let it be known in no uncertain terms that he felt the "town company" had made only token contributions to the bridge fund in proportion to their land holdings. In an editorial titled: "A Few Facts about Public Affairs," October 4, 1881, he took this potshot at Glover:

> J. N. Glover & Co. must rule the property for which they have already received a price, or do their best to ruin the prospects of the real owners. They are a blight upon the place, standing between our city and the prosperity to which it is entitled. They foster no enterprise but such as pays them tribute. It is a known fact that they have driven trade from our town on former occasions and continue to do so. Let it be fully known that they control our city, and prosperity will cease to be a characteristic of the place.

This excerpt is part of a long article bashing Glover that Cook liked so well he ran it for three consecutive weeks in the *Times*.

The city elections in the spring of 1882 gave Cook ample opportunity to continue the attack. He repeatedly called for competitive bidding for laying water mains in the streets and denounced the town "bosses" for wanting to control a monopoly without regard to cost or inconvenience to the townspeople. He berated the city council for postponing such an important decision. Furthermore, Cook advocated councilmen being elected from districts rather than at-large. "It is well understood," he printed, "that a majority of the present city council can be advantageously spared, that is, laid on the shelf, or bottled, to improve with age."[10] There were two groups of candidates: the Citizens' Ticket headed by J. N. Glover and the Peoples' Ticket headed by R. W. Forrest, the latter who opposed monopoly, according to Cook. The councilmen for the most part were the same on both tickets.

Cook claimed the real name of one of the "bosses" was "A. M'Cannon." That might have been the item that raised A. M. Cannon's blood pressure to the boiling point. March 29, 1882, Cannon called on Cook with his future son-in-law, Bascom H. Bennett, the cashier of his bank. Mounting the stairs to the *Times'* second floor office on the east side of Howard Street, they found Mr. and Mrs. Cook and a baby alone at the time. Cannon brandished papers he wanted Cook to sign. Upon his refusal, Cannon drew a revolver. Using an iron bar, Cook knocked the gun out of Cannon's hand, whereupon Bennett produced a gun. In the ensuing melee a couple of bullets hit the stove pipe, blood splattered from the contact Cook

Bascom Bennett
(Photo from Spokane Falls Illustrated, *1889)*

Francis and Laura Cook with six of their eleven chilren in 1890, from left, Clara, Frank, Katie, baby Chester, Laura May and Silas (seated). *(Photo from Adi Song, great granddaughter of Francis and Laura Cook, courtesy Tony and Suzanne Bamonte)*

made on his opponents' heads, and a case of type was upset. Mrs. Cook escaped downstairs where a crowd gathered. Cook chased his opponents to the street, where Cannon again threatened to kill Cook as he renewed the attack.

Both Cannon and Bennett required a physician to stitch up their scalp wounds. They each posted a bond of a thousand dollars on charges of assault to commit murder. However, when a grand jury met in Cheney the following month, no indictment was brought against them. The fact that J. N. Glover was foreman of the jury, claimed Cook, probably had something to do with the verdict. Nevertheless, both sides recognized the need to suspend the hostility. Cook retracted his statement about Cannon's name and stated that the late unpleasantness was wholly the outgrowth of a newspaper controversy and differing opinions regarding the management of municipal affairs.

Perhaps his articles had some effect, as Glover was narrowly defeated in his bid for mayor. Robert W. Forrest was re-elected, with George A. Davis, Samuel T. Arthur, Dr. L. H. Whitehouse, G. M. Palmtag, Dan M. Drumheller, W. C. Gray and Rev. S. G. Havermale voted in as councilmen. Cook had tried to upgrade his paper the previous summer by making it an evening daily. As this proved to not be economical, he sold out nine months later, in April 1882, to D. S. Herren. Even though Herren changed the name to the *Spokane Independent*, the die was cast, and publication ceased that year. [11]

After leaving the field of journalism, Cook devoted his time to developing the 640 acres on Spokane's South Hill that he purchased from the Northern Pacific Railroad. This property, covering approximately the area from Tenth to Thirty-sixth avenues, Division Street east to Hatch, included a lake, which Cook named Mirror Lake. As he began to develop the land for residential purposes, he preserved the region around the lake as Montrose Park.

Becoming somewhat affluent, Cook built a nine-bedroom mansion for his large family (he and his wife, Laura, were the parents of eleven children) in 1892.

The Cook family home on the South Hill.
(Photo courtesy SPLNWR)

Perched on top the South Hill at Twelfth and Grand Boulevard, the house afforded a superb view of the town. In return, it presented an impressive sight. St. John's Episcopal Cathedral presently occupies the same location.

Like many others who were heavily mortgaged, Cook was hit hard during the Panic of 1893, costing him his wealth, the trolley line, most of his property on the South Hill, and eventually his Victorian home. Within a few years, Jay P. Graves, a mining and real estate tycoon, acquired most of Cook's holdings. By 1904, he and a few other property owners in the vicinity donated over 90 acres, at the center of which was Cook's Montrose Park, to the City of Spokane. At this time, the name was changed to Manito Park.[12]

Recognizing the need for early acquisition of park land, Cook bought the top of Mount Carlton, locally called "Old Baldy," in 1908. He and his son Silas laboriously built a road to the top. After Cook donated this site, Spokane County paid him $30,000 dollars for his road. In 1913, the name officially became Mount Spokane when it was transferred to the State of Washington for a state park.

On June 29, 1920, at the age of 69, Cook died of cancer. This tall, handsome, bearded man was very intelligent and scrupulously honest, but could lay no claim to being a diplomat. Not afraid to "tilt at windmills," in his younger days he never shied away from locking horns with the "big shots." Perhaps the best

On October 26, 2007, the monument at left was dedicated to Francis H. Cook in Riverside Memorial Park, where Cook is buried. It acknowledges Cook's many contributions to the early development of Spokane. Family members who attended the memorial ceremony, shown from left, were: Nancy Swanson, Kathleen Cook, Laura Poulin, Lori Ashe, Marcia Harken, Dave Fray, Gwen Yoke and Charles Yoke. *(Photo courtesy Tony and Suzanne Bamonte)*

and most concise summation of his character was the comment by Mrs. Frank L. Paine (Agnes Cowley) at the time of his death: "Independence was always a characteristic. His advanced ideas often met with little enthusiasm."[13] It is likely that Francis Cook deserves a bigger place in Spokane history than he has been accorded. In 1925, J. Orin Oliphant, professor of history at the State Normal School, now Eastern Washington University, wrote:

> Cook belonged to that small class of unusual men whose vision leads them into enterprises for which the common lot of mankind is not ready. He was a promoter of worthy enterprises, but his enthusiasm induced him frequently to sponsor movements which were not at the time profitable. Time, however, has proved the worth of his faith, and those who came after him have gathered unto themselves the fruits of his foresight and pioneering labors. Francis H. Cook occupies in the annals of the Spokane country an honored place as one of its foremost builders.[14]

By October 1883, the population of Spokane Falls reached an estimated fifteen hundred residents. Before the end of the decade, two complementary events would help propel a tremendous spurt of growth and secure Spokane's status as the hub of the Inland Northwest. The most exciting was the discovery of gold in North Idaho (followed within months by an even greater wealth of silver). The gold was discovered on Prichard and Eagle creeks, tributaries of the North Fork of the Coeur d'Alene River, by Tom Irwin, Andrew Prichard and their small prospecting party. It sparked a stampede of miners to the Coeur d'Alenes in the fall and winter of 1883 and into the spring of 1884. Coinciding with the announcement of the gold discovery was the completion of the Northern Pacific Railroad's transcontinental line in September 1883. The railroad officials could have created no better drawing card than the lure of gold to attract customers for their newly opened line.

Construction of the Northern Pacific Depot in 1883, looking west from Howard.
(Photo from Spokane and the Inland Empire *by N. W. Durham, 1912)*

If Spokane Falls had been "wide open" before, it moved at a fevered pitch now. Prospectors poured into town to stock up on supplies and equipment, merchants were busy, town lots were selling, the hotels were full, and the atmosphere was electric with anticipation. Public gambling existed in all the hotels and saloons. Brawls were frequent. "It was nothing unusual to get up in the morning," recalled Dr. Edward Pittwood, a dentist, "and hear of some 'tinhorn' having been shot during the course of a quarrel over a gambling game. But the community paid little attention to affairs of this kind."[15]

When Mattie (Martha) Hyde, one of the town's first schoolteachers, came to Spokane Falls, she could not get over the large number of playing cards all over town. The streets and vacant lots were littered with them. There were heaps beneath the windows of the downtown buildings. They ran down the gutters

and blew in the wind. To a newcomer this was an astonishing display. The explanation was simple enough. It was the custom for a loser in a card game to ask for a new deck. Thereupon, the old cards were thrown on the floor, tossed out the window or into the street.[16]

By the time the snow melted in the mountains, the gold seekers scrambled up Canyon Creek, Nine Mile Creek, Big Creek and Milo Gulch on the South Fork of the Coeur d'Alene River and began staking their claims. Eagle City

Mattie Hyde and Murray were already established towns on Prichard Creek. With only a few exceptions, most of the great silver strikes in what is now known as the Silver Valley were located in a surprisingly short period of time, within about five months.[17] That region would become one of the richest mining districts in the world.

The two ends of the Northern Pacific were joined by a golden spike on September 8, 1883, at Gold Creek, Montana. The following day, those shiny threads of steel ended Spokane's isolation from the East and made immigration into the region much easier. Spokane Falls prepared for a big celebration.

Five trains en route from New York carrying Henry Villard, president of the line, and an impressive entourage of noted dignitaries and capitalists from both the United States and Europe, an estimated total of three hundred people, were due to arrive throughout the day on September 9. As the first town in Washington Territory to greet the esteemed entourage, the residents of Spokane Falls took their role seriously. Invitations had been sent to nearby military forts and towns. The town was cleaned and decorated. A banner hung across Howard Street from California House read: "Spokane Falls Gem City of the Inland Empire Gives First Greeting From Washington Territory to our Eastern Visitors." Flags were flown, evergreen garlands were draped from balconies and entwined around pillars. Over at the new Echo Flour Mill, the older girls and women, including Susan Glover and her niece, Lovenia Culver, decorated the second floor in anticipation of a grand reception. There were to be speeches, music and handshaking. The first train was expected early Sunday morning.

Sunday morning came. Everyone trooped to the depot and waited ... and waited. The first train passed through town at 6:00 p.m. The second section arrived ten or fifteen minutes later. Henry Villard briefly disembarked from the train to make a few appropriate comments. So that people could see him, he stood in the barouche that was to take him on a tour of the town. But he failed to see the welcoming decorations downtown.

General Ulysses S. Grant and other dignitaries did not arrive until eight or nine o'clock on one of the other trains. By that time, only the hardiest of the men were left to shake hands with the former president of the United States. The band played, a bonfire was lit, and the day's excitement was over. However, what mattered most was the intoxicating realization that Spokane Falls was finally connected by rail to the outside world.

New construction and additional businesses contributed to a growing city. However, the frontier appearance of the town remained, as houses were not yet painted in 1883. A second bridge crossed the Spokane River, this time at the foot of Post Street. Eventually, the wooden bridge became so rickety that sand bags had to be hung on the sides during high water to keep it from collapsing into the river. By 1888, it was declared unsafe.

Henry Villard
(1835-1900)

The immeasurable importance of the Northern Pacific Railroad's transcontinental line to the Northwest was met with a corresponding degree of celebration upon its completion. This photo was taken in Spokane Falls the day after the golden spike ceremony, held on September 8, 1883, at Gold Creek, Montana, west of Helena. Completion of the long-awaited northern transcontinental railroad was the most important event of the decade and, within a few short years, transformed Spokane Falls from a little pioneer settlement to a booming metropolis. *(Photos courtesy SPLNWR)*

Construction of Gonzaga College on the north side of the river finally got underway. Bricks were molded out of the clay found on the banks of the bay below the campus. Although day laborers were hard to find, the superintendent managed to hire five Chinese workers. The college would open four years later in 1887. The new school drew students from all around the Northwest.

A new newspaper, the *Spokane Falls Review,* began publishing on May 19, 1883. Succumbing to the eloquent praise by a friend about Cheney as a "coming Chicago," Frank M. Dallam left Hayward, California, for Washington Territory and a new opportunity in journalism. The owners of Cheney's two newspapers were not interested in selling, so Dallam took a look at Spokane Falls. Although the owner of the *Chronicle* was not ready to sell either, A. M. Cannon and other leading citizens encouraged Dallam to start a Republican paper in opposition to the Democratic *Chronicle.*

Dallam set up shop in the abandoned, drafty one-room schoolhouse set among the pine trees south of First Avenue. Little did he realize the influence and role his newspaper would play in the future of this fledgling town. Printed weekly, the *Review* contained primarily local news, such as an observation on the number of covered wagons that had already reached Spokane Falls: "The white topped vehicles of slow transportation, by which the sturdy immigrant conveys his household goods from populous states out into the new and undeveloped Northwest, are common objects hereabouts already so early in the season."[18]

Both papers touted the future of Spokane Falls and encouraged migration to this quarter of the state. Names of newcomers and visitors registered at the six hotels were printed regularly. From its first issue, the *Chronicle* included items of regional news and national issues. Of great amusement today are the remarks regarding "The Woman Question":

> We do not believe that three percent of all the respectable women in this country would vote at political elections if they were legally accorded the right. But nothing disheartens the female ranter, who neglects her home duties, and trots about the country shrieking to the gaping sisterhood, to shake off "fetters," to ape the ways of mankind and claim free warren in that domain, no matter what that includes. It is apparent that even the best of women do not lean to the soundest and most stable wisdom, either in private or public life, and even if they did, they would not get control of their sex in politics, and so, universal female suffrage would be the most reckless of all experiments.[19]

Nevertheless, the legislature of Washington Territory did see fit to enfranchise women by amending a bill defining citizenship and qualifications to vote to include women.[20] Gov. W. A. Newell signed it into law November 23, 1883.

Some gentlemen encouraged the ladies to vote. Mary Hadley Grimmer (Mrs. J. Mel Grimmer) said Mr. Nash came by to take her to the polls. Jim Glover saw to it that his reluctant wife got there although she did not want to go at all, which

The first Post Street Bridge and the lower Spokane Falls in the late 1880s. *(Photo courtesy SPLNWR)*

is a bit surprising as the first territorial election in Spokane Falls had been held in her house and her husband was the town mayor.

A visitor to the town in 1886 observed with great interest a local election in progress. "In Washington Territory the lawmakers have possessed enough of good common sense to extend the right of suffrage to the ladies," wrote Theodore Gerrish, "and they use it too. All through the afternoon I saw them going to and from the polls, on foot and in carriages, interested, quiet, intelligent, and refined, sacrificing neither position nor character by the act."[21]

However, when the suffrage bill was re-enacted January 18, 1888, a number of men in the state were up in arms! Headlines in the *Review* for January 19, 1888, proclaimed:

The Jig is Up
Gov. Semple Weakens at the Last Hour
In defiance of the Wishes of the People
He Signs the Dangerous
Women's Suffrage Bill

The Spokane Board of Trade, a forerunner of the Chamber of Commerce, was incensed and met with some prominent citizens (male) to draw up a plan of action to prevent this folly on the part of the legislature. They announced the circulation of petitions in eastern Washington and northern Idaho requesting Governor Eugene Semple to veto this bill. They even appealed to the ladies of Spokane Falls for support against this measure. It was deemed that a woman "unsexed" herself if she voted.[22]

An article reprinted by the *Spokane Falls Review* from Murray, Idaho's *Coeur d'Alene Sun* took a firm stand against women serving on juries. "The domestic circle cannot be invaded by political hucksters to drag the mother away from the cradle, the maiden from her lover, or the lady from her parlor to mix in the filthy pool or serve as jurors in criminal cases before the bar ... The idea is to degrade womanhood, instead of elevating and ennobling it."[23]

Not everyone shared these opinions. A mass meeting in the interest of women's suffrage was held in the Opera House on January 18, 1888. Mrs. Charlotte Hamblen recorded in her diary that the meeting was well attended. Among those addressing the group were Rev. May Jones and Col. W. W. D. Turner, brother of Judge George Turner. The next morning the *Review* printed a negative report of the meeting and its small attendance. Upset, Mrs. Hamblen wrote in her diary for January 19: "The *Review* is full of downright lies regarding the mass meeting last night. Nobody but the most unprincipled editors would print such utterly false reports."

The final disposition of the franchise bill was determined when a test case was held in Spokane August 14, 1888. Nevada M. Bloomer sued three election judges because they refused to accept her ballot. Former Supreme Court Judge George Turner (later a U.S. senator), George M. Forster and James M. Kinnaird argued that the act enabling women to vote was in conflict with the Organic Act of the territory. The intent of the founding fathers of the constitution of the United States based on English law, contended Turner, was that the word "citizen" referred to males only. The territory could not pass a bill contrary to the U. S. Constitution. "In 1852, when this act was passed, the word 'citizen' was used as a qualification for voting and holding office, and, in our judgment, the word then meant and still signifies male citizenship, and must be so construed." Judges Langford and Allyn of the Fourth District of the Territorial Supreme Court concurred.[24] It would be twenty two years before the women of Washington State could legally vote again, and thirty one for the entire nation.

The confidence the town fathers had in Spokane Falls becoming a trade center began bearing fruit. John D. Sherwood, who lived on the second floor of the Wolverton Building overlooking Riverside Avenue, observed that the street life in 1884 was proof of it:

> There were cowboys from the Big Bend who gave us interesting exhibitions of horse breaking and pony racing; miners loading their pack trains; Canadian boatmen from the Upper Columbia buying merchandise to smuggle across the line; Chinamen selling fine gold washed from the sands of the Columbia; lumber-jacks and ranchers all buying and trading or blowing-in their savings for a good time.[25]

Still, the town was small enough that cries of "fire" and pistol shots served, as they always had, to alert the townsmen. Up at the Glover house, Jim's niece, Lovenia Culver, awoke about four in the morning of November 28, 1884. From her window she could see the light of a fire two blocks away on the north side of Riverside near Mill Street. She hastily awakened the other members of the household, especially her cousin Wyley, who was a member of a hose company.

The fire had started in the rear of a one-story building in which T. J. Brunk sold glassware and Alexander W. McMorran operated a drugstore. (Ironically, McMorran would lose everything by fire two more times!) To the west stood W. M. Wolverton's two-story brick on the corner. In the rear of Brunk's and fronting Mill were more wooden stores. In the opposite direction, a two-story frame housed A. Rudolph's bakery. From there a continuous row of wooden structures extended around the corner and down the west side of Howard Street toward Main.

If not for the new waterworks and street mains with hydrants, the entire business district of the city would probably have been destroyed. As it was, Rolla

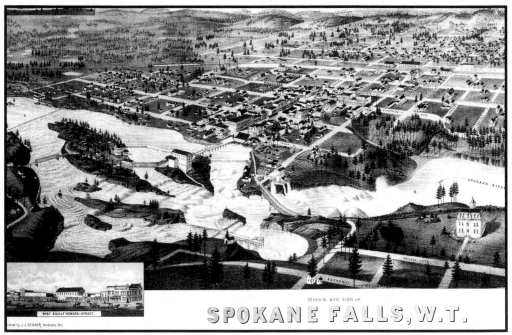

A bird's eye view of Spokane Falls, 1884. This offers a good perspective of where the three spans of the Howard Street Bridge were located. The bridge at the center was at Post Street. *(Courtesy Nancy Compau)*

Jones down at the plant kept the pressure up, providing plenty of water. The firemen performed nobly in spite of the cold, being drenched with water, and the difficult location of the fire. Within two hours they extinguished the blaze. In addition to burning Brunk's building, the fire ate its way under the roofs of Wolverton's brick building on one side and Rudolph's bakery on the other, severely damaging those top floors. Two attorneys lost their law libraries and offices, Sergeant Moore his signal service, and John Sherwood his personal possessions. All had been tenants on the second floor of Wolverton's building.

Nevertheless, the new waterworks had proved its worth, although everyone agreed the town urgently needed a fire bell. In October, only a month before, the *Spokane Falls Review* reported that Spokane Falls had better protection against fire than any other city on the coast, and fire insurance should be reduced. After this superb

One of the volunteer fire department's hose carts in 1886. *(Photo from Mark Danner's Patsy Clark Collection, courtesy Tony and Suzanne Bamonte)*

performance by the volunteer firemen, the city felt safe from any great conflagration in the future.

A year earlier, the town's first major fire had graphically illustrated the need for an adequate water system and fire department. Early in the morning January 19, 1883, at a frigid 26° below zero, fire took out half a block of buildings from its origin in F. Rockwood Moore's store on the southeast corner of Howard and Front all the way south to the alley. It consumed Charlie Carson's restaurant, Robert Forrest's grocery, Porter's drugstore, and the post office. To provide a firebreak, Rima's jewelry store south of the alley was purposely sacrificed.

Sketch of the first major fire in Spokane Falls, which was on the southeast corner of Howard Street and Front Avenue, January 19, 1883. *(Sketch from William and Clara Gray's (Chapter V) personal memorabilia, possibly originally printed in the* Chronicle*)*

The men formed a bucket brigade from the river, their only means of fighting the inferno. It was almost ludicrous, as nearly as much water slopped on the firefighters as got to the fire. But a point was made. Thirteen brick buildings were erected that year, and a volunteer fire department became a reality. Rescue Hose Company number 1 and Spokane Hose Company No. 2 each had a complement of seventy-five men.

The city contracted a private company to install a water pumping system with two Holley pumps in the basement of the Echo Flour Mill. However, work slid to a halt by August 1884 for lack of funds. Thirty businessmen came to the rescue by forming an association into which each man donated a thousand dollars to complete the job. The successful demonstration by the volunteer firemen at the Wolverton building fire in November made purchase of the waterworks by the town an easy matter early in 1885, thus reimbursing the private owners. The old town well in the center of Main and Howard streets became a thing of the past.

Spokane Falls was growing up, although pine trees still stood in the middle of Riverside Avenue. Roller skating provided entertainment for young and old as they nightly crowded the Casino Roller Rink on the southwest corner of Mill and Sprague. Street crossings connected the wooden sidewalks along the south side of Riverside, a long needed improvement. By August, the city employed men daily to water portions of Mill, Howard and Riverside to keep down the dust. The *Morning Review* warned the citizens that horse racing with the Indians on Sundays violated the "blue laws."

On September 26, 1885, the *Spokane Falls Review* made a startling announcement: "If the plant is put in this fall, Spokane Falls will be the first city in the United States to be lit entirely by electricity." To say that a mere ten arc lights would illuminate the city was either an admission of how tiny the town was or sheer optimism on the part of the newspaper. Nevertheless, power poles popped up alongside the California House and up Howard Street. Those picturesque falls in the river were beginning to show their potential. A little-known fellow, George A. Fitch, came to town with a Brush dynamo said to have been dismantled from the old steamship *Columbia* that ran between Portland and San Francisco. Fitch installed his machinery in the basement of the Echo Flour Mill on Glover Island. Generating only four kilowatts, it powered ten street lights scattered between Washington and Monroe south to the Northern Pacific tracks and one on the north side near the road to Colville. From such a humble beginning, this marvel laid the foundation for the development of hydroelectric power in the Pacific Northwest and was the first commercial hydro plant west of the Mississippi River. All this occurred only three years after Thomas A. Edison's steam plant began producing electricity in Menlo Park, New Jersey.[26]

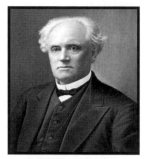

William Pettet
(Photo from Spokane and the Inland Empire, Deluxe Edition *by N. W. Durham)*

F. Rockwood Moore
(Photo from the 1890 Spokane Falls and Its Exposition *souvenir book.)*

Recognizing the future of electricity, William Pettet, his nephew Frederick Chamberlain, Frank Rockwood Moore and Horace L. Cutter bought out Fitch the next spring. As the Spokane Falls Electric Light and Power Company, they hired Henry M. Hoyt, the Edison representative in Seattle, to build an Edison incandescent electric light plant. Hoyt arrived in June 1886. The new plant, located in a bay of the river near Bridge Avenue, went into operation later that year. Built of heavy timber and rough planking, it gave the appearance of a rather crude structure. However, the new generator produced thirty kilowatts, and electric service expanded up Post Street and over to Howard. The unit from the Echo Mill

Horace L. Cutter
(Photo from the 1890 Spokane Falls and Its Exposition *souvenir book.)*

This scene of the upper falls shows Spokane Falls Electric Light and Water Power Company's plant in the foreground and the waterwork's pumping station on Crystal (now Canada) Island. The large building visible behind the pumping plant is the Echo Mill on Glover Island. *(Photo courtesy SPLNWR)*

was moved to this central station. Liking what he saw, including Horace Cutter's niece Laura Grace, Hoyt returned the following year to become a permanent resident. He and Miss Cutter were married in 1891.

The demand for electricity soon made it apparent that more wattage was needed, but local funds could not be found. The company, therefore, turned to eastern investors, the Edison Electric Light Company of New York. At the request of their new partners, the company was reorganized as the Edison Electric Illuminating Company of Spokane Falls. By the spring of 1888, another new plant, looking more like a two-story frame house, began operating just west of the C&C Flour Mill. With four times the capacity, that company offered twenty-four hour service for the first time and extended lines into the residential areas. One went up Howard Street as far south as Sixth Avenue; the other line ran along Pacific as far west as Chestnut Street in Browne's Addition.

It was soon evident that this new plant would still not be equal to the demand for electricity. New industries, streetcar lines and residents all became eager consumers. Nevertheless, the eastern stockholders could see no great future in electricity and refused additional money for plant expansion. Whereupon, the Spokane stockholders decided to gamble by purchasing the lower falls themselves for another power plant. The principle stockholders – F. Rockwood Moore, John D. Sherwood, Herbert Bolster, William S. Norman and Cyrus R. Burns – incorporated as Washington Water Power Company on March 13, 1889. In 1891, Washington Water Power (now Avista Utilities) bought out Edison

Electric and began to systematically build new dams and absorb its competitors along the Spokane River.

Other signs of modernization appeared in the city by the falls. The telegraph had arrived with the railroad, but when telephone poles were erected, the *Spokane Falls Review* considered it an unnecessary affectation of a large city. An editorial wondered why anyone would use a telephone in a town so small a boy could run a message to any part of the business district in two minutes.

In 1884, Charles B. Hopkins, pioneer newsman, began purchasing old military telegraph lines connecting the region's military forts and began converting them to telephone lines. Although his primary interest was to connect his newspaper office in Colfax to the outside world, by December 1886, he had secured the necessary equipment and opened an exchange in the Hyde Block in Spokane Falls. Upon completion of the exchange, Hopkins sold it to William S. Norman. On December 6, 1886, telephone service was inaugurated in Spokane Falls, with thirty-five customers. Among those listed in the first directory were Mr. Walker Bean (in whose grocery store the first telephone set was installed), Daniel Dwight, Sam Glasgow, Mrs. W. C. Gray, W. S. Norman, Spokane Hardware, Harl Cook, Washington Brick, Lime and Sewer Pipe Co., Dr. Pittwood, Dr. B. F. Burch, Mrs. Sylvester Heath, Dr. J. E. Gandy, McNab Drug Co., and the *Chronicle*.

Telephone set inside the Spokane Falls telephone exchange in 1887. *(Photo from the Elsom Collection, Ms 162, courtesy MAC/EWSHS)*

The constant sound of carpenters' saws and the pounding of nails filled the air in 1887 as 36 business buildings, 25 miscellaneous buildings and 532 dwellings, including cabins, arose. A new gas works, Spokane Falls Gas Light Company, began supplying heat and lighting for these new dwellings. Excavations began for a sewer system, but it apparently received very little attention from the city council, as only 525 feet of drains were laid. Shoppers could walk almost the entire length of Howard Street on wooden sidewalks, and branch railroads sprouted north and south from Spokane. Browne and Cannon donated the site for the first city park, Coeur d'Alene in Browne's Addition, although it would not be developed until 1891. In the midst of all this development, in spite of laws to the contrary, the cows still wandered at will throughout the town.

Looking south on Howard Street, circa 1886. The California House is on the left, at the northeast corner of Front and Howard and across the street to the right are Glover and Gilliam's City Stables. On the opposite corner is the Glover Block.
(Photo from Spokane and the Inland Empire *by N. W. Durham, 1912)*

A major development in 1887 was the completion of Sacred Heart Hospital. The tall, sturdy Mother Joseph (Esther Pariseau) of the Sacred Heart, a member of the Sisters of Charity of Providence, accompanied by Sister Joseph of Arimathea, arrived May 1, 1886, from Vancouver, Washington Territory, to build Spokane's first hospital.[27]

The sisters bought land from the Rev. Havermale on May 21 and, in order to supervise the construction, they moved into a rough shanty on the grounds. It has been said they began their ministry to the sick there on June 13, 1886.[28]

On the second of July, the cornerstone for Sacred Heart Hospital was laid with Bishop Junger of Vancouver, W.T., officiating. By the seventh, the stonework was completed and the framework could begin for the two-story brick veneer building measuring 51 by 81 feet. A mansard roof with dormers comprised the third story. Facing south, the hospital stood on slightly elevated ground, about one-half block north of Front Avenue between Center (McClelland) and Park (Browne) streets.

The one hundred-bed hospital opened January 27, 1887, with a staff of five Sisters of Providence under Sister Joseph of Arimathea as Superior, six doctors and six employees. The demand for hospital space grew rapidly, requiring an

Looking southeast over the Spokane River at the east end of Spokane Falls in the 1880s. *(Photo from the Don Neraas Collection, courtesy Tony and Suzanne Bamonte)*

A view of Spokane Falls in 1883. The site of the Post Street Bridge is in the foreground. The California House, the town's first proper hotel, is at the center with the City Stables, owned by John W. Glover (brother of James) and Lane Gilliam, to its right. The south channel of the Spokane River, in the center of the photo, was dammed during the 1890s by Washington Water Power, creating the lagoon in present-day Riverfront Park. *(Photo from Mark Danner's Patsy Clark Album, courtesy Tony and Suzanne Bamonte)*

addition which was completed October 17, 1888. Placed perpendicular to the original building, the new wing was connected to it by a narrow passageway. By 1901, a similar north-south wing was built on the east end. When Jim Hill bought the property in 1908 for the Great Northern Railroad, Sacred Heart Hospital relocated up the hill on Eighth Avenue.

Sacred Heart Hospital's main building, located on Front just west of Browne, was constructed by the Sisters of Providence in 1886. Two additional wings were added, one in 1888 and the other in in 1901. *(Photo courtesy Tony and Suzanne Bamonte)*

During her forty-six years of Christian service, Mother Joseph established eleven hospitals, seven academies, five Indian schools and two orphanages in Oregon, Washington, Montana, Idaho and British Columbia. In the state of Washington, she erected hospitals in Vancouver, Walla Walla, Yakima, Olympia and Spokanc. On May 1, 1980, a statue of Mother Joseph was placed in Statuary Hall, Washington, D.C., to represent Washington State. A statue of Marcus Whitman had been placed there earlier.

Spokanites never lost their love of horse racing. It was the impetus for the first Spokane County fair, which was held on Francis Cook's property on the South Hill in 1886. In 1887, there were three groups devoted to trotting and pacing contests: the Gentlemen's Riding Club, the Spokane Drivers' Club, and the Falls City Racing Club. It was also observed in the *Morning Review* on June 6, 1888, that probably no city in the country had such a large number of ladies noted as graceful equestrians.

In 1887, Dr. Charles Penfield, F. Rockwood Moore, Horace Cutter and Thomas S. Griffiths of the Gentlemen's Riding Club decided a permanent racetrack was needed. Under the auspices of the Washington & Idaho Fair Association, they raised $5,000 from the community and purchased land at the foot of the north

The driving park and grounds of the Washington & Idaho Fair Association, which were completed in time for the annual fair in the fall of 1887. *(Photo from* Spokane Falls Illustrated, *Hook and McGuire, 1889)*

hill, where they put in a half-mile of track and erected a thirty-stall stable and grandstands. It was completed in time for the annual fair in the fall of 1887 and was proclaimed to be the "fastest track west of the Mississippi." A baseball field in the center of the track provided a place for baseball games to entertain spectators between horse races. Eventually the fairgrounds and racetrack moved to larger quarters, and the land was sold to D. C. Corbin, who platted it as Corbin Park Addition in the 1890s. The fairgrounds became Corbin Park. Years later, the park was redesigned by the Olmsted Brothers, a renowned landscape architectural firm from Brookline, Massachusetts.

The general population was warned that horses would be impounded if not tied to a hitching ring, and several runaways a day were causing problems downtown. Other inconveniences associated with traveling by horseback opened the way for public transportation. However, the noble horse provided the power for the first streetcars.

The Spokane Street Railway Company was incorporated on December 17, 1886, by Henry C. Marshall, Andrew J. Ross and John J. Browne. On April 15, 1888, two fine grays made their appearance, pulling a vehicle along the tracks laid from downtown Division Street out First Avenue to Browne's Addition, around Coeur d'Alene Park, and returning through Cannon's Addition. Gaily decorated with American flags, the coach carried members of the city government, newspaper reporters, J. J. Browne, president of the line, and A. M. Cannon. A large crowd watched this historic event, and photographs were taken. The approximately four miles of track were covered without incident as there was no friction experienced on the curves. That evening a banquet was held at the Grand Hotel, where speeches praised this new advance in the city's progress. This was the second streetcar in the state – only Seattle had a similar one. Although A. J. Ross has been credited with being the principal motivator of the Spokane Street Railway, he soon sold his shares to Browne and Cannon (who then sold their shares in 1889).

On December 20, 1887, the Spokane Falls City Council had also granted a franchise authorizing construction of a motor line, a completely different concept. This franchise was given to Francis Cook (the initiator and president of the line), T. J. Dooley, Horatio Belt and E. A. Routhe for a period of 30 years. With a $25,000 loan made by the Provident Trust Company, construction began in the spring of 1888. On November 16, 1888, the Spokane & Montrose Motor Railroad, powered by a wood-burning steam engine, began operations as Spokane's first *motor* trolley.

This photo of Spokane's first trolley line, the Spokane Street Railway, which connected Browne's Addition to downtown Spokane, was taken during the streetcar's first trip, April 15, 1888. Bill Shannon was the driver and John Simonson the conductor. *(Photo from the Jerome Peltier Collection, courtesy Tony and Suzanne Bamonte)*

In appearance, the Spokane & Montrose looked more like a train than the current concept of a streetcar. Traveling on a narrow-gauge track, the nine-ton locomotive burned wood to get up a head of steam. Going downhill to town the locomotive led, but on the return uphill trip the engine had to push one or two cars, each holding twenty passengers. It was said there was no schedule whatsoever. It simply ran when the engine could make it, announcing its approach with a whistle. Housewives shuddered as it belched dirty smoke and showered sparks upon wooden roofs, igniting small fires. Lawyers were kept busy with the many lawsuits that resulted.[29]

Cook's Spokane & Montrose line initially consisted of a square-shaped engine and two passenger coaches. The route began between Front and Riverside and provided transportation to the Spokane Heights (top of Grand Hill). The streetcar traveled south on Washington Street, through an underpass below the Northern Pacific tracks, to Fifth Avenue. There it traveled east to a rock-cut on Bernard Street between Sixth and Seventh avenues. From there it proceeded to a point where the Rockwood gate posts now stand. It then continued west on Sumner to the site of the present St. John's Cathedral, then south on Grand Boulevard to Montrose (Manito) Park.

Cook's original Spokane & Montrose Motor Railroad, circa 1889, on Washington Street, just south of Spokane's first viaduct, which provided passage under the Northern Pacific Railroad tracks. When the line began operations in 1888, the viaduct was not yet completed, so early trips began near this point. *(E. E. Bertrand photo, courtesy MAC/EWSHS, L86-1040)*

THE NORTHWEST MAGAZINE, APRIL 1890.

18

from Colville to Spokane Falls, but it is not very probable that they will come down this year.

CHURCHES AND SCHOOLS.

Spokane Falls is well supplied with churches and schools. To speak of the growth and development of Eastern Washington in general and this city in particular, without mentioning prominently the work of the Jesuit fathers, would be to leave out one, if not the greatest factor in its civilization and advancement. To attempt to tell the story of the band of pious and zealous men, would be to write the history of the State for the past fifty years and that is far more than the scope of this article contemplates. Our artist has given some idea of their work and progress in the education of the people, in the accompanying sketch. The little frame building in the upper left hand corner of the picture shows the beginning, and the handsome brick structure in the center of the five acre tract of high ground overlooking the city and gently sloping to the banks of the beautiful Spokane, shows the later building that became necessary to accommodate the fast-growing school which the Jesuit Fathers founded here years ago, realizing as they did that the first principles of good citizenship consist of a good, sound, practical education. Had the sketch been made a few months later, it would have included a third and much larger building for which the plans are already drawn, that will cost $360,000 and be ready for occupancy at the beginning of the next scholastic year. The present superior of the order in Spokane Falls is Father Mackin, to whose pious zeal and splendid executive ability, coupled with sound business judgment, much of the success of the past few years is due. There has not been an enterprise looking toward the advancement of Spokane Falls, of which the order through him has not been an ardent supporter, and many are the persons in the city who to-day can bear testimony to his benevolence. Under the Jesuit care is the Gonzaga College, St. Ignatius Preparatory School and Convent of the Holy Name.

The Episcopalians have one church, All Saints, and under its protection, are a school for boys and one for girls.

There are three Presbyterian churches in the city; and a university, and girls seminary.

Three flourishing churches and the Spokane Methodist College represent the Methodist denomination.

There are two Baptist churches, a German Lutheran society and one Unitarian church in Spokane Falls.

The public schools are in excellent condition, increasing daily in efficiency and in numbers. Physical culture is promoted by a carefully prepared system of calisthenics; music is regularly taught; and science has its proper place in the course of study. A general onward movement is noticeable along the length of the educational line, and has the hearty sympathy and co-operation of the board of education, teachers and citizens. The public school is the basis of our growth, and whatever tends to strengthen and develop this system has the cordial support of the people.

STREET RAILWAYS.

There are at present four systems of street railways in Spokane Falls and it is safe to say that no city in America of its size is so well supplied in this matter. There is sixteen and one-half miles of road now being operated and twenty-five miles additional road that will be in operation before the middle of summer, making a total of forty-one and one-half miles of street railway tracks. In no other way will Spokane show such great change and improvement as in this year's development of the street railway systems. Miles of new track will be laid and the very latest and most improved methods of locomotion will be used. To-day Spokane Falls has the very best electric street railway in the United States, with the most perfect and complete equipment of rolling stock, appliances, etc.

The Ross Park Electric Street Railway Company was incorporated on the seventeenth of April, 1888, with a capital stock of $30,000 which was afterwards increased to $150,000, the entire cost of road being $300,000. The incorporators were G. B. Dennis, H. N. Belt, C. R. Burns, Cyrus Bradley and I. S. Kaufman. The officers are G. B. Dennis, president; E. J. Webster, vice president; H. N. Belt, general manager; S. Heath, treasurer; and C. L. Marshall, secretary. The board of directors consist of R. W. Forrest, A. P. Wolverton, Cyrus Bradley, W. H. Marshall, I. S. Kauffman, G. B. Dennis, H. N. Belt, Cyrus R. Burns, T. F. Conlan and S. Heath. They are all old and substantial citizens.

Transition by means of electricity was demonstrated as a practical success four years ago and it is fast being adopted as a method of rapid transit.

The Thomson-Houston Electric Company built a road one mile in length at Crescent Beach, Massachusetts, for the Lynn & Boston Railway Company and operated but one car. It accomplished all that was claimed to the satisfaction of the most critical. This system is generally accepted in the principal cities and towns of the States but the finest roads have been constructed at Boston, Washington, D. C., Omaha, Council Bluffs and Spokane Falls; the first four named being thoroughly inspected

Francis Cook's motor line wound to the top of Grand Boulevard from Washington Street, 1890. *(From the April 1890 edition of the* Northwest Magazine*)*

During the 1880s, Spokane Falls experienced one of its greatest periods of growth. From a country crossroads of 350 inhabitants in 1880, it grew to a fair-sized city of about 18,000 by the spring of 1889. Ten banks had been established instead of two, with deposits of over two million dollars. Lumber production was estimated at $150,000 per month; the flour mills put out 300 barrels a day; the surrounding area had been recognized for its agricultural potential and was being developed; and trade in the stores had increased proportionately. The brick, lime and granite quarrying businesses found their products in the many handsome, large, multi-storied buildings in the business section of town. The first public drinking fountain, located on Howard Street near Riverside Avenue, was installed in 1888 by T. M. Harrington, owner of the Fountain Chop House. Streets, however, were still unpaved, so it was necessary in the spring for men with teams to scrape the mud from the streets and load it into wagons to be hauled away. Should the mud be too watery, it would leak through the wagons, and the task had to be done again in a few weeks.

The building trades continued to prosper in 1888 as 600 new homes were built. In the first seven months of 1889, permits were taken out for $115,000 in new homes (about half the actual finished cost, including J. N. Glover's at $30,000 and W. C. Gray's for $15,000) and over $900,000 in other types of buildings. That year, houses were officially numbered for the first time, with the river separating north from south addresses and Howard Street being the dividing line east and west for the southern part of town. On the north side, Monroe was designated as the east-west divider. In 1891, the dividing streets were changed to Division for the east-west numbering and Sprague Avenue for north-south.

As the population of Spokane grew, so did the need for more schools. In 1888, only Central School on the south side of town and Bancroft with four rooms on the north side of the city comprised the school district. Next came four-room Lincoln in Cowley's Addition and Webster with two rooms in Heath's Addition on the north side. These were followed in 1889 by Franklin, Logan and Bryant.

Women in the work force were primarily in the following occupations: dress-making, hair dressing, millinery or nursing. A third of the boarding and lodging houses were run by women; about half the music teachers were women; only one laundry had a woman proprietor, the others were operated by Chinese (most of the cooks in the hotels were also Chinese). There was one woman wholesale grocer, no lawyers, and about six of the forty nine physicians were females. A fifth of the restaurants were owned and operated by women, and of the two stenographers in town, Katherine Kelliher was one.

At the other end of the social scale, away from the work-a-day world, were the beautiful homes sprouting up on the vantage points of the South Hill, in the lovely residential areas of Cannon's and Browne's additions, and in the fashionable Ross Park area. All of this development was made possible by the wealth pouring into town from the Coeur d'Alene mines, the construction of railroads, and the sale of real estate.

Riverside, looking east from Post before the fire. By this time, Riverside had become the financial and commercial center of downtown Spokane Falls. Many of the town's most substantial and impressive commercial buildings can be seen in this photograph. However, they were all destroyed in the 1889 fire. *(Photo from the Don Neraas Collection, courtesy Tony and Suzanne Bamonte)*

Many of Spokane's newcomers were men of university education from the eastern United States with well-educated wives. At the same time, a number of immigrants from Europe were equally successful in business and investments. Together they pursued an elitist lifestyle so grand and gracious it has never been duplicated here. It survived over two decades, probably until World War I.

Under the pen name of Lady Albion, a Mrs. W. A. Mears described the social atmosphere:

> Water, earth and air unite to crown Spokane the ideal, the peerless queen of cities. The Hill [South Hill, especially along Seventh Avenue] is very aristocratic and receives on Wednesdays when carriages and coupes, hansoms and gurneys climb the spacious streets and throng the wide avenues with their fair freight. The heavy portiere is lifted and the smiling visitor glides into the perfumed presence of the mistress of the mansion, where, clad in classic robe or dainty empire gown, she nestles mid downy pillows, silken soft. Coals glow in the brazier, and anon a gentle aroma floats through the room from the Russian samovar where the tea is brewing, while fingers like rose leaves stray softly, yet busily among the dainty cups. Thursday is reception day in Browne's Addition and this center of wealth and fashion is just as gracious in its dispensation of pleasant hospitality as the Hill.

Mrs. Mears went on to predict that the very choicest residential portion of town would be around Cliff Park on the top of the south hill cliff.[30]

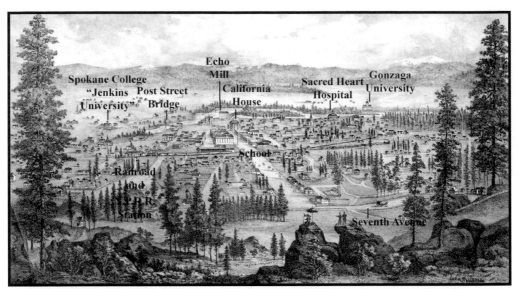

Sketch of Spokane Falls, looking north from Cliff Drive, prior to the Great Fire of 1889. Much of the development shown here was destroyed in the fire. *(Sketch from Taylor and Jefferson, Real Estate and Investors' Agents, courtesy SPLNWR)*

Never had the future looked brighter. Although some residents were struggling to make Spokane a refined and culture-centered city, other aspects of entertainment remained strictly frontier western. "A Limb Show" was booked for July 24 and 25, 1889, at the Falls City Opera House. Lida Garner's Female Burlesque Company, noted for its attenuated costumes, was touring the area. No doubt as many "bald-heads" well down front enjoyed the performance in Spokane as when it had played in Wallace, Idaho, a few days earlier.

A serious fire the previous September (1888) destroyed a complete block except for Glover's small brick building on the southwest corner of Front and Howard. The *Morning Review* called for an adequate water system and more reliable fire protection than just volunteers. Even a few horses to pull the fire trucks would help. The editorial advocated a condemnation of all wooden "shanties" in the valuable downtown area as fire traps that should be removed before more fires occurred. (Later events took care of the situation in only four hours.)

The summer of 1889 was hot and dry. On May 18, a fire erupted in Orr's livery stable on Main Street between Mill and Post. A house on Front and Stevens burned on June 13. Mrs. Anna Stratton, Mrs. J. J. Browne's grandmother, recorded in her diary on June 20: "[there is] hardly any water, none for watering the lawn and not much for use in the house." On June 21 fire broke out among some lumber. Down in Shantytown[31] several buildings went up in smoke in two separate fires. In July, Mrs. Stratton commented almost daily about the lack of rain:

July 8: There has been only one little [rain] shower since the 29th of May. It is very dry and dusty.
July 10: O! so dry and scorching hot.
July 12: Another warm, dry, dusty day. Yesterday it was 90°.
July 14: No rain, sun is scorching hot.
July 18: The heavens appear to be brass and the earth iron under our feet.
July 19: Oh! so hot, air is hot as fire. O! send us a shower if it can please thee, our kind benefactor.

In downtown Spokane, the usual dusty streets became increasingly annoying to the populace, prompting editorials and letters to the newspapers about the intolerable nuisance and the brown haze over the city from the dust. They demanded the city send out sprinkling carts daily from four in the morning until eight in the evening. On July 27, seven buildings burned on the north side of Riverside eastward from Ziegler's Hardware on the corner of Howard. It had begun in Stegmeyer's paint shop and was attributed to spontaneous combustion.

The entire Northwest suffered from the drought and drought-related fires. Seattle lost its business district on June 6; Vancouver, Washington Territory, had a serious fire on June 22; and Ellensburg went up in smoke on July 4. As the season wore on, tar dried on roofs and wooden boards became tinder dry.

August 4 was just one more day of unrelieved heat. Those who could escaped to the nearby lakes, including Rolla A. Jones, the Water Department superintendent. According to the following day's *Spokane Daily Chronicle*, about 6:15 that Sunday evening, smoke curled out of a third-story gable window of Wolfe's lunch counter and lodging establishment on Railroad Avenue. Five restaurants, four saloons, two combined eateries and drinking establishments, a cigar and tobacco shop, and a thirty-one-room hotel crowded the space between Post and Lincoln streets. These wooden buildings faced the Northern Pacific passenger depot and non-elevated railroad tracks to the south of it. Wolfe's was the third building west of Post and slightly northeast of the depot.

Within ten minutes of the alarm, firemen arrived on the scene. They connected hoses to hydrant after hydrant, but nothing happened. There was no water. Curious onlookers did not expect the blaze to amount to much, even as adjoining structures caught fire. But the buildings were too dry, and the usual southwest wind carried the embers to the next block and the next and the next. Then a strong wind came up from the northeast, creating a draft to fan the flames, while the upper current from the opposite direction drove the conflagration north toward the river. The flames seemed to go hundreds of feet into the air, lighting up the sky as darkness fell.

By this time it was apparent nothing would stop the fire. The night became hideous with the shrieks of women and children, the hoarse shouts of men, the

Looking north from Railroad Avenue after the fire. *(Photo from Mark Danner's Patsy Clark Collection, courtesy Tony and Suzanne Bamonte)*

rattle of wagons, and snorting of frightened horses. The tolling church bells and the shrill whistles of the locomotives trying to move the railroad cars lined up on the track away from the fire added to the confusion. Above all could be heard the constant roar of the flames. Embers and burning fragments were carried for miles. Big pieces of heavy tin roofing were found the next day on the prairie to the northeast.

May and Daniel H. Dwight had gone downtown earlier that Sunday from their home on West Pacific. As the fire grew, they hurried to the Falls City Opera House on the southwest corner of Riverside and Post, and got tubs from Bonne & Lindsey's grocery store on the ground floor. Putting a tub filled with water at each window, Dwight stationed a man with a broom at each one to keep the window frames wet. As the windows were on the fourth floor and there were no other openings, he hoped to keep the window frames from catching fire and so save his building. South of the Opera House were one-story wooden buildings.

On August 6, Dwight wrote to his mother-in-law describing their brave fight:

> May stood bravely by one with her broom and water. By this time the flames were down to Sprague St. and spreading rapidly. The chief of the fire department now began to blow up the buildings with dynamite ahead of the fire to try to stop it [along Washington and Lincoln streets]. Every few minutes there was a deafening roar and some frame building went into the air a hundred feet or more and dropped a heap of ruins. A few minutes more and our glass began to crack & I had to order May downstairs and out of the building to get her away from danger. We kept all the window frames wet for a few minutes longer – a dynamite bomb blew up a building about 20 ft. south of us – another just to the west. A few minutes more and with one great burst the flames jumped through the Opera House windows and also leaped to the roof on the outside. Galbraith and I ran downstairs for our lives. When I got to the head of the hall stairs,

I ran into room #1 and seized my great antique oak desk and dragged it out, for it contained all of my receipts and papers. I hauled it down the stairs, but just as I got to the Opera House entrance, the smoke and flames whirled round the corner and swept into the doorway with such blinding force that I had to let go of everything & leave the desk about three feet from the sidewalk & run for my life. Mr. Galbraith lingered a moment to get a few clothes and papers and when he came to the stairs, they were a sheet of flames and his exit was cut off. His only escape was to jump – which he did from Dr. Hanver's window on the corner, fully 20 ft. above the sidewalk. He is here at our house and hasn't stepped on his feet for two days, but no bones were broken & he will probably be around in a few days. The great block burned out and the street sides fell in, in almost no time it seemed. By blowing up the buildings west of us the fire was stopped at Lincoln St. on the west, but they rolled on down Riverside Ave., sparing neither five story brick blocks nor frame shanties. I can't describe the terrible rush & confusion, the glare of the flames, and the roar of the dynamite blasts, but those who went through it will never forget it. Men who were at the Chicago fire say this was just like it only the area burned is not so great. Mr. Galbraith said he never saw anything like it except the battles of the war which he passed through and you know he has bullet marks enough to prove what he says. In about three hours everything was in ruins. The burned district covers between 75 to 100 acres I should judge. When it was at its height part of the crowd got panic stricken and fled to the outskirts of the city. But I must stop describing it now – this is only a very little part of all that was crowded into that two or three hours.

At midnight the first section of the Howard Street bridge burned as well as some of the logs in the millpond. The Post Street and Division Street bridges escaped. Twenty city blocks were completely gone and 27 partially destroyed. Only the great empty, smoldering hulls of brick buildings greeted the morning light. Thirty-two major business buildings were burned.[32]

Although accounts vary as to the cause of the fire, what started as a small, seemingly manageable fire at Wolfe's lunch counter soon turned into a raging firestorm. Every catastrophe must have a scapegoat, or so it would seem. In this case it was Rolla Jones, superintendent of the Water Works, who was accused of either taking the keys to the water pumps with him to Coeur d'Alene Lake, or of leaving in charge an inexperienced person, George C. Bartoo. Actually, neither accusation was correct, but to save the city fathers, Jones and Bartoo were permitted to resign the day after the big fire. Bartoo, the chief engineer at the pumping plant, was perfectly competent. The day of the fire, some work had been done on the water mains at the foot of Post Street, and the main valves had not been reopened. After one

The burned out shell of the Glover Block at the southwest corner of Howard and Front after the devastating fire of August 4, 1889.
(Photo courtesy MAC/EWSHS, L86-1055)

of the workers went to check, the pressure dropped at the plant and water arrived up at the fire. By then, it was too late.[33]

The newspapers carried complete and almost blow-by-blow accounts of the advance of the flames. The *Spokane Falls Review*, in its first issue after the fire, August 6, reported on page one: "On Front Street the flames darted in every direction. It soon cleaned out a number of little frame buildings occupied mainly by Chinamen and disreputable women among which was one magnificent brick structure known as the Synagogue." To the east of the Windsor Hotel (formerly California House) had lived Kittie Lewis, Essie Russell, Dollie Bell with her boarder Gypsie Lovering, and several Chinese.

Fire stories were swapped, including the ludicrous. One account told of a lady who was so distraught she rushed along the street carrying her baby upside down oblivious to his protests. One gentleman went to the aid of a lady trying to save items from her home and came out of her house carrying a small pegging awl. Another fellow dashed into a lovely home full of books, paintings and beautiful furniture. He saved a small kerosene lamp. One woman wrung her hands demanding to know where the fire was – she was surrounded by it.

Cold, hard statistics paint a more complete picture of the destruction. Approximately 800 businesses and private residences housed in 300 buildings were gone. Thirty of those buildings had brick or masonry walls. Sacred Heart Hospital treated 120 patients as a result of the fire. Some 2,000 were left homeless. Fortunately there was only one fatality: George Davis, who jumped from a second-story window of the Arlington Hotel.

A panoramic view of the burned district, looking southwest from the Echo Mill. Tents and makeshift structures in which to conduct business were set up amidst the rubble. Streets in right foreground are Front and Mill (now Wall). *(Photo from Mark Danner's Patsy Clark Collection, courtesy Tony and Suzanne Bamonte)*

Chapter VII

ALICE IDE HOUGHTON

**Alice Houghton, about age 45, a member of the Board of Lady Managers
for the World's Columbian Exposition held in Chicago in 1893.**
(Photo from History of Washington, *American Publishing Co., 1893)*

"Seek not to walk by borrowed light,
But keep unto thine own;
Do what thou doest with thy might
And trust thyself alone!"[1]

These words by an unknown nineteenth century poetess were used in the
New Year's Day supplement of the *Spokane Spokesman* in 1892 to introduce a biographical sketch of one of the city's leading real estate agents, and

Interior of the Frankfurt Block outside the real estate office of H. M. Williams and Mrs. Alice Houghton before Spokane's Great Fire of August 4, 1889. *(Sketch from* Spokane Falls Illustrated, *1889)*

the only woman in the field, Alice A. Ide Houghton. They aptly described her persistence and self-confidence. But then, what woman without a strong conviction of her abilities would enter a business field dominated by the founding fathers and civic leaders as the only woman in that profession?

Mrs. Houghton's venture into real estate began in the spring of 1887 with little or no capital. It might have been in conjunction with an uncle, Chester D. Ide, and a cousin, Clarence W., who opened a real estate office in the Jamieson Building at that time. Alice proved very adept at selling, and by the next year when the Ides withdrew for other pursuits, she became a partner in the firm of H. M. Williams & Co.

Alice's executive ability, shrewd judgment, unflappability, and unwavering persistence led to almost instant success. In the first two years she was associated with Williams, sales exceeded two million dollars. It was said her personal worth was over $100,000[2] – not a small accomplishment for two and a half years as a neophyte businesswoman. In the summer of 1889, the firm of Williams and Houghton rented rooms 24 and 25 in the prestigious Frankfurt Block on the southwest corner of Howard and Main streets. A brochure put out by the Retail Trade Bureau that year identified Mrs. Houghton as being a very remarkable woman.[3]

Alice was born August 18, 1848, in Montreal, Canada, to Frederick J. and Atlanta (Glover) Ide.[4] She was the fourth child of seven. When Alice was eight years old, the family moved to Mondovi.[5] One of her two brothers, George, died during the Civil War. In 1878, Mr. and Mrs. F. J. Ide moved to Durand, Wisconsin, where most of their married daughters were living.

She was only 16½ years old when, on January 16, 1865,[6] she married the prosecuting attorney of Peppin County, Wisconsin, Horace E. Houghton, a man almost twice her age. They had two children: son Harvey W. (or Harry, as he is listed in most of the censuses) in 1868 and daughter Idell in 1872. There had hardly been time for more formal education than what she received at a seminary for young ladies in Mondovi, Buffalo County, Wisconsin.

In pursuing his profession as a lawyer, Horace Houghton attained some prominence in Peppin County, first as district attorney for twelve years, then in the state legislature. In 1873, he was elected to the house of representatives, and in 1879, to a term in the Wisconsin State Senate representing Buffalo, Peppin and Trempleau counties. Although a number of men around the state urged him to accept the Republican nomination for governor, he had to decline because of poor health. Thought to be suffering from Bright's disease, Houghton looked westward for a more healthful climate.

He followed the lead, and probably the advice, of some of the Ide family who had joined a wagon train for Walla Walla, Washington Territory, in 1878. Alice's uncle Chester D. Ide, his wife Lucy and three sons spent a year in Dayton, Washington, before moving to Spokane County. The following year, they located in the town by the falls. That same year, 1880, Gilbert Ide, Alice's younger brother, decided to leave the family farm. After working a year on a ranch in the Palouse country, he, too, settled in Spokane Falls, where he established a livery stable.

Horace Houghton arrived in March 1884. In just two months, his health was so improved that he went back to Wisconsin to close out his affairs. He returned in July and was followed by Alice and the children in September. She was accompanied by her younger sister, Victor Anna, the widow of Horace's brother, Harvey Houghton, and Victor Anna's three-year-old daughter, Helen. Their parents also migrated to Spokane Falls in 1884. Houghton opened a law office with George M. Forster as his first partner.

Young, attractive, energetic Mrs. Houghton settled in on Fourth Street between Lincoln and Monroe on a lot they bought from A. M. Cannon. With her beautiful singing voice, Alice soon became involved in every musical activity in the community.

In Spokane Falls, the primary source of social activity had always centered around music in some form, from a handful of townspeople singing Christmas carols together to elaborate charity balls a decade later. Amateur theatricals first made an appearance in the winter of 1879 with "The Last Loaf." Several other plays were given that winter with people journeying from as far as Colfax and Colville to see them. So successful were they that a profit of $1,000 was realized. Elocutions and concerts performed by the schools, churches and lodges, with an occasional traveling troupe, played to packed houses. Between 1881 and 1885, only one musical group had been formally organized, the German Concordia Society, an all-male chorus.

In March 1886, two performances of the operetta *H.M.S. Pinafore* were staged by local talent. Harry Hayward, Walker Bean, Dr. E. P. Penfield and Ralph Clarke played the lead roles. It is interesting how soon after *Pinafore* was produced for the first time ever (1878) that Hayward staged this ambitious and successful production for the little community of Spokane Falls. It was directed by Walker Bean, and Jennie Patterson was the accompanist. Among the "bevy of pretty and vivacious sisters, cousins, aunts" reported the *Morning Review* were: Alice and Idell Houghton, Clara Gray, Katie and Josephine Clarke, Lulu Kelly, F. May Williams and Emma Cannon (A. M. Cannon's sister). This was not the first time Alice had sung in *H.M.S. Pinafore*. While living in Durand, Alice's older sister, Ada Prindle, organized two performances of the operetta, which they presented in January 1880. Four of the Ide sisters, who frequently sang before audiences in Durand and other nearby towns in Wisconsin, had lead roles and received glowing reviews in the local newspapers.

Following the success of *H.M.S. Pinafore*, on April 15, 1886, fifty music-loving citizens of Spokane Falls formed the Arion Society. Their next production, *Mikado*, was presented in Joy's Opera House on December 27 and 29, 1886. The cast of forty-two, plus nine members of the orchestra, also performed the opera in Coeur d'Alene. Walker Bean, J. D. Sherwood, Ralph Clarke and Alice Houghton (as one of the three little maids from school) played some of the leading parts. Unfortunately the Arion Society ceased functioning after these two popular performances. In a sense, it did revitalize when most of its members became part of the Mozart Club in December 1892 and transferred the Arion treasury to the new organization.

As neighbors of the A. M. Cannons, the Houghtons easily became part of Spokane Falls society. They attended all the fancy parties at the Cannon home and entertained in return. Mrs. Houghton served on various committees for a variety of community functions. Wherever the Cannons, Brownes, Grays, Glovers and Zieglers were, so were the Houghtons. Whenever she was requested to sing for a benefit, Alice readily accepted. One such occasion was held at Joy's Opera

House on May 22, 1885, to raise money for uniforms for Pynn's Brass Band. Daughter Idell was also on the program.

The Ides were a close-knit family. Frequent visits were made back and forth by the Durand and Spokane Falls members of the Ide and Houghton families. Two of Alice's uncles – Chester D. and Daniel B. Ide – and their families, the latter of whom migrated in May 1886, lived four blocks east of the Houghtons. Alice's brother Gilbert lived with their parents, but Victor Anna and her daughter made their home with the Houghtons. In 1885, Gilbert moved to Colville where he became a pioneer and prominent citizen in that community. After building and operating the Columbia Livery Stables

Horace E. Houghton
(Photo from the 1890 Spokane Falls and Its Exposition *souvenir book)*

for a year, he was elected sheriff of Stevens County. On November 4, 1885, Victor Anna married Col. Isaac N. Peyton. They would have two sons: Horace C., born February 1891, and Harlan Ide in January 1894.

Judge Houghton quickly became known as one of the ablest legal minds in town. Where the appellation of "judge" came from is unknown as he never served on the bench in either Wisconsin or the state of Washington. Perhaps it was a mark of respect similar to the "captain" extended to men as captains of industry, or the many "colonels" who served in the Civil War, regardless of rank. Nevertheless, Houghton formed a law partnership with Frank Hyde Graves early in 1886.

On April 6 of that year, Houghton was elected city attorney and served three terms until he was fired in 1892 as a result of a legal opinion he gave contrary to the wishes of the city council about an upriver water project. He claimed F. Lewis Clark had no right to sell river water to anyone, nor did the Spokane Falls Water Power Company or the Washington Water Power Company. W. W. D. Turner replaced him, and the Upriver Water Plant was completed March 1, 1896.

Misfortune struck the Houghton household early in May 1886 when Horace collapsed while addressing a jury in the courtroom. His condition, from which he eventually recovered, was considered critical after a diagnosis of "softening of the brain." This domestic crisis is probably what prompted Alice to enter the working world. Commercial work was not unknown to her. Before coming to Spokane Falls, Mrs. Houghton had a millinery shop in Durand. This time, however, she entered real estate. It was at a most propitious time, as the booming Coeur d'Alene mines meant an influx of potential buyers of property.

In 1887, Alice had an option on the land that became the Houghton and Callahan Addition in Spokane, roughly enclosed by Perry east to Crestline, and Fourteenth south to Twenty-first. When the option was about to expire, she asked her sister Agnes's husband, Denton J. Callahan, of St. Paul, to buy the property. They agreed that she would sell the land and divide the profits. After a disagreement arose with Callahan, the Houghtons sued for half of the unsold realty in 1891. However, the state supreme court ruled that according to the agreement, Callahan would hold the title. Alice's half-interest was in the profits only, not in the unsold real estate.[7]

The Houghtons' experiences were probably not any different from many other people in Spokane, particularly those dealing in selling their own real estate rather than acting exclusively as an agent for someone else. Alice might not have intended to pursue a full-time career in the beginning, but her talents, abilities and ambitions soon found an avenue of gratifying expression. Financial success and peer recognition are not easily discarded. The Houghtons moved to a new home a block farther west in 1888 on the southwest corner of Fourth and Cedar.

Trips to the East were more than visits to family. Upon returning, Mrs. Houghton was frequently interviewed by the *Morning Review*. Although she was a retiring woman by nature, she never missed an opportunity to promote her adopted city, such as when a sleeping-car conductor was giving false impressions of Spokane to travelers. "She straightened him up with plain and logical reasoning."[8]

It is unlikely Alice realized it at the time, but she was laying the groundwork for not only a future career, but for her life. In Chicago, she met a man associated with the German Board of Immigration and promptly suggested bolstering German migration to the Inland Empire through his German newspaper. From her observations, Alice forecast a large increase in population during 1889. The *Morning Review* made its own observation: "As a type of the genuine western business lady, Mrs. Houghton has no superior, and as a devoted wife and tender mother but few equals."[9]

That Alice's wit and intelligence were easily discernible upon first meeting was evidenced in a letter Adelaide Sutton Gilbert wrote to her parents describing a party at the Tiger Hotel in Burke, Idaho. "In the party were two very jolly ladies from Spokane and between them we nearly killed ourselves laughing. One of them about 50 – is a Mrs. Houghton – a real estate dealer. Her husband is a judge and holds some official position – has his office and she has hers – he says

Interior view of Mrs. Houghton's real estate office in the Eagle Block, 1890.
(Sketch from the April 1890 issue of the Northwest Magazine*)*

she makes more money than he does – she made $25,000 one year. She is as bright and as smart as a steel trap – very stylish – dresses beautifully."[10]

Being an astute business woman, Mrs. Houghton knew that the best advertising was good public relations. This meant more community involvement than just social or musical events. She subscribed $500 toward the construction of D. C. Corbin's Spokane Falls and Northern Railway. When Seattle suffered a disastrous fire, Alice donated $50 to the city's relief fund. Shortly thereafter, when Spokane experienced its own conflagration, Williams and Houghton, like many of the people in the business district, had no insurance to cover their losses. However, their assets were mostly in residential property, rather than in structures within the fire zone, so their losses were not as significant as some.

After the 1889 fire, Alice opened her own real estate firm in the Eagle Block, branching into mining investments and insurance. Her business soon became one of the largest and most profitable of this type in the Northwest. She placed ads in the *Spokane Falls Review* advertising herself as the sole agent for the Bonners Ferry town site, gateway to the Kootenai Mining District. She was the secretary-treasurer of the Bonners Ferry Company, and vice president of the Northwestern Mining and Agricultural Company dealing in mining and farm loans.

Important events in Washington Territory in 1889 claimed local interest. The seven Spokane County delegates had met in Olympia from July 4 to

August 22 to help write the new state constitution. Statehood was granted on November 11, 1889. Elections that month sent Judge Houghton, along with H. W. Fairweather, Eugene B. Hyde and B. C. Van Houten, to the first legislature as members of the senate. Seven men represented Spokane County in the house of representatives.

Idell Houghton left Spokane in the fall to attend a young ladies' seminary in Lake Forest, Illinois, with Josie Clarke. Later that year, on December 4, these two young ladies served as maids-of-honor at the double wedding ceremony for Katie Clarke and her cousin, Mamie Pope. For this outstanding social event, Mrs. Houghton wore a black velvet dress trimmed with black lace. The entire front of the gown was filled with a network of crocheted lace. She wore diamond accessories.

Alice Houghton's reputation continued to rise. An article in the *New York Sun*, reprinted in the *Spokane Falls Review* on December 18, 1890, said Mrs. H. E. Houghton was one of the most remarkable women in the Northwest. The article went on to extoll her success through the investments she had made in timber, coal and desert lands, as well as in numerous town sites, notably Bonners Ferry and Post Falls, all quite unusual for a woman. They stated she was worth $500,000 from an original investment of only $100.[11] However, be that as it may, hard cash was scarce. Taxes went unpaid from 1887–1890 on property the Houghtons

Alice Houghton as she appeared in the 1890 *Spokane Falls and Its Exposition* souvenir book.

owned. Some of these were for as little as seven dollars to seventy. However, when the tax delinquent suits came up in court in 1893, they were dismissed because the Houghtons paid the back taxes.

Alice remained actively engaged in community involvement or social activities in the early 1890s. A group of women met January 25, 1891, to form a new Sorosis club, a professional women's association. As a founder and also the club's first president, Mrs. Houghton entertained fifty-five members in her home the next month. Weekly meetings were designated for discussions on science, art, literature and authors. Should there be a fifth week in a month, the topic would relate to political or legal subjects. On October 24, 1891, Mr. and Mrs. Houghton served on the reception committee for the dedication of the Review Building.

Alice's recognition as a woman of ability went beyond Spokane. In September 1890, just prior to the Northwestern Industrial Exposition held in Spokane, in which Alice participated, the governor appointed her one of the two state representatives to the Board of Lady Managers (often referred to as the Women's Commission) for the World's Columbian Exposition to be held in Chicago in 1893.

Alice's position inaugurated innumerable trips and speaking engagements around the state and to the "Windy City." She traveled throughout Washington to organize women's clubs to support the Columbian Exposition. As chairwoman of the women's division for the state, she was looking for outstanding examples of women's work: art, needlework, etchings on metals, modeling in clay, pen and ink sketches, illustrations for periodicals, published books, inventions, historical relics, curios, and any other interesting products from women's hands. Frequent press releases reported on the interest in the fair and the progress of her recruitment campaign.

Trips to Chicago to attend the meetings of the Board of Lady Managers could last as long as a month. Alice was the chairperson of the Lady Managers' Transportation Committee and also served on the Machinery Committee. Melissa D. Owings of Olympia, the other representative from Washington, was chairperson of the Livestock Committee. Mrs. Owings was the wife of Washington's former secretary of state and was prominent in reform and political circles.

When Congressman Frank of Missouri introduced a resolution to abolish the Women's Commission, Mrs. Houghton went to Washington, D.C., where she interviewed the representatives from Oregon, Washington, Idaho and Wisconsin. The result of her visit to the capitol, she felt, was favorable to their cause. Of the 115 women making up the commission, only eight were professional or self-supporting. There were two physicians, two newspaper workers, two lawyers, one artist, and a real estate agent, Alice Houghton.

Diplomatic relations between Italy and the United States were at a standstill. When it was learned that Italy refused to send an exhibit to the fair, Alice suggested to Mrs. Bertha Honore Palmer, president of the Board of Lady Managers, that she contact Queen Margherita personally. As a result, Italy was among the first to announce its committee under the special patronage of the queen. She sent her personal collection of historical laces, which had never before left Italy. Some were nearly 3,000 years old, having come from Egyptian and Etruscan tombs. Contemporary works of Italian women were also included.[12] The June 1892 issue of the *Northwest Magazine,* published in St. Paul, Minnesota, pointed out the credit for the Italian exhibit must belong to Mrs. Houghton.

On every trip east Alice extolled the grandeurs and future of the state of Washington. Finding a great deal of interest in westward migration, but very little knowledge regarding the Pacific Northwest, she continually advocated hiring representative people for the Washington State Pavilion who could talk to the fair attendees about the state.

Five thousand dollars had been appropriated for the women's department by the state, while the Fair Commission received ten times that amount. In addition to collecting the items for the women's exhibits, Alice had to arrange for their shipping, insurance, and for setting up the exhibits at the fair. She was also charged with the responsibility of decorating the room.

The Woman's Building, designed by a woman and decorated with statues created by a woman, stood in the northwestern part facing a man-made central lagoon. It measured 400 by 200 feet. On one side was the Illinois State Building and, on the other, the Horticulture Building. The final report of the Washington World's Fair Commission included a section on the Woman's Department. In part it read:

> The department was given quarters in the west end of the north wing of the state building, adjoining the educational exhibit. The collection of decorative needlework, china painting, decorated native wood panels, old family heirlooms, and the like, certainly demonstrated the fact that the ladies of the Evergreen State enjoy an atmosphere of culture and refinement that would do credit to many older communities.

> Mrs. Houghton also earned the thanks of the commission by draping and decorating the reception rooms of the state building, the expense of which was defrayed from the funds of the board of lady managers.[13]

In her dedication address, Mrs. Palmer commented: "Even more important than the discovery of Columbus, which we are gathered together to celebrate, is the fact that general Government has just discovered woman."[14]

The main decoration was a frieze of eighty-six panels of native woods, painted by the women of Spokane, showing fruits, flowers, birds, fish and landscapes of the country. One was the head of Spokan Garry, chief of the Spokane tribe. Other contributions from Spokane included a fine exhibit of lace by Mrs. J. T. Weeks, drawn work by Mrs. Otis Sprague and Mrs. A. M. Cannon, and fine embroidery by Mrs. W. J. M. Hale.

The official published report on exhibits at the exposition stated in its resume of the woman's department from Washington State: "The 85 varieties of woods and sea mosses of Washington exquisitely mounted on embossed cards by Miss S. C. Hyatt and 300 specimens of the State flora prepared by Mrs. George Crane of Spokane, elicited much favorable comment."[15] The Tacoma Women's Club furnished a huge sandstone vase which was made from one block of stone and weighed over seven thousand pounds. It was placed on the lawn in front of the state building and contained a huge planting of native rhododendrons.

When Mrs. Houghton had held a meeting May 27, 1892, at the Hotel Spokane to solicit the painting of the panels, she was joined by Mrs. Samuel C. Slaughter of Tacoma, the state art director for the fair. Although Alice suggested making this group a world's fair club, Mrs. Slaughter urged the ladies to form an art league for the advancement of all forms of art. Accepting this latter recommendation, the Spokane Art League was formed. Many meetings were held to further the work for the exposition, but eventually the members turned to the writing of papers and discussing artists and their works.

The Columbian Exposition was a fabulous success and over twenty million attended, but it coincided with the Panic of 1893 that subsequently plunged the nation into a depression. Banks failed and many lost fortunes.

Alice Houghton's photograph as it appeared on the frontispiece of the *Spokane Spokesman's* "Annual Illustrated Supplement," January 1, 1892.

During the first four years of the 1890s, Alice and her husband had borrowed more than twenty thousand dollars, often with other people, using various properties for security. Sometimes interest was paid on the loans, occasionally some of the principal, but many times nothing was repaid. Consequently, there were a number of civil suits by the Hypotheekbank, Traders National Bank, and individuals to reclaim the outstanding debts. Failing to appear in court, the Houghtons defaulted, and various parcels of their property were sold in 1894.

As the Panic of 1893 brought a general slow-down of business in Spokane, because of the contacts Alice had made during the Columbian Exposition, she looked toward Chicago. She opened a real estate office there in December of 1893. Again, Alice shared her time between Chicago and Spokane. She also had another reason to travel east; in November 1894, daughter Idell married Herbert C. Phillips of Pennsylvania and moved to Pittsburgh.

There had been continual campaigning for women's suffrage after the state bill had been declared unconstitutional in 1888. Surprisingly, Mrs. Houghton was president of the anti-suffrage movement. One would have expected that a per-

The Northern Pacific Railroad's exhibition car that was outfitted for the Columbia Exposition in Chicago, 1893. *(Photo courtesy Haynes Foundation Collection, Montana Historical Society, Helena, Montana)*

son actively engaged in business, who was as well known as she was throughout the state, would have wanted to express her political opinions as well, but for the most part, Alice held traditional ideas about the role of a wife and mother. However, when a unit of the National Temperance Union was formed in 1895 by men and women opposed to saloons, Alice was one of the organizers.

For all practical purposes, by 1895, Mrs. Houghton made her home permanently in Chicago, where she continued to promote the wonders of Washington State. She became the manager for a railroad emigration bureau that directed home seekers to the Pacific Northwest. She appealed to the people in Washington State to send exhibits of grains, grasses, vegetables, fisheries, building stones, minerals and polished wood. The Great Northern and Northern Pacific railroads offered to ship these items without charge. In this manner, Alice pointed out: "We can obtain a great deal of advertising, attract a good deal of attention, and interest both investors and home seekers."[16] She also promoted Washington in a monthly article she wrote for the *Homeseeker's Journal*, owned and published by A. H. Ford,[17] and gave innumerable speeches to encourage emigration to the state.

The Chicago Western Society, of which Alice was president and served as hostess, held a reception in the Northern Pacific's exhibition railroad car. Built for the 1893 World's Fair, the car cost $50,000. The floor was inlaid with wood from every state in the Northwest. Along the sides stood stuffed animals and birds ranging from the Dakota teal duck to a Rocky Mountain sheep. In glass cases were ore samples. It was a visual demonstration that the country west of Chicago could produce everything desirable for the comfort of mankind.

These endeavors appear to have been short-lived, however. By 1896, Alice again opened her own office, this time dealing in mining investments. The next year she formed a partnership with Archibald G. Brownlee.

In the spring of 1897, Judge Horace E. Houghton suffered a stroke. The previous winter he had worked arduously in the state senate, having been re-elected to a second term. Although he seemed to be recovering from his exhaustion, he became ill in April. By August, Houghton seemed well enough to travel to Chicago, where his wife resided. His daughter, Idell Phillips, accompanied him.

A second attack occurred at St. Paul. After a few days, the doctors decided he could continue his journey. In Chicago, a third stroke claimed his life on August 23, 1897. His death at the age of 62 came as a shock to friends in Spokane. This prominent and popular figure was described as a man of high character, considerate to a fault with his family, and always generous in his contributions to charitable causes.

His former law partner, Frank Graves, said of Judge Houghton: "His was a character singularly lovable and admirable. His life in this state marked him as a man in the broadest sense of high honor and unswerving devotion to the great things of humanity. His death is a loss to the community in which he lived and to the state."[18] Washington State Governor John R. Rogers sent a message of condolence to the family.

Funeral services for Judge Houghton were held at A. G. Brownlee's residence on August 26 with interment in Rosehill Cemetery, Chicago. At this time the Houghtons' son, Harvey, was living in Colville, where he had moved around 1893 to work with his uncle, Gilbert Ide. However, by 1900, he had left the state of Washington. He returned to Wisconsin, his state of birth, where he lived with his wife Nellie and their children.

Alice's mother, Atlanta Ide, who had been making her home with Judge Houghton in Spokane, returned to Durand, Wisconsin, to live with her daughter, Ada Prindle. She passed away in 1904. Her body was returned to Spokane, and she was buried next to her husband in Greenwood Memorial Terrace.

Alice continued her business interests in Chicago after her husband's death, but had no listing in the 1899 *Chicago City Directory*, although her business partner, Archie Brownlee, did. The next year, on May 18 1900, the *Buffalo County Herald*, Mondovi, Wisconsin, carried the following item:

> Mrs. Alice Houghton, widow of the late Hon. H. E. Houghton, formerly of Durand, was recently married [May 16] to a wealthy Denver gentleman [Brownlee]. Mrs. Houghton grew up in this neighborhood, her parents being Mr. and Mrs. F. J. Ide. She has been engaged in the real estate and mining property business in recent years and has been very successful. A recent deal netted her a snug fortune.

No announcement of Alice's marriage to Brownlee appeared in the Spokane newspapers.

Archie and Alice moved to Denver, where they resided for five years. By 1905, they were in Idaho Springs, a small mining town twenty miles west of Denver, where Brownlee was president of the Stanley Mines Company.

Brownlee, who was nine years younger than Alice, passed away January 16, 1912, at the age of 55, in Idaho Springs. Alice had him interred next to her first husband, Horace Houghton, at Rosehill Cemetery, Chicago. Following Archie's death, Alice moved back to Denver, where she was vice president of the Western Metals Company. Her last listing in the directory there was 1918. Alice died on August 19, 1920, one day after her 72nd birthday. She was buried on the other side of Horace in Rosehill Cemetery (where her interment record states 68 as her age).

Alice Ide Houghton Brownlee was a living example of what an able and brilliant woman could accomplish regardless of the times in which she lived. She was as successful as any man in the line of business she chose. Yet, all biographies point out that she was always mindful of her duties as a wife and mother and was a popular patron of society, as if it were necessary to pigeon-hole her as a woman and not as an individual person.

Dr. Mary Archard Latham

Dr. Mary A. Latham, as she appeared in the
***Spokane Spokesman's* "Annual Illustrated**
Supplement," January 1, 1892.

An advertisement announcing the imminent arrival of Dr. Mary Latham ran for a couple of months in the local newspaper in 1887. In this way Spokane Falls was introduced to its first female physician. Although there is inconclusive evidence, there are written references that she was the first woman doctor to practice medicine in Washington Territory, or at least the first to have been licensed in Washington.

Dr. Mary Archard[1] Latham moved to Spokane Falls in the fall of 1887. With her were sons Frank, 21, James, 17, and Warren, 15. Her husband, Dr. Edward

Hempstead Latham, was to settle his affairs in Cincinnati and follow in a short time. It took him almost two years. In the meantime, Dr. Mary Latham, a woman of great energy and ability, set to work in the rapidly growing town by the falls. She rented a house from Henry Brook on the southwest corner of First and Stevens. Here she opened a combination office and residence in the fall of 1887.

Dr. Latham quickly rose to the top of her profession as a specialist in the diseases of women and children, enjoying the respect and friendship of the community. A large practice followed. From the beginning of her practice in Spokane, Dr. Latham announced plans for a private hospital where women could stay while undergoing treatment or during an illness. It would include a pharmacy and resident physician. In this respect she was ahead of her time.

However, her talents were not limited to medicine. In spite of the continuous demands of her profession, Mary also found time to indulge in literary pursuits. One of her first publications in Spokane Falls was "For Ladies Only," a booklet encompassing the four "H"s: house, home, hygiene and health.[2] Proceeds from its sale were to go toward the establishment of a prospective home for women and children.

In its 1891 Christmas issue, the *Spokane Review* carried one of Mary's pieces of fiction written expressly for the holiday. A sad story, it tugged at the heartstrings, but had a happy ending. In it Mary used a number of Indian words indicating that she had at least a speaking acquaintance with the Spokane Tribe's tongue. As a person who knew Latin and Greek and translated articles from German, Dr. Latham obviously had an ear for sounds and picked up languages easily.

As well as writing for newspapers, Dr. Mary also wrote for magazines and was rapidly earning a reputation as a writer of fiction. At least one novel, *A Witch's Wreath*, came from her talented pen. One reader described it as having been written in the author's usual forcible style, decidedly realistic, and predicted it would be a masterpiece of fiction.[3]

Those words could also be used to sum up Dr. Latham's approach to life. There was nothing "wishy-washy" about her. With characteristic enthusiasm, she espoused many worthwhile causes in the community. The July 28, 1889, issue of the *Spokane Falls Review* honored her, along with the Baptist minister May C. Jones, as good and noble women of Spokane Falls. Part of the article read: "Dr. Latham's record as a lady and Christian, doing good deeds is incomparable. The smiles that lit up the sad faces as I passed with her through the Sisters' Hospital [Sacred Heart] told more plainly than words can tell that she was a frequent and welcome visitor. Mrs. Latham is an earnest worker in home mission fields and never gives up on a good cause."

Dr. Edward H. Latham, 1901. *(Photo courtesy Washington State University)*

Into this climate of respect, recognition and a prosperous practice, Mary's husband finally arrived in Spokane Falls at the end of July 1889, and announced he would purchase a home and locate here.[4] From time to time, while Dr. Edward Latham had been winding up his affairs in Cincinnati, items had appeared in the newspaper about his expected arrival.

The Lathams' entrance into the medical field had been somewhat unusual. Mary and Edward were married July 28, 1864, when she was not quite 20 years old and he was 21. To them were born three sons: Frank A. in 1866, James A. in 1870, and Warren A. in 1872. When the boys were still young, Edward enrolled at the Cincinnati School of Pharmacy, graduating in 1882. He then went on to earn a degree in medicine two years later from the Miami Medical College, also in Ohio.

Next, Mary entered the Cincinnati College of Medicine and Surgery, no small task for a woman with three children and a home to care for. While she was a student, the Cincinnati General Hospital permitted women to practice in its clinical wards for the first time. Mary Archard Latham graduated in 1886 at the age of 42.[5]

Mary was born in the fall of 1844, in New Richmond, Ohio, to James and Jane W. Archard, and was a granddaughter of an early settler of Ohio. There were at least three other girls in the family: Jennie, Laura and Louisa. Mary received her primary education in the district schools and at Clermont Academy.

Chapter VIII

Edward Latham, born in Columbus, Ohio, in April 1843, was the sixth of seven children. His father, Bela Latham, was a postmaster for a number of years and a bank director. Bela died when Edward was quite young, and an uncle, Allen Latham of Kentucky, became his official guardian. Nothing more is known of Edward's early years. Eventually, he and Mary Archard met and were married.

Together the Drs. Latham began the practice of medicine in Cincinnati. There probably were not many husband-wife teams in the medical profession at that time. It took an extraordinary amount of determination, courage, energy and fortitude, which Mary exhibited in abundance. But it also required a husband who was sympathetic, understanding and supportive.

Although Mary had lived in the Ohio River Valley all her life, it became apparent that a healthier climate was necessary. The couple chose Spokane Falls in Washington Territory, perhaps because one of Mary's sisters already lived there – hence, the advertisements in the newspaper.

At the time of Edward's arrival, Mary and the boys were residing at South 508½ Howard Street between First and Railroad Avenue. Frank was a druggist, James worked for Holley, Mason & Marks as a plumber, and Warren was a plumber's assistant for the Falls City Plumbing & Heating Company.

Mary now had offices in the recently opened Frankfurt Block, a four-story brick building on the southwest corner of Howard and Main. This central location was one of the best. Among the forty-four tenants were Gardner and Fred Chamberlin[6] who dealt in real estate; Blake and Ridpath, lawyers; Herman Preusse, architect; Spokane City Water Works office, Rolla A. Jones, superintendent; and the offices for Goetz and Baer, proprietors of the Coeur d'Alene Theatre. Numbers 24 and 25 down the hall were occupied by the real estate firm of H. M. Williams and Mrs. Alice Houghton. No other building had a more prestigious group of tenants.

Five days after Dr. Edward Latham's belated move to Spokane Falls, the central business district was destroyed in the fiery holocaust of August 4, 1889. Both Mary's office and the family's apartment were total losses, which were not covered by insurance. Immediately after the fire, Edward and Mary opened a dispensary at the rear of the former Louis Ziegler home on the southeast corner of Stevens and Sprague.[7] Mary shared the burden of caring for the burned-out townspeople by offering, through an advertisement in the newspaper, to treat free of charge any fire victim who was unable to pay for medical services.

By the first of October, the Lathams found a residence on Havermale Island but still practiced out of the office and dispensary at Stevens and Sprague. When the Blalock Block was completed to the west across Stevens, they moved their office and residence there.

During the first year Edward was in Spokane, it became apparent he was not going to gain the same spontaneous prominence Mary had been accorded. He worked some at his profession, kept busy with his photographic hobby and, unfortunately, drank rather heavily.[8] In January 1891, Edward was accepted for the position of resident physician with the Colville Indian Reservation in Nespelem at a salary of $1,200 a year.[9] Over one hundred miles from Spokane, the agency provided housing only for a single man. Dr. Edward Latham became the first permanent white doctor to live and work on the reservation.

Consequently, Edward departed for a frontier-style existence in a harsh and semiarid land. Certainly, his life on the reservation would be the extreme opposite of what it had been socially and professionally in Cincinnati. Back in Spokane, Mary's reputation continued to rise.

In 1891, Mary became involved with a group of doctors adhering to the biochemic system of medicine. It was based on the theory that "any disturbance in the molecular motion of the basic cell-salts in living tissue constitutes disease, the cure of which consists in restoring the proper balance in the cell-salts by administering small doses of the same mineral salts in molecular form."[10] They did not believe in the germ or microbe theory, and instead claimed that disease was caused by a lack of some component in the blood.[11]

Dr. Mary Latham, as a person who professed a philosophy of progress in medicine, found in the biochemic system the type of new idea that sparked an interest in her.[12] As a result, Dr. Latham joined forces with the Biochemic College after its incorporation the next month in Spokane. With a capital stock of $10,000, its stated purpose was to accept students for the study of medicine.[13]

Located in Dr. George W. Carey's offices at #23 and #24 in the Tull Building, the college staff consisted of Carey as dean and teacher of biochemistry and cellular pathology; the physicians: Mary A. Latham, obstetrics; Charles Rodolf, anatomy and histology; Will Wood, physiology; Miss Nina Wood, materia medica[14] and therapeutics. Carey's wife, Lucy, taught hygiene. Amazingly, there were three instructors by correspondence: Dr. Joseph B. Chapman of Seattle, materia medica and therapeutics; Dr. William Chapman of Columbus, Washington (now Maryhill), diseases of women and children; and M. Doutti Walker, M.D. of Dundee, Scotland, theory and general practice of biochemistry.[15] As early as 1890, a branch office of the Washington Biochemic Medical College of North Yakima appeared in the *Spokane City Directory* with Carey's office location.

A closer look at the biochemic school personnel reveals that Charles C. Rodolf first appeared in Spokane in 1887 as a lawyer with W. W. D. Turner and George M. Forster, then as a bookkeeper, a life insurance broker, and accountant, and finally in 1892 as a biochemic physician and editor of the *Northwest Journal of Biochemistry* with the Tissue Remedy Company. Will Wood had been a carpenter two years previously.

George W. Carey showed up in Spokane about 1890 as a physician. However, his medical education was self-taught, having read under Dr. Odell and Dr. E. Y. Chase of Oregon. Taking exception to many of the theories of the regular school of medicine, Carey was wide open to accept Schussler's "Theory of Therapeutics." Convinced that this point of view was valid, Carey was determined to establish a college where the principles of biochemistry could be taught correctly. He was even issued a diploma to put his college on a working basis.

Before becoming a paper physician, Carey worked as an associate editor for the Yakima *Signal*. After moving to Spokane, he erected a sign on the corner of the picket fence around his home on Augusta near Ash, announcing it to be the residence of "Doctor Carey." That did not satisfy the State of Washington, as he was arrested in August 1891 for practicing without a license. The following June, Rodolf received a similar charge.[16]

The qualifications, or lack thereof, of Mary's associates probably did not bother her. She was intensely loyal to her friends and, at times, had her own personal concepts of right and wrong. For the two or three years the medical school existed, no known records survive to tell how many students attended Carey's college or whether or not any diplomas were issued. By 1895, Carey and Rodolf had left town.

Among the community projects Dr. Mary espoused was the need for a public library. There had been various endeavors in the 1880s to establish a permanent library, generally through private clubs or labor unions, but none had survived. Following the successful Industrial Exposition the year after the 1889 fire, which established Spokane as a well and functioning city again, Mary felt attention could once more be focused on the next important matter – that of good literature. In a letter to the editor of the *Review,* she called for a subscription program to get the library going. As a starter she offered a complete set, nicely bound, of the *Encyclopedia Britannica*. In 1891, two separate libraries – one started by the Sorosis Club and the other by local labor unions, whose reading rooms were for members only – joined forces. Mary was one of the library's greatest benefactors and was elected to the board of directors as a representative of the business patrons. In 1894, it became the Spokane City Library, a municipal tax-supported institution (now the Spokane Public Library). It was located in the new City Hall at Front and Howard streets, the old site of the California House.[17]

In addition to the library, and her tireless work on behalf of children and the poor and helpless, Mary befriended animals. She recognized the need for and actively supported a Humane Society and served as its secretary and treasurer.

From the time of Dr. Latham's arrival in Spokane, she very wisely invested in real estate. One of her holdings, along with her son James, was more than a quarter-section near the town site of Mead. As horticulture was another facet of Mary's diversified interests, she purchased the following from the Mix Nursery in Moscow, Idaho: 2,000 apple trees, 1,000 pear trees, 200 cherry trees, 2,000 prune trees, 4,000 grape vines, 5,000 blackberry and 10,000 raspberry vines – a rather ambitious orchard. Mary agreed to pay ten-percent interest semi-annually on the cost of $6,000. Her task was to prepare the land, plant, care for the trees and bushes, and replace any dead ones for the years 1893 and 1894. She hired J. M. Boyd to work on the orchard.

At the end of the century, a horticulture society was organized for the purpose of discussing the various methods of protecting fruit and trees from invasion by insects. Dr. Latham served as the group's first vice-president.[18]

A physician's demanding profession leaves few spare hours. Somehow Mary managed to donate her time as well as her verbal patronage to any cause she considered important. In addition, there were three grown sons at home needing a mother's love. She did not spare herself, and wasted no time in strictly social or recreational pursuits.

Surely no woman received greater praise than that written about Mary Archard Latham in the *Spokane Spokesman's* "Illustrated Annual Supplement," January 1, 1892. Part of a biographical sketch read:

> In nearly every community there is one who is a mediator between wretchedness and wealth, a person whom the affluent respect and the needy love, a person who preserves the ray of summer to dispel the gloom of winter, one who condemns wrong, but pities the wrong-doer, one who has sentiment without sentimentalism, shrewdness without cynicism, dignity without haughtiness, one whose heart pities the suffering, but does not confine that pity to an imaginary field of action, one who believes in human nature, whose nature has not been soured by disappointments, who is too liberal to heartily espouse a creed or sect or religion, who conciliates all doctrines in universal good will to all – such a character is Dr. Mary A. Latham. Probably no woman in all Washington has so many friends as she. Many of the poor into whose lives she has thrown sunshine regard her as their patron saint.

Dr. Mary A. Latham, Isabella Club delegate from Washington State to the Columbian Exposition in Chicago, 1893. *(Photo from* History of Washington, *American Publishing Co., 1893)*

A fellow practitioner said of her: "I believe that Mrs. Latham's career, brilliant as it has been in this city, is only in its beginning, for with her indomitable energy she will go on until the highest success is hers."[19] Prophetic as these words were intended, Mary was closer to the peak than anyone realized.

One more plum came her way. Mary received the appointment as chairman of the Queen Isabella Association for the World's Columbian Exposition to be held in Chicago in 1893. The Isabellas, made up primarily of doctors and lawyers, supported women's suffrage, and stood for equal rights and for competition with men on an equal basis. There was an out-and-out power struggle between this independent association and the government-sponsored Board of Lady Managers, to which Alice Ide Houghton belonged. The Board of Lady Managers preferred to demonstrate the philanthropic accomplishments of women and their handiwork, and were interested in general reform rather than equal rights. They lobbied for a separate woman's department at the fair in Chicago. The Isabellas rejected a separate board for women and felt they should be members of the general fair board with the men. In the end, the Woman's Department was established as a separate pavilion at the fair, and the Isabellas constructed their building two blocks from the entrance to the fairgrounds.

There is no indication this conflict carried over to Spokane, but it would indicate that Dr. Latham was known as advocating women's rights, including the franchise. Other than collecting money for the statue of Queen Isabella and the erection of a clubhouse at the fair, no other duties seem to have been associated with this assignment. Nevertheless, the appointments of Dr. Mary A. Latham and Mrs. Alice I. Houghton illustrate their recognition as prominent women in the state of Washington.

There was one attribute Mary lacked – financial acumen. As strong willed as she was, she probably would not have listened to or followed advice anyway. Her world began to fall apart in 1895. Mix Nursery and S. J. Genoway brought suit against Mary, Edward and an H. Warner for $2,800 still owed on the trees purchased from them plus $600 in damages. At the trial in May, Mary retorted that the trees given to them to plant had been inferior, diseased and imperfect. Nevertheless, Judge Moore awarded Genoway and the four Mix brothers (as Mix Nursery) a judgment of $1,279.80 plus eight-percent interest per annum. However, Mary was back in court on July 7 with an injunction to stop a sheriff's sale of some of her property to satisfy the Genoway-Mix settlement. In response, Genoway filed an attachment on three lots Mary owned in the Lidgerwood Park Addition.[20] In addition, J. M. Boyd sued Mary for $3,300 in back pay for the work he had done in connection with the orchard a year and a half earlier.[21] At the June 10th trial, Boyd received a writ of garnishment against Mary.

In July, Mary and Edward sparred before Judge Jesse Arthur. In suing Mary for divorce, Edward contended she had intentionally and without cause deserted and abandoned him about 1888 and ever since had continued to live separately and apart from him. Although Mary denied the charges, Edward received a divorce July 18, 1895. Represented by attorney Daniel W. Henley, Mary asked for alimony. She was granted $300 to be paid in installments of $50 twice a year. Neither ever remarried.

About 1893, Mary had moved her family from downtown to 1122 East Gordon. Her plans for a women's hospital finally materialized. Located a block away at 1024 East Gordon, the Lidgerwood Sanitarium opened in late 1896 or early 1897. Mary also made her residence at the hospital. It seems to have had a short life, as it was not listed in the 1899 *Spokane City Directory*, although Mary's office and home remained at that location. The next year she reopened a downtown office in the Hyde Building. Both Warren and Frank married during the 1890s, leaving only James still living at home.

During this time, another lawsuit faced Mary and Edward over property they had previously owned west of Spokane. As one of the parties who had at one time or another held title, they were accused of not having paid any funds toward interest or principal. At the trial on June 8, 1897, the judge awarded the plaintiff, North American Loan & Trust, $595.30 plus $150 in attorney fees from all the defendants.

One would expect that Mary would have learned something about making more careful investments and having an empathy with her creditors. Such was not the case. She was described as being "liberal-minded." Quite literally, she was a classic example of "one marked by generosity and open-handedness who was not bound by authoritarianism, or strict in the observance of traditional ways." More and more, Mary fit this category as the new century progressed. She subscribed to series of books, but never paid for them and was sued by the publishers.[22] Other legal entanglements ensued.

Then tragedy struck on April 20, 1903; Mary's son James was killed instantly by a Northern Pacific train at Division and Railroad Avenue. For the preceding two years, James had worked as a brakeman for the N.P. This blow sent Mary reeling. Already in questionable physical health, she also began suffering from mental problems; psychologically, she was never the same again. Mary seemed to have had a closer relationship with James than with the other two boys.

As a result of non-payment for one of her book subscriptions, a default was filed September 28, 1903, and Mary was ordered to pay the $20.25. In order to satisfy this debt, the court ordered the sheriff to sell Mary's orchard property and the three lots in the Lidgerwood Park Addition. After advertising in the *Daily Chronicle* five times between March 10 and April 7, 1904, the sheriff sold the property to the Lyon Slater Company for $47.25 – the amount owed them plus court costs.[23] While this was going on, another miniscule suit appeared against Mary. One Edgar A. Sherwood was awarded $35.90 against her.[24]

Less than a week later, Mary received another summons to court. Earlier in the year, Mary had employed Paul Mueller, a carpenter, to work on a one-story frame house, a barn, cow shed and wagon shed on a quarter-section north of her orchard. Mueller worked six weeks and claimed Mary owed him $104.85. She retorted that thirty cents an hour was adequate and forty-five cents an hour was not a reasonable amount for the work done.

Mary then filed a countersuit listing the following charges that Mueller owed her for the following: treatment of his wife, $50.00; renting them a room, $1.00 per month; providing wood, $2.00; medicine, $5.00; hiring a team of horses, $5.00; hiring a horse, $2.00; carpets loaned, $3.00; meals for his wife, $2.50; a loan to Mueller, $20.00 in gold coin. The total was $90.50. In Mary's opinion, it was a standoff. Not so, declared the court. Mueller received $117.70, plus $26.40 costs. Since Mary could not or would not come up with the cash, a lien was placed against her property, and it was to be sold.[25]

Apparently Mary finally recognized her costly mistakes, but her method of dealing with them was a bit unorthodox. She began putting her property in the name of a third party in order to keep it out of the hands of her creditors. As might be expected, the scheme backfired.

Jennie H. Johnson had entered Mary's life around 1898 when she had appeared at Mary's office, pregnant, with nowhere to go. As was typical of Dr. Latham, she took Jennie home where her child was born. The infant lived only two weeks. In the years since, Jennie had apparently become involved with Mary's son James, and they had become engaged. After James's death, she had moved to Butte, Montana.

As James's death had left her devastatingly lonely, Mary invited Jennie to Spokane, claiming Jennie was all Mary had left. Mary's health had always been precarious, and she promised Jennie that in exchange for taking care of her, Jennie would receive all the property James and Mary had. Jennie jumped at the chance, arriving March 25, 1904. The same day, Mary purchased a store in Mead about three blocks from her home, where she then lived. She transferred the store to Jennie "in trust" and for temporary purposes only. Purportedly, Jennie gave Mary a power of attorney to sell the property or do whatever she wished with it. Mary told people the business belonged to Jennie. It was an act Dr. Latham would come to regret.

Earlier, in the summer of 1898, Mary had temporarily deeded all her property to her son James while she traveled to the Yukon. When she returned from the Yukon, she forgot or delayed having James return her property to her. James died without a will, and Mary suddenly faced the real possibility that Edward, from whom she was divorced, would receive half the property she had bought and paid for. Thinking to protect herself, Mary drew up a deed, signed James's name, and dated it prior to his death. In it Mary gave the properties "in trust" to James G. Scribner, a miner she possibly met in the Yukon. Scribner in turn supposedly gave her two powers of attorney to handle the property in whatever way she deemed best.

Jennie proved to be no "dummy." After working at the Mead Mercantile, a combination grocery, dry goods and drug store for a couple months, Jennie sold the property. When she learned the title had been transferred to Scribner, Jennie went to court to question the validity of that warranty deed. At stake were the titles to fourteen lots and five hundred acres of land near Mead that Jennie said James left to her as his fiancee. Furthermore, Jennie claimed Mary was concealing the will in an effort to defraud her rights. Jennie vigorously denied giving Mary a power of attorney.

The trial over the Mead property began August 10, 1904. Although Mary denied the existence of a will by her son James, which Jennie insisted she had, Judge Henry L. Kennan directed Dr. Latham to produce her son's will or show cause why she should not be held in contempt of court. Mary produced what she called "will forms," obvious forgeries written is Mary's flowery style, stating James bequeathed his assets to a Jennie C. Johnson, not Jennie H. Johnson.

The big question became: who was Jennie C. Johnson? Dr. Latham proceeded to explain she was a married woman, separated from her husband, who came to Mary in the spring of 1902. She remained with Mary until her child was born. Mrs. Johnson was considering a divorce. As a friendship developed between the two women, James also became rather fond of Mrs. Johnson. She had been making her living traveling around the country selling household rubber products. This was the Jennie Johnson to whom James intended to leave his estate, but he died before he could execute a will.

According to Dr. Latham's story, Mrs. Johnson changed her mind about a divorce and returned to Salt Lake City to her husband and children. Dr. Latham described her as being a member of the Swedish nobility who spurned the $15,000 involved. In fact, she did not even know about the property and was now someplace in Europe. Attorneys for Jennie H. Johnson challenged this glorified tale after Mary Burmoid, a domestic for five years in the home of Dr. Latham, claimed that the only Jennie Johnson who had ever lived there was Jennie H. Johnson.

Upon the insistence of Judge Kennan that she search her home more diligently for her son's will, Mary brought more made-up wills to court. Some detailed possessions; others did not. She did acknowledge having some papers at the Exchange National Bank. Court was dismissed for half a day to allow Mary to go to the bank. She found no will. Finally, nine days into the trial, the judge rescinded his order for Dr. Latham to produce the will.

Mary explained to the court that she had deeded the store property to Scribner under the power of attorney she held from Jennie in order to protect herself from being defrauded by Jennie. Then she wrote to Scribner asking him to re-deed the property to her and enclosed a check for $1,500 – unsigned.

Attention turned to the powers of attorney Mary claimed to have. Both Jennie and Scribner went to the auditor's office to examine the records. Both denied executing the papers on file. They subsequently filed articles revoking any such power of attorney to see if she could be prosecuted for forgery. As Mary expressed it: "to see what kind of a jackpot I have got myself into."[26]

The sad truth of the matter was that Mary simply could not understand how Jennie or Scribner had any claim to property she had bought and paid for. They had not invested one cent. It seemed proper and reasonable to her to use the law for her own purpose, such as avoiding attachments for debts, but at the same time to ignore it when it suited her to do so.

She claimed that Scribner had assumed there would be a marriage between them. When he realized there would not, he turned on her "with the fury of any angry childish woman to help this woman [Jennie] do me up."[27]

The *Spokesman-Review* found that Dr. Latham provided good copy and gave the trial front-page coverage. The judge took the case under advisement until April 3, 1905. The court came to the conclusion that Jennie was the rightful owner, and the defendant unlawfully and wrongfully withheld possession of the real estate. A judgment of $1.00 was to be paid to Jennie plus court costs. On April 29, Judge Kennan overruled a motion for a new trial.

Early on Sunday morning, May 7, the building that housed the Mead Mercantile went up in flames. Dr. Latham was charged with arson. Her immediate reaction was to send two letters to the *Spokesman-Review*. She had her housekeeper, Nellie Stansbury, copy one of them, signing it with the fictitious name of Mrs. A. R. Smith. In essence, the letter was to provide an alibi stating that Dr. Latham had always stood high in the community and was home in bed the night of the fire. "Jealous enemies are trying to make trouble for her," said the writer. Mary signed the second letter, proclaiming her innocence and stating she had not been in the store for two hours before the fire broke out. She also denied that anything had been removed from the store prior to the fire. The *Spokesman-Review* printed the letters on May 10, although no one at the newspaper recalled who had delivered them.

As usual, Dr. Mary confronted the controversy before consulting anyone. Her strong sense of self-preservation was automatic. Whenever there was a problem, she followed the same course: indignant denial, then fabrication of stories to extricate herself.

Two days before the trial was to begin, Mary's attorneys, Daniel W. Henley and Alphonso G. Kellam, asked for a two-week postponement, claiming the defense's key witness was ill. Dr. J. L. Smith, a physician in Colbert, signed an affidavit that George Messner, Mary's next door neighbor and son of Dr. John Messner, a veterinarian who shared an office with her, was suffering from a severe attack of gastritis and nervous prostration. A trip to Spokane for any reason would jeopardize his life. However, when Spokane County Sheriff Howard B. Doak went to Mary's house, he saw Messner through the glass in the front door sitting in the living room. By the time the sheriff was admitted, Messner was upstairs in bed. Postponement of the trial was not granted.

On June 10, 1905, twelve men were chosen for the jury. Monday morning, June 12, the trial began in Superior Court with Judge Miles Poindexter presiding.

The State's most damaging witness against Mary was Melville Logan, a young fellow who took care of Mary's horses. On the night of the fire, Logan had gone to a dance about a mile north of Mead. He returned home around 2:00 a.m., the same time as Mrs. Stansbury and Charlie Harding. While he was unhitching the team, Harding rode up and asked Logan for a half-pint of whiskey. Seeing a light at the store, which was unusual at that hour, Logan crossed the road. He found Dr. Latham in the store fully dressed, including a hat. Giving Logan the whiskey, Mary asked him to return to move some drug bottles belonging to Dr. Messner. Dr. Latham explained that she and Messner had had a disagreement and decided on separate offices.

Logan made two trips carrying drug bottles to the barn, after which he took the horses behind the barn to water them. Before he could remove their harness, he heard the roar of flames. When questioned by the prosecuting attorney, Richard M. Barnhart, according to *Spokesman-Review* on June 14, 1905, Logan responded as follows:

> "Was anybody in sight when you looked out and saw the store afire?" asked Mr. Barnhart.
> "Yes."
> "Who?"
> "Dr. Latham."
> "What was she doing?"
> "She was standing near the side door of the store watching the fire."
> "Did she make any outcry?"
> "None at all."[28]

Logan then told how he ran two blocks to awaken O. H. Winkler, who had property in the barn, as he was afraid the barn would burn, too. When he returned, Mary had crossed the street and was watching the fire from there. Logan suggested alerting Mr. Cushing who had a nearby store, but Mary replied, "Let him sleep."

Later in the day, Logan found a number of items from the store in a former blacksmith shop run by George Messner. There stood the furniture from Messner's and Latham's office; the soda fountain including the tables, chairs and pictures Dr. Messner had in the store; and George Messner's barber shop equipment that had been on the second floor of the store on Saturday. The blacksmith shop had been cleaned just a few days before the fire.

Logan also testified how he and Dr. Messner had packed Dr. Latham's books into boxes and barrels on Friday night preceding the fire. He then drove with Dr. Messner to Frank Tibbetts's place to rent the building where they moved the books on Saturday. Although Messner told Logan the books belonged to him, they contained only Dr. Latham's name in them.

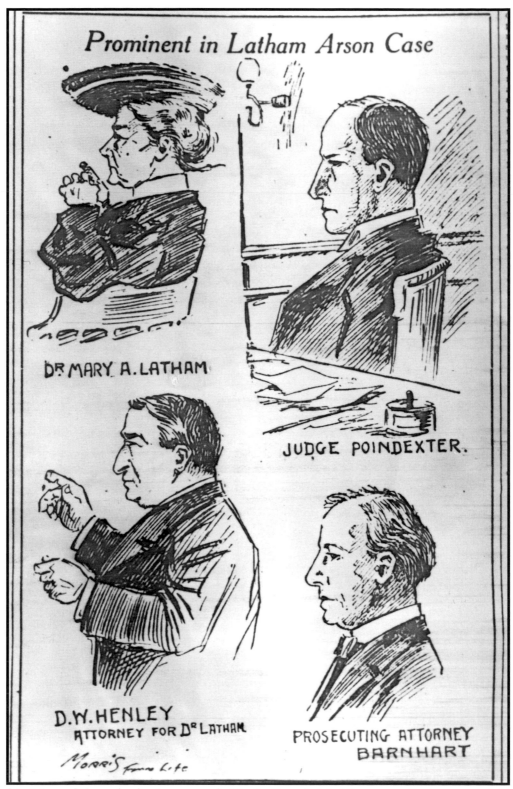

Sketches of the principal persons in Dr. Latham's trial for arson that appeared in the *Spokesman-Review* on June 14, 1905.

Sensational evidence came from Mrs. Sadie Riley of Green Bluff. The previous November, Mary was playing cards at Mrs. Riley's home. In response to a question about the property litigation, Mary commented that if Jennie Johnson won, it would not do her any good. She would never live in the store. "She'd have to get up pretty early to beat Mrs. Latham," retorted Mary.[29]

Henley tried to discredit Mrs. Riley's remarks by questions about her previous employment by Dr. Latham. Mrs. Riley denied that she and her husband had been fired. They had left because Mary was so far behind in Mr. Riley's wages that they had to go. She also denied they wanted Mary to pay them in advance, or that she was giving this testimony to get even with Mary for discharging them.

Some letters were introduced as further evidence to substantiate the contention Mary burned the building out of spite. These letters, in which she expressed her feelings about Jennie, had been written to J. S. Scribner while the ownership of the store was in question. By the time that litigation began, Jennie had moved into Spokane, so she was not living in Mead at the time of the fire.

When Dr. John Messner took the stand, he described his first meeting with Mary a year earlier. His friend J. W. Prall brought Dr. Latham to set his broken leg. The next month, at Prall's request, Messner began to operate a veterinary business at Mary's store. Prall also suggested Mary sell Messner an interest in her store, as he knew something about drugs, but Messner was not interested in the store. Messner boarded at Mary's, and his son George lived next door. In addition to Mrs. Stansbury, the housekeeper, Clarence Binkley, a laborer, also lived in the Latham home. There was a kitchen attached to the rear of the store where they all ate lunch and dinner. Breakfast was served at the house.

Upon being questioned about the books he and Logan moved, Dr. Messner claimed he had a bill of sale for them dated April 7. No money changed hands, as Mary applied the $150 purchase price to what she owed him. Although Messner shared an office with Mrs. Latham in a small building connected to the store, he paid no rent. Supposedly, he supervised the work at her orchard and ran Mary's livery stable.

Ten days before the fire, Messner accompanied Mary to her attorney's to discuss a transfer of the goods in the store to settle some debts. At that time, Henley advised Messner to move his personal belongings from the store to avoid any confusion during litigation. However, Messner did not know that an assignment of the merchandise had actually been made to Edward C. Gove until Mary returned from Spokane about 6:00 p.m. on Saturday, May 6. William J. Niedermeyer, a real estate broker and notary, later confirmed the transaction had taken place that day, though he did not remember to whom the assignment was made.

Upon learning of this assignment, Messner, his son George, Mr. Winkler and several other men immediately started moving his things out of the building. The reason he gave to his helpers was that he and Mary had had a falling out. The men worked until nearly midnight, after which Messner drove to the home of Mrs. Annette Franzen on Peone Prairie, arriving about 1:30 a.m. Although his calling on Mrs. Franzen was supposedly by previous arrangement, her tenant, Mr. Rouse, was the one who awakened to answer the door. Mrs. Franzen was asleep and acted surprised at Dr. Messner's calling so late. The next day Messner drove Mrs. Franzen to Spokane to find a dentist as she had a toothache. He seemed to be in no hurry to get to town, as it took him four hours to drive the twelve miles.

Mary Latham was called to the witness stand. She reiterated that Gove was coming Sunday morning to get the stock in her store. Upon arriving back in Mead Saturday evening, she had gone into the kitchen to wash some dishes before moving them. She had built a fire in the stove that stood close to the wall adjoining the main storeroom. She claimed she went home at midnight, meeting George Messner, who had also been working late. The two of them walked home together. She said she knew nothing of the fire until George awakened her. However, it was Mrs. Stansbury who responded to George's pounding on the dining room door, yelling that "the town was burning up."

A long parade of witnesses appeared for both the prosecution and the defense. Prior to the start of the trial, George Messner had been charged with perjury and was held in the county jail. Twice Mary's attorney tried to see him. At first the sheriff refused, and later he said there had to be a jailer or deputy present. Mr. Henley finally resorted to a court order to see his key witness in private.

By four o'clock Saturday, June 17, both cases had been presented. Over the objections of both attorneys, Judge Poindexter called for their closing arguments. Following the judge's instructions, the jurors retired at 10:30 p.m. They reached a verdict at 1:00 a.m.

Court reconvened Sunday morning. The jury found Dr. Mary A. Latham guilty of arson based on circumstantial evidence, but recommended leniency because of her age of 60 years and her sex. After the trial, Mary collapsed. As the sheriff hesitated taking her to jail in her physical condition, she was permitted to go to the home of friends, the J. W. Poseys, under the care of a nurse.

On June 20, Dr. D. C. Newman examined Mary and diagnosed her as having had a stroke. He filed an affidavit in court stating she was in a very nervous state and could possibly have a second one. She needed absolute rest and quiet and could not safely be moved for several days. The court sent Dr. George A. Gray for a second opinion, who reported he did not think Mary's health would be threatened by jail until bond was posted. Nevertheless, Dr. Latham remained at the Posey residence at 412 South Hogan.

On June 27, Dr. John Messner was also charged with arson. Annette Franzen posted the $500 cash bond for his release.

Two days later, Warren and Carrie Latham, and Louisa Kellogg (possibly Mary's sister) put up the $2,500 for Mary's bond. Perhaps this encouraged Dr. Latham to leave the confines of the Posey residence. That evening she walked out at 9:30 to go to town to meet James. All day she had talked about her son's coming. Alarmed at not being able to prevent her departure, the Poseys alerted the police. On the ride to town, Mary talked to herself and cried. When she descended from the streetcar at Howard and Riverside, Officer George Miles met her. This thwarting of her deluded mission precipitated a scene on the street corner. Miles managed to get her to the police station where she broke down completely, weeping and wailing. They returned her to the Posey home by taxi. The *Spokesman-Review* headlined the story the next morning:

Dr. Mary A. Latham
Creates a scene
Woman convicted of arson
Appears to be crazy

It was believed her mind had been shattered by recent events. (Ironically, Dr. Latham's testimony only six years earlier had helped send Susan Glover to the hospital at Medical Lake as being mentally unstable.)

On July 1, a three-column headline screamed on the front page of the *Chronicle* that Dr. Mary A. Latham was starving to death. In the two weeks since the trial, she had eaten only half a box of strawberries. She was getting progressively weaker. Her attorney requested the case be continued until she could come to court. Dr. Newman expressed the opinion Mary would never be able to appear if she continued in her present condition. Other than her unexpected journey to town two evenings earlier, she had not left her bed and refused all nourishment. Judge Poindexter continued the case for a week.

Mary had convinced herself that if she remained ill and unable to appear in court, the judge would never be able to pass sentence. She allegedly tried to take drugs to make herself sick. Fortunately, her friends were aware of the situation and prevented her from damaging her health further with drugs. Although Mary supposedly required complete rest and quiet, Dr. Messner, Mrs. Franzen and Warren visited her frequently.

Finally, on July 20, Judge Poindexter sent doctors Gray and W. F. Morrison to the Posey home to examine Mary. Following their report, a bench warrant was issued for Dr. Latham to attend court. She arrived in an ambulance and was carried into the courtroom on a cot by four sheriff's deputies. As the news of the sentencing had been kept quiet, the courtroom was empty of spectators. It was a pathetic scene. Mary lay on the cot with her head buried in her arm. She spoke only twice: to answer her attorney and, raising herself on her elbow, to ask for her son James.

The defense filed a motion for a new trial, claiming the State erred in permitting the decision on the property litigation to be entered as evidence. Furthermore, they felt the State went to extremes in cross-examining the witnesses, prejudicing the jury. The evidence was completely circumstantial.

"If ever a conviction was secured in a court of justice through malice, prejudice, hatred and perjured testimony, this is the one," argued D. W. Henley. He pointed out that Mrs. Latham had a large feeling for humanity and had performed many kind and graceful acts. "The day has never been so disagreeable, the night so dark or the patient so poor that the defendant has remained away when her services were required." Henley concluded by pleading for leniency.[30]

Judge Poindexter overruled the motion for a new trial. "This is one of the most aggravated cases which ever came under my observation," said the judge. "The defiant attitude of the defendant during the trial and her false testimony on the witness stand certainly do not recommend leniency to the court. I am convinced from the evidence that she is guilty." Judge Poindexter thereupon sentenced Mary to four years of hard labor at the women's prison at the Washington State Penitentiary in Walla Walla, fined her $1,000 plus court costs of $586.40. She returned to the Posey home.

When a reporter from the *Spokesman-Review* interviewed Mary at the Posey home, she maintained her innocence. The building belonged to her. There was no insurance on it, so she felt she had a right to burn it if she wanted to.

A new visitor showed up at Mary's bedside: John W. Prall, in the company of Messner and Mrs. Franzen. Prall told Mary that if a sufficient sum of money were raised, it could buy her time and freedom. Money could do anything. He and Messner could pay off Prosecuting Attorney Barnhart for a thousand dollars, another thousand to Judge Poindexter, less to the other county officials, and fifteen hundred dollars on the bond. Prall graciously offered to take only a hundred dollars for his services. Terrified of going to prison, Mary was ready to clutch at any straw. Once the prosecuting attorney was satisfied and the bond forfeited, Prall continued, she did not need to be more than a hundred miles from Spokane. After four or five years, she could return and resume her practice of medicine if she wished.

No problem. This sort of thing was done every day. The clincher was Prall's claim to be a secret service agent who could go anywhere, have access to any records, and knew what the grand jury was going to do. There was also the little matter of the death of Mrs. O. H. Winkler of Mead, the wife of Prall's hired man whom Mary had treated. Although Prall said he knew Dr. Latham was not guilty, in light of the recent case, he told her the prejudice against her would send her to prison for life for manslaughter. He said she could never get out of it – not even for a million dollars. It was really simple. All Mary had to do was turn over her ownership of 360 acres of land adjoining Mead to Prall, who would then mortgage it to raise the needed cash.

What a scenario. But, Mary believed him! The next day Messner informed her that Prall needed an additional thousand dollars to distribute among the sheriff, deputies and bailiffs. In Mary's confused mind, she thought that as long as she was putting up her own money she might as well take their advice and get out of town. She was perfectly willing to have Prall settle with the officials. He assured her the statutes of limitation on the manslaughter and arson charges would run out in five years, at which time she could safely return.

Mary left the Poseys on Saturday night, July 22, bound for Mead and lying in the bottom of a wagon driven by William A. Glasson, who had worked for her on her farm. Sunday night about 10:00 p.m., Dr. Messner and Mrs. Franzen drove Mary to Rathdrum. Upon learning his mother had left the Poseys, Warren went to Mead, where he found Prall and his wife ensconced in Mary's home. Prall claimed he held a mortgage on the farm and Mary's personal possessions. When Warren asked to see the papers and offered to pay it off, Prall refused to show him the mortgage or to tell Warren where his mother had gone.

It is possible that Warren, fearing for his mother's safety, reported her missing. Forfeiture of her bond had not been requested out of sympathy for Warren, who was considered to be an exemplary young man. In all decency, he could not have refused to put up his mother's security.

By Tuesday morning, the hunt was on for a woman driving a horse and buggy alone in northern Idaho. At one time, the sheriff's office announced they were only two hours behind her. On Wednesday, July 26, Dr. Latham was reported to have been at the Schroeder ranch about forty miles north of Rathdrum. Spokane County Sheriff Doak was searching the road he thought she had followed. However, he also ordered an observer at Fourth of July Canyon.

One report on July 29 said that pursuit of Dr. Latham had been abandoned. Another claimed she had been located. Although it was speculated that Mary had either made it to Canada by train, was being harbored by friends somewhere in the wilderness of Idaho or, most commonly believed, that she had taken her own life, she was captured on Sunday night, July 30. Deputy Sheriffs McDonald and Merritt of Kootenai County arrested Mary while she was eating dinner at the house of a bachelor named Moseley about four miles from the Schroeder place. For five days Mary had been wandering on foot in the heavily timbered country. She had abandoned her buggy when her horse got loose and ran off. For a few days, her dog had been her sole companion, until she left him at a farmhouse. Saturday morning, she had again appeared at the Schroeders, who found her in their kitchen fixing breakfast. They notified the local sheriff. Sheriff Doak was alerted and left on the train for Rathdrum Saturday night.

After spending the night at Moseley's, Mary and the Kootenai County deputies headed for Rathdrum by wagon, meeting Doak on the way. Mary was reputed to have said, "Here's a familiar face." They arrived in Spokane on the midnight train early Tuesday morning August 1, whereupon Mary finally saw the inside of the Spokane County jail. Bail was increased to $10,000.

During her absence, on July 28 attorneys Henley and Kellam filed suit against Dr. Latham for $1,180 plus costs for fees owed them for the past two years. She had given them a promissory note for $900, of which $400 was now due. In addition, they filed a writ of garnishment against E. M. Heyburn, believed to have some of Mary's personal property or effects in his control. When apprised that her attorneys were suing her for legal services, Mary retorted: "Yes, isn't that terrible? Those people had five cases for me, and lost every one of them. I don't see why they want to sue me."[31]

Denying that she had tried to escape, Mary claimed she had been camping with friends from Cincinnati, Mr. and Mrs. W. A. Bushnell. They had wired her to meet them in Rathdrum. According to her story, with their large camping wagon and Mary's buggy, they camped for a week at a place northeast of Spirit Lake, Idaho. She did not know the officers were looking for her until Sunday, but by that time she was on her way back to Spokane. The Bushnells left on Saturday, and Mary said she would have returned earlier except her horse ran away. The sheriff completely disregarded Mary's story, as she had been seen at three different farmhouses during the week with no evidence of any companions.

On August 2, in an interview with a reporter from the *Chronicle*, Mary said she was just too tired and sick to think. However, without hesitation, she managed to diagnose her problem, as follows:

> If I could have remained up there and had perfect peace of mind, I might have rallied, but I know I never will get well here [in jail]. I have not been up and have not eaten nor drank [*sic*] anything since I have been here. My trouble is only a recurrence of the trouble which I had after the trial, and in medical terms we call it shock. In a way it is a cyclone of force on the nerves, and the nerves collapse. Under favorable condition this strain can be overcome, but often a patient so affected never regains the normal condition.

This statement completely negated her earlier comment that she was on her way back to Spokane when arrested.

Legal actions against Dr. Latham continued. On August 5, she was sued by the Spokane Drug Company for $83.26 owed them for drugs and supplies purchased over the past two years. Four days later, although Dr. Latham and her attorneys had arrived at an agreement resulting in the withdrawal of her suit, Jennie Johnson initiated action to recover the value of the store, which she placed at $1,450. The judge decided neither party could recover damages against the other. He dismissed Jennie's suit as having been fully settled. The land was now in Jennie's possession and the title in her name.

Was it worth it? It would be difficult to justify that it was. The recordings in the title books resemble yo-yos, as Mary's Mead property bounced back and forth monthly, sometimes daily, during 1904 and 1905.

In the fall of 1905, Messner, Prall and Mrs. Franzen were charged with trying to defraud Mary out of a mortgage security. On October 20, when Mary arrived in court from jail accompanied by Warren, she was in good health and spirits. Her testimony was marked by wit and humor. She told how Prall asked her for $3,600 to bribe the county officials, advising her to get out of town and let him and Messner settle her legal affairs. But when her tenant, W. A. Glasson, refused to sign the mortgage for her ranch over to Prall, a new plan had to be devised. Their plan, according to Mary, was for her to cross the Rocky Mountains, float down the Missouri River in a houseboat, and escape to freedom in Mexico. Mary's desire for escape was so strong that she had deluded herself into believing wishful thinking was reality.

E. H. Sullivan, counsel for the defense, tried to infer that a jilted romance with Dr. Messner led Mary to turn conspirator and implicate the defendants. According to his account, when she found out there would be no marriage because Messner loved Mrs. Franzen, she took revenge by "squealing" on her friends and inventing the fraud charge. After all, Sullivan proclaimed, the gentlemen were only trying to help her, at Mary's insistence, get beyond the reach of the law.

Taking the witness stand, Prall assured the court his only motive was to help a friend. He was going to use the money to pay her attorneys, other incidental expenses, and for a cash bond so Mary would be permitted to go somewhere quiet where she could rest. Furthermore, as a good friend, Prall had offered to look after Mary's property while she was in prison. If she would deed the property to him, he could subdivide it into forty or less acre sections and sell it. After paying any indebtedness and expenses, he would make an even division of the profits between Dr. Latham and himself.

On October 30, Superior Court Judge D. C. Carey found the defendants guilty of conspiracy to defraud. He sentenced J. W. Prall to a year in jail plus a fine of $500. Dr. Messner received a six-month jail term and a similar fine. Charges against Mrs. Franzen were dismissed.

Mary entered the women's prison at Walla Walla on January 9, 1906. However, on the first of April the following year, she was paroled. Her health was so poor she was not expected to live. She was not officially discharged until February 4, 1908.[32]

Upon arriving back in Spokane, Mary again denied being guilty of the offense for which she had served time. Neither had she asked for a pardon. "Any attempts to secure such action were made by my friends, and I had nothing to do with it."[33] She resumed the practice of medicine in the Van Valkenburg Block. She made her home at 724 West Spofford.

Mary filed a complaint against John and Sarah Prall for $655.30. Between January and June 1905, Mary had sold them merchandise worth nearly $500. They also owed her $57.60 for medical services. While she was in prison, Mary had left $100 worth of surgical instruments in their care, which they had used and refused to return. Judge Kennan suggested both parties come in and talk about the case without cost to either. (There seems to be no record as to the disposition of Mary's charges.)

While Mary was in prison, Warren Latham left Spokane for four years. It is possible that during this period he ran a Christian home for men in Ames, Iowa. Frank was in Tacoma in 1900, but returned to Spokane for short periods. After 1916, his name no longer appeared in the *City Directory*. He did not seem to be as close to his mother as Warren, who was always there when she needed him. In the last few years of Mary's life, Warren and Carrie, who had no children, lived next door.

During the 1930s, Warren had a sheet metal shop on North Washington Street. He hired non-union men to make galvanized iron duct work in case he needed it. Although he could not pay them very much, he provided room and board. The unions were not happy about the situation. Warren was a very religious person, but in a non-formal sense. He disliked any control over his affairs from the government, labor unions, or anyone else. In this respect he was very much like his mother.[34]

On February 9, 1911, Mary was arrested again – this time for performing a criminal operation, i.e., an abortion. A seventeen-year-old "delinquent" girl confessed that Dr. Latham had operated on her the previous November. It is easy to understand how Mary's sympathies could persuade her to try to help a young woman in whatever way she could. Bond of $1,500 was posted. This was not the first time Mary had been charged with an illegal surgery. Shortly after her release from prison three years earlier, she had been arrested, though the charge was later dismissed. At that time she commented, "Life has nothing for me except trouble and I look for nothing else."[35]

This new complaint hung over Mary's head until November when the prosecuting attorney recommended the charges be dropped. After reviewing the evidence, he felt it possible a conviction could not be had. Instead he convinced Mary to retire permanently. He described her as being aged, in broken health, and a woman whose mental condition was very much impaired. This time she kept her word.

In January 1917, one last act of kindness led to Dr. Latham's death. She consented to care for a twelve-day-old infant who was suffering from pneumonia. Unfortunately, Dr. Latham contracted pneumonia from the baby. She was taken to Sacred Heart Hospital, where she passed away on January 20, 1917, at the age of 72. She was survived by her sons Warren and Frank; one grandchild, Frank's son, Edward Chester Latham; her ex-husband, Edward Latham; three of her sisters and a niece.

The following anonymous quote may well have applied to Mary Archard Latham's life:

> What is human life without some purpose or end which may be attained by industry, order and exercise of moderate abilities? Great abilities are rare and often accompanied by qualities which make the abilities useless to him who has them and even injurious to society.[36]

EPILOGUE

Dr. Edward Latham gained recognition as a photographer. A feature article in the *Oregon Sunday Journal* in 1904 stated: "Dr. Latham … has without a doubt the finest collection of Indian photographs in the Northwest."[37] It was Latham who made the oft-quoted remark that Chief Joseph died of a broken heart. Dr. Latham's photographs have become increasingly important in documenting the reservation period for Northwest Indians. For that reason Edward Latham has been noted as being historically noteworthy.[38] When Mary was enjoying immense popularity in Spokane, Edward buried himself in a remote region. When he did receive acknowledgement for his work, it was Mary's blackest hour.

Edward seemed to have licked his drinking habits. In January 1905, he wrote to the Indian agent: "Captain I have reformed and am strictly on the Water Wagon. I am giving these fellows all good advice and offering myself as the terrible example."[39]

Unfortunately, being a reservation physician did not mean Edward was a top-notch doctor. Captain Webster, the Indian agent for the Colville Reservation, in his staff efficiency report of 1909, commented that Latham was out-of-date, had not kept up with his profession, had vegetated and hibernated at Nespelem for eighteen years. Although he was kind and charitable, he was too old and indolent to be efficient. Webster gave him a classification of "fair."[40] At this time Edward was 65 years old. Nevertheless, after retiring from Nespelem in 1910, he accepted another reservation assignment, going to Inchelium in February 1911. For the next eight years, he was the government doctor for the southern half of the Colville Reservation.

Edward passed away May 21, 1928, at Lakeside, Chelan County. His photographs were disbursed. Some he had given to Professor Edmond S. Meany a quarter of a century earlier; others were sent to the Indian Agent, Albert M. Anderson. A number of his pictures have been credited to Edward S. Curtis as well as to T. W. Tolman. One of Dr. Latham's Lakeside neighbors was a professional photographer, Lawrence D. Lindsley, who acquired a lot of the doctor's glass negatives. Some of these were printed under Lindsley's copyright. The two largest collections of Latham's work can be found in the University of Washington Photographic Collections and the research library at the Eastern Washington State Historical Society (Northwest Museum of Arts and Culture).

Edward and Mary are buried side-by-side in Greenwood Memorial Terrace, Spokane. Their headstone simply reads: "Edward H. Latham and Mary his wife." On April 4, 2007, a monument honoring Dr. Mary Latham as Spokane's first female doctor was dedicated near their grave sites. The monument was erected and dedicated by the Fairmount Memorial Association in cooperation with the Spokane Police Department History Book Committee and the Spokane Law Enforcement Museum. The inscription on the monument summarizes her life and professional career and includes the following:

> The final years of Mary's life were undeserving for such a kind and caring woman. Mary and her husband divorced in 1899 and, in 1903, her son James, a brakeman for the Northern

Pacific Railroad, was killed when struck by a train at Division Street and Railroad Avenue. From that time on she suffered severe bouts of depression and dementia...

... neither Mary nor Edward remarried and are buried side by side at Greenwood Cemetery. Although Mary's accomplishments in Spokane outshone Edward's and she had created a name for herself as a professional woman during a time when few women had careers outside the home, the original headstone reads: "Edward H. Latham and Mary his wife."

This photograph was taken at the dedication of the monument honoring Dr. Mary Archard Latham at Spokane's Greenwood Memorial Terrace on April 4, 2007. Shown here are individuals who were involved in the creation of the monument through either Fairmount Memorial Association, the Spokane Police Department History Book Committee or the Spokane Law Enforcement Museum (from left): Kathy Panas, Carl Ellis, Duane Broyles, Dave Clark, Coleen Prescott, Jack Pearson, Dave Prescott, Rae Anna Victor, Susan Walker, Tim Hattenburg, Emily Sue Pike, John McGregor, Glen Whiteley, Suzanne Bamonte and Tony Bamonte. *(Photo courtesy Emily Sue Pike)*

Chapter IX

Rebuilding After Spokane's Great Fire

The Crescent Block immediately after the fire. The Crescent Store, which took its name from the building, was due to open for its first day of business on August 5, 1889. As the only retail dry goods store to survive Spokane's Great Fire of August 4, it was automatically guaranteed success. To the credit of its owners, prices were not raised to take undue advantage of the disaster. Banks, mortgage offices and insurance companies were responsible for the majority of the temporary business signs on the building, as shown above. *(Photo courtesy SPLNWR)*

In his diary following the Great Fire of Sunday, August 4, 1889, John A. Meyers, a night miller for the Centennial Mill, wrote: "It has been very smoky through the ruins for days. The heat has been intense and sultry all week."[1] By Monday morning, the city was under martial law with soldiers holding bayonets at the street corners and guarding the vaults in the shells of burned banks. All unburned saloons were closed, and no curiosity seekers were allowed into the burned area. Those who had legitimate business were issued passes. Only by counting the streets could one tell what locality one was in.

Instead of shaking their heads in dismay, men shook hands over the ashes and vowed to build Spokane up "bigger than she ever was before."[2] Demolition work started immediately. Debris was used to fill the gulch from west of the

After the fire, business commenced in tents until they were banned in 1890. This photograph is looking east along First Avenue. *(Photo courtesy SPLNWR)*

C&C Flour Mill southeast toward Riverside and Howard, and dumped in the river between small islands. Banks opened up in the Crescent Block, distinguished from each other only by hastily painted signs on a piece of paper or on a cloth. Diagonally northeast, on the corner of Lincoln and Riverside, the O.K. Livery Stables were used for offices.

Within a week, Spokane Falls became a tent city, like a battlefield. The *Chronicle*, insurance companies, real estate firms, the telegraph company, and tobacco shops were among those conducting business in the large tents sent from Portland, Fort Walla Walla and Fort Sherman. Especially visible were the dozen or more gambling tents, the largest being Dutch Jake's beer garden on the north side of Riverside between Post and Lincoln. Operated by "Dutch Jake" Goetz and Harry Baer, the saloon eventually reached Main Street to the north with additional tents and covered an area 50 by 150 feet.

Dutch Jake's saloon, 1889, stretched from Riverside to Main. Note the gulch beneath the bridge and part of the tent saloon. *(E. E. Bertrand photo courtesy MAC/EWSHS, L93-66.278)*

Telephone and telegraph offices shortly after the fire. The piled wire was probably used to replace burned lines. The same building also served as the Electric Light facility. *(Photo from the Elsom Collection, courtesy MAC/EWSHS, L94-36.337)*

The carpenters and brick layers went to work with hammer, saw and trowel as Sherwood, Cannon, Browne, Glover, Blalock, Bennett and many others rebuilt. Six of these new buildings were on their original sites and retained the same name as their predecessor. Eleven buildings rose to six stories, while the Daniels and Frankfurt (and eventually the Review Building in 1891) reached seven. These massive buildings, framed of wood but with bearing walls of granite and brick, faced Riverside Avenue, demoting Howard to a side street. Five hundred new buildings were begun after the fire, and it took twenty columns in the newspaper to list all of them. Had they been placed in a row, they would have stretched nearly a mile and a half. As many would later regret, it was all accomplished on borrowed money.

Fire Station No. 1 at 418 West First Avenue, built after the 1889 fire, became the department's headquarters. It was abandoned as a fire station in 1938 but is still standing today. *(Photo from* Spokane Police and Fire Departments Illustrated, *1902, by the Spokane Police and Fire Department Pension Board)*

After the 1889 fire, it became clearly evident that a volunteer fire department was no longer sufficient to protect the growing city, and a permanent department was established with paid personnel. Both fire stations on the south side of the river had been destroyed in the fire. Fire Station No. 1 was soon built and was ready for occupancy by December 1889. It became the fire department's headquarters.

Construction also resumed as quickly as possible on the three streetcar lines that had begun before the fire. Although a great number of people lived in the upper stories of the downtown commercial buildings, developers of new additions needed to entice potential property buyers with public transportation. Few people had their own horse and carriage. Streetcar lines, both electric and cable, soon reached out in every direction to areas slated for development. These were profitable ventures and competition became fierce. To attract riders, parks were often developed along the streetcar lines. Natatorium Park was the most popular of the destination parks and entertained crowds of visitors for three-quarters of a century, though it ceased to be a trolley park in 1929.

J. D. Sherwood, F. Rockwood Moore, Herbert Bolster, Henry Brook and other large shareholders in Washington Water Power, who were already involved with the development of the power plants along the river, planned to utilize that source of energy for their people-mover. With others, they organized the Spokane Cable Railway Company in May 1888. From the initial southern terminus at the Northern Pacific tracks on Monroe Street, the cable cars were to run north to Boone Avenue, then west to the company-owned Twickenham Addition in the general area of where Fort Wright would be built several years later.

A bridge over the Spokane River at the west end of Boone Avenue ran diagonally northwest. It was a high wooden double-deck structure with a narrow, single-track road on top for the cable car and a wider, planked wagon road underneath. With its center section visibly lower than the two ends, it gave the appearance of a roller coaster. The cable line used the bridge for less than a year,

The cable car bridge across the Spokane River headed west into the Twickenham Addition. Note the wagon road below it. *(Source of photo unknown)*

and Twickenham (later Natatorium) Park became the western terminus. The upper deck approaches to the bridge had been removed a long time before the bridge washed out in the flood of 1894. It was never rebuilt.

The route on the south side followed Monroe Street to the Northern Pacific tracks. There it was necessary for any passengers wishing to continue to walk two blocks across the tracks to get to the southbound cable car to the Cable Addition, where homes designed by architect Kirtland Cutter were being sold. The cable car climbed Monroe Street to Fourteenth Avenue, then east to Division Street. A major obstacle facing the cable company was the need for a bridge at Monroe Street to connect the line from Twickenham to the South Hill.

Looking northeast over the first Monroe Street Bridge, which opened in 1889.
(Photo from Spokane and the Inland Empire *by N. W. Durham, 1912)*

To build the bridge at Monroe Street, which was designed to also accommodate wagon and pedestrian traffic, the cable company coerced the city into putting $15,000 into a joint venture. The company contributed $12,500, with the adjacent property owners responsible for another $15,000. Although the cable line opening was announced on September 1, 1889, it was a little optimistic. Problems plagued construction, delaying the opening of the bridge and start of the cable cars. On September 7, 1889, there was a landslide on the south bank caused by dumping large volumes of ash and other debris from the recent conflagration. In addition, placement of the center span across the turbulent river was hazardous and required a great deal of caution. The formal opening of the $200,000 road occurred three weeks after the prematurely announced opening.

The bridge was a narrow, spindly-looking trestle structure, built largely of wood reinforced by some steel rods. It, as well as the cable railway, was fraught with difficulties from the beginning. The city did not believe the bridge to be safe

An 1890 sketch of an elegant streetcar on the Ross Park Railway, the first electric line in Spokane Falls. *(From the* Northwest Illustrated Magazine*)*

and refused to pay its share of the cost. Further settling of the south bank in February justified their delay, and the city engineers declared it unsafe. After the needed repairs were completed, city officials approved the bridge on May 1, 1890, and paid their debt, only to have the bridge burn down 84 days later. It would be two years before it was replaced by one of steel construction.

After the bridge burned, the Spokane Cable Company had to resort to horse-drawn cars to cross the river via the Post Street Bridge. By using the Spokane Street Railway tracks, they could connect to their southbound cable line. Due to financial difficulties, this portion of the line was suspended altogether in 1894. The north-side route had long since been converted to a standard-gauge electric line and had been largely absorbed into the Spokane Street Railway (many of whose shareholders owned stock in the cable company).

Ross Park Railway streetcar. *(Photo from the Jerome Peltier Collection, courtesy Tony and Suzanne Bamonte)*

The "Cadillac" of all the systems was the highly touted Ross Park Street Railway, Spokane's first electric line. By July 1889, power poles had been installed

View of the Ross Park electric railway crossing the Dennis and Bradley's Addition. The line crossed the Spokane River about a hundred yards upstream from the present Trent (formerly Olive) Avenue Bridge before turning north on Hamilton Street and east on Illinois Avenue. *(Sketch from the April 1890 issue of the* Northwest Magazine*)*

in the center of Main Street. At a hundred feet apart and thirty feet high, the neatly painted poles had gilded cross brackets to support the trolley lines between double tracks. The cars, built by the Pullman Company, contained red plush seats running the length of each car. At the center of one side stood a small coke-burning stove to provide comfortable heat in winter. Courtesy was stressed, and every lady was offered assistance in entering or departing the cars.

Quickly dubbed the "gold plate" line because of the gilt balls on top of the center poles, this first electric line was incorporated principally by G. B. Dennis and Cyrus Bradley, along with eight or nine other prominent Spokane men. From Post Street, the route ran east on Main to Bernard. There it went one block north before continuing east on Front (later Trent Avenue and now Spokane Falls Boulevard). It passed south of what would be the location of the Schade Brewery (built in 1903) and crossed its own wooden bridge running west-east into the Dennis and Bradley's Addition. (After the bridge washed out in 1894 and the city built a new one on Olive, now Trent, the line was rerouted to pass in front the Schade Brewery location.) The electric line traveled north on Hamilton, passing its car barns at Desmet Avenue, to Illinois Avenue. Following the curve of Illinois, it bisected the Ross Park Addition, ending about Regal Street.

The old Ross Park Railway car barn was later purchased by McGoldrick Lumber Company and became part of its operation. Photo dated 1923. *(Libby Studio photo courtesy Jim McGoldrick)*

Nearly five thousand people rode the line on opening day, November 16, 1889. The winter that year was particularly snowy. At one time, as many as two hundred men were employed to shovel the snow day and night in order to keep the line open.

In January 1890, it was reported that Spokane Falls had almost seventeen miles of public transportation. An addition of twenty-five more miles was anticipated by the middle of summer, some of which was provided by a second electric line, the City Park Transit Company, which opened that year. Seven miles of double track were laid along Sprague Avenue from Monroe, then north on Division to the Lidgerwood Park area.

The *Electrical World*, a weekly publication printed in New York, carried an article on the electric railways in Spokane Falls in their issue of May 10, 1890. In conclusion it stated: "This is one of the very few successful attempts to supply electric energy from water power, and our neighbors in the Northwest are to be congratulated upon having accomplished that in the trial of which so many have failed." The estimated cost of power to run the electric streetcars was three dollars a day. The savings was apparently enough to entice the Spokane Street Railway, with its horse-drawn system, and Cook's stream-powered line to begin converting to electricity. Within a few years, all of the lines were running on electricity.

As the streetcar system rapidly expanded, the existing lines became embroiled in numerous lawsuits and court cases over joint use of various streets or bridges, which often required the police or other city officials to intervene. In addition, City Hall and the mainline railroads were often contentious forces. The city objected to the streets being perpetually torn up (partly due to replacement of original track with that suitable for electric lines), and the railroads, with safety and scheduling concerns, did not want the streetcars crossing at grade.

Having become the leader in water-power production along the Spokane River, the Washington Water Power Company had a decided advantage when it began to compete in the streetcar business. It systematically began absorbing beleaguered streetcar lines. By the end of the century, as a full-service utility company with nearly no competition, it had developed a temporary monopoly. Cook's Spokane & Montrose was the only early streetcar line that remained independent of Washington Water Power. In 1902, Jay Graves acquired the line, which he reorganized the following year as the Spokane Traction Company. Its rapid development and expansion soon provided Washington Water Power with a major competitor.

There was plenty of other activity after the fire. The spring of 1890 found civic pride greater than ever. It provided substance to the prediction made by State

The 1890 Industrial Exposition Building, located between Sheridan and Hatch on the north side of Sprague Avenue. The building measured approximately 380 by 220 feet. *(Photo from Mark Danner's Patsy Clark Album, courtesy Tony and Suzanne Bamonte)*

Senator H. E. Houghton three days after the fire. The *Review* used his comments as an editorial. In part, Houghton stated:

> The forthcoming year will be the most prosperous ever witnessed in Spokane Falls.... This will make all classes of business good and so stimulate growth in the city.... Leaving us in possession of one of the finest cities in the west with abundant resources to support it.... The general activity that will ensue, the prosperity of all classes of business will bring here thousands of new men who will add to the capital to be invested, thus insuring an era of wonderful growth in the city.

To prove that Spokane Falls was alive and well, the citizenry planned an Industrial Exposition. The city council aided in beautifying the city by calling for all tents to be removed within the fire limits by the first of August. L. C. Dillman donated land between Sprague and Riverside, six blocks east of Division for the exposition building. C. B. Seaton was hired as the architect while F. Lewis Clark served as president of the fair. Charles W. Robinson was employed as manager. Many prominent men served on the executive committee: A. A. Newbery, A. M. Cannon, Jay P. Graves, Cyrus R. Burns, F. Rockwood Moore. Among the directors were: J. N. Glover, J. J. Browne, H. O. Tilton, H. N. Belt, John R. Reavis, H. L. Wilson, E. J. Brickell, and W. H. Lynch.

In spite of a carpenters' strike in September, the fair opened on October 1 and ran until November 3. Opening day, with an estimated attendance of 12,000, featured a parade and a number of speeches. F. Lewis Clark delivered the welcoming address, while Mayor C. F. Clough contributed some appropriate remarks. W. H. Calkins was the orator of the day. The 150-member chorus from the Spokane Musical Society provided some musical selections. The Fourth Infantry Band and the band from the Second Regiment of the National Guard rendered patriotic tunes. Seated on the platform were the outstanding men of the community, but missing were any women. Lane C. Gilliam acted as the floor manager for the brilliant ball held that evening.

October 28 was Ladies' Day, at which time the ladies voted for the married man and the single man deemed the most popular. A. M. Cannon won with 920 votes, and F. Lewis Clark was named the favorite of the single gentlemen. Deciding to have the same contest for the ladies, the men gave Mrs. Horace Cutter only fifty-one more votes than Mrs. Alice Houghton. Mrs. Jennie Cannon was the third choice for the most popular married woman. Single ladies judged the favorites were Fanny Watson, Josephine Clarke and Idell Houghton.[3]

Declaring the fair a huge success, the city bought the building for $75,000 with the intention of making the exposition an annual event. Unfortunately, the wooden building burned September 10, 1893. The arson fire took only one-half hour to consume the structure, which had not been insured.

Growth and expansion was also seen in the addition of new schools. The six-room frame Central School, on the present Lewis & Clark High School site, was moved in 1890 to Fifth and Washington to make room for a separate high

Spokane High School, renamed South Central after North Central High School opened in 1908. *(Photo from the Don Neraas Collection, courtesy Tony and Suzanne Bamonte)*

school building. Erected in 1883 as a two-story, four-room grammar school, two more rooms were added to the building in 1885 for a high school. Seven students comprised the first public graduating class in May 1891. This building was later moved farther east and was used for the Sacred Heart Parish School. Spokane High School opened September 1891,[4] as did Emerson and Lakeview (Whittier). The Spokane Kindergarten Association, founded March 21, 1894, had a specific goal: to establish free kindergartens as part of the public school system. Along with a similar association in Seattle, they succeeded in getting a law passed through the legislature. In the fall of 1898, two kindergartens opened in Spokane, the first free ones in the state. By 1900, Spokane would have one high school, sixteen grade schools and nine kindergartens in operation.

After nine years, it was decided to revise the city charter. In a special election on September 27, 1890, fifteen prominent men were elected to draw up the charter.

Looking west along Riverside Avenue from Washington Street in 1890. The number of five- and six-story buildings in this photo illustrate how quickly Spokane rebuilt after the Great Fire of 1889. *(Photo courtesy SPLNWR)*

It passed by a majority vote of the people on March 25, 1891, and was signed by Mayor C. F. Clough on April 1, 1891, one of his last mayoral acts before the newly elected mayor took office. The new charter, under the guiding hand of Judge Houghton, provided for five wards with three representatives from each. The city boundaries were extended to twenty square miles, and "Falls" was dropped from the city's name.[5] The post office made the change official a month later. The dividing lines for numbering the city streets were changed from Howard to Division for east-west locations on both sides of the river, and to Sprague Avenue instead of the river as the north-south designation.

In June 1891, Mayor David B. Fotheringham ordered the closing of saloons and variety theatres on Sundays. Harry Baer, coproprietor of the Coeur d'Alene Theatre, responded with the terse comment: "If they want to kill the town, they are going at it just right."[6] Nevertheless, the Coeur d'Alene complied. However, Baer's partner, Dutch Jake, installed an automatic beer dispenser on the sidewalk outside their emporium. Costing $10,000, the machine stood five feet high and three feet wide. A sign beside it read: "Today is Sunday, please do not put a nickel in the slot. The mayor and law forbids it." Men queued up to spend their nickels. Water washed the glass and beer followed. The next morning, $500 was found in the lobby. Although the machine was used only once because of a malfunction, Goetz took it to Chicago's Columbian Exposition in 1893.[7]

Chapter IX

As 1893 dawned, another prosperous year was anticipated. Spokane had established itself as the trading and railroad center of the Inland Northwest, with branch lines radiating in every direction. In the preceding twelve months, the railroads had hauled over 506 million pounds of freight into Spokane. One million dollars had been spent on new buildings, the Echo Mills had been rebuilt after its destruction by fire in 1892, and A. M. Cannon had almost finished the new Marble Bank building. But as the year progressed, a severe depression descended upon the United States, aptly dubbed the "Panic of 1893."

Spokane was hit hard. Businesses closed. Banks were over-extended. Of the ten banks in town, seven closed their doors permanently. The first to go was A. M. Cannon's Bank of Spokane Falls on June 5, 1893. Twenty-four hours later, the Washington National and the Washington Savings, both of which Cannon had an interest in, suspended payments. Then the Citizens National shut its doors. On July 26, Glover's First National became insolvent. The Browne National Bank lasted until November 22, 1894. Glover sacrificed his personal fortune to pay back his depositors. Browne managed to liquidate nearly all the deposits and subsequently was able to pay off all his obligations. The three early developers of Spokane – Glover, Browne and Cannon – were bankrupt. They had lost everything. Of the three, only Browne eventually recovered his fortune. By the end of 1895, only the Exchange National, the Old National, Spokane & Eastern Trust Company, and Traders National survived as strong banks.

As business fell off, tenants could not pay their rents, and building owners were unable to meet their mortgage payments. Extensive foreclosures occurred during 1893-1896. Following the 1889 fire, in their exuberance to rebuild the city, many property owners who lost their homes or businesses to the fire became excessively mortgaged. The Northwestern and Pacific Hypotheekbank (the Dutch word *hypotheek* is translated "mortgage"), which had been chartered two months before the fire, held the majority of these mortgages. It charged its borrowers eight to ten percent interest, of which five percent was paid to its Dutch investors. When Isaac C. Jolles arrived from Holland in 1896 to evaluate the Dutch-owned Hypotheekbank holdings, he reported to stockholders:

> I have never seen a small town ... which offers such an overwhelming impression of monumental buildings.... Its people were too extravagant during its early development and many over-reached themselves to force its development when they should have been cautious and allowed natural growth to occur.[8]

Northwestern and Pacific Hypotheekbank ended up owning twenty-five percent of the central part of the city. It held over millions of dollars worth of buildings, commercial sites and thousands of acres of farm land for which there were no buyers. Many private homes had also been heavily mortgaged to the Hypotheekbank.

Spokane City Hall and the annex (at the far left) for the police and fire departments, designed by architect Willis A. Ritchie, was completed in 1894 and demolished in 1913 to make way for the Union Station. *(Photo courtesy SPLNWR)*

In spite of the depression, some construction continued in Spokane. A new city hall rose on the site of the California House. Begun in 1892, the city hall suffered a setback when a fire on September 13, 1893, demolished the main structure. When completed, the main building housed the city offices, Spokane City Library, Chamber of Commerce, and the municipal court. An attached annex on the north side of the building (facing Howard) became the city's largest fire station and the police headquarters. The fire station was located in the larger section and the police station was sandwiched between it and the main building.

As early as December 1891, the county commissioners were calling for plans for a new courthouse. Civil War veteran Colonel David P. Jenkins had already donated land on West Broadway and given $1,000 toward its construction. A contest held for the best design was won by Spokane architect Willis A. Ritchie who had just designed the city hall, as well as other courthouses in the state.

Work began in October 1893 under contractor David B. Fotheringham, former Spokane mayor (1891-1892), and finished in November 1895. This construction project provided a stimulant for Spokane's faltering economy. As the building was not fully occupied when it was completed, some of the employees lived there. It was said the smell of cabbage cooking permeated the hallways.[9]

Spokane County Courthouse, located on West Broadway, shortly after its completion in 1895. Willis A. Ritchie was the architect and David B. Fotheringham the contractor. This photograph was taken before there were any sidewalks, paved roads or landscaping around the courthouse. *(Photo courtesy SPLNWR)*

To add to the gloom of the depression, flooding in the spring of 1894 washed out three of Spokane's bridges. However, by fall, some encouraging news reached the townspeople and created a flurry of excitement. The United States announced the possibility of building another military post in the Northwest. The proposal required a thousand acres of suitable land with a free water source and other financial obligations. But in return, it would mean an expenditure of approximately half a million dollars for construction, plus the men stationed at the fort would be drawing steady paychecks. Spokane's economy needed that fort. Arthur A. Newbery was sent to Washington, D.C., to lobby for it.

Forty thousand dollars had to be raised locally, of which $15,000 was to be in cash and the balance in land. Donations raised $4,500, a concert sponsored by the ladies brought in $1,200, and 565 acres of land worth $10,000 had been donated. Just when it seemed as if any further source of funding had dried up, the women stepped in with a major capital campaign. The idea of a "Fort Christmas Tree" was proposed. Some have credited Alice Houghton with the suggestion. Whether or not it was her idea, she certainly was one of the first promoters. Donations ranged from a mince pie to a 25¢ harmonica to a $125 shotgun. There were curling irons, rheumatism medicine, dental work, paint, pickles, plumbing work, a gold watch, ladies' hats, a bicycle and even a colt. People gave what they could. Tags listing the gifts were hung on a Christmas tree in the Auditorium Theatre. Admission tickets to the party, which had been postponed until December 31, 1894, and chances on the presents sold for a dollar.

It turned out to be a hilarious event. F. Lewis Clark drew a turkey, Herbert Bolster got a pair of eyeglasses, George Adams drew the harmonica, and Burgess L. Gordon's three-year-old son won the fifteen-dollar Kodak camera. The tree raised $4,500, enough to ensure the fort would be built in Spokane. The impact on the economy was not immediate, as the first federal appropriations were still a year and a half away, but more importantly, it served to break the reticence of the townspeople. For the first time, strangers and acquaintances had worked together as a community toward a common goal. Fort George Wright was commissioned in 1899.

Slowly the economy improved. Investors in Spokane began receiving dividends from the mines in British Columbia and Idaho's Coeur d'Alenes. The North Idaho mines were producing tons of silver-lead concentrates per month, and in the area around Republic, Washington, about one hundred claims had been located. In addition, a new type of gold was being harvested in northern Idaho – the coveted white pine. As the timber stands were being exhausted on the East

This aerial photo provides a perspective of Fort Wright at the top and Natatorium Park at the bottom, separated by the Spokane River. *(Photo from the Wallace Gamble Collection, courtesy Tony and Suzanne Bamonte)*

The Phoenix Sawmill, located at what is now Wall Street and Spokane Falls Boulevard, was built on the site of S. R. Scranton and J. J. Downing's sawmill, Spokane's first commercial business, which they operated from 1871 until James Glover bought them out in 1873. Seven successive sawmills operated on this site until 1944. The Phoenix mill was the longest running, from 1898 to 1927. The last sawmill at this site was the Long Lake Lumber Company, 1927 to 1944. *(Photo from the Jerome Peltier Collection, courtesy Tony and Suzanne Bamonte)*

Coast, capitalists in the timber industry began looking to the Northwest, which contained huge stands of virgin white pine and other valuable species. The new riches meant innumerable changes in Spokane.

With this fresh income, men began buying up real estate from the Northwestern and Pacific Hypotheekbank at depressed prices. The mortgage company had fallen on difficult times; as was the case with those who earlier were the subjects of foreclosures, the company had expenses on the properties it held with no related income. It declared bankruptcy on March 30, 1898. Some who took advantage of the opportunity to purchase real estate from Hypotheek were: F. Lewis Clark, Charles Sweeny, D. C. Corbin, Patrick Welch, Aaron Kuhn, James Comstock, Robert Paterson, James Monaghan and David Ham. As Spokane author John Fahey has pointed out, the Panic did what the fire had not. It closed out the pioneer builders, and turned over their ground to a new group of men, largely speculators and developers, who would influence Spokane for the next thirty years.[10] With Sweeny's purchase in 1904 of the Rookery, Riverside, and Spokane National Bank buildings, the Hypotheekbank's ownership of the central business district came to an end.

Looking northeast from about Front Avenue (Spokane Falls Blvd.) and Post Street, circa 1896. Milling flour was an important component of Spokane's economy during this time. The numbered structures are: (1) the first C&C Flour Mill, (2) second C&C Spokane Flour Mill (today the Flour Mill contains shops and restaurants, including the popular Clinkerdaggers), (3) Frederick Post's flour mill, (4) brick addition to the Centennial Mill, (5) Centennial Mill, (6) Howard Street Bridge, (7) Falls View Hotel, and (8) the former Frederick Post house. (City Hall now occupies the site of numbers 7 and 8.) *(Photo courtesy SPLNWR)*

Looking north over the second Monroe Street Bridge in 1895. Note the partial fill in the gulch to the right of the bridge and the livery stables on the present site of the Spokane Public Library. *(Photo courtesy SPLNWR)*

Riverside Avenue looking east from Stevens Street around 1895. The Oregon Railway and Navigation's ticket office was in the corner building at the left and Kemp & Hebert's department store was in the Green Building just east. The Tull (also known as the Marion) Block on the far right was later replaced by the Paulsen Building. The Granite Block, just east of the Tull Block, was on the site of the present Paulsen Medical and Dental Building. The piles along the edges of the street of horse manure and mud from street cleaning, much of which was done by prisoners, were a familiar sight. *(Photo from Mark Danner's Patsy Clark Album, courtesy Tony and Suzanne Bamonte)*

With the advent of more spending, Spokane's "Barbary Coast" became more wide open than ever before. There were the Theatre Comique, the London, the O.K., the Louvre, People's and, of course, the Coeur d'Alene – all designed to gather in the easy money from the area's miners who were in town, or anyone else who patronized their establishments.

The Comique, located in the second building west of Mill (Wall) on the north side of Main, claimed to have the best band, which was very important in attracting business. Each evening before the show began, the band gave a concert in front of the theatre playing popular tunes of the day. How easily one could be enticed to listen to "Sidewalks of New York," "After the Ball," "Two Little Girls in Blue," "A Bird in a Gilded Cage," and "Maggie Murphy's Home." Inside, a glass of beer cost only a nickel and included a free lunch plus a great show. However, once inside, a single glass of beer was never enough, and these entrepreneurs knew it.

The activities of the gambling houses did not go unrecognized by the general population. Reform movements were continually underway. In 1895, the Washington State Legislature passed an act "to prohibit the employment of females in places where intoxicating liquors were sold as a beverage." In Spokane, that law was largely ignored.

The same year the city council passed an ordinance outlawing the variety theatres, but the mayor vetoed it. It is possible the council knew this would happen, and the bill was an attempt to save face with their law-abiding constituents. Ministers called upon the mayor to close down the box-rustling theatres. "Box rustlers" referred to attractively costumed young women who greeted the male patrons and escorted them to the screened boxes around the theatre from which they could watch the performance. Their job was to persuade the customers to order champagne, beer and whiskey at double or triple the price at the bar. (What rankled the patrons was the practice of selling cheap whiskey for as much as the traffic would bear.)[11]

Eventually the variety theatres became so bold that they staged a parade down Riverside Avenue at four o'clock in the afternoon during good weather. First came the uniformed band followed by the male performers of the current shows. Behind them in smart carriages with well-groomed horses rode the "painted la-

This band, shown circa 1900, was employed by Jacob "Dutch Jake" Goetz and Harry Baer, owners of the Coeur d'Alene Theatre at the southeast corner of Front Avenue and Howard Street. The band paraded through town to attract customers to the Coeur d'Alene, the fanciest of the variety emporiums. *(Photo courtesy Sally Jackson, whose grandmother, Theresa Kulhanek, is at the center of the middle row.)*

dies" in their feathers, boas and flashy dresses.[12] Obviously, the parade always drew an interested and fascinated audience. From office windows or curbside, men jostled for an advantageous viewpoint as all business stopped for the duration of the parade.

The largest and fanciest of the variety emporiums was the Coeur d'Alene run by Dutch Jake Goetz and Harry Baer. It contained three bars, a gambling room, a café, a dance hall, a Turkish bath, and rooms for rent. Its faro tables could accommodate a thousand men at a time and operated twenty-four hours a day, seven days a week. Col. George Clarke recalled going into the Coeur d'Alene with his grandfather, A. M. Cannon. All the dealers were women who wore tuxedos, but with no shirt underneath. The *Spokesman-Review* came right out and called the Coeur d'Alene a "department store of vice and immorality."[13] They were probably right.

During one of the "reform waves," Dutch Jake offered the use of his largest barroom on a Sunday to any minister who would use it for religious services. Three ministers accepted this challenge and, on November 3, 1901, three to four hundred men filled the room. While they waited, the big mechanical pipe organ pumped out tunes and the electric fountain kept flashing its myriad of colors. As the ministers took their positions near the staircase leading to the gambling rooms, the organ was turned off, the men were asked to remove their hats, and the services began with singing. But the fountain kept twinkling its rainbow of lights throughout the services, and the waiters were kept busy, as there was no interruption of the regular business. The hymns and messages of salvation were accompanied by the clink of glasses, the noise of shuffling feet, the murmurs of tipsy men, and the loud calls of the waiters placing their orders. All the while, Dutch Jake was everywhere shaking hands, and snatching his derby off his head whenever he remembered it was there. Each time he passed the bar, he ordered free drinks for everyone standing there.

The crowd listened attentively to the appeals of the ministers to forsake sin and attend church. Free Bibles were distributed to all who wanted one as long as the supply lasted. The services closed by singing "Nearer, My God, to Thee." But as the crowd filed out in an orderly manner, the siren voice of the big pipe organ urged them to stay.

The campaign to close down the variety theatres continued. The *Spokesman-Review* opened a strong drive against the wine rooms with their couches and the private boxes, which were closed off by a curtain. It was not until 1907 that Ren Rice, the new chief of police, ordered the saloon keepers to remove the couches and the curtains by May 31. Although some proprietors grumbled about not being able to stay in business without the liquor solicitation in the closed boxes, all saloons and restaurants complied with the order. Next, out of respect for the Sabbath, the taverns were required to screen their windows and keep their doors shut (while open for business) until evening on Sundays. Then the saloons were ordered to close from 1:00 to 5:00 a.m. On January 13, 1908, Mayor C. Herbert Moore closed the saloons and variety theatres in compliance with the laws of the state. In spite of lengthy petitions from downtown businessmen in opposition, Spokane experienced its first "dry" Sunday. Finally, the variety theatres closed permanently when the State of Washington outlawed gambling in 1908. Recognizing a new era, Goetz and Baer added two floors to the Coeur d'Alene and converted it into a proper hotel.

The merchants in town got tired of the muddy or dusty streets and petitioned the city council for paving. Some wanted asphalt, others macadam, and some recommended vitrified brick at an estimated cost of $1.50 to $2.00 per square yard for the brick. As it was, the city had been paying sixty dollars per block each year for sprinkling the streets and eighty dollars for the crossings, not to mention the additional cost of removing mud from the streets in the spring. Finally, after more than a decade of discussions about paving the streets, in 1898, a concerted effort got underway. It was only a year later, on September 15, 1899, that Spokane's first automobile appeared on its newly paved streets.

This photo taken on Wall Street around 1900 shows the first telephone building in Spokane (on right) and the condition of the streets. *(Photo from the Elsom Collection, Ms 162, courtesy MAC/EWSHS)*

The Board of Health announced that people could no longer keep boxes of manure or other refuse in the alleys. The ponds were drained for Liberty Park, and cinder bicycle paths were created on Pine, Mallon and Third Avenue for the growing number of cyclists. Arlington Heights was renamed Hillyard in honor of Jim Hill, who in 1892 had brought the Great Northern, the second transcontinental railroad into Spokane.

Up on Seventh Avenue and in Browne's Addition, elaborate mansions were rising by the score in the late 1890s. Many were designed by Kirtland K. Cutter, and were built for the mine owners and railroad entrepreneurs with their newfound wealth. The "Age of Elegance" continued, but with different players. By 1909, a *Spokane Blue Book* printed the accepted protocol for the social elite.

Overlooking Spokane from Sixth and Wall (in the area known as "The Hill") in 1896. *(Photo courtesy SPLNWR)*

Appointed days for visiting a lady "at home" were established by the area in which she lived: Wednesdays for "The Hill" and Thursdays in Browne's Addition. Formal calls were not to exceed fifteen minutes and were made between 3:00 and 6:00 p.m. Married men were expected to call with their wives once or twice a year. If this was not possible, his calling card was left with his wife's.

The proper attire for gentlemen called for a dark frock coat and trousers of a lighter shade for morning or afternoon dress. Accessories included a silk hat, a light colored scarf and gloves of a shade suitable for street wear. "Full dress" required a black swallow-tail coat, black trousers, and a low-cut black or white vest. Black patent leather shoes, immaculate linen, a small white lawn tie and pearl studs completed his fashionable look.

No description for the rules of dress for women was included. However, one was to avoid discussions of religion, politics or scandals when calling. Calls in return for invitations were to be made promptly within a week, and dinner or parties required a more timely response, usually within three or four days.[14]

New Year's Eve balls at the hotels, "coming out" parties for debutantes in their own homes, charity balls, and euchre (card) parties were popular entertainment for the social group. "Thimble parties" were afternoon gatherings where the young ladies spent their time with fancy work while being entertained with musical selections.

During the 1890s, while the men pursued their professions, politics and fraternal organizations, the ladies organized a variety of clubs and societies. The Ladies'

Matinee Musicale became the first women's "club" in Spokane. Begun in the spring of 1889, it was made up of women musicians and music lovers. Sorosis began in 1891 and Cultus Club in 1892. Started March 20, 1896, the Spokane Floral Association had as its purpose to provide flowers for the annual Spokane Fruit Fair (predecessor to the Spokane Industrial Exposition, then the Spokane Interstate Fair). They later branched out to beautifying the parks, placing drinking fountains on the streets, and campaigning for free swimming pools. The Amethyst Club studied literature, as did the Ross Park Twentieth Century Club, which began meeting January 15, 1898. The Spokane Red Cross appeared July 13, 1898. There was a D.A.R. chapter in Spokane and a Wednesday Afternoon Literary Club for the intellectual and social edification of its members.

Although some of these groups took an active part in the community, notably the Red Cross, WCTU units, and the Kindergarten Association, the majority of the women's groups were more social in nature. Some limited the number of members and concentrated on cultural experiences, such as studying foreign countries, giving or sponsoring musicales, and in general providing an afternoon once or twice a month of social enrichment for its members. Fashionable tea gowns with diamond and precious jewels were worn in rooms decorated with bowers of fernery and an abundance of harmonious floral arrangements. Hostesses vied with each other to provide an elaborate setting and refreshments.

Within another decade, the direction of women's organizations changed in interest to charitable and benevolent institutions and projects. The *Coast* magazine for November 1907 featured Spokane and an article "Women's Work in Spokane" by Mrs. W. H. Allen. She told how a group of prominent society women raised funds for the new St. Luke's Hospital by selling candy and lemonade at a minstrel show they sponsored, running the Interstate Fair for a day, and manning the streetcars, during which the lady conductor stopped any well-known businessman and escorted him to the car. Instead of the usual five-cent fare, it was apt to be five dollars. In a few weeks, these industrious women raised $7,536, enough to furnish twelve rooms for the hospital.

The Florence Crittenton Home and the Women's Hotel[15] were run entirely by women. Once a year, the largest department store gave a generous percentage of the day's sales to those institutions. The Federated Women's Clubs banded together to purchase a site and raise funds to erect a club building for the use of the women's clubs. (It was built in 1909 at Ninth and Walnut.) The women were also asked to raise $20,000 to furnish the new $160,000 YMCA building.

As one lady put it: "We are busy women here. Every day brings new duties and added responsibilities. Churches must be built, homes must be beautified, organizations for mutual help and assistance must be formed, hospitality must

Looking east along Sprague Avenue in the early 1900s. Davenport's Restaurant is visible on the right. In a few short years, all the buildings to the right of the restaurant would be demolished for the construction of the renowned Davenport Hotel. *(Photo courtesy SPLNWR)*

be extended to the strangers that throng our gateways, but we are willing, happy and content, for we know we are aiding, in our humble way to build up a great city that shall be a good home for us, a joy to our children and shall endure until generations shall have reaped with pleasure the results of our earnest heart-felt efforts."[16]

The 1900 U.S. Census tabulated Spokane's population at 36,848. Then the population exploded and tripled in the next decade, reaching 104,402 by 1910. Spokane again over-built as the business district spread to the east and south. Gone were Spokane's "baby" years. The "teens" ended with the abolition of gambling in 1908 and alcohol at midnight on December 31, 1915. Soldiers soon began marching off to fight in two world wars. From its humble beginning, in less than two generations' time, Spokane assumed its new importance as the largest metropolis between Minneapolis and Seattle with new frontiers to conquer.

Chapter X

Carrie Adell Green Strahorn

Carrie Adell Strahorn on her honeymoon, Chicago,
1877. *(Photo courtesy Idaho State Historical Society)*

Although Robert Edmund "Bob" and Carrie Adell "Dell" (or Della) Green Strahorn did not move to Spokane until 1898, they were conspicuous members of the community during the early part of the 20th century – Bob in building railroads and public utilities and Dell in the social and cultural scene. Their involvement with the western part of the United States had begun many years earlier. It is no exaggeration to say that the Strahorns contributed more than any others to the settlement of the West. Yet somehow they seem to have become lost in the annals of the Old West. Carrie Adell's story is unique because of her many unlikely experiences for the time period in which she lived.

Chapter X

Like her friend Anna Browne, Dell does not fit into the stereotypical image of the "Victorian" lady. That she would spend a night with twenty-six men in one room, albeit with her husband, that she knew how to use firearms and would, that she rode on the cowcatcher of a train over the Continental Divide, or would be the first woman to do a myriad of other things, does not fit the conventional pattern of the period. Still, Carrie Adell Strahorn was a Victorian lady in the sense that she was modest, refined, cultured, well-educated, womanly, home-loving, and completely devoted to her husband and his career. When circumstances required that she ride astride rather than the preferred sidesaddle, she always kept a long skirt in her saddlebag, and donned it immediately upon dismounting from her horse.

Born January 1, 1854, Dell grew up with two sisters in Marengo, a small rural Illinois town northwest of Chicago. Her father, John W. Green, a noted surgeon, was the first doctor west of Chicago to administer an anesthetic. In his home, he established a liberal atmosphere that did not embody the usual Victorian restraints. His exceptionally intelligent and talented daughters were permitted to pursue their own abilities and as much education as they desired. Harriet (Hattie), four years younger than Dell, graduated from the Chicago Woman's Medical College and became well known in the Chicago medical profession. She also established an excellent reputation in literary circles. The eldest daughter, Mary, who was two years older than Dell, married Dr. W. B. Waters of Chicago. Carrie Adell, the middle child, attended the University of Michigan at Ann Arbor. She had an outstanding singing voice and also studied under some of the foremost American and European teachers. One newspaper article described Dell as having a voice of unusual sweetness, which assured her a successful career as a vocalist.[1] She also became a writer of some note.

If it is possible to inherit traits such as stamina, indomitable spirit, fortitude, determination, loyalty and the ability to make the best of any situation, then Dell had the right ancestors. Her mother had accompanied her surgeon husband during the Red River campaign of the Civil War and shared every danger of field and hospital. Dell's paternal grandparents had been founders of Greenfield, Ohio, and her own parents were pioneers of northern Illinois. Ironically, Dell said she never wanted to be a pioneer of any place because she had listened to so many old-timers' stories that invariably began: "Now back in '49, or I remember the spring of '50." Neither did she want to be called the oldest settler in a town or to be one of the early ones in any state history. Fate, however, decided that she would be the first non-Indian woman to traverse many regions still marked on the school maps as "unexplored." With unbounded courage, good humor, an unquenchable interest in people, and inquisitiveness about every geographical feature of the land, she never became blasé or bored. Today her life story reads like a novel.

The humble beginnings of Robert Strahorn, the man Carrie Adell Green was to marry and spend her life with, was radically different than the refined and rather privileged life of Adell's experience. He was born on May 15, 1952, in Center County, Pennsylvania. At the age of four, he moved with his family to a farm in Illinois. His formal education ended at age ten. On his own by his early teens, he moved to Sedalia, Missouri, and learned the printer's trade. For health reasons, at the age of 18, he moved to Denver and began working as a newspaper reporter, editor and correspondent.[2]

While in Denver, Strahorn met and feel in love with Lettie Dean, a young woman originally from Marengo, Illinois. Sadly, she became terminally ill and expressed a desire to return to her old home. Gallant Bob took her home and nursed her for the few months before she died. As fate would have it, Lettie and Adell Green had been childhood friends and close college classmates at Ann Arbor. Dell helped Bob tenderly care for Lettie and stood beside him at her funeral. When he left Marengo, Bob and Dell began corresponding.

After several years of letter writing, Dell and Bob were married September 19, 1877. The wedding took place at 8:15 Wednesday evening in the Greens' home before a hundred and fifty guests. As the Marengo Cornet Band struck up a lively tune, the bridal party entered the spacious and beautifully decorated parlor. The local newspaper reporting the event listed the wedding gifts and their donors: the complete works of Dickens, fifteen volumes; Bancroft's six-volume history of the West; a fancy pin cushion; an elegant library edition of Whittier's poems; a set of bureau mats and a tidy; three glass and silver pickle dishes; a bud vase; silver forks; linen towels, and a porcelain pudding dish.[3] They were not exactly practical necessities for the frontier.

Before their marriage, Strahorn had been a newspaper reporter during the Sioux Indian Wars of 1875-76. He was with General George Crook in the Wyoming and North Dakota campaigns against Sitting Bull, Crazy Horse, Dull Knife and Little Wolf. An early-day Ernie Pyle, Strahorn rode in the front lines to get his stories, using his rifle as effectively as his pen. His articles appeared in the *New York Times*, the *Chicago Tribune*, and the Denver *Rocky Mountain News*.

Following that period, Strahorn wrote and published a book on the resources of Wyoming. Fortuitously, this book came into the hands of railroad tycoon Jay Gould as he was about to embark upon an ambitious expansion of his Union Pacific Railroad. Gould wanted wholesale immigration west of the Missouri River so that businesses would be established and shipping tonnage waiting for him before his railroad got to those remote areas. It did not bother Gould that this was somewhat in reverse of the usual procedure. He recognized in Strahorn the talent he needed to report graphically and statistically on the resources of the West and their potential, whether mineral, agricultural, timber or whatever. Strahorn was then to compile this information into a book of several hundred pages, followed by a veritable flood of leaflets, maps and folders, and an eight-page monthly newspaper titled *The New West Illustrated*. Some of these writings would be printed in foreign languages and distributed overseas. It was this barrage of leaflets and folders generously spread around that enticed settlers to move into Colorado, Utah, Wyoming, Montana and Idaho. Strahorn was also expected to write half-a-dozen other books on as many different territories and states in great detail.[4] This was perhaps the biggest public relations job ever undertaken, but at age 25, Bob Strahorn's ambition knew no bounds.

Gould's recruitment of Strahorn came within a week after their marriage. Following a short honeymoon in Chicago, the newlyweds took the train to Cheyenne. Bob had no intention of leaving his bride alone in that frontier town so far from her home and friends. However, he had to get permission and passes from the Union Pacific officials for Dell to accompany him. When he approached them, the railroad officers blanched at the thought of a woman, especially a refined lady like Dell, enduring the rough roads and trails, the unknown dangers from Indians, all kinds of weather, the terrain from mountains to alkali deserts, and the crude and primitive housing conditions. But Bob and Dell were insistent, and Bob issued an ultimatum: he would only accept the offer if they allowed Carrie Adell to accompany him. Consequently, Cheyenne became only a home base for an occasional day's rest. Their real home would be the stagecoach and saddle for many years to come. Thus began their "stagecoach honeymoon" from which this husband-wife team fused into a lifetime partnership. In fact, Dell always referred to her husband as "Pard."

With her beloved husband, Carrie Adell traveled by train, by ship, by stagecoach, by horseback through mud and desert heat from Alaska to Mexico, and Omaha to Hawaii. No route was too perilous, no transportation too rough, no housing too primitive. She saw it all, mile after mile, until six years and thousands of miles had rolled by. She would later chronicle these adventures in newspaper articles and a bestselling memoir.

Salary was something Bob completely forgot to ask about, and Dell, Victorian lady that she was, assumed her husband would take care of her and never gave finances a thought. As Bob was long on courage, confidence and expedients, they headed for Salt Lake City with only ten dollars to cover the next three months' expenses. The Mormon capital was to be their headquarters while covering Utah, Montana, Idaho and western Wyoming.

Not wanting to miss a thing, these eager young travelers selected the most advantageous seat on the train – the cowcatcher! The view was sensational, but so

Crossing the Dale Creek Bridge on the cowcatcher of a Union and Central Pacific train in 1877. *(Photo from* Fifteen Thousand Miles by Stage, *1911, by Carrie Adell Strahorn)*

was the feeling of rolling pell-mell over the Continental Divide while clinging to the iron supports in the face of a gale. Two miles west of the summit, the train rolled into the Dale Creek crossing. This 650-foot bridge was held up by spidery steel legs 150 feet above the canyon floor where a minute stream could be seen.[4] Next the train plunged into a snow-shed, followed by a tunnel. The Strahorns could not see even a glimmer of track, let alone each other. To be in total darkness was much worse than seeing any potential danger ahead. For the rest of that journey, they decided to ride in a quiet corner of a Pullman car. Dell's regular letters to her parents never mentioned the cowcatcher pass.

An equally unusual experience was attending a dance a thousand feet under-ground, held in the Colorado Central Mine near Georgetown, Colorado, in No-vember 1877. The entrance to the mine opened at an elevation of 12,000 feet. Eight rows of lights illuminated the quarter-mile-long tunnel draped in bunting that led to a large underground cavern. Blasted out of the heart of the mountain, this room later housed the hoist and other machinery for the mine. The ladies wore their finest gowns. A gorgeous ballroom had been created by the brilliant lights and gay hangings covering the rock walls. Over the years, the Strahorns would attend many balls, a number of which were given in their honor, even though Bob never learned to dance. The settings ranged from unfinished school-houses to elegant resort hotels, but none equaled this first one for uniqueness.

Chapter X

The stagecoach played a big part in Dell's early married life. Perhaps no other object associated with the Old West has been more glamorized than the stagecoach. Realistically, among all the modes of conveyances, it was certainly one of the most abominable. The stage was a clumsy, awkward thing that swayed from side to side, back and forth, making motion sickness a common malady even for seasoned travelers. When the coach was filled, as it usually was, the poor persons sitting in the middle were often caught in an unenviable position.

Should a passenger happen to drift off into sleep, invariably the wheels either fell into a chuckhole that sent one clutching the air for something to hang on to, or hit a rock, throwing the whole coach to one side with a bone-jarring jolt. At the very least, the passenger's head banged against a cross rod or side brace. Sometimes the sudden lurch sent a fist into a neighbor's eye. About the time everyone settled down again, someone would get a cramp and everyone had to readjust his position to provide relief for the aching muscle. If the jostling of the coach did not keep a person awake, there would always be a passenger who decided to tell his life story – in the middle of the night.

In dry weather, one ate and smelled the dust, in wet one slopped in the mud. Still the old transportation wagon went lumbering along. During the summer it traveled twenty-four hours a day, whereas the winter schedule called for no traveling at night. The stopping and starting was generally in accordance with the distance to be covered and the condition of the roads. It might stop from 4:00 p.m. until 7:00 a.m., or it might travel until 11:00 p.m. with a call to start again at 3:00 a.m. They usually laid over on Sundays. Stage stations were from ten to twelve hours and twenty miles apart. Once every twenty-four hours, there would be a "home" station, where supplies were stored and some semblance of defense was provided.

Accommodations along the stage routes were crude at best. The furniture at stations often consisted of only a few boxes or kegs to sit on. For overnight stays, passengers often shared a common room that was frequently overcrowded, and an empty spot on a bare floor with a leaky roof above might provide the only sleeping accommodations. Seldom was there a cloth to cover the unfinished pine board tables. The dishes were heavy and course. Any glasses were thick and dull. The tip of the cream pitcher was invariably gone, the sugar bowl cracked, and the condiment bottle dirty from greasy hands. Over all buzzed a swarm of flies in warm weather. Occasionally a station would be spotlessly clean and the tables loaded with palatable food, a veritable oasis in the wilderness. At Lost River Junction (now Grouse, Idaho), Dell looked in vain for the usual "one-holer" behind the cabin. When Bob inquired, the station tender bawled, "My Gawd! There's the whole territory of Idaho out there, what more does she need?"[5]

Stagecoach runaways did occur. Once when Dell was traveling with her sister, Mary Waters, they had remained aboard although a number of others had gotten out for a bit of exercise. The driver was off his box, and the team made a sudden dash for freedom down the corduroy road. The reeling carriage sent the few remaining occupants, including Dell and Mrs. Waters, flying around like feathers. One stalwart gentleman managed to climb out a window in true John Wayne fashion, work his way to the front, and bring the six horses under control.

This, indeed, was the frontier in fact, not fiction, in the late 1870s and early 1880s. By means of the stagecoach, the Strahorns traversed and researched Colorado, northern Utah, southern Idaho, and Montana, touching into Oregon and eastern Washington. They went to Dillon, Deer Lodge, Bellevue, Ruby Camp, Leadville, Lake City, Gunnison City, Central City, Boise City, Canyon City, Virginia City, Nevada City, Diamond City, Baker City and Salt Lake City. Then on to the Bitterroot Valley and Hell Gate Valley, to Fort Benton, Fort Hall, Fort Ellis, and Fort Walla Walla; to Ogden, Oneida, Black Foot, Helena, Missoula, Laramie, Pueblo, Santa Fe, Georgetown, Denver and Challis. They covered Idaho Springs, Soda Springs and Colorado Springs – not necessarily in that order – and Spokane Falls.

The Strahorns traveled into towns so recently thrown together that the hotels, if there were any, had been built of green lumber. As the boards dried, they shrank, leaving gaps. The Strahorns carried their own bed linens. Not infrequently did they have to hang sheets, clothing or newspapers on the walls in order to give Dell a shred of privacy from the curious eyes in the cubicle next door.

The couple spent several winters in Omaha, where Bob sorted through his copious notes and wrote his books. On the fringe of civilization, Omaha had no paved streets and few crosswalks. After one of the usual hard winter rains one day, Dell sallied forth, quite smartly dressed, to do some shopping. At the first intersection, she confidently stepped into the street – and was stuck! The more she wiggled and twisted trying to get one foot loose, the deeper the other one sank in the mud. Even pulling her feet out of her overshoes did not help. She was absolutely trapped. There she remained until a strong gentleman came along and pried her out.

In newspaper columns Dell wrote, she described in a humorous vein the romantic history, the social life, entertainment and conditions of the people already in the new land, as well as the grandeur of the scenery. Throughout her narrative, she wove the ridiculous and amusing episodes. One year alone, forty-five articles were published in the *Omaha Republican,* as well as in other eastern newspapers. She used two pen names: Emerald for her maiden name of Green, and A. Stray for Adell Strahorn.[6]

In addition to covering the territories and towns by stagecoach, the Strahorns in time explored every cave and waterfall, climbed innumerable mountains including Pike's Peak, snowshoed, shot-the-rapids, and thought nothing of taking days out of their way to see something they had heard about. Bob was constantly being besieged for more statistics and facts until he literally became a walking encyclopedia of the Far West. Since his pamphlets and papers were sent all over Europe, as well as the United States, each town wanted that kind of publicity and went out of its way to make the Strahorns' stay as pleasant as possible. In the first six months of 1880 alone, Dell figured they had covered 25,000 miles by steamboat, railroad and horseback, plus 3,000 miles by stage. Some eastern papers commented on that trip as being the most remarkable one in any woman's history, but more adventures were to come.

In the fall of 1880, when the Marshall and Goff Stage Company started the first public transportation into Yellowstone National Park, Dell and Bob were to be their first passengers. Although a number of people advised against the trip so late in the fall, they set out the first of October from Virginia City, Montana Territory, for the 120-mile journey to the Marshall Hotel, built by George W. Marshall and John B. Goff. This was the first hotel in Yellowstone Park and, unbeknownst to the Strahorns, who were the hotel's first guests, it was only partially finished. Consequently, the accommodations were rustic at best. Although Yellowstone had been declared the first national park eight years earlier, there were still no adequate roads and tourist facilities were primitive.

George Marshall served as the Strahorns' guide during their stay in Yellowstone, during which time they toured about four hundred miles, mostly on horseback. They followed the same old Indian trail General Oliver O. Howard had used three years earlier while pursuing the Nez Perce. By the time they reached the east side of the park, snow had begun to fall. Because the trails were considered too dangerous for a sidesaddle, Dell had to use a man's saddle, which she was not used to. She became so stiff and sore that tears rolled down her cheeks and she wanted to scream with pain, but this indomitable woman was not about to stay behind and miss something. Once, she opted to remain on the horse to eat her lunch, because she was afraid if she

Camping under the stars in Yellowstone. *(Photo from* Fifteen Thousand Miles by Stage, *1911, by Carrie Adell Strahorn)*

got off, she would never make it back on. It later took three men to help her off her horse because she was too stiff to dismount by herself. Even Bob admitted that "of all our horseback ventures, that 400-mile jaunt through Yellowstone Park was the worst." However, according to Bob's account, they "reveled in its virgin freshness of unmatched wonders." He went on to say:

> Never again could we hope for the thrills of first sight of that November garb of snowy purity and glory of setting of its strangely awe-inspiring features. Its pine forests were a glorious mass of glittering icy jewels, the congealed remnants of geyser and hot spring moisture projected on every hand. It was as if the rubies and diamonds of the universe had been left frozen upon twig, leaf and forest monarch on those frosty mornings of brilliant sunshine, to reflect the array of multi-colored springs, geysers, canyons, falls and the surpassing glory of richest autumnal garb.[7]

In recalling only the beauty and inspiration of what would have been a miserable experience for others, Bob and Dell exhibit why they were so successful in their portrayals of the West. It was due in no small part to the fact that Dell seldom missed a mile, never complained and enthusiastically greeted the next journey. No matter what the difficulties, the Strahorns never lost their enthusiasm, wonder or awe.

Their first visit of several to Spokane came late in the year of 1880. Although Dell thought she was going to have a week's rest in Walla Walla, she soon found herself in a stage bound for Lewiston and points north. A ferry took them down the Snake River from Lewiston to Almota. One of the interesting sights along the way was wheat being loaded on steamboats from the top of the Snake River bluffs through flumes some two to three thousand feet long. A guide was sent ahead with saddle horses and a couple of pack horses to set up camp near the Spokane River. At Colfax, the Strahorns caught the Kinnear stage.

Dell described their first view of the town by the falls:

> The virgin grandeur and beauty of the Spokane country appealed to us as no other place had done in all our travels. The little village of four or five hundred people straggling over the parklike openings among the pines impressed us as one of the most picturesque in America. As we stood on the banks of the beautiful river and saw its wonderful falls with the magnificent valley, its rich bunchgrass carpet then yellow as gold in its autumn garb and recalled the vast grainland empire stretching to the southeast and southwest, the wonderful mines opening up nearby on the east [the Coeur d'Alene mines], the ample forests, and the possibilities for power, the majesty of the situation made Bob declare that "Here will be the greatest inland city of the whole Northwest."[8]

Dell's perception of the economic potential was apparently greatly enhanced by thirty years' hindsight or from the impression gained during subsequent visits. The Strahorns' first visit to Spokane was three years prior to Andrew Prichard's announcement of gold in the Coeur d'Alenes (the mines did not begin to develop until after that announcement), and five years before electricity powered by water would appear in Spokane Falls.

Although it was late fall, the Strahorns camped out, but they ate most of their meals at the California House. Actually, little time was spent in town, as they visited Medical Lake and bathed in the soapy water; rode out to the Little Spokane River; and saw Coeur d'Alene and the fort there. Their time was limited as they wanted to catch a boat to Portland before winter set in.

Hoping to gain some time, they rode ahead of their guide on the return to Colfax. Somewhere north of Spangle, they got off the road and ran into a band of migratory Indians. Realizing there was nothing they could do except follow instructions, they dismounted. Several young warriors went through their saddlebags, making signs by pointing to their mouths and tipping their heads back as if looking for whiskey. They carried none. When one of the Indians found Dell's medicine case, he led her to a tepee where an Indian woman was writhing in agony. Dell shook her head, but the fellow was adamant. The only thing Dell could think to do was to give her a large dose of bicarbonate of soda, accompanied with a bit of dramatics – and many earnest prayers for help. One or the other worked because, after the simple remedy came back up, the squaw was relieved of her stomach cramps. However, her husband decided to keep this magic elixir and would not return the bottle.

Bob and Dell were not restrained from remounting their horses, but before they could leave, the large Indian said: "Spokane," pointed to the sun, made a circle upon the earth and to the point overhead. After pointing to himself and saying "Spokane" again, he indicated five or six ponies and two blankets. He concluded with "white squaw, me buy." As near as the Strahorns could determine, the Indian said he would be in Spokane at noon the next day to buy the "white squaw," Dell, and would give Bob a certain number of horses and blankets. With that, the Strahorns hastily left in the opposite direction from Spokane.

Portland they found to be an architectural beauty, the best built town of 20,000 people anywhere west of the Mississippi River. Seattle, on the other hand, was not that impressive. To Dell it was only a place for an optimist to dream of maritime power and great commercial docks. The town was a veritable mud hole with its cow-path streets meandering over the hills. "Our feet came out of the mud," she wrote, "with a sock-sock-sock that was as ludicrous as it was annoying."[9]

Perhaps no trip back home to Marengo was more pleasant than the one in September 1882, when Dell's parents gave a reception and dinner for seventy friends in honor of the Strahorns' fifth wedding anniversary. Bob's gift to Dell was an elegant diamond ring.

After six strenuous years, Strahorn's publicity work (some have called it propaganda) was finished. He entered upon the second phase of his career, that of empire building. In so doing, he became his own best example of how to take advantage of western opportunity.

From the time of their first fact-finding trip to the Pacific Northwest, Strahorn had been impressed with the vast and varied resources of the region. The endless possibilities for the future led him to bombard his superiors, all the way up to Jay Gould himself, to build the Oregon Short Line between the Union Pacific's tracks at Granger, Wyoming, and the Oregon Railway & Navigation at Huntington in eastern Oregon for the connection to Portland. Strahorn was soon asked to make confidential reports on the railroad traffic possibilities and to advise them on the merits of likely routes. In 1883, the Oregon Short Line was under construction. It has been described as being strategically the most important railroad in the Pacific Northwest, and all the credit belonged to Strahorn.[10]

In 1883, with three others, Bob formed the Idaho and Oregon Land Improvement Company to build and service some of the towns needed along the route of the new railroad. Thus, Dell found herself looking at where her new home was to rise, Caldwell, Idaho Territory. Actually, all she could see was the stark white, desolate glare of alkali, some gray sagebrush and greasewood bushes. There was not a house nor a road, not a tree nor a blade of grass, let alone water. She did not know whether to laugh or cry. Yet, she knew her sobbing had to be buried so deep her sweetheart would never know it was there. Success hung on laughter and courage.

As general manager and vice president of the Improvement Company, Bob plunged into obtaining rights-of-way and building irrigation works, roads, bridges, telegraph lines, hotels, houses, and depots. The political details alone would have overwhelmed a less energetic person. Although the stations and terminals were for the benefit of the Union Pacific line, the railroad had no financial interest in the Improvement Company. The capital had been furnished mainly by former Senator C. A. Caldwell of Kansas and Andrew Mellon, a future ambassador to Great Britain and longtime treasurer of the United States. The only way the company could realize a profit was from the sale of the town sites and suburban lands.

In their "brood of children," as Dell referred to them, were the newly located towns of Shoshone, Hailey, Mountain Home, Caldwell, Payette and New Weiser in Idaho and Ontario, Oregon. At one time, the Strahorns maintained homes in three different places, including Denver. The trips from one town to another were tedious, dusty, irksome and frequently at unseemly hours. Still, Dell participated as frequently as she could cajole Bob into taking her along.

Front Avenue, Caldwell, Idaho, circa 1886. The Strahorns lived above the Land Office until their ranch house was built. *(Photo courtesy Ted Williams of Caldwell, Idaho)*

One round-trip drive between Caldwell and Weiser, about a hundred and fifty miles, could have been anyone's undoing. Near Ontario was a bad, rocky ford of the Payette River. As they began to climb the opposite bank, a piece of harness broke. The inexperienced colts, which Bob had acquired shortly before at Jim Clement's ranch, thrashed around until the wagon tongue broke. Fortunately, Clement was able to extricate them from the water and patch the tongue.

On the way home, darkness overtook them before they reached the ford of the Boise River. Directly above the ford, a highway bridge was under construction, making the crossing a perilous task even in daylight. In the pitch-black night, Bob gave the horses free rein to pick their own route across the stream. In so doing, the team unluckily straddled a large boulder which broke the wagon tongue where it had previously been mended. Water poured into the wagon. Standing on the seat as the water swirled around their feet, the Strahorns waved a lantern and shouted for help. Their anguished cries managed to awaken the construction crew camped nearby, who came to their rescue. A long plank was laid from the bridge pilings to the wagon, and Dell and Bob had to crawl up this on their hands and knees. Then they groped their way along the bridge stringers for several hundred feet to shore. Dell was grateful the extreme darkness hid the rushing water and saved her from becoming dizzy. A misstep would have plunged them to the icy floodwaters below. Bob recalled that the trip concluded with a two-mile walk home.[11]

Early in 1884, church groups began forming in Caldwell. The Christian Church, the Methodists, and Baptists held services in the schoolhouse. By June, the Baptists erected a church across the railroad tracks (Tenth and Chicago streets today). Since there was no Presbyterian group, nine or ten women met October

21, 1885, to form the Ladies' Presbyterian Building Society. Dell was its first president and strongest promoter. By December, the ladies had raised two hundred dollars toward a church. They held ice cream socials, oyster suppers, bazaars, lunch stands – anything they could think of to raise money. At their musical concerts, Dell was always featured in a lead role.

In November 1887, Dr. William Judson Boonc, a just-graduated missionary, visited Caldwell and reluctantly accepted the job as pastor. He held services in the Baptist church until the Presbyterian building was ready in April 1888. With those same determined women, Dr. Boone established the College of Idaho at Caldwell on land donated by Strahorn. Boone always gave credit to Dell as being a founder of the college. The Strahorns remained lifelong supporters of the school. After Dell passed away, Bob built a library, Strahorn Hall, for the college as a memorial to her. It has been said that Strahorn Hall stands on the site where Dell sat in the wagon while Bob laid out the town in his mind.[12] This is likely to be more romantic fiction than actuality.

By 1885, the Strahorns had given up their other residences and took up a homestead a mile outside Caldwell, which they affectionately named "Sunnyside." Their home had an open-door policy that encouraged single men and other townspeople to visit evenings or come out for Sunday dinner. Not infrequently did the gregarious Bob invite four or five house guests. This meant chickens in the pot, cakes in the oven, and bread in the pan to an unlimited degree. In summer there was fruit to preserve, pickles to make, jellies to be boiled, conserves to be mixed, cooked, bottled and labeled. Dell had to be ready for callers at any hour of the day, to take friends and strangers for a drive around the countryside as well as be prepared to go with Bob whenever possible. Domestic help was

"Sunnyside," the Strahorns' ranch outside Caldwell, Idaho, in 1887. *(Photo courtesy Ted Williams of Caldwell, Idaho)*

about as obtainable as green grass on the alkali flats before irrigation. Eventually she was able to hire a Chinese houseboy named Charlie.

One of the Strahorns' neighbors was Frank Steunenberg, who became a governor of Idaho in the 1890s. Many a time, Bob and Frank leaned on the Steunenberg gate to finish a chat. It was this same gate that Harry Orchard boobytrapped December 30, 1905, killing Steunenberg in retaliation for his calling out the militia during the labor disputes of 1899 in the Coeur d'Alenes.[13]

Although Caldwell was over a thousand miles from her hometown, Dell's parents visited her there several times. Her sister and niece, Mary and Louise Waters, as well as other longtime friends, also made the journey to Caldwell. Even family visits were not beyond freakish accidents. In the fall of 1883, Dell escorted a young cousin home to Chicago from Denver aboard the Kansas Pacific Railroad. Upon passing from the dining car to their sleeper, the train suddenly lurched, knocking Dell's purse out of her hand into the darkness outside. There went all her money, baggage claim tickets, bank checks and all her many railroad passes, including a Pullman pass. It was too great a loss to ignore, so Dell notified the conductor, who had the train back up three miles. Although the train crew searched the area with lanterns, no handbag was found.

Dell decided she would have to leave the train. The nearest station with lodging was thirty miles away, where they were obliged to sleep in the section house. The morning train returned them to Magnolia, where the section men were to take them on a handcar back to the site of the missing purse. Upon alighting at Magnolia, Dell discovered the men had already left – in the wrong direction. As no other assistance was available, the only recourse was to trudge down the track three or four miles in the rain. The conductor had warned her of tramps in the area, so Dell borrowed a revolver from the telegraph operator, the lone resident of Magnolia.

When they had nearly reached the site of search, a gentleman came along in a fine carriage driving a pair of gray horses. Dell declined his offer of aid, but before he had gone very far, their glad shouts at finding the purse with its precious contents brought him back. Mr. Malony insisted on taking them along toward Denver until the carriage Dell had wired for met them. Malony, a cattle king who had just finished a new house on his ranch, was hosting a large dancing party there the next night. Wouldn't they accept his cordial invitation to attend? As Dell felt her responsibility as chaperone rather keenly, she decided she had better return her cousin to her parents before the sudden mutual admiration could become more involved. Thereafter, her young cousin teased Dell for spoiling her chances for the best romance of her life.

Bob's intention from the very beginning had been to comfortably and firmly establish the pioneers of those days and then move on. By the fall of 1888, his towns in southern Idaho were on their own, and it was time for the Strahorns to leave. The Union Pacific entered the picture again as they wanted Bob to come east, but they also wanted him to go to Alaska. They compromised by sending Dell, accompanied by the Waterses, to Alaska while Bob went to Chicago to attend the Republican National Convention.

The steamship *George W. Elder* plied the waters of the Inland Passage north from Vancouver, B.C., with stops at Wrangell, Juneau, the Douglas Islands, Chikat, Sitka and Killisnoo. As could be expected, Dell visited the native peoples' towns, attended potlatches, and climbed up the Muir Glacier.

While in Chicago, Bob arranged with a distant relative by the same name to buy the Hailey Hot Springs with the intention of building a luxury hotel and swimming pools at the site. It was the only venture of Bob's that Dell really opposed. She felt it did not present a broad enough scope for his abilities.

No sooner was construction underway outside Hailey than the Union Pacific requested Bob to write six new pamphlets of over one hundred closely printed pages on Colorado, Utah, Montana, Idaho, Oregon and Washington. The deadline for distribution: ninety days! It was a Herculean task, but Bob accomplished it. In spite of their moving from Salt Lake City to Denver to Omaha and finally Chicago in search of a place that was comfortable and quiet while the writing was in progress, Bob was completely exhausted when the work was finished. The doctors said he had used up all his physical strength. One doctor predicted Bob probably would not live through the winter. Even Dell's physician father pessimistically advised the only hope lay in absolute rest in a warm climate. Bob and Dell chose Pass Christian, Mississippi, on the Gulf of Mexico.

By the latter part of April 1889, Bob had recovered sufficiently for the Strahorns to journey to Chicago to buy the furnishings for the Hailey Hot Springs Hotel. In typical Strahorn fashion, the resort was touted as being the very finest. The two-story building contained a number of bathing rooms, a ballroom, pavilion, parlors, dining room, billiard room, a ten-pin alley, porcelain bathtubs, and rooms for resting after bathing in the mineral waters. The hotel even had its own electric light plant. The grounds were to be fully landscaped with thousands of trees, three lakes for swimming, boating and fishing, and stocked with a hundred and fifty registered pedigreed shorthorn cattle and a small band of fine horses from Kentucky. However, after only one successful summer, the partnership with the wealthy Robert Strahorn of Chicago (Bob's relative) proved not to be a happy one. Knowing Dell's feelings about the project, Bob sold out in the fall of 1890. (The following July the hotel burned and was not rebuilt.)

Chapter X

An opportunity opened up for Bob to join Nelson Bennett, a highly successful railroad builder, and C. X. Larrabee, a Montana banker, in their construction work along Puget Sound. James J. Hill, president of the Great Northern Railroad, had revealed that the western terminus of his line would be at Fairhaven (now part of Bellingham) on Bellingham Bay. He also publicly promised great docks for his proposed fleet of ocean liners that would connect Washington State with Alaska and the Orient. With these plans on the horizon, Bennett and Larrabee formed the Fairhaven Land Company. Among the other men involved was Jim Wardner of Coeur d'Alene mining fame. With the great resources of minerals, forests, agriculture and fisheries close at hand, and a harbor location opposite the ocean entrance to Puget Sound, it was natural to dream big, speculate heavily and enthusiastically in a surefire future. Along with some other ambitious insiders, Bob launched the real estate venture of South Fairhaven, expecting it to be a second Brooklyn or at least another Oakland. As in southern Idaho, Bob was involved in land speculation: buying the land, providing services of water, streets, etc., and planning to sell the lots at a profit.

Then Hill changed his mind and stopped the Great Northern in Seattle. With no railroad into Fairhaven, there would be no population growth, no transportation for products. Nor did Hill build the promised docks for seagoing vessels. It meant total ruin for Robert Strahorn.[14] The bubble burst almost simultaneously with bank failures in London in 1890, which eventually contributed to the Panic of 1893. The Fairhaven fiasco left a bitter dislike for Hill, which Strahorn carried for years. Eventually he got even.

Intuition told Bob there was still money in conservative New England. On borrowed funds, the Strahorns left for the East in the winter of 1891. Basically, Bob's purpose was to sell municipal warrants[15] for cash-starved western towns to eastern bankers. For this doubtful venture, Bob opened an office in Boston.

While living in Massachusetts, and then in an apartment on Madison Avenue in New York City, Dell was able to continue her study of music. Bob was still on the road, going up and down the Eastern Seaboard, as well as back and forth to the West. His expertise as a persuasive salesman was severely tested.

One of Strahorn's supporters was C. J. Lord, president of the Capital National Bank at Olympia. The state of Washington was badly in need of a state capitol building. In order to finance it, the legislature decided to issue special state warrants to be repaid only out of the sale of the plentiful state land. Lord was to furnish the funds as needed, relying on Strahorn to sell the warrants in the East.

Construction had started and Bob had made some advance sales of the securities when the State Capitol Commission stopped issuing the papers on some technical ground. In reality, although it was a shock at the time, it was a reputation-saving occurrence for Bob, as all Washington State land sales ceased for many years as an aftereffect of the 1893 panic. Payment on those warrants would have been impossible, and Bob's credibility would have been badly damaged.

Strahorn branched out into promoting corporate bonds, thereby raising billions in cash and credit to finance western towns, counties and states to pay for the construction of thousands of miles of railroads and ocean lines, and for building canals from such rivers as the Colorado, Columbia and Missouri.[16] Although Robert Strahorn's enduring reputation was as a railroad tycoon, he also organized, promoted and constructed various public utilities, including plants to provide power for electric rail lines and water for irrigation systems. However, the greatest result of his seven years in the East was the contacts made with bankers and powerful lending institutions and the understanding Strahorn gained of the inner workings of large-scale financing. This knowledge would in due time provide Strahorn with the millions needed to reach the pinnacle of his personal achievements and eventually to build a mansion in Spokane.

Bob worked so intensely and wholeheartedly at every enterprise he undertook that his physical health was repeatedly tested. He saw little business advantage in civic or social clubs; although he was a member of the Spokane Club and a few other organizations, he was not much of a "joiner." Dell really had to work hard to make her husband see the humorous side of life and encourage frequent respites from his commercial endeavors.[17]

Between 1890 and 1898, the Strahorns spent a portion of each year in Spokane and the vicinity, or elsewhere in the Rocky Mountains.[18] They enjoyed camping in the wildernesses of Idaho, Colorado or British Columbia with compatible friends. Frequently, Dell's sister and husband, W. B. Waters, of Chicago, accompanied them. An avid hunter and fisherman, Bob was never happier than the times spent out-of-doors.

By 1898, the doctors advised Bob to leave the eastern climate and return to the West. That year, they decided to make Spokane their permanent home. However, as Bob needed a complete rest and warm climate, the Strahorns spent the winter in Hawaii. The islands were unspoiled and unhurried. Bob and Dell explored the islands by steamer, stagecoach, horseback and on foot. They rode the waves in outrigger canoes, and Bob fished for shark. On their last day in Honolulu, unaware a storm was approaching, they went for a ride in an outrigger. They were caught in high waves, which overturned the canoe. Dell swallowed quantities of salt water every time she went down, but Bob never loosened his grip on her. Fortunately, everyone reached shore safely. As a result of this accident, Bob suggested there should be a lifesaving station on Waikiki Beach.[19]

The Strahorns continued to travel, either for business or pleasure. They spent the next couple winters in Mexico and Cuba, and in 1901, they attended the inauguration and ball for President McKinley. They were also honored American guests at the elaborate ceremonies in Vienna when Franz Joseph handed over Austria to Kaiser Wilhelm.

The Strahorns lived in the Spokane Hotel, then in downtown apartments in the Van Valkenburg and Hyde buildings, before purchasing the J. J. Browne residence in October 1902. The purchase price for the house at 2216 West First Avenue and seven lots was $35,000. The house sat under pine trees, and the well-landscaped grounds included some rare trees and flowers gathered from distant lands. There was every modern luxury throughout the four floors. Bob presented the house to Dell as a 25th wedding anniversary gift. Having made some money with Jay P. Graves in a British Columbia mine, Strahorn hired leading architect Kirtland K. Cutter to remodel the house at a cost of $100,000.

While this work was in progress, Carrie Adell and Bob celebrated their anniversary with a six-month trip to Europe. One of the highlights of their trip was attending Pope Leo XIII's Silver Jubilee in March 1903. Dell took copious notes and collected brochures, postcards and pictures from each country visited. She painstakingly made a scrapbook of these items, with notes on the history, the people, the weather, and her own impressions. Among Strahorns' numerous

The Strahorns' home at 2216 West First Avenue in Browne's Addition in the early 1900s. *(Photo courtesy MAC/EWSHS, L87-189)*

The elaborate reception room at "Strahorn Pines" in Browne's Addition, 1902.
(Photo courtesy MAC/EWSHS, L86-1266)

scrapbooks, the one on this European trip, at 536 pages, was the "grand-daddy" of them all.

The mansion in Browne's Addition was more than the Strahorns felt they needed for their personal comfort, but they considered it necessary for entertaining. "Strahorn Pines" became a many-gabled Elizabethan half-timbered style home, the first in Spokane to have a hot-water steam-heating system. The twenty-room house included nine bathrooms, ten fireplaces and a single-lane bowling alley in the full basement.[20]

In a sense it was a house of contrasts: the bedrooms were rather plain looking, the entry hall dark and cluttered, and the connecting music and drawing rooms so ostentatious it is difficult to imagine a more elaborate reception room in all of Spokane. It contained onyx-topped tables, gilt chairs with flowered satin seats, American Beauty rose satin panels on the walls, a costly silk Aubusson flowered carpet, and cupids painted on the ceiling in which was centered a graceful chandelier with swags of crystal beads and prisms. Lace curtains and velvet draperies hung at the windows. The most unusual piece of furniture was a high, straight-backed, narrow-seated settee, covered in a floral pattern. The satin fabric covering the back was pleated to the center in a sunburst effect where it was gathered into a cluster resembling a pompom. Satin flowered pillows reclined in the corners. There could not have been a comfortable inch in the entire piece.

Animal motifs were abundant throughout the house. In the paneled entry hall was an umbrella stand that combined a standing bear and a monkey at the top, a narrow swan chair, and bird pictures in enormous gold picture frames. In the library, a large wooden bear stood by Bob's desk and a smaller one sat on top. In the basement billiard room, a stuffed cougar head hung over the mantel.

Crocheted pieces covered every surface in the paneled dining room, with a hunting-scene tapestry topping the wainscoting. A built-in buffet and half-oval table displayed cut-glass bowls including a punch bowl and cups. The mirror over the fireplace reflected plates and crystal vases. Above the round dining table hung a massive brass chandelier that challenges description. There were four individual lamps with tapered square shades and a large round center shade trimmed with a four-inch beaded fringe. Around the room stood matching Queen Anne chairs.[21] In contrast, a glassed-in porch at the back of the house overlooked the Spokane River. With wicker chairs and magazines tossed on the table, it was likely the most relaxed room in the house.

Dell's favorite room was her study, where her drop-leaf desk stood in the corner overlooking First Avenue. On it could be found a bear-head paperweight. She surrounded herself with literally hundreds of photos of people collected over the years of their endless travels. They were on the walls, the plate rail and in the glass-doored bookcase. Over the door frame hung a souvenir outrigger canoe. On her rocking chair was a brightly colored flowered slipcover.

Dell Strahorn, 1911, at her desk where she wrote *Fifteen Thousand Miles by Stage*.
(Photo courtesy MAC/EWSHS, L88-507)

Well ahead of other large homes of the period, the entire Strahorn mansion was electrified. Yet, the lamps on the desk or nightstand had to be connected to a ceiling chandelier or wall sconce with hanging cords, as there were no wall outlets.

Strahorns also invested in at least two other properties in Spokane. One was a ten-room modern colonial house directly south, on the corner of Hemlock and First Avenue. This $15,000 investment also included a lot directly across the river on which stood a large barn and garden tract, which was used by Strahorn's manservant. Other employees in the Strahorn home included a cook, maids and a housekeeper.

In spite of frequent absences on business or pleasure trips, the Strahorns did enjoy their home. Their oc-

The Strahorns outside their home on First Avenue. Like their neighbor to the west, Amasa Campbell, Strahorns had their own shiny black carriage, well-groomed horses, and uniformed coachman. Although Spokane was approaching a population of one hundred thousand, Bob and Dell still enjoyed horseback riding. In addition to their horses, they also had a bulldog and later black Labradors. *(Photo courtesy MAC/EWSHS, L84-25)*

cupancy of the mansion was during the heyday of Spokane's "Age of Elegance." Carrie Adell moved into the very core of fashionable society. Their home, "The Pines," was known for its hospitality. When Bob had a meeting with a large number of men, Dell entertained their wives in her gracious home. Receptions for four hundred were accomplished easily.

Dell loved to give unusual parties with great attention to detail. On Halloween 1919, members of the Fortnightly Bridge Club were greeted by an old witch silhouetted against the light shades. Inside they were ushered into a mysterious place where dim lights revealed grotesque Halloween creatures. Draped in sheets to add to the spooky effect, the guests mingled among marble statues dressed in costume, chandeliers draped in different colors or hidden in deep fringe, and heads of witches, elves and jack o'lanterns illuminated by Christmas tree lights. Light globes were hidden in false faces with weird caps. The motto in the entrance hall set the tone: "Oh, to be a child again, just for tonight." The refreshment table at The Pines held Halloween-patterned China, the ice cream molds were topped with pumpkin sticks, each with a fortune for the guests. The French pastries were shaped in Halloween designs. Thirty-eight people enjoyed the unique evening.

Robert E. Strahorn, circa 1912.
(Photo courtesy Idaho State Historical Society)

The Strahorns were very devoted to each other and were partners in every sense of the word, but in appearance, they presented quite a contrast. In her fifties or sixties, Dell's naturally curly hair had turned gray. She was double-chinned with a mature figure and erect posture. She looked and dressed like a fashionable matron with a lavish wardrobe. In contrast to his five-foot six-inch, rather stout wife, Bob was over six feet tall and very thin. At 59, he still carried himself ramrod straight, possibly a result of his years as an Indian War correspondent with General Crook. He wore his black hair in a pompadour, a style in which the hair was combed straight up in front above his broad and high forehead. Bob had bright piercing gray-brown eyes, a sharp slightly aquiline nose, and a mustache above a firm mouth and chin.[22]

Rev. Boone of the College of Idaho described Dell as a woman "of vision, cheerfulness, ability to establish confidence, to make the best of any situation, and loyalty."[23] All who knew her acknowledged Dell to be a brilliant person. She was widely known in Spokane for her civic, charitable, educational and religious work. One of Dell's contributions was her role in the construction of the Women's Club building. In 1905, the Athenaeum Club, of which Dell was an honorary member, began a movement to build a club house for women's organizations. Dell served as chairman of their committee to interest other women's groups. However, she resigned as the movement got underway because she did not want to accept credit for this project, which rightfully belonged to the club. The Women's Club house became a reality in 1909 when it was erected at Ninth and Walnut.

Although the Strahorns had many harrowing experiences during their early days of exploring the unsettled West by stagecoach, such adventures were not over.

Late in the fall of 1909, Bob and Dell were returning from the East over the Northern Pacific when the train derailed about 2:00 a.m. Down an embankment went their car, landing nearly upside down, but enough on its side to block the window. Everything was topsy-turvy: bedding, luggage, clothing, car seats, and Bob and Dell. The most frightening aspect was the thought of the big car heater just beyond the wood partition with its hot coals being upside down as well. The door to their drawing room was jammed by debris making an exit there impossible. Then they were drenched with ice cold water as the upturned water tank and broken pipes sent water everywhere. They hoped the water would also put out the fire in the heater.

The crew members chopped through the roof to release the trapped passengers. Dell suffered a few bruises, but Bob had a badly crushed leg. In what dry blankets could be found the passengers spent the remainder of that long night huddled on the embankment or down in the bottom of the borrow pit. The relief train finally arrived at 9:00 the next morning. The company surgeon, recognizing Bob, passed up his injuries as nothing much to worry about. Bob did not receive the surgical aid he needed until they got back to Spokane.

The climax of Dell's activities was the writing and publication in 1911 of a book describing their early years in the unfolding West: *Fifteen Thousand Miles By Stage.* In addition to over two hundred photographs, it also contained illustrations by renowned Montana artist Charles Russell, who was a personal friend. So well received was this book that Harvard University asked if she would collaborate with them in preparing a book on the West. Unfortunately, it is not known whether or not this project was ever carried out.[24] A Fresno, California, newspaper review ranked her book a classic equal to Mark Twain's *Roughing It* and Francis Parkman's *The Oregon Trail: Sketches of Prairie and Rocky-Mountain Life.*

Carrie Adell Strahorn, circa 1912.
(Photo courtesy Idaho State Historical Society)

Bob was so proud of Dell that he hosted a surprise dinner party at the Hall of the Doges above Davenport's Restaurant on September 19, 1911. No expense was spared for this white-tie affair. The finest china, silver and crystal graced the immaculate white-clothed round tables. The theme of the dinner was illustrated at the end of the room where a large painted replica of a stagecoach

The Hall of the Doges above Davenport's Restaurant, September 19, 1911, decorated for the occasion of Strahorns' 34th wedding anniversary and the release of Dell Strahorn's widely celebrated *Fifteen Thousand Miles by Stage*. The decorations, including the tepees in the back, depicted their early travels in the West.
(From the Davenport Hotel Collection, courtesy Walt and Karen Worthy)

Davenport's Restaurant at the southwest corner of Post and Sprague, circa 1912.
(Photo from Vintage Postcards From Old Spokane, *courtesy authors Duane Broyles and Howard Ness)*

and horses hung, while at the sides of the room Indian tepees had been erected. Around the room were ten-foot-tall limbs of leaves and bouquets of chrysanthemums. Crossed tomahawks, greenery and flowers decorated the rectangular head table. Suspended above were the dates 1877-1911 in pink asters. Place cards and menu cards both had hand-painted covers of western scenes featuring an old stagecoach in the center. On the back of the booklet was a sketch of chaps, spurs and a western hat. Music was provided by the Davenport orchestra and singing by the Elks Quartet.

Since this was the occasion of their 34th wedding anniversary, Strahorn presented his wife with a six-page tablet of sterling silver pages, bound with gold cord and tassels. On the cover was a stagecoach and "six," representing the number of years of exploration of the unsettled West, embossed in gold. The signature of each guest, all 174 of them, had to be secured in advance for the engraving plates to make up the booklet. They represented a veritable "Who's Who" of Spokane society: John and Charlotte Finch, Amasa B. and Grace M. Campbell, Patrick Welch, W. H. and Harriet Cowles, J. J. and Anna Browne, Mr. and Mrs. N. W. Durham, Patrick "Patsy" and Mary Clark, Austin and Katherine Corbin. Other guests included the Dodsons, Rutters, Happys, Comstocks, Patersons, Wakefields, Hamblens, Graveses and the Burbridges.

One page of the tablet quoted testimonials about her book: "A delightful book without a dull page or a dull paragraph," said the *Argonaut*. From the *New York Sun* came: "A romantic story of the development of a country from savagery to civilization." The Toronto *Globe* wrote: "A narrative that is readable and fascinating from cover to cover," and the *San Francisco Chronicle* printed: "A prose epic stored with delightful anecdotes and unique experiences."

Adell Strahorn was a member of the Esther Reed Chapter NSDAR, the first chapter in Spokane. In October 1970, eighteen members formed a new Spokane chapter, which they planned to call the Carrie Adell Strahorn chapter. The national DAR considered Dell as "too modern," so it was named the Jonas Babcock Chapter, in honor of Dell's maternal great-grandfather who had fought in the Revolutionary War.[25] This was not the only time Dell was commemorated. During the 1880s, a school in Hailey, Idaho Territory, had been named the Della High School, and there is a peak near Hailey called Della Mountain. Bob named the junction point in Adams County, Washington, of his "high line" with the old mainline of the Milwaukee Railroad for Dell's home town, Marengo.

At the time Strahorns decided to make Spokane their home, this large area was serviced only by the major lines of the Northern Pacific and the Great Northern (both of which were then largely controlled by James J. Hill), Bob felt certain that other major railroads – the Milwaukee and the Union Pacific – would soon enter the Pacific Northwest. Bob conceived a plan to bring the lines together into one combined facility in Spokane and planned to convince Edward H. Harriman of the Union Pacific to build it. Having worked for the Union Pacific under Gould, he was partial to that line. He was also well aware of the personal, almost fanatic, rivalry between Harriman and Hill.

With his characteristic western boldness and energy, Strahorn set out to assemble the vast amount of detailed information needed to present to Harriman. His general plan was twofold: (1) to build the shortest line possible to Portland from Spokane, a distance of 368 miles, naming it the North Coast Railroad[26] (later consolidated with other Harriman lines in the Northwest as the Oregon-Washington Railway & Navigation Company, a subsidiary of the Union Pacific), and (2) to install a connection at Wallula west through the Yakima Valley to Puget Sound, a distance of 250 miles. Necessary feeder lines to Walla Walla, Lewiston, and four electric railroads up tributary valleys from Yakima would be included in the approximately thousand miles of track. At the same time, he needed to convince the Chicago, Milwaukee and Puget Sound (later the Chicago, Milwaukee, St. Paul and Pacific, known simply as the Milwaukee Road), controlled by John D. Rockefeller Sr., to bring their main line through Spokane instead of forty-five miles south, with only a spur into the city, as planned.

Strahorn's $2.1 million purchase of the Tacoma and Eastern Railway and construction in the Yakima Valley caught J. J. Hill's attention, Considering this an invasion of his territory, Hill immediately began putting every possible obstacle in Strahorn's way – physical as well as legal. However, by 1905, Bob felt he had established an invincible position with strategic rights-of-way, engineering, terminals and construction ready for negotiation with Harriman. Because of the capital such a project required, Hill would naturally suspect Harriman was the backer. Therefore, the only way Harriman would agree was that all negotiations had to be secret and handled in such a roundabout way that no one would ever be able to tie Strahorn in with anyone in particular. Accordingly, Strahorn bought real estate, made surveys, built tracks and organized the Spokane Union Terminal, paying for everything by personal check. It drove the newspapers and railroad people wild. Who was his backer? Even during the depression of 1907, construction continued in Spokane. (Harriman laid off 8,000 men on other jobs in order to keep this project moving.)[27]

So carefully was this connection concealed that when Sam Stern, the Union Pacific attorney for the Spokane district who suspected Harriman's interest, wired for instructions on a disputed fee with Strahorn for some property in Marshall Canyon, the answer came back: "Not interested in Strahorn. Soak him [in court]."[28] The Sterns and Strahorns had both lived at the Spokane Hotel in 1901, had socialized on a regular basis and become good friends. Like everyone else in town, Stern was in the dark as to whom Bob could be representing. Not until 1910, when a thousand miles had been surveyed, a hundred miles of track completed in the Yakima Valley, and bridges over the Columbia and Snake rivers built, did the Harriman people themselves announce the relationship with Strahorn.[29] That complete secrecy earned Bob the nickname of "The Sphinx."

In 1911, in the midst of bringing the other major lines to Spokane, the Harriman interests sent Strahorn to the Willamette Valley, where Hill was making overtures in competition with the Southern Pacific. Strahorn purchased the Portland, Eugene & Eastern properties, which were pieces and parts of an electric line, and embarked upon a three-year, large-scale expansion. As a result, this line connected with and became a subsidiary of the Southern Pacific into California.

When the Strahorns first went to Oregon to work on this undertaking, Bob asked Dell to decide whether or not they should transfer their home to Portland. In a letter to Anna Browne, she

An illustration depicting Robert E. Strahorn as "The Sphinx" from *The Spokane Book, A Collection of Personal Cartoons* by William C. Morris, published in 1914.

confided: "I surely cannot say yet that we will. I am hoping that a few months will even convince him that it is not the thing to do. I love my friends and home too much to give them up."[30]

Bob and Dell returned to Spokane periodically for visits of several weeks' duration to just a few days. On one visit, Anna Browne left a bouquet of flowers at The Pines for Mrs. Strahorn. The loveliness of the flowers and the thoughtfulness of her friend prompted Dell to stay over an extra day just to enjoy them. In her thank-you note, Dell penned: "You always do such beautiful things for your friends. What dear good people we have in Spokane, I never met their like anywhere else and I am always proud to say that Spokane is our home."[31]

As the Spokane project progressed, grade crossings of four miles through the city were eliminated by construction of overhead tracks. This, too, was Strahorn's concept. Not one cent did the city have to pay, in contrast to railroad buildings in other towns. The total cost of the project was a $110 million project, of which $22 million had been spent in Spokane. Strahorn's efforts to bring other transcontinental lines with their branches into Spokane at one terminal

On September 15, 1914, people lined the Monroe Street Bridge for the golden-spike ceremony celebrating the completion of the Union Terminal and the Oregon-Washington Railway & Navigation Company's bridge, along with the Milwaukee Road's entry into Spokane. This was one of two bridges built in Spokane under Strahorn's direction. The Milwaukee signed a 99-year lease with the Union Pacific (of which the OWR&N was a subsidiary) was to use this bridge, which was subsequently demolished during the preparations for Expo '74. *(Photo from the Jerome Peltier Collection, courtesy Tony and Suzanne Bamonte)*

culminated with the driving of the golden spike on September 15, 1914. This took place where the tracks on the railroad bridge joined midway over the Monroe Street Bridge. The observation car of the Union Pacific stood on the west end of the track and the observation car of the Milwaukee Road on the east. In between waited the local and railroad dignitaries. In a velvet-collared top coat and derby hat, Bob and other officials hit the spike with a silver hammer. Dell watched over Bob's shoulder. Crowds stood on the Monroe Street Bridge, some with umbrellas to protect them from the drizzly weather. Following the ceremonies, a magnificent banquet was held at the Davenport Hotel, where Strahorn was presented with the golden spike.

Harriman died in 1909, so he did not live to see the fruition of his faith in Strahorn. He had issued just one injunction: "Whatever happens, Strahorn, don't get licked!"[32] He did not. As most of Bob's operations had involved long and bitter warfare with the Hill interests, this moment of acclaim must have been sweet, indeed. After twenty-five years, Bob had managed to get even with Hill for the debacle in Bellingham by putting the Harriman line in the strongest possible position in the Pacific Northwest, and accomplishing it right under Hill's nose. (Ironically, when Hill died in 1909, Strahorn was invited to deliver the eulogy at his funeral.) Even the *Spokesman-Review,* which had opposed the project, asserted in later years: "Where other men saw vast expanses of territory unsettled, he [Strahorn] saw them as they would be when settled and comprehended at the same time the process of their settlement."[33] The completion of the project made Spokane the most important railroad center west of Omaha,[34]

In the early 1970s, the two familiar depots of the Great Northern on Havermale Island and Strahorn's Union facility of on Trent Avenue were torn down and the tracks and bridges removed for Expo '74. The result was the beautiful Riverfront Park and a revitalization of Spokane's core area. Only the Northern Pacific's passenger depot and trackage remain. One could almost say that in the end, Hill won out.

Strahorn's Portland, Eugene & Eastern project for the Southern Pacific ended in 1914 also and marked the end of major railroad construction in the United States. At the age of 62, Strahorn could easily have rested on his laurels, but railroad operation was monotonous to him as compared to the excitement of railroad building. He had always wanted to build a road of his own, and found the spot in Oregon between Bend and Klamath Falls. In 1915, he incorporated the Oregon, California and Eastern Railroad with plans for four hundred miles of trackage beginning at Klamath Falls and working north. Despite all of Bob's previous monumental successes in railroad development, and sinking thousands of his own money into this project, his line was never profitable. Unbeknownst to Bob, Dell even mortgaged their home in Spokane to help with the finances. Ten frustrating years dragged by, but the timing was all wrong; independent railroad construction was a thing of the past. The government regulations (strangulation, as Strahorn put it) completely finished off an era in western development. Fortunately, Bob was at least able to redeem the mortgage on their Spokane home.

During America's participation in World War I, many movements were started to cheer the boys at the front. One of these was donating cartons of cigarettes. While living at Klamath Falls in 1917, Dell read about this project in the Portland *Oregonian.* Although she deplored the use of tobacco, she wrote to N. W. Durham, chairman of the Spokane County Council of Defense, suggesting a similar campaign here, not knowing the *Chronicle* had already done so. To start the ball rolling, Dell subscribed twenty cartons for Washington State soldiers abroad. Whenever she was in Spokane, Dell donated her time to the Red Cross and loaned her automobile and driver for their use. In another patriotic action, Mrs. Strahorn sent a United States flag to the Della High School in Hailey, asking an old friend, T. E. Picotte, to present it to the school in her name.[35]

As more and more of Bob's time was involved in legal entanglements necessitating his presence in San Francisco, the Strahorns more or less moved there in 1920. Maintaining their home in Spokane, they returned each September to celebrate their wedding anniversary.

Dell's health deteriorated the last year of her life and, after a month's illness she passed away March 15, 1925, at the age of 71. Her younger sister, Dr. Hattie Lacey of Los Angeles, and niece Louise Waters Johnson of Spokane had been with her throughout her last illness.

Funeral services for Carrie Adell Strahorn were held at the First Presbyterian Church on March 21. Many friends and representatives of pioneer families of Idaho, Montana, Oregon, Washington and California attended. Masses of roses, carnations, daffodils, tulips and calla lilies banked the church. Pink and white rosebuds covered the gray casket. A longtime friend, the Reverend W. J. Boone of Caldwell, delivered the eulogy:

Carrie Adell Strahorn, circa 1911. *(Photo from* Fifteen Thousand Miles by Stage, *1911, by Carrie Adell Strahorn)*

Mrs. Strahorn's personality had much to do with the success of her life and the success and happiness of many others. The inspiration of her character, her talk, her emotions set things in action. She was energy personified. The radiance of her, her wonderful good cheer in unfavorable circumstances, her power to recover from defeat were all there. Time and again her way was not rosy, and her road was full of obstacles. She was always loyal to her friends, high and low, rich and poor. There was no one like Mrs. Strahorn.

On the way to the Strahorn mausoleum in Riverside Memorial Park cemetery, the funeral cortege swept through the grounds of the Strahorn residence and paused briefly under the windows of her study where she had written *Fifteen Thousand Miles by Stage*.[36]

At the time of her death, a number of Northwest newspapers carried articles and editorials on her life. The *Spokane Daily Chronicle* printed a special memorial folder in her honor. Dell was credited with being the first white woman to completely explore and describe Yellowstone National Park, Glacier National Park, and Rocky Mountain National Park in north central Colorado. She was one of the first persons to depict the wonders of Alaska. Years earlier, in his *Spokane and the Inland Empire,* Nelson W. Durham praised her accomplishments with the following statement:

Not a few of the far west's foremost men in business, professional and political life, join her noted husband in gratefully ascribing much of their success to Mrs. Strahorn's untiring encouragement and general helpfulness in her home, social and public activities at the period in their lives when such help meant everything to them.[37]

Perhaps the *New York Times* summed it up best when it described her history-making effort in creating homes and communities as "Mothering the West."

Epilogue

Two and a half years after Dell's death, on October 5, 1927, Robert Strahorn remarried. He and Miss Ruby Garland were married in San Francisco. The Southern Pacific Railroad furnished a director's car for their leisurely trip to New York, where the couple embarked on a two-year honeymoon around the world. In 1929, after returning to their home in San Francisco, Bob sold his property in Spokane. Ruby opened an interior decorating studio in San Francisco, and Bob invested in half-a-dozen business properties within a three to five minute walk of their residence at the Palace Hotel. The investments included the largest and finest wholesale dry goods store on the Pacific Coast, the largest wholesale and retail men's clothing and novelty goods, the very best close-in apartment house, and a moderate-sized hotel. But as fate would have it, during the Great Depression, he fell victim to overwhelming odds and lost his fortune and properties.

Ruby Garland Strahorn passed away May 1, 1936, at the age of 53, and was buried in the Strahorn mausoleum at Riverside Memorial Park. Although Bob undertook no new business ventures, in 1942 he wrote his autobiography, "Ninety Years of Boyhood," which has never been published. Robert Edmund Strahorn died on March 31, 1944, less than two months shy of his 92nd birthday. After cremation, his ashes were also interred in Spokane. He remained an incurable romanticist to the end as he expected to have two angels waiting for him in heaven!

The Strahorn mausoleum at Spokane's Riverside Memorial Park in 2010. *(Photo courtesy Tony and Suzanne Bamonte)*

Notes and Sources

Chapter I – Spokane Falls, 1870s

Notes

1. Two spellings have been used for Jasper Matheny: the 1870 U.S. Census, Marion County, Oregon, and the 1872 *Salem City Directory* used Matheney. However, the 1871 *Salem Directory* listed him as Matheny. Various newspaper articles have spelled the name both ways. Since the *Weekly Mercury*, the official newspaper of Marion County, July 26, 1871, carried an advertisement for a sheriff's sale signed by J. N. Matheny, sheriff, the author accepted it as the correct spelling.

2. *Spokesman-Review*, January 1, 1903, part 2.

3. For a detailed account of Glover's journey from Lewiston to Spokane Falls, see Bond, *Early Birds in the Northwest*, chapter 25.

4. Seltice Lake, located between the Holiday Hills recreation area and Barker Road, was drained about 1894. It is usually spelled Saltese.

5. This makeshift road came over the bluff from Altamont Boulevard to the flat below, which later became known as Union Park.

6. There was a small island, Glover's Island, west of Havermale Island. Following the 1889 fire, the river between the two was filled in with rubble. About 1895, the south channel of the river was dammed by Washington Water Power to provide power for the Phoenix Sawmill, creating the present forebay or lagoon in Riverfront Park. The smaller islands or outcroppings of rock were also filled in, as below the Flour Mill, or were dynamited out, leaving just the two main channels where the river flows through Spokane today.

7. The muley saw was the forerunner to the circular saw. It consisted of a water-powered crosscut saw that could only cut on the down stroke as the blade moved up and down in a reciprocating manner.

8. For the story about Richard M. Benjamin, see Bond, *Early Birds*, chapters 22 and 23.

9. Rising. "Spokane Historical Notes." Hereafter Rising. "Notes."

10. Some of the early land acts, such as the Preemption Act of 1841, authorized the acquisition of government land by meeting a requirement of physically occupying the land (i.e. squatting on it). Although the term might presently carry a negative implication, it was a legal means to acquire land.

11. *Spokesman-Review*, January 1, 1903, part 2.

12. Cochran, *Exploring Spokane's Past*, p. 16. LaPray Bridge was located three and one-half miles upstream from Long Lake Dam on the Spokane River.

13. Lockley. *Impressions and Observations*, p. 6.

14. For the story of the Bassett family, see Bal, *Fairchild: Heritage of the Spokane Plains*, chapter 3.

15. Rising. "Notes," p. 1.

16. The name was changed to Paradise Prairie in 1885.

17. *Spokesman-Review*, August 21, 1899, p. 8. The Downings were also the first white people at Grand Coulee, but their tenure was interrupted by the Nez Perce uprising of 1877. Later they lived in Walla Walla, then settled on a farm in Dayton where Downing died in 1889. Mrs. Downing married J. R. McClure and resided in Pendleton.

18. Rev. Cowley in DAR Family Records, v. 4, p. 176. The Royal Anne cherry tree was given to the DAR about 1907. From the wood of this tree a pedestal was made upon which a bust of George Washington rests. It is now part of the collection at the Northwest Museum of Arts & Culture (MAC). Mr. and Mrs. Bradbury with their three sons lived north of France on Glenrose Prairie. This could possibly be the Bradbury who worked for Frederick Post (as mentioned in Williamson manuscript, p. 21.)

19. A great deal of controversy has existed about the location of Jim Glover's first store. However, there is sufficient evidence to place it as described. Among these are Rev. Cowley's writing that Glover's store was on Howard between Front and the river in the middle of the block, not in the middle of the

block between Howard and Mill. (*Spokane Chronicle*, "Spokane '89 Revisited," July 22, 1964, p. 3, a reprint from a Cowley memoir of 1888.) In an interview in 1897, General Merriam said: "Captain Conrad lived at Mr. Glover's residence across Howard Street from the now City Hall (California House site). A large livery stable subsequently located on the site of Mr. Glover's residence." *(Spokesman-Review*, August 16, 1897, p. 1.)

20. Just how many of the Matheny children lived in Spokane Falls with their father is uncertain. Glover recalled four children, while James Perkins of Colfax said seven, which concurs with the U.S. Census of 1870 as taken in Salem, Oregon. Yeaton said Matheny brought his son and a housekeeper to Spokane. Williamson stated there was a son, Lee, and a daughter. It is also unclear as to whether the housekeeper was a niece or his deceased wife's sister. It is sufficient to say a housekeeper and some children lived here with Matheny.

21. Rising. "Notes," p. 16.

22. Ibid., p. 17.

23. *Spokesman-Review,* July 5, 1896.

24. Williamson, p. 73.

25. Cushing Eells and Elkanah Walker were protestant missionaries to the Spokane Indians from 1838 to 1847. They were recalled from their small settlement, the Tshimakain Mission, on Walker's Prairie several miles northwest of the falls at the time of the Whitman massacre. (See Clifford M. Drury, *Nine Years Among the Spokane Indians*.)

26. All three letters are in the Eells Northwest Collection, Whitman College.

27. Stillman. "Recollections of Henry T. and Lucy A. Peet Cowley," p. 21.

28. There were many chiefs and sub-chiefs among the three bands of Spokanes. Although the white people considered Garry the head chief of the Spokanes, there really was no such position recognized by the Indians themselves. (Jessett, p. 93.) Nevertheless, Spokan Garry was certainly referred to and addressed as a chief by the white residents at the falls and had had this title extended to him more than twenty years earlier by Governor Stevens.

29. Stillman manuscript, p. 6.

30. Spokane County. Record of Deeds, p. 100. Filed for the record May 31, 1880. Although Glover always gave 1875 as the year of Sheet's survey, the original survey plat is dated as beginning July 29, 1874, and completed August 9, 1874, and is signed by Sheets. U.S. Federal Bureau of Land Management.

31. Bell. *Spokesman-Review.* 1925. Interview by William S. Lewis.

32. Ticor Title Insurance Co. Records.

33. Williamson, p. 46.

34. Durham, v. 1, p. 372.

35. Rev. Cowley. *Spokane Daily Chronicle,* n.d..

36. Durham, v. 1, p. 338.

37. Some sources list a Miss Whitehouse as being the first teacher in the school that opened in April 1879 (i.e. Edwards, p. 126 and Durham, v. 1, p. 586, who repeats Edwards). However, Dr. Leonard Waterhouse and his family were pioneers of 1878, which is confirmed in the 1880 U.S. Census for Spokane County. Dr. Louis Whitehouse did not arrive until after that time. Durham, v. 2, p. 486, states that the daughter of Dr. Waterhouse was "for three terms teacher of Spokane's first school." Clara Gray (chapter V of this publication) recalled her name correctly as Anna Waterhouse.

38. Although most sources give the second location of the schoolhouse as being on the site of the Davenport Restaurant, SW Post and Sprague, a look at the map of 1884 indicates that block to be empty. There are a couple of buildings one block south that certainly could have been the little one-room school. Therefore, the author is inclined to accept the location described in *News For An Empire* by Ralph E. Dyar, who quotes Frank Dallam, founder of the *Spokane Falls Review*, p. 4, as saying: "It stood in the middle of the block and back from the street, in the block west of the Pacific Hotel [then on the SE corner of Post and First] and just south of the Davenport Hotel." For a year, 1883-1884, Dallam put out his newspaper in the old school building before moving to the second floor of the Union Block, SE Howard and Front, above the Pantheon Saloon. Edwards, p. 204, confirms this location: "Buildings being scarce he [Dallam] could only secure the old school house, a mere shell of a structure, sitting nearly opposite where the Pacific Hotel now [1900] stands."

39. *Spokan Times*, June 19, 1879.

40. Ibid., April 24, 1879.

41. The Union Park Addition is that area approximately between Pittsburg east to Regal, and Third

Avenue south to Seventh.
  42. Edwards, p. 296.
  43. *Spokane Daily Chronicle*, November 21, 1924.

Sources

Allard, William Albert. "Chief Joseph." *National Geographic*, March 1977.

Bal, Peggy. *Fairchild: Heritage of the Spokane Plains*. Privately printed, 1976.

Becher, Edmund T. *Spokane Corona*. Spokane, WA: C. W. Hill, 1974.

Bell, Oliver N. Unidentified newspaper article, n.d. EWSHS.

Bond, Roland. *Early Birds in the Northwest*. Nine Mile Falls, WA: Spokane House Enterprises, 1971-1972.

Cochran, Barbara F. *Exploring Spokane's Past*, Rev. Ed. Fairfield, WA: Ye Galleon Press, 1984.

DAR Family Records, v. 4, 1935.

Drury, Clifford M. *Elkanah and Mary Walker, Pioneers Among the Spokanes*. Caldwell, ID: Caxton Printers Ltd., 1940.

————. *Tepee in His Front Yard*. Portland, OR: Binford & Mort, 1949.

Durham, Nelson W. *Spokane and the Inland Empire*. Spokane-Chicago-Philadelphia: S. J. Clarke Publishing Co., 1912, v. l.

Edwards, Rev. Jonathan. *An Illustrated History of Spokane County, State of Washington*. W. H. Lever, 1900. Eells Northwest Collection. Penrose Memorial Library. Whitman College, Walla Walla, Wash.

Jessett, Thomas E. *Chief Spokan Garry*. Minneapolis, MN: T. S. Dennison & Co., Inc., 1960.

Kensel, W. Hudson. "Spokane: First Decade." *Idaho Yesterdays*, v. 15, no. 1 (Spring 1971).

Lockley, Fred. "Impressions and Observations." *Oregon Journal*, January 17, 1934.

Marion County, Oregon. 1870 U.S. Census.

Nash, Lucius G. "When Game Roamed Spokane." Newspaper article November 16, 1941. EWSHS.

Rising, Henry. "Spokane Historical Notes," a collection of James N. Glover's recollections of early days in and around Spokane. EWSHS. MsSc 137, ca.1917.

Salem, Oregon, City Directories, 1871, 1872. Oregon State Library, Salem.

Spokane County Land Records. *Record of Deeds*, Book "A." Spokane County Courthouse.

Spokesman-Review. Various issues.

Spokane Daily Chronicle. Various issues.

Spokan Times. Various issues.

Stillman, Edith Cowley. Manuscript. Spokane Public Library, Northwest Room.

————. "Recollections of Henry T. and Lucy A. Peet Cowley." Westminster Congregational Church, Spokane, Wash., 1879-1954.

Ticor Title Insurance Co., Spokane, Wash.

United States. Interior Department. U.S. Bureau of Land Management. Spokane Office, Spokane, Wash.

Williamson, A. J. Manuscript, 1922. EWSHS.

Wynecoop, David C. *Children of the Sun, a History of the Spokane Indians*. Wellpinit, WA: Privately printed, 1969.

Chapter II – Susan Crump Glover

Notes

1. Thornton, J. Quinn, *Oregon and California in 1848*, tells much of the story of this overland journey.

2. Mrs. Tabitha Brown's letter in the *Oregon Historical Quarterly*, (June 1904), pp. 199-205, summed up the journey as being pleasant and prosperous until after passing Fort Hall. Mrs. Brown, also an emigrant of 1846, wrote: "... there was 60 miles of desert without water, mountains to climb, cattle giving out, wagons breaking, emigrants sick and dying, hostile Indians to guard against by day and night to save horses and cattle from being stolen. ... Out of the hundreds of wagons only one came through [Canyon Pass] without breaking." Nevertheless, after work was done on the road to improve it, most of the Oregon-bound emigrants followed the Applegate Cut-off. After the emigration of 1847, it was definitely established as a road to Oregon. This southern route is now incorporated into major highways.

3. *Colonial Home*s, pp. 111-113. The *Oregon Statesma*n, April 8, 1931, p. 4 states that the post office was in the Jason Lee house.

4. Crump's donation claim was located about ten miles south of Salem in Sec 4, Township 9 South, Range 3 West of the Willamette Meridian.

5. Copy of the Marriage Certificate, Marion County, Oregon, as recorded September 5, 1868.

6. There were two Richard Williams who were prominent in early Oregon: one was a lawyer who became a U. S. Congressman, the other was involved with the Oregon Steam Navigation Co., which had a virtual monopoly of transportation on the Columbia River between Portland and the Snake River. When he retired from the marine business, Captain Williams settled in east Portland where he became president of the First National Bank of East Portland. In Glover's biographical sketch in Durham's *Spokane and the Inland Empire*, v. 2, it states that Glover became associated with the Hon. Richard Williams of Portland in the operation of his ferry. *Spokane Falls Illustrated*, 1889, p. 34 identifies Williams as an ex-Congressman, now of Portland.

7. Marion County, *Oregon Court Journal*, August 5, 1868, p. 191.

8. Root, "Philip Glover Family History" manuscript, p. 66.

9. Lucius G. Nash, *Spokesman-Review*, January 11, 1942.

10. Crump's body was returned to Salem and buried in the Odd Fellow's Cemetery, now the Pioneer Cemetery, following services at the Christian Church of which his mother was a charter member. At the request of Crump's lodge, the complete text of his letter was printed in the newspaper so that young men might take warning of Crump's sad fate and heed his dying advice to avoid even the chance of temptation. This newspaper clipping was in Lovenia Culver's scrapbook. (EWSHS. MsSc 220)

11. Mrs. L. Ella Masterson Hewitt, "Memories of Spokane," Old Timer's Page, *Spokesman-Review*, April 23, 1950.

12. John Glover had three children by Caroline Stanley, who died of tuberculosis September 3, 1879. Wylie A., born in 1866, lived in Spokane from 1884-1895 or 1896, then went to Grand Forks, British Columbia. He passed away in 1946. Mary Helen, born 1871, taught music as a Catholic nun in Pendleton, Oregon, before returning to Portland where she died on March 7, 1957. Lillian Pearl died at the age of four years, five months on October 5, 1882, at the home of James Stanley, her maternal uncle who homesteaded east of Salem. The 1880 U. S. Census lists both John and George Glover as residing with James and Susan in Spokane Falls.

13. The deed was recorded February 21, 1880 (Ticor Title Insurance). F. Rockwood Moore would build a fortune in railroading, mining and real estate. In 1889, he built a grand and imposing mansion on West Seventh Avenue at the head of Howard Street. Judge George Turner, lawyer and U. S. senator, bought the home after Moore died in 1896. The house was torn down in 1940.

14. Frances Maurer Schneider, Sacramento, Calif., Glover's grandniece and daughter of Lovenia Culver Maurer, in a letter June 15, 1978, recalled her mother mentioning a child. No documentary evidence has been located of an infant born to Jim and Susan.

15. Letter from Venia Culver to her parents June 27, 1883. (EWSHS. MsSc 220)

16. Barouche (b-rush): a four-wheeled carriage with a driver's seat high in front, two double seats inside facing each other and a folding top over the back seat. (*Webster's Dictionary*, 1973)

17. Lovenia Culver's "Journal."

18. Spokane Methodist College was built on land donated by Colonel David Jenkins, who also made considerable monetary contributions. Since Venia was only fifteen and sixteen when she attended the "college," it must have resembled more a high school than the present day college. The school was short-lived, closing in May 1892. However, the street still bears the name it received from the location of the school, College Avenue.

19. The original copy of this story can be found at EWSHS, MsSc 220. In Venia's scrapbook, part of MsSc 220, are copies of the commencement program and the newspaper article reviewing the program dated June 25, 1884.

20. Letter from Venia Culver to her family dated March 27, 1884.

21. Venia entered Willamette University on September 7, 1885, residing in Salem during the school year. Brother Jimmie graduated the next year, and Venia's father, William B. Culver, was elected a representative to the Oregon State Legislature. In June 1887, Venia graduated and began teaching in a one-room school at Liberty, four miles south of Salem. It is probable that she taught until the family moved into a new house in Salem that Jimmie built in 1892 following the death of their father. Frank also lived there until his marriage in 1895. Venia and her mother devoted many hours working in their church. In 1899, Venia married a widower, Rev. Ezra Maurer, a pastor of the Evangelical Association Church, which later merged with the Methodist Church. To them were born two boys and five girls. Venia passed away October 18, 1952.

22. *Morning Review*, August 28, 1887. Although the house was extensively remodeled in 1911 and again during World War II, the building (now apartments) still stands on the southeast corner of First Avenue and Oak Street.

23. The Bank of Fairweather and Brooke opened in Sprague, Wash., on May 6, 1882. Six years later, they incorporated as the First National Bank of Sprague.

24. *Spokane Falls Illustrate*d, p. 42. It should be noted that the wall sconces, the tapestry coverings on the walls in the hall, mezzanine and dining room, as well as the dining room chandelier, are not Glover originals. These items, as well as six more bathrooms, were added later, perhaps during the Patrick Welch occupancy.

25. "Articles of Separation" between James N. Glover and Susan T. Glover, Spokane County Courthouse, microfilm.

26. Ibid., p. 2, no. 1.

27. It would seem that at least some of Glover's shares of stock, notes, mortgages, etc., had to have been purchased with salaries earned during the twenty-three years of legal marriage. If not, then why had Susan signed every deed for properties sold or given by Jim, including the parcel to Frederick Post in 1876?

28. Spokane County, Superior Court Journal. Microfile no. 2430. The divorce complaint was amended March 31, 1892.

29. *Spokane Daily Chronicle*, April 4, 1892. According to the Kootenai County, Idaho, Marriage Records, 1881-1900, v. 1, Book B, p. 132, Jim and Esther were married by F. J. Salman, minister, with John Glover and Wm. Franklin Leslie, Esther's brother, as witnesses. Perhaps to ensure that there could be no question as to the legality of their marriage, Jim and Esther were married a "second time" in Rathdrum on October 12, 1892, with Henry Melder, Pro. J., officiating and witnessed by Geo. M. and Sarah J. Melder. Book B, p. 153.

30. *Spokesman-Review,* July 3, 1899.

31. *Spokane Daily Chronicle,* July 3, 1899.

32. Jules L. Prickett resided at 825 West Seventh Avenue, two houses west of August Corbin, and remade his fortune after 1893 from mining, real estate, loans and insurance.

Sources

Bancroft, Hubert Howe. *History of Oregon.* v. 1, 1834-1848. San Francisco: The History Co. Publ., 1886.

Becher, Edmund T. *Spokane Corona: Eras & Empires.* Spokane, WA: C. W. Hill Printers, 1974..Bond, Rowland. *Early Birds in the Northwest.* Nine Mile Falls: Spokane House Enterprises, 1971-1972.

Cox, James W. "Memoirs of Early Salem." *Marion County History,* v. 3 (June 1957).

Cross, Harry M. "The Community Property Law in Washington." *Washington Law Review,* v. 49, no. 3, 1974.

Culver, Lovenia. Sixteen letters to her family in Salem: June 17, 1883–December 31, 1884. EWSHS. MsSc 220.

———. Autograph Book. EWSHS. MsSc 220.

———. Journal, 1882-1884. Transcript provided by Frances Maurer Schneider.

———. Scrapbook. EWSHS. MsSc 220.

Dictionary of American History. McKinley Memorial Edition, 1901.

Durham, N. W. *Spokane and the Inland Empire.* Spokane-Chicago-Philadelphia: S. J. Clarke Publishing Co., 1912, vols. 1, 2.

Edward, Rev. Jonathan. *An Illustrated History of Spokane County, State of Washington.* W. H. Lever, 1900.

General Statutes and Codes of the State of Washington. Arranged and annotated by William Lair Hill. San Francisco: Bancroft-Whitney Co., v. l, 1891.

Glover, Susan T. Letter to Louisa Glover Culver, June 6, 1883. EWSHS. MsSc 137.

Hodgkin, Frank and J. J. Galvin. *Pen Pictures of Representative Men of Oregon.* Portland, OR: Farmer & Dairymen Publ., 1882.

Hook, Harry H. and Francis J. McGuire. *Spokane Falls Illustrated,* August 1, 1889.

Jackman, E. R. and R. A. Long. *Oregon Desert.* Caldwell, ID: The Paxton Printers, Ldt., 1964.

Marriage Certificate of James N. Glover and Susan T. Crump, certified copy, EWSHS. MsSc 137.

Maurer, Ruth, daughter of Lovenia Culver Maurer. Correspondence with author.

McArthur, Lewis A. "Earliest Oregon Postoffices." *The Oregon Historical Quarterly*, v. 41, no. 1 (March 1940).

Meacham, Walter. "Barlow Road." Oregon Council, American Pioneer Trails Assoc., 1947, reprint.

Morgan, Dale. *Overland in 1846*, 2 vols. Georgetown, CA: The Talisman Press, 1963.

Morning Review. Various issues.

Oregon Historical Quarterly, v. 5 (June 1904).

"Pioneer Homes in Oregon," Colonial Homes, v. 6, no. 4 (July-August 1980).

Portland Oregonian. November 1, 1981.

Railway Review. Spokane, WA. Issue no. 2 (July 1981).

Rising, Henry. "Spokane Historical Notes." EWSHS. MsSc 137.

Root, Mabel Glover. "Philip Glover Family History." Manuscript, 1966. Oregon Historical Society, Portland, OR.

Salem, Oregon, City Directories, 1871 & 1872. Oregon State Library, Salem, OR.

Schneider, Frances Maurer, daughter of Lovenia Culver Maurer. Correspondence with author.

Spokane Daily Chronicle. Various issues.

Spokane City Directories, 1885-1899.

Spokane County, County Clerk. "Articles of Separation," August 28, 1891. Microfilm #2430.

Spokane County, Superior Court. *Journal*, January 1892-October 1892.

Spokane County, Superior Court. Records, 1892 & 1899.

Spokane Falls and Its Exposition, souvenir booklet, 1890.

Spokane Falls Review. Various issues.

Spokesman-Review. Various issues.

Steeves, Sarah Hunt. *Book of Remembrances of Marion County, Oregon, Pioneers of 1840-1860*. Portland, OR, 1927.

Thornton, J. Quinn. *Oregon and California in 1848*, v. 1, New York: Harper & Bros., 1849.

Ticor Insurance Co., Spokane, Wash.

Washington Territorial Censuses, 1885 & 1887.

Williams, Edgar & Co. *Illustrated Historical Atlas Map, Marion & Linn Counties, Oregon, 1878.* Reprint.

Williamson, A. J. "Spokane Pioneer of 1876." Manuscript, n.d. EWSHS.

U.S Censuses: 1850-1880.

Ziegler, Margaret (Mrs. Louis). Scrapbook in private collection.

Chapter III – Anna Stratton Browne

Notes

1. *Spokesman-Review*, ca. 1929.

2. *Spokane Chronicle*, June 2, 1914. "Back Trails".

3. Letter to Anna from Browne, April 28, 1878, from Colfax, W. T. (EWSHS. Ms 21, This collection, which contains the J. J. Browne papers, was used extensively.)

4. "Back Trails".

5. Letter to Anna from Browne, April 21, 1878. (EWSHS. Ms 21)

6. In some accounts Mrs. Browne said the cow belonged to Jim Glover. However, Glover only mentioned keeping a cayuse on the prairie and nothing about a cow. Having a young family, it would seem more likely that the Cowleys would have had the cow.

7. This experience made a vivid impression on Anna as she retold the story in many later interviews: namely 1914, 1929 and 1932. Each time it became more colorful. The version presented here came from an article written in 1904 by Mrs. W. W. Foote for the *Spokesman-Review* and later printed in *The History of the Big Bend Country,* pp. 997-1000. The author feels this is perhaps the most accurate of the accounts.

8. "Back Trails." The approximate location today would be 1717 West Pacific Ave.

9. *Spokane Chronicle*, April 15, 1934. Pioneers: "Men of Steel."

10. Although no reference was ever made to siblings, Browne wrote to Royal Centre, Indiana, prior to his marriage, inquiring about Andrew Browne and a Mary E. Browne (a sister?). The postmaster replied May 11, 1874, that Andrew Browne had lived there in 1868 and was somewhere between 35 to 40 miles of there at that time. For a fee of $7 he would go and look him up. He expressed the belief that Mary E. Browne was dead. No further correspondence was preserved, and it is likely J. J. did not have the $7 to send for further investigation.

11. Durham, v. 1, p. 584.

12. Letter from Rev. Stratton to Anna, April 1, 1887, (EWSHS. Ms 21)

13. Letter from Mary Stratton to Anna, n.d. (EWSHS. Ms 21)

14. Letter from Browne to Anna, September 22, 1883. (EWSHS. Ms 21)

15. Letter from Browne to Anna, November 13, 1884. (EWSHS. Ms 21)

16. Mrs. Browne's comment raises the question as to the relationship between Browne and Glover

after five years. Perhaps they managed to work together except where politics were involved.

17. Letter from Browne to Anna, February 1, 1886. (EWSHS. Ms 21)

18. This school, located at 622 West Second Avenue, was short-lived. It is listed in the 1890 Polk Directory with Geo. A. Way as principal. In 1892, Way was a bookkeeper for the W. A. Cracker Co.

19. Anna Whittlesey Stratton's diary, June 18 and 20, 1889. (EWSHS. MsSc 174)

20. Letter from Browne to Anna, June 21, 1888. (EWSHS. Ms 21)

21. Letter from Anna to Earle, November 21, 1889. (EWSHS. Ms 21)

22. Letter from Anna to Alta, January 27, 1890. (EWSHS. Ms 21)

23. Browne owned the paper until 1897 when he sold it to W. H. Cowles, whose descendants remain the sole owners. The purchase price was given in a letter from S. R. Flynn to Browne, February 25, 1890. (EWSHS. Ms 21)

24. Fisher died August 15, 1902, and was interred in the Browne plot at Fairmount Cemetery. Mary Stratton Fisher lived to be 93, passing away March 21, 1927.

25. Anna Stratton's diary, December 9, 1891. (EWSHS. MsSc 174)

26. Browne again revealed his attitude toward his children by referring to twenty-year-old Guy as a dear boy, never a young man. To J. J., they were always children. Although Browne placed his sons in good positions in his banks, he was never able to let go of the reins and let them assume responsibilities and develop maturity.

27. The Browne grandchildren included: Guy's children: Karl (born ca. March 1901), Marjory (Peggy, April 26, 1904), and John Jay (October 11, 1905); Alta's son, Dale Hamilton (ca. 1905); and Earle's daughters: Hazel (February 3, 1907) and Anne (1908). Irma's children were: Alta Francis Ross (December 31, 1908), Marshall B. Ross (Bud, May or June 1910), and Jack Ross (ca. 1912). Hazel had twin girls, one of whom lived only a few days. The surviving twin was named Jean (April 16, 1910). Anna Sweeley was born April 1, 1913. A third Sweeley granddaughter was named Maryland.

28. Letter from Browne to S. R. Flynn, December 10, 1910. (EWSHS. Ms 21)

29. Letter to Anna from Everett Sweeley, March 4, 1913. (EWSHS. Ms 21)

30. Letter to Anna from Adell Strahorn, February 4, 1914. (EWSHS. Ms 21)

Sources

Browne, Anna S. Diary, 1927. EWSHS. MsSc 197

———. Letters to and from J. J. Browne, to her mother and from various family members. EWSHS. Ms 21.

Durham, N. W. *Spokane and the Inland Empire*. Spokane-Chicago-Philadelphia: S. J. Clarke Publishing Co., 1912, vols. 1, 2.

Edwards, Jonathan. *An Illustrated History of Spokane County, State of Washington*. W. H. Lever, 1900.

Fahey, John. *Inland Empire, D. C. Corbin and Spokane*. Seattle, WA: University of Washington Press, 1965.

———. "When the Dutch Owned Spokane." *Pacific Northwest Quarterly*. (January 1981) v. 72, 1.

History of the Big Bend. Western Historical Publ. Co., 1904.

Jones, Sylvia Case and Myra Frederickson Casady. *From Cabin to Cupola*. Seattle, WA: The Shorey Book Store, 1971.

Newsclippings: unidentified and undated.

Spokan Times. Various issues.

Spokane Chronicle. Various issues.

Spokesman-Review. Various issues.

———. Interview with Mrs. E. G. Taber, ca. 1929.

Strahorn, Carrie Adell. Letters to Anna Browne. EWSHS. Ms 21.

Stratton, Anna Whittlesey. Diaries, 1887, 1889-1894. EWSHS. MsSc 174.

Chapter IV – Jennie Clarke Cannon

Notes

1. Kane's *Illustrated West*, p. 9.

2. Jim Glover said at the time of A. M.'s death that the Cannons came to Spokane in September (*Spokesman-Review*, April 8, 1895). However, Mrs. W. C. Gray recalled that the Warners were at the falls when they arrived October 8, 1878, and that the Cannons plus seven more families were here by the end of November. ("Told by the Pioneers," p. 175).

3. Durham, v. 1, p. 339.

4. *Spokesman-Review*, April 8, 1895.

5. Ibid., September 8, 1893.

6. It is interesting to note that the Indians, primarily the male members, seemed to seek out the white women with their ailments rather than a white doctor.

7. The gully, known as Little Wolf Ditch, fanned out in a V shape from the block where the Crescent Court now stands (between Main and Riverside at Wall) to the river. It has since been filled, largely by fire debris that was dumped into the gully after the Great Fire of 1889.

8. *Spokane Falls Illustrated*, p. 44.

9. After Cannon's death, the house, too, suffered from irreplaceable neglect. When the property was sold to the First Presbyterian Church in 1910, the house was moved to the north side of Fourth Avenue near Madison and converted into apartments. It was torn down in 1937 after fire destroyed the top floor.

10. Letter from Anna Browne to J. J. Browne, November 15, 1884.

11. Unfortunately, it was not possible to find more information about George Clarke's death. The earliest newspaper available on microfilm for 1883 is the month of May.

12. *Spokan Times*, April 22, 1882. The ongoing feud between the owners of the two newspapers erupted in violence when A. M. Cannon and son-in-law B. H. Bennett armed themselves, stormed into Cook's second-story apartment above his newspaper office and, under threat of death, demanded a retraction of an unfavorable statement printed in the *Times*. In spite of the presence of Cook's wife, Laura, and their infant child, shots were fired. Cook, however, managed to overpower Cannon and Bennett by some well-directed blows with a stove iron, sending both to the hospital. Despite sufficient probable cause, neither Cannon or Bennett were ever charged of a crime.

13. This unique little building was a landmark in Spokane until 1953 when it was torn down to make way for a four-story addition to the Crescent Department Store.

14. Dr. Ludlam is the same doctor who had taken care of Clara Gray (chapter V of this publication) two years earlier.

15. *Spokane Review*, September 11, 1893.

16. *Spokane Chronicle*, January 13, 1894.

17. Ibid.

18. Fahey. "When the Dutch Owned Spokane," p. 5.

Sources

Browne, J. J. Letters. EWSHS. Ms 21.

Durham, N. W. *Spokane and the Inland Empire*. Spokane-Chicago-Philadelphia: S. J. Clarke Publishing Co., 1912, v. 1.

Dyar, Ralph E. *News For An Empire*. Caldwell, ID: Caxton Printers, Ltd., 1952.

Edward, Rev. Jonathan. *An Illustrated History of Spokane County, State of Washington*. W. H. Lever, 1900.

Fahey, John. "Requiem For a High Roller." *Spokane Magazine*, October 1979.

———. "When the Dutch Owned Spokane." *Pacific Northwest Quarterly*, January 1981.

Gray, Mrs. W. C. "Told by the Pioneers." Works Progress Administration, 1937-38.

Hawthorne, Julian, editor. History of Washington, v. 2. New York: American Historical Publ. Co., 1893.

Hook, Harry H. and Francis J. McGuire. *Spokane Falls Illustrated*, August 1, 1889.

Hyslop, Robert B. *Spokane's Building Blocks*. Spokane, WA: Privately printed, 1983.

Kane's Illustrated West, v. l, no.3 (December 1886) Portland, OR: T. F. Kane, Editor & Publisher.

Morning Review. Various issues.

Portland, Oregon, City Directories, 1872-1878.

Spokan Times. Various issues.

Spokane County, Court Records, Civil Index: #7691, 8322, 9012, 10036, 10068.

Spokane Daily Chronicle. Various issues.

Spokane Falls and Its Exposition, 1890.

Spokane Falls Review. Various issues.

Spokane Review. September 8, 1893.

Spokesman-Review. Various issues.

United States Census, 1870. Oregon State.

———. 1880. Washington Territory.

Washington Territory. Special Census, 1885 and 1887.

Ziegler, Maggie. Scrapbook in private collection.

Chapter V – Clara Smiley Gray

Notes

1. For a more complete review of W. C. Gray's career, see N. W. Durham, *Spokane and the Inland Empire*, pp. 205-208. Of Gray's family, one sister, Fannie (Mrs. Frank Mercer), came out to Spirit Lake, Idaho, and a brother, Samuel, resided in St. Johns, Oregon.

2. *Spokesman-Review*, February 15, 1931.

3. Gray gave this price in "The Back Trail" articles in the *Spokane Daily Chronicle*, June 29, 1914. Mrs. Gray, however, recalled the price of the lot as being $250 in the *Spokesman-Review*, "Keeping House in Spokane Thirty Years Ago," April 23,1911.

4. *Spokane Daily Chronicle*, January 19, 1936, interview with W. H. Smiley. The exact number and names of the people at Spokane Falls at any given time is almost impossible to determine as people's reminiscences varied. Where did the carpenters come from who worked with Gray on his hotel? Perhaps he employed them in Walla Walla, and they returned there when the job was done. This has never been clarified.

5. "Mrs. W. C. Gray," *Told by the Pioneers*, v. 2, Works Progress Administration, 1937-1938, p. 171.

6. Herbert Gaston, "The Back Trail," *Spokane Daily Chronicle*, June 24, 1914. Another version of the incident in which Nellie dropped the food on the floor so the dinner was spoiled for Clara and the boys was told in the W. P. A. Writers' Project, v. 2, p. 168. In any event, Clara had to cook another meal.

7. Mail to Spokane Falls came through Walla Walla. In one article, Mrs. Gray is reported to have said there was no mail service for six months that winter, but this seems unlikely.

8. *Spokesman-Review*, December 25, 1924.

9. Conflicting dates have been given for this dance. Some articles report it to have been Thanksgiving, 1878. Common sense dictates this as unlikely since construction on the hotel would only have been in progress six weeks at the most. If, indeed, the weather was already so severe as to freeze Clara's dress, it would take some very hardy (or foolhardy) persons to have a dance in an unheated room when a comfortable place was available. Furthermore, the Grays did not move into the kitchen lean-to of the hotel until after Thanksgiving.

10. Polonaise: an elaborate overdress with a short-sleeved fitted waist and a draped overskirt.

11. *Told by the Pioneers*, v. 2, p. 169.

12. According to Gray, there were ten rooms on the second floor; Mrs. Gray said eight. Either way, the rooms were tiny and could measure no more than 8 by 10 feet or 10 by 10 at most.

13. Gray recalled having 18-20 beds in the "corral." That would seem to be quite a few in a half-story attic. Perhaps he was referring to sleeping spaces on the floor where a man could spread his blankets.

14. There seems to be a bit of confusion about the time of year this Indian scare occurred. In the *Spokesman-Review* article "Keeping House in Spokane Thirty Years Ago," April 23, 1911, Mrs. Gray recalls it as happening in July 1879. However, in "The Back Trail" series of articles in the *Chronicle* for June 24, 1914, she gives the time as being in the early winter of 1879. Since the camas blooms in May and the Indian women dug it between salmon seasons (August to October), it would seem more likely that this event happened in the fall. When Rev. W. H. Cowley came to Spokane, he said he met the Indians when they returned from digging camas in October 1874. (Durham, v. 1, p. 371.)

15. The camas, a member of the lily family, is an edible root which was a staple food for the Indians. The stems and blossoms resemble a wild hyacinth. It grows about one to two feet tall and blooms in May. It is a small, white, flat tasting vapid onion when removed from the ground, but black and sweet when prepared for food. It is excellent, especially when boiled with meat. If kept dry, it can be preserved a long time. After being pounded, the camas could be baked into loaves like bread. (Clifford Merrill Drury, *First White Women Over the Rockies*, v. 2, 148 footnote.) Although widely used by the Indians, the camas root does not seem to have been adopted by other people as a source of food.

16. Milton S. Bentley, interview by William S. Lewis. (W. S. Lewis papers, EWSHS. Ms 25)

17. *Spokane Daily Chronicle*, "The Back Trail," June 24, 1914.

18. *Spokane Daily Chronicle*, November 21, 1924.

19. *Spokan Times*. Various issues.

20. Robert Hyslop, *Spokane's Building Blocks*, p. 33 and several photographs of California House.

21. *Spokane Daily Chronicle*, January 4, 1883.

22. Daniel H. Dwight papers (EWSHS. Ms 136).

23. *Morning-Review*, May 18, 1887, p. 1. Contrary to articles published some time later, this fire occurred in 1887, not 1888.

24. Ibid., October 2, 1887.

25. Letters to Mrs. W. C. Gray from Dr. Ludlam dated December 26, 1890, and Dr. Carlson, 1891, can be found in the W. S. Lewis papers (EWSHS. Ms 25).

26. *Spokesman-Review*, February 15, 1931.

27. Ibid., December 18, 1929.

Sources

"Back Trail, The," *Spokane Daily Chronicle*. Various issues.

Becher, Edmund T. *Spokane Corona: Eras & Empires*. Spokane, WA: C. W. Hill, 1974.

"Deaths in Marysville," 1870-1918. California State Library, Sacramento, Calif.

Drury, Clifford Merrill. *First White Women Over the Rockies*, v. 2. Glendale, CA: The Arthur H. Clark Co., 1963.

Durham, N. W. *Spokane and the Inland Empire*. Spokane-Chicago-Philadelphia: S. J. Clarke Publishing Co., 1912, vols. 1, 2.

Edwards, Jonathan. *An Illustrated History of Spokane County, State of Washington*. W. H. Lever, 1900.,

Fargo, Lucile F. *Spokane Story*. Minneapolis, MN: The Northwestern Press, 1950.

50th Anniversary Program, Telephone Service, 1936. Betts Collection. EWSHS.

Hook, Harry H. and Francis J. McGuire. *Spokane Falls Illustrated*, August 1, 1889.

Hyslop, Robert B. *Spokane's Building Blocks*. Spokane, WA: Privately printed, 1983.

"Keeping House in Spokane Thirty Years Ago," *Spokesman-Review*, April 23, 1911.

Letters to Mrs. W. C. Gray. William S. Lewis papers. EWSHS. Ms 25.

Marysville, Calif., Directory, 1870-1871.

Morning Review., Various issues.

"Seminary Reminiscences." n.d. California Historical Society, San Francisco, Calif.

Spokan Times. Various issues.

Spokane Daily Chronicle. Various issues.

Spokane Falls Review. Various issues.

"Spokane Pioneer Reminiscences," *Spokane Daily Chronicle*, November 15 and 21, 1924.

Spokesman-Review. Various issues.

U. S. Works Progress Administration, Federal Writers' Projects. Washington State. "Told By the Pioneers," v. 2. 1937-1938.

Vancouver (Wash.) *Columbian*. March 27, 1977.

Chapter VI – Spokane Falls, 1880s

Notes

1. Louis Yale comments. *Spokesman-Review*, May 24, 1925. Also Francis Cook in the *Spokan Times*, June 30, 1881.

2. Jack Cartwright reminiscences.

3. *Spokan Times*, March 24, 1881.

4. *Rawhide Press*, January 17, 1981, and the *Community Press*, January 14, 1981.

5. *Spokane Falls Review*, July 28 and November 23, 1889. One can only wonder whether or not a male minister would have evoked the same over-reaction from the newspaper.

6. First Baptist Church. "Historical Summary," ca. 1928.

7. "From the NW corner of Sec 19, T 25 N, R 43 E, west 160 rods [1/2 mile] to the quarter post, south 160 rods to the center of Sec 24, T 25 N, R 42 E, East 480 rods [1 1/2 miles] to the SE corner of the N1/2 of sec 19, T 25 N, R 43 E, East 80 rods [1/4 mile], then N. 160 rods [1/2 mile], E. 80 rods [1/4 mile] to the SE corner of the SW1/4 of Sec 17, T 25 N, R 43 E. Thence north to and across the river to a point 200 feet from the high water mark. Meandering in a westerly direction from the high water mark to the west line of Sec. 18. South along the section line to the point of beginning." (Spokane Falls, Articles of Incorporation, W. T., November 29, 1881, sec. 1)

8. *Spokane Chronicle*, September 28, 1881.

9. Letter from Thomas Symons to S. E. Symons of Saginaw, Mich. (EWSHS)

10. *Spokan Times*, March 18, 1882.

11. *Spokane Independent*, University of Washington Libraries, Pacific Northwest Collection, microfilm. Herren's name has been given erroneously as Herron or Herring in other publications. Herren and Son were the publishers.

Notes and Sources

12. In 1953, the Spokane County Pioneer Society monument committee considered putting a marker in Manito Park to commemorate Francis Cook. Unfortunately, this project was not carried out. (*Spokane Chronicle,* October 31, 1953)

13. *Spokesman-Review,* June 30, 1920.

14. J. Orin Oliphant.

15. *Spokane Chronicle*, July 29, 1914.

16. Ibid., July 15, 1914.

17. Magnusen, p. 16.

18. Dyar, p. 6.

19. *Spokane Chronicle*, June 29, 1881.

20. Code of Washington Territory. Sec 3050, Chapter 238. Amended November 23, 1883.

21. Gerrish, p. 180.

22. *Spokane Falls Review*, January 19, 1888.

23. Ibid.

24. Nevada Bloomer v. John Todd, J. E. Gandy and H. A. Clarke. Laws of Washington Territory, 1888, pp. 599-623.

25. N. W. Durham, *Spokane and the Inland Empire*, v. 1, p. 404.

26. Bond, pp. 214-218. Also "*The History of the Electrical Industry in Spokane and the Inland Empire,*" 1959.

27. *Sacred Heart Hospital Chroniques*, the journal written in French by the Sisters of Providence, which states the sisters left Vancouver on April 30. As it was an overnight journey to Spokane, they arrived here on the first of May.

28. *Morning Falls Review*, June 14, 1890.

29. *Spokesman-Review*, May 18, 1936.

30. *Spokane Falls Review*, January 1, 1890.

31. "Shantytown" at this time was located on the land disputed between Rev. H. T. Cowley and the Northern Pacific Railroad: the area between Mill on the west to Division on the east, and from Sprague south to the alley between Sixth and Seventh avenues. (*Spokane Falls Review,* September 11, 1889. Also Durham, v. 1, p. 432.)

32. Durham, v. 1, pp. 415-417; *Spokane Falls Review*, August 6, 1889; *Spokane Falls and its Exposition, 1890*, p. 7; *Spokane Falls Chronicle*, August 5, 1889 and August 3, 1964; Andrews, p. 131; and Hyslop.

33. *The Falls* (a weekly journal), June 4, 1976, interview with C. Hubert Bartoo, a retired Spokane fireman and son of George C. Bartoo.

Sources

Anderson, Fred O. "How the Present Spokane County Developed." Manuscript, 1965.

Andrews, Ralph W. *Historic Fires of the West*. New York: Bonanza Books, 1966.

Articles of Incoporation. Spokane Falls, Washington Territory.

Askman, Allegra. "A New Story About an Old Fire." *The Falls*, a weekly journal. Spokane, WA, v. 2, no. 25 (June 24, 1976).

Atlases: Ogle, 1912; Metzger, 1941.

Bond, Roland. *Early Birds in the Northwest*. Nine Mile Falls, WA: Spokane House Enterprises, 1971-1972.

Carrere, John F. "Spokane Falls, W. T. and Its Tributary Country." Spokane Falls: City Council and the Board of Trade, 1889.

Code of Washington Territory. Sec. 3050, chapter 238, 1883.

Commemorating a Half Century of Continuous Electric Service, 1889-1939. Washington Water Power.

Community Press. Spokane, WA, January 14, 1981.

Cook, Francis H. *The Territory of Washington, 1879*. Reprint. Edited by J. Orin Oliphant, 1925. Cheney, WA: State Normal School.

Crosby, Edward J. *The Story of the Washington Water Power, 1889-1930*.

Durham, N. W. *Spokane and the Inland Empire*. Spokane-Chicago-Philadelphia: S. J. Clarke Publishing Co., 1912, v. 1.

Dwight, Daniel H. Letters to his mother-in-law, Mrs. Mary Wills, August 6 and 11, 1889. Private Collection.

Dyar, Ralph E. *News For An Empire*. Caldwell, ID: Caxton Printers, Ltd., 1952.

Electrical World. Weekly. New York: W. J. Johnston, Ltd., v. 15, no. 19 (May 10, 1890).

First Fifty Years. Westminster Congregational Church, 1879-1929. Spokane, WA: Empire Printing Co., 1929.

Gerrish, Theodore. *Life in the World's Wonderland*. Biddeford, ME: Press of the Biddeford Journal, 1887, chapter 8 "Spokane Falls."

Hamblen, Charlotte. Diary, 1888. EWSHS. MsSc 211.

"Historical Summary," First Baptist Church, ca. 1928.

"History of the Electrical Industry in Spokane and the Inland Empire." Washington Water Power, 1959. Manuscript.

Hyslop, Robert B. *Spokane's Building Blocks*. Spokane, WA: Privately printed, 1983.

Jones, Sylvia Case and Myra Frederickson Casady. *From Cabin to Cupola*. Seattle, WA: The Shorey Book Store, 1971.

Kalez, Jay. *Saga of a Western Town, 1872-1972*. Spokane, WA: Lawton Printing, Inc., 1972.

Landmarks. Winter, 1982, v. 1, no. 2.

Laws of Washington Territory. Olympia, W. T., 1888, Chap. 51.

Magnusen, Richard G. *Coeur d'Alene Diary*. Portland, OR: Metropolitan Press, 1968.

Morning Review. Various issues.

Phipps, T. E. Manuscript on the Washington Water Power Co., December 31, 1916.

Oliphant, J. Orin. Introduction to *The Territory of Washington*, 1879 by Francis H. Cook. Reprinted by the State Normal School, Cheney, Wash., 1925.

Pratt, Orville C. Spokane Public Schools: *A Brief History* and the Annual Report for 1942-42. Spokane, WA, June 1943.

Railway Review. "Northern Pacific and Spokane, 1881-1981." Spokane, WA, no. 2, July 1981.

Rawhide Press. Weekly. Wellpinit, WA, January 7, 1981.

Renz, Louis T. *Construction of the Northern Pacific Railroad Main Line During the Years 1870-1888*. Walla Walla, WA, 1973.

Schoenberg, Wilfred P., S. J. *Gonzaga University, Seventy-five Years, 1887-1962*. Spokane, WA: Lawton Printing Co., 1963.

Spokan Times. Various issues.

Spokane Chronicle. Various issues.

Spokane Falls and Its Exposition, souvenir book, 1890.

Spokane Falls Review. Various issues.

Spokesman-Review. Various issues.

Spokesman-Review Supplement. "The Washington Water Power Company, 75 Years: 1889-1964."

Stratton, Anna Whittlesey. Diary, 1889. EWSHS, MsSc 174.

Symons, Thomas. Letter. EWSHS.

Chapter VII – Alice Ide Houghton

Notes

1. *Spokane Spokesman*, Annual Illustrated Supplement, January 1, 1892, p. 45.
2. Hook and McGuire, p. 24.
3. Ibid.
4. There is a great deal of discrepancy in the year of Mrs. Houghton's birth. *The History of Washington* (1893) gives it as 1850. The cemetery records say she was 68 when she died in 1920 which would place her birth year as 1852. However, the 1860, 1870 and 1880 U.S. Censuses, as well as the Washington Territorial Census of 1885, are all consistent with her having been born in 1848. Therefore, the author accepted that year as being the most accurate date.
5. All the biographical sketches of Mrs. Houghton state that her family moved to Durand, Wisconsin, from Canada. However, the *Buffalo County Herald* in Mondovi for December 7, 1878, told of F. J. Ide, "one of our oldest and most respectable citizens moved to Durand with his family." Only Gilbert was still at home, as all the girls were married and most of them lived in Durand. When Alice married A. G. Brownlee, the same newspaper commented that she grew up in "this [Mondovi] neighborhood."
6. Vital Statistics, Buffalo County, Wisconsin. Mrs. Houghton has given the year of her marriage inaccurately as 1866.
7. *Spokesman-Review*, November 20, 1891. Civil suit #5480.
8. *Morning Review*, April 21, 1889.
9. Ibid.
10. Letter from Adelaide Gilbert to her parents, February 12, 1889. (EWSHS. MsSc 225)

11. *Spokane Falls Review*, December 17, 1890.

12. Weimann, p. 137.

13. State of Washington. Final Report, p. 23.

14. Memorial of the World's Columbian Exposition, 1893, p. 154.

15. Johnson, p. 488.

16. *Spokesman-Review*, June 3, 1895.

17. Despite efforts to locate copies of this magazine, they could not be located either through the Spokane Public Library inter-library loan or the Illinois State Historical Society.

18. *Spokesman-Review*, August 25, 1897.

Sources

Avery, Bailey. *The Northwest: Illustrated Monthly Magazine.* St. Paul, MN, April 1890; June 1892.

Boughton, Jennie. "Spokane from Memory." Spokane: Stake Print & Publ. Co., 1941.

Chicago Historical Society, Chicago, IL. Correspondence with author.

Durham, N. W. *Spokane and the Inland Empire.* Spokane-Chicago-Philadelphia: S. J. Clarke Publishing Co., 1912, vols. 1, 2.

Edwards, Jonathan. *An Illustrated History of Spokane County, State of Washington.* W. H. Lever, 1900.

Evans, Elwood, editor. *State of Washington.* Published by the World's Fair Commission of the State of Washington, 1893, for distribution at the World's Columbian Exposition.

Gilbert, Adelaid Sutton papers. EWSHS. MsSc 225.

Hawthorne, Julian, editor. *History of Washington*, v. 2. New York: American Historical Publishing Co., 1893.

History of the Big Bend Country. Western Historical Publ. Co., 1904.

Hook, Harry H. and Francis J. McGuire. *Spokane Falls Illustrated.* Minneapolis: F. L. Thresher, August 1, 1889.

Johnson, Rossiter, editor. *History of the World's Columbian Exposition*, v. 2. *Exhibits.* New York, 1898.

May, George, descendant of Sarah Ide Hunter, Fair Oaks, CA. Correspondence with author.

Memorial of the World's Columbian Exposition by the Committee on Ceremonies. Chicago, IL: Stone, Kastler & Painter Publishers, 1893.

Morning Review. Various issues.

Peyton, Avery, descendant of Victor Anna Ide Houghton Peyton, Spokane, Wash. Interview with author May 22, 1984.

Spokane Daily Chronicle. August 24, 1897.

Spokane City Directories.

Spokane County Court Records. Civil Index Numbers: 3098, 5381, 5400, 5480, 5514, 5515, 5528, 5580, 5583, 5627, 6650, 6667, 6760, 6761, 7046, 7106, 7316, 7406, 7499, 8475, 8485, 9712, 10525, 23169

Spokane Falls and Its Exposition. Buffalo & New York: Matthews-Northrup & Co., 1890.

Spokane Falls Review. Various issues.

Spokane-Review. Various issues.

Spokane Spokesman. "Annual Illustrated Supplement," January 1, 1892.

Spokane Spokesman. April 23, 1892.

Spokesman-Review. Various issues.

Sunday Review, "The Stage in Early Days," December 24, 1893.

Washington Territorial Censuses, 1885, 1887. Microfilm.

Washington State World's Fair Commission. Biennial Report. Olympia, WA: State Printer, 1891 & 1892.

———. Final Report. Olympia, WA: State Printer, 1894.

Weimann, Jeanne Madeline. *The Fair Women.* Chicago, IL: Academy Chicago Publishers, 1981.

Williamson, A. J. Manuscript. EWSHS.

Chapter VIII – Mary Archard Latham

Notes

1. Although Archer is frequently used in more recent published writings, original historical documents indicate the family's name was Archard.

2. No copy of this work, which was reported in the *Morning Review* on August 18, 1888, has been found.

3. *Spokane Spokesman*, Annual Illustrated Supplement, January 1, 1892, p. 37. No record was found of a book by that name having been printed.

4. *Spokane Falls Review*, July 30, 1889, "City Items."

5. Letter to the author from the Office of Medical Alumni Association of the University of Cincinnati Medical Center, Cincinnati, Ohio, July 5, 1978.

6. Gardner and Fred Chamberlin were nephews of William Pettet.

7. *Spokane Falls Review*, August 6, 1889.

8. Gidley, p. 97.

9. National Archives. Bureau of Indian Affairs.

10. *Spokane Review*, May 24, 1891, and the *Spokane Chronicle*, May 30, 1891.

11. A theory attributed to German pathologist Rudolf Virchow, 1821-1902.

12. *Spokane Spokesman*, Annual Illustrated Supplement, January 1, 1892, p. 37.

13. *Spokane Review*, June 11, 1891.

14. Materia medica refers to substances used in the preparation of drugs.

15. *Spokane City Directory*, 1892, p. 66.

16. *Spokane Review*. Various issues.

17. At the end of 1905, the library moved into the Carnegie Library building on Cedar between Riverside and First Avenue on land donated by A. M. Campbell.

18. Edwards, p. 246.

19. *Spokane Spokesman*, Annual Illustrated Supplement, January 1, 1892, p. 37.

20. Block 111, lots 6, 7, 8 on Gordon Avenue between Nevada and Morton. Civil Court Cases #9033 and #9041.

21. Civil Court Case #9262.

22. Civil Court Case #15539.

23. Civil Court Case #18317.

24. Ibid., #20415.

25. Ibid., #18996.

26. Ibid.

27. Ibid.

28. *Spokesman-Review*, June 14, 1905.

29. Ibid.

30. *Spokane Chronicle*, July 20, 1905.

31. *Spokesman-Review*, August 1, 1905.

32. Washington State Penitentiary Parole Record, v. 2.

33. *Spokesman-Review*, January 21, 1908.

34. Interview with Robert Hyslop, June 15, 1982.

35. *Spokesman-Review*, February 10, 1911.

36. Author unknown. The late Dr. Carl P. Schlicke of Spokane, Wash., jotted down this quotation while in medical school, but did not identify the source. It is used here with his permission.

37. Gidley, p. 13.

38. Ibid., p. 20.

39. Ibid., p. 112.

40. Ibid., p. 113.

Sources

Edwards, Jonathan. *An Illustrated History of Spokane County, State of Washington.* W. H. Lever, 1900.

Gidley, Mick. *With One Sky Above Us, Life on an Indian Reservation at the Turn of the Century.* New York: G. P. Putnam's Sons, 1979.

Hook, Harry H. and Francis J. McGuire. *Spokane Falls Illustrated.* Minneapolis: F. L. Thresher, August 1, 1889.

Morning Review. Various issues.

National Archives. Record Group no. 75. Bureau of Indian Affairs. Central Files, 1907-1939, Washington, D. C.

Schlicke, Carl P., M.D. *Working Together.* Fairfield, WA: Ye Galleon Press, 1980.

Spokane City Directories.

Spokane County Court Records. Civil Index numbers: 9033, 9041, 9262, 9886, 11947, 15539, 16416, 18317, 18996, 19384, 20415, 20806, 20867, 25611

Spokane Daily Chronicle. Various issues.

Spokane Falls Review. Various issues.

Spokane Review. Various issues.

Spokane Spokesman, "Illustrated Annual," January 1, 1892.

Spokesman-Review. Various issues.

University of Cincinnati Medical Center, Cincinnati, Ohio. Correspondence with author.

Weimann, Jeanne Madeline. *The Fair Women*. Chicago: Academy Chicago, 1981.

Chapter IX – Rebuilding After Spokane's Great Fire

Notes

1. *Spokesman-Review*, August 13, 1916.

2. Daniel H. Dwight in a letter to his mother-in-law, August 6, 1889. In a private collection.

3. *Spokane Falls Review*, October 20, 1890.

4. North Central High School opened September 1908, at which time the Central High became South Central High School. When South Central burned on June 21, 1910, all of the city's high school students used North Central until Lewis & Clark was completed on April 10, 1912.

5. According to the Office of the Secretary of State, the "Falls" was dropped from Spokane's name in 1890. Durham gives the date as March 1891, v. 1, p. 438. *Editor's note:* Actually, the name was officially changed by Article XV of the 1891 City Charter. That article specified the name change was subject to a separate vote and required a majority. Voting took place on March 25, 1891. The Mayor's Certificate, which certified the passage of the 1891 City Charter and Article XV, was signed by Mayor Clough on April 1, 1891. It provided the vote count for the passage of Article XV: 1129 in favor and 513 opposed.

6. Durham, v. 1, p. 439.

7. *Spokane Daily Chronicle*, August 1, 1964; *Spokesman-Review*, August 8, 1911.

8. For a more detailed account of the Dutch involvement in Spokane, see Fahey, "When the Dutch Owned Spokane," *Pacific Northwest Quarterly*, January 1981.

9. *Community Press*, July 4, 1979.

10. Fahey. "Building Blocks," p. 79.

11. *Spokane Daily Chronicle*, July 9, 1964.

12. Durham, v. 1, p. 484.

13. Dyar, p. 124.

14. *Spokane Daily Chronicle*, May 12, 1960.

15. The Women's Hotel opened in September 1904 in the Denee Building at Sprague and Madison, which had just been vacated by St. Luke's Hospital (formerly the Spokane Protestant Sanitarium) because its new building on Summit was ready for occupancy. The hotel provided housing accommodations for unmarried women.

16. Allen, p. 490.

Sources

Allen, Mrs. H. W. "Women's Work in Spokane," *The Coast*, November 1907. Seattle: The Coast Publishing Co.

Browne, J. J. Letters. EWSHS, Ms 21.

Community Press, July 4, 1979.

Durham, N. W. *Spokane and the Inland Empire*. Spokane-Chicago-Philadelphia: S. J. Clarke Publishing Co., 1912, vols. 1, 2, 3.

Dyar, Ralph E. *News For An Empire*. Caldwell, ID: Caxton Printers, Ltd., 1952.

Edwards, Jonathan. *An Illustrated History of Spokane County, State of Washington*. W. H. Lever, 1900., *Electrical World*, v. 15, no. 19 (May 10, 1890). New York: W. J. Johnston Co.

Fahey, John. "Building Blocks." *Spokane Magazine*, July 1981.

———. "When the Dutch Owned Spokane." *Pacific Northwest Quarterly*, v. 72, no. 1 (January 1981).

Ferris, Joel E. "The Cable Cars." *Spokesman-Review*, April 13, 1958.

Hyslop, Robert B. *Spokane's Building Blocks*. Spokane, WA: Privately printed, 1983.

Morning Review. Various issues.

Northwest Magazine, v. 8, no. 4 (April 1890). St. Paul & Minneapolis: E. V. Smalley, Editor & Publisher.

Pratt, Orville C. Spokane Public Schools: *A Brief History*.

Spokane Daily Chronicle. Various issues.

Spokane Falls & Its Exposition, 1890.

Spokane Falls & Its Tributary, 1889.
Spokane Falls Review. Various issues.
Spokesman-Review. Various issues.

Chapter X – Carrie Adell Green Strahorn

Notes

1. Carrie Adell Strahorn's scrapbook, p. 100, in private collection.
2. Durham v. 2, pp. 5-6
3. *Marengo Republican*, Mrs. Strahorn's scrapbook, p. 70, in private collection.
4. "Ninety Years of Boyhood," unpublished autobiography of R. E. Strahorn, 1942, p. 36. Hereafter referred to as "Ninety Years." The original manuscript is in the Terteling Library, College of Idaho, Caldwell, Idaho. A microfilm copy is available from the Idaho State Historical Society, Boise, Idaho.
5. "Ninety Years," p. 155.
6. Carrie Adell Strahorn scrapbook, in private collection.
7. "Ninety Years," p. 154.
8. Carrie Adell Strahorn, *Fifteen Thousand Miles by Stage*, p. 314. Hereafter referred to as *Fifteen Thousand*.
9. Ibid., p. 363.
10. Dr. Albro Martin of Harvard University in a lecture at EWSHS on October 16, 1981, "Hill or Harriman, What difference did it make to Spokane?" made this statement.
11. "Ninety Years," p. 208 and *Fifteen Thousand*, pp. 536-541.
12. *Boise Statesman*, March 23, 1936. In 1967, a new library was erected on the campus, Terteling Library. Strahorn Hall, which is listed on the National Register of Historic Places, is now used for classes in history, foreign languages, sociology, psychology, and English.
13. Fahey, p. 209.
14. "Ninety Years," p. 217.
15. Warrant: a short-term obligation of a governmental body, such as a municipality, issued in anticipation of a revenue.
16. "Ninety Years," p. 227.
17. *Fifteen Thousand*, p. 418.
18. Durham v. 2, p. 11
19. *Hawaiian Gazette*, a semiweekly newspaper, March 7, 1899.
20. *Where the Washingtonians Live*, 1969. Also see "The Pines," home of Mr. and Mrs. Robert E. Strahorn, a leather covered photo album, EWSHS. A year after Strahorn sold the house in 1929, it was converted into eleven apartments. The building was torn down in 1974 as a result of neglect and termites. The site was black-topped for a parking lot in 1977 for the adjacent Cheney Cowles Museum (now the MAC/Northwest Museum of Arts & Culture).
21. Part of the Strahorn dining room (the fireplace, doors, wall covering and sconces) are in the MAC's collection.
22. Stern, p. 545.
23. *Spokane Daily Chronicle*, March 16, 1925.
24. *Spokane Daily Chronicle*, July 10, 1913.
25. The Esther Reed Chapter was founded by Elizabeth Tannatt and other patriotic women on June 14, 1900. This information was provided in 2010 by Doris J. Woodward of the Jonas Babcock Chapter.
26. "Ninety Years," p. 250. This line should not be confused with the Spokane, Portland & Seattle built by the Great Northern, i.e., Hill, in 1907.
27. "Ninety Years," p. 256.
28. Ibid., p. 248.
29. Quiett, p. 537.
30. Mrs. R. E. Strahorn to Mrs. J. J. Browne, June 10, 1912. (EWSHS, Ms 21)
31. Mrs. Strahorn to Mrs. Browne, April 23, 1914. (EWSHS, Ms 21)
32. "Ninety Years," p. 238.
33. "Ninety Years," p. 266, also the *Spokesman-Review*, November 1914.
34. Quiett, p. 538.
35. Picotte started the *Wood River Times* in Hailey and remained its editor for nearly forty years. Of the three newspapers begun in Hailey, only the *Times* survived. It is now named the *Wood River Journal*.

Notes and Sources

The Della High School building was torn down around 1919. Rebuilt, the name was changed to Wood River High School.

36. *Spokesman-Review,* March 22, 1925.

37. Durham, v. 2, p. 11. It is noteworthy that Carrie Adell Strahorn was one of the few women Nelson Durham wrote about in his three-volume set on the history of Spokane and its surrounds.

Sources

Bird, Annie Laurie. *Boise, the Peace Valley*. Caldwell, ID: The Caxton Printers, Ltd., 1934.

Durham, N. W. *Spokane and the Inland Empire*. Spokane-Chicago-Philadelphia: S. J. Clarke Publishing Co., 1912, v. 3.

Fahey, John. *The Days of the Hercules*. Moscow, ID: University Press of Idaho, 1978.

Hayman, H. H. *That Man Boone*. Caldwell, ID: The Caxton Printers, Ltd., 1948.

Knight, Oliver. "Robert E. Strahorn, Propagandist For the West." *Pacific Northwest Quarterly*, v. 59, 1 (January 1968).

McDonald, Lucile and Werner Lenggenhager. *Where the Washingtonians Lived*. Seattle, WA: Superior Publ. Co., 1969.

News Tribune, Caldwell, ID, November 5, 1937.

"Pines, The," leather covered photo album with interiors of the Strahorn home. EWSHS. MA 13.

Portland Oregonian, October 6, 1927.

Quiett, Glenn Chesney. *They Built The West*. New York and London: D. Appleton-Century Co. Inc., 1934.

Spokane Daily Chronicle. Various issues.

———. Special memorial folder in honor of Mrs. Strahorn, March 1925.

Spokesman-Review. Various issues.

Stern, Samuel S. "Western Personalities, Robert E. Strahorn." *Sunset Magazine*, 27:5 (November 1911).

Strahorn, Carrie Adell. *Fifteen Thousand Miles by Stage*. New York and London: G. P. Putnam's Sons, 1911.

———. Three scrapbooks in private collections.

———. Silver tablet. R. E. to C. A. Strahorn, 1911. EWSHS.

Strahorn, Robert E. "Ninety Years of Boyhood." Unpublished autobiography,. 1942. Mimeographed copy in author's possession.

Yarber, Esther. *Land of the Yankee Fork*. Salt Lake City, UT: Publishers Press, reprint 1970.

Ziegler, Margaret. Scrapbook in private collection.

Index

Index

Index

Index

Index

Index

Index

Index